Angels of Efficiency

Angels of Efficiency

A Media History of Consulting

FLORIAN HOOF

TRANSLATED BY DANIEL FAIRFAX

OXFORD

UNIVERSITY PRESS

OXFORD
UNIVERSITY PRESS

Oxford University Press is a department of the University of Oxford. It furthers
the University's objective of excellence in research, scholarship, and education
by publishing worldwide. Oxford is a registered trade mark of Oxford University
Press in the UK and certain other countries.

Published in the United States of America by Oxford University Press
198 Madison Avenue, New York, NY 10016, United States of America.

First published in German in 2015 as *Engel der Effizienz: Eine Mediengeschichte
der Unternehmensberatung* By Kontanz University Press
© English translation Oxford University Press 2020

Library of Congress Cataloging-in-Publication Data
Names: Hoof, Florian, author. | Fairfax, Daniel, translator.
Title: Angels of efficiency : a media history of consulting /
by Florian Hoof ; translated by Daniel Fairfax.
Other titles: Engel der Effizienz. English.
Description: New York, NY : Oxford University Press, [2020] |
Translation of: Engel der Effizienz : eine Mediengeschichte der Unternehmensberatung. |
Includes bibliographical references and index.
Identifiers: LCCN 2019034775 (print) | LCCN 2019034776 (ebook) |
ISBN 9780190886363 (hardback) | ISBN 9780190886370 (paperback) |
ISBN 9780190886387 (updf) | ISBN 9780190886394 (epub) | ISBN 9780190886400 (online)
Subjects: LCSH: Business consultants—History. | Consulting firms—History. |
Corporate culture—History. | Industrial management—History. |
Mass media in counseling—History.
Classification: LCC HD69.C6 H6613 2020 (print) |
LCC HD69.C6 (ebook) | DDC 001—dc23
LC record available at https://lccn.loc.gov/2019034775
LC ebook record available at https://lccn.loc.gov/2019034776

1 3 5 7 9 8 6 4 2

Paperback printed by Marquis, Canada
Hardback printed by Bridgeport National Bindery, Inc., United States of America

The translation of this work was funded by Geisteswissenschaften International – Translation Funding
for Work in the Humanities and Social Sciences from Germany, a joint initiative of the Fritz Thyssen
Foundation, the German Federal Foreign Office, the collecting society VG WORT and the Börsenverein
des Deutschen Buchhandels (German Publishers & Booksellers Association).

" . . . we are on the road to our ideal, a self-perpetuating system of management . . ."

—Henry L. Gantt, *Work, Wages, and Profits,* 1919

"You can also visualize who will be the next man at the machine. You can visualize if there is going to be a change. You can visualize that the planning department is at fault in not getting work in the second set of hooks. You can visualize the names of the best workers. [. . .] Your chart department is the greatest visualizing device of all."

—Frank B. Gilbreth, *Visualizing the Problem of Management,* 1921

"The medium of visualization [. . .] is an automatic machine that takes the raw material of management and converts it into a finished uniform article by the law of transfer of skill, just the same as any other automatic machine."

—Chester B. Lord, *Management by Exception,* 1931

"The slide rule is a small symbol carried in one's breast pocket and sensed as a hard white line over one's heart. If you own a slide rule and someone comes along with big statements or great emotions, you say: 'Just a moment, please—let's first work out the margin for error and the most-probable values.'"

—Robert Musil, *The Man Without Qualities I,* 1921–1930

Contents

Acknowledgments

This book is the English translation of my thesis, a project I was involved in between 2007 and 2011. Special thanks go to the Studienstiftung des deutschen Volkes, which financed this project through a doctoral stipend, to Vinzenz Hediger, who vigorously supported my undertaking regardless of disciplinary boundaries, and to Dirk Baecker, who has contributed to the success of this work with crucial advice. I would also like to thank the jury of the Geisteswissenschaft International, represented by the jury chair Luca Giuliani for awarding the translation prize and financing the English translation. A thorough revision of the German manuscript was enabled by an invitation as a scientist in residence at the University of Sydney Business School, and more particularly by Sebastian K. Boell. The Institute for Advanced Study on Media Cultures of Computer Simulation at Leuphana University of Lüneburg provided generous resources for preparing the translation. I also carried out helpful conversations relating to the translation with Oliver Gaycken and Scott Curtis. I like to thank the translator Daniel Fairfax and Oxford University Press for their extraordinarily good cooperation, especially Norman Hirschy for his constructive feedback on the translation.

David Gugerli and Daniela Zetti gave me the privilege of developing my thoughts as a guest at the ETH Zurich in the concluding phase of the project. I received valuable feedback at conferences or in conversations with the aforementioned individuals, as well as Monika Dommann, Thomas Elsaesser, Lea Haller, Herbert Kalthoff, Alexandros-Andreas Kyrtsis, Dan Streible, and Chris Wahl. Thanks to the doctoral forums of the Studienstiftung des Deutschen Volkes, the colloquium "Form Labor" at Zepplin University in Friedrichshafen, the colloquium on the history of technology at the ETH Zurich, and to Tobias Röhl and Herbert Kalthoff, as well as the colloquium for the Sociology of Knowledge at the Johannes Gutenberg University in Mainz. I would like to acknowledge Andrea Genrich and Petra Memmer (Landesmuseum für Technik und Arbeit in Mannheim), Sammie L. Morris (Archives and Special Collection Purdue University, Indiana), and Wolfgang Rabus and Carsten John (Corporate Archive of Daimler AG). Further thanks go to the Bibliothèque Historique de la Ville de Paris, where I was able to write a significant portion of the manuscript, to the Research School in Bochum for partly financing my archival trips, and to the Lehrstuhl für Filmwissenschaft at the Goethe University in Frankfurt for financially supporting the German book. I would also like to expressly acknowledge the extremely good cooperation of Konstanz University Press, their editorial board (Monika Dommann, Wolfgang Essbach, Michael Hagner, Albrecht Koschorke, Kirsten Mahlke, Christoph Menke, Bernd Stiegler, Dieter Thomä), and particularly Alexander Schmitz, whose critical yet constructive reading is responsible for much of this book's success. Finally, the most important thanks of all: without Nika Mossessian this book could never have been written. I also thank my parents, as well as Anne and Ruth for their help with the manuscript's legibility in the earlier stages of the project, and Helen for her mathematical expertise.

Introduction

Angels of Efficiency

The history of consulting as a form of knowledge begins with the case of a dead man in a telephone booth. The site of this tragic event is the Lackawanna railroad station in Montclair, New Jersey, an outer suburb of New York City. On a sunny day, June 14, 1924, the corporate consultant and film pioneer Frank B. Gilbreth embarked on a trip to Manhattan. He needed to organize a visa for a planned journey to Europe, to attend the Prague International Management Conference. But he never got that far. During a phone call with his wife, he suffered a heart attack and died. The ensuing newspaper obituaries not only highlighted his services to managerial practices, but also laconically noted that, with his idiosyncratic methods, he had brought about his own downfall. Together with his wife, Lillian, the first woman in the United States to receive a doctorate in industrial psychology, Frank belonged to the first generation of modern corporate consultants. The specialty of their consulting firm, Gilbreth, Inc., was lab-based consulting, the filmic analysis of motion in industrial labor processes, with the goal of raising worker productivity. In the end, as some of the obituaries implied, Frank succumbed to the stress of an optimized life. In any case, the circumstances that afternoon resulted in one of the first publications of modern consulting appearing posthumously. Three months after his death, the magazine *Management and Administration* publicized the consultancy model used by Gilbreth, Inc., "The One Best Way to Do Work," an article which consists of a grammar of motion, defining seventeen elementary motor acts.[1] With these "therbligs" (an anagram of the name Gilbreth), all the motion episodes occurring in industry could be modeled. The text assigned a specific symbol to every therblig and compared different strategies of labor organization in the workplace through flow charts and graphs. Individual therbligs were assigned to specific

---

[1] Frank Gilbreth and Lillian Gilbreth, "Classifying the Elements of Work: Methods of Analyzing Work into Seventeen Subdivisions," *Management and Administration* 7, no. 8 (1924): 151–54; Frank Gilbreth and Lillian Gilbreth, "Applications of Motion Studies: Its Use in Developing the Best Methods of Work," in *Management and Administration* 7, no. 9 (1924): 295–97. The seventeen therbligs are "search," "find," "select," "grasp," "transport loaded," "position," "assemble," "use," "disassemble," "inspect," "pre-position for next operation," "release load," "transport empty," "rest for overcoming fatigue," "unavoidable delay," "avoidable delay," "plan."

Angels of Efficiency. Florian Hoof, Oxford University Press (2020) © Oxford University Press.
DOI: 10.1093/oso/9780190886363.003.0001

time units, which allowed businesses to calculate labor activities in advance. This consulting model, based on hundreds of filmed motion studies conducted by Frank and Lillian Gilbreth since 1912, was an initial prototype of a simulation system for human labor. Having recorded motion patterns, the Gilbreths subsequently synthesized them in the therblig system. This system involved "at least a hundred variables that are important [. . .] and our list contains several thousand variables." Since this list was not to be relayed to potential customers of their corporate consulting firm, the Gilbreths reduced their framework to a simple, clear model: "We have adopted a 'Wheel of Motion' not altogether unlike the 'Wheel of Life' of Hindus, for explaining therblig study to the employees of our clients."[2] One of the first models of corporate consulting is thus a wondrous mix of Hindu/Buddhist symbolism, the latest technologies in cinema and the principle of graphic representation (see Figures 1 and 2).

As one of the earliest visual models of consulting, this piece appeared toward the chronological end of the time frame of this book (between 1880 and 1930), during which time—as my central hypothesis has it—the use of media in business and industry rapidly expanded. As the earlier example shows, the use of charts, graphics, photographs, and film increased to the point that they became self-evident components of corporate management. Consultants and managers themselves also became passionate filmgoers and pondered the role that film could play as a new communication medium for businesses. In what follows, I will examine, from the perspective of the history of film, media, and knowledge, the visual culture that arose as a result of this phenomenon. There are only a few preexisting studies that are concerned with media in a business context and could thus offer orientation to my endeavor. Elspeth H. Brown explored the role played by photography in large corporations, while Brian Price and Richard Lindstrom have tackled Frank Gilbreth's biography.[3] Some preliminary considerations on how to conceive of film in relation to business have, however, come from research carried out on industrial cinema.[4] Occupying the zone between

[2] Ibid., 295.

[3] Elspeth H. Brown, *The Corporate Eye. Photography and the Rationalization of American Commercial Culture: 1884–1929* (Baltimore: Johns Hopkins University Press, 2005); Brian Price, "One Best Way: Frank and Lillian Gilbreth's Transformation of Scientific Management, 1885–1940" (PhD diss., Purdue University, 1987); Richard Lindstrom, "Science and Management: Popular Knowledge, Work, and Authority in the Twentieth-Century United States" (PhD diss., Purdue University, 2000).

[4] Florian Hoof, "'The One Best Way': Bildgebende Verfahren der Ökonomie als strukturverändernder Innovationsschub der Managementtheorie ab 1860," *montage a/v* 15, no. 1 (2006): 123–38; Vinzenz Hediger and Patrick Vonderau, eds., *Films That Work: Industrial Film and the Productivity of Media* (Amsterdam: Amsterdam University Press, 2009); Scott Curtis, "Images of Efficiency: The Films of Frank B. Gilbreth," in *Films That Work: Industrial Film and the Productivity of Media*, ed. Vinzenz Hediger and Patrick Vonderau (Amsterdam: Amsterdam University Press, 2009), 85–99; Vinzenz Hediger, Florian Hoof, and Yvonne Zimmerman, eds., *Films That Work Harder: The Global Circulation of Industrial Cinema* (Amsterdam: Amsterdam University Press, forthcoming).

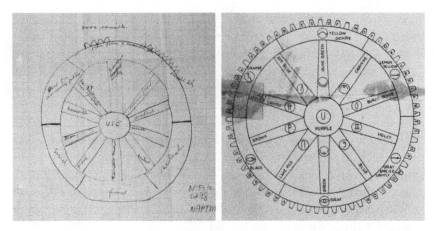

Figures 1 and 2 From the sketch outline of the Wheel of Motion. The results of roughly ten years of filmic motion analysis, reduced to an easily communicated analytic framework for corporate consultants.

film, media, and economic history, my study draws on this work, describing the culture of rationalization resulting from industrial films and situating it as a part of the history of corporate consulting.

This much can be said right away: the form of knowledge emerging from this work has proven to be extremely stable, and it continues to prevail in present-day forms of corporate consulting. In this regard, the Wheel of Motion is an exemplary model that intended to clarify the relations existing between the different variables contained within. It is not sufficient to implement a single change at a single point in a single labor activity. "The variables affect all of the therbligs and must be all carefully considered in order to obtain The One Best Way to Do Work." All conditions must be thought of in an equilibrium with the center of the model: *use*. "The more *use*, the more production."[5] There are two kinds of therbligs. On the one hand, they can be a "method of attack,"[6] with which changes in the existing corporate structure can be undertaken. On the other hand, they can aid in the comprehension and representation of a new type of knowledge: consulting knowledge.[7]

This form of knowledge is subject to very particular demands. It must be modular and flexible, and it must also follow a persuasive, stable inner logic. Changes undertaken, or considered, in the framework of a consulting commission must

---

[5] Gilbreth and Gilbreth, "Applications of Motion Studies," 295. Emphasis in the original.
[6] Ibid., 297.
[7] Here, I take the term to refer not only to knowledge in the strict sense, but also as an epistemological concept, as proposed in historical epistemology.

be confirmed with the clients, and at the same time communicated within the enterprise. It is only in this way that innovations can be successfully implemented. Consulting knowledge involves a knowledge of potentiality. It vacillates between an ideal-typical form—in this case, the system presented in the Wheel of Motion—and its profane realization as "transferable data."[8] It must address the utopian character of potential future changes in an enterprise, and at the same time appear practicable and capable of being carried out. The model of the Wheel of Motion stands for this balancing act between mundane improvements and the utopian potential for efficiencies that could be tapped into. It nonetheless promised a reproducible benchmarking (to use the vocabulary of today's corporate consultants) of human motion and labor performance, setting verifiable and comprehensible standards, and thus creating "the managerial conditions which will permit The One Best Way to Do Work."[9]

Against the backdrop of the great success of corporate consultants in the 1910s and 1920s, it seems as if consulting knowledge provided them with "the sacred knowledge of the Brahmins."[10] Corporate consultants appeared in industrial enterprises as a media version of angels of efficiency. With their "symbolistically rationalized magic"[11] and their "mimetical actions of a magician,"[12] they succeeded in creating new, unprecedented efficiency potentials. These angels of efficiency were not, however, messengers of an opaque mediality; considered from the standpoint of economic and media history, they were an apparition of differentiation that was firmly grounded in the mortal world.

The field of corporate consulting, and the knowledge tied to it, represented a new sensory system that promised to guide disoriented industrial management through moments of technological and social upheaval. The "disenchantment of the world" brought about by rationalization and intellectualization, as diagnosed by Max Weber,[13] is paradoxically accompanied by a process of idealization in the consulting industry and in the talents it cultivated. The manner in which, in the course of time, the rather profane activity of a corporate consultant was given an almost religious elevation, can to a large degree be traced back to the careful media presentations of the first consultants (Fig. 3). This special status bestowed on corporate consulting is no coincidence. Rather, it is a constitutive condition for the branch's success.

[8] Ibid., 296.

[9] Ibid., 297.

[10] Max Weber, "Religious Groups (The Sociology of Religion)," in *Economy and Society*, ed. Guenther Roth and Claus Wittich (Berkeley: University of California Press, 1978), 458.

[11] Ibid., 407.

[12] Ibid., 400.

[13] Max Weber, "Science as a Vocation," in *From Max Weber: Essays in Sociology*, ed. H. H. Gerth and C. Wright Mills (New York: Oxford University Press, 1946), 129–56.

Figure 3 The corporate consultants of the 1910s–1920s used media to present themselves as angels of efficiency. An employee of the corporate consulting firm Gilbreth, Inc., surrounded by cyclegraphic recordings.

The circumstances portrayed earlier could go down in history as an episode in the expiring age of thermodynamics, as the last stirrings of an outmoded understanding of labor and production, in which workers are little more than human machines. It could be supposed that they have little in common with today's knowledge-based branches of industry. Like the Lackawanna railroad station, now closed, the consultancy practices of the time and the businesses tied to them could be understood as relics of the distant past. The station building may still be standing today, but its façade is now adorned with an oversized advertisement for the video store chain Hollywood Video, which had an outlet at the site until its 2010 bankruptcy. The age of local video stores may be over, and the structures, as well as the perceptions, of industrial management may have radically changed. And yet, up to the present day, very little has changed in consulting knowledge, as the model of the Wheel of Motion prototypically embodied it. There are two reasons why this is not such a surprise.

First, the present object and purpose of consulting processes is still identical with that of the 1920s. Its goal is to change a status quo, but also to moderate this process, to legitimize it, and to lead it to an optimal conclusion. Local considerations internal to the workplace may also play a role in management resorting to external experts. That this strategic deployment of corporate consultants is not a new phenomenon can be seen in the opinion given by Frank B. Gilbreth on the quarreling sections of a Berlin firm, and on his status as a corporate consultant for the company: "In other words they have all been fighting for a long time and they want me to be the buffer wheel."[14] With his Wheel of Motion consulting model, Gilbreth could do their bidding, and not only in a metaphorical sense. Second, the consulting business of this period is one of the driving forces behind a new order of knowledge which imposed itself on business affairs at the turn of the century and which continues to the present. Today, it is the formation of complex processes, and not a concern for the loss of energy within thermodynamic systems, that is at the center of thinking in this area. As the example of the fractious Berlin firm shows, attention increasingly came to focus on technical and social factors, which were difficult to comprehend with the standard laws of thermodynamics. These were replaced with graphic consulting models, with which a pragmatic improvement of labor processes was to be achieved. Thinking in large-scale energy systems was replaced with thinking in modular consulting structures. Up to the present day, this paradigm shift has determined the effect that a microeconomic perspective has had on business efficiency.

A good sixty years later, in the early 1980s, Tom Peters and Robert Waterman, two consultants from the consulting firm McKinsey & Company, developed the McKinsey 7-S Framework (see Figure 4). Almost identical, in its visual form and conception, to the Wheel of Motion, it also served the purposes of business analysis. The consulting model developed in the 1920s had set itself the target of detecting efficiency reserves in bodily labor processes in the workplace, which went unrecognized before their cinematic visualization.

Peters and Waterman pursue a very similar objective, since they also seek to optimize something that is not visible. Their model does not, however, focus on the individual body of the worker, but on the enterprise as a whole. The framework of their analysis consists of seven variables, called "levers," with which they strive toward a definition of the existing "workplace culture" and the changes that need to be undertaken. It is no longer individual workers, and their motion sequences, that stand in the center of corporate consulting, but the logistical coordination of the entire business. This model does not describe firms as mere structures, but as complex systems. While business structures, such as hierarchy levels, are perceptible and visible in their institutionalized form, this does not apply to workplace culture, which evades standard forms of empiricism and

---

[14] F. B. Gilbreth, letter to L. M. Gilbreth, November 12, 1914, Gilbreth LOM, SPCOLL, Purdue University Libraries, NF 91/813-6.

McKINSEY 7-S FRAMEWORK ©

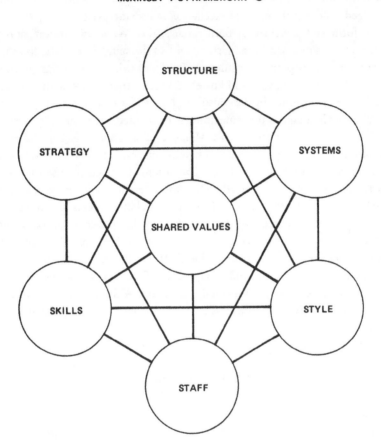

Figure 4 The 7-S Framework developed by McKinsey & Company sought to define and visualize invisible components of business organizations, such as "workplace culture."

representation. If Frank B. Gilbreth's filmic studies served to shed light on previously imperceptible motion procedures, then the McKinsey 7-S Framework has the purpose of enabling an articulation and discussion of the amorphous object that is workplace culture. In order to concretize an invisible object, Gilbreth resorts to the idea of an infallible, conclusive grammar of motion. The McKinsey 7-S Framework, meanwhile, resembles a self-contained molecular structure. Gilbreth's indivisible therbligs here take on the form of atoms forming the nucleus of the organization. It is with these construction elements that the culture of a workplace can be described, analyzed, and transformed. Whereas Gilbreth still loudly promised the "One Best Way to Do Work," McKinsey & Company envisaged a successful "search of excellence" in the enterprise.[15]

The form and structure of both models, the "Wheel of Motion" and the McKinsey 7-S Framework, can also be seen in the standard analytic tools used by present-day corporate consultants. BCG Growth-Share Matrix, Balanced Scorecard, SWOT Analysis, and Porter's 5 Forces Analysis are analytic tools in which the form assumed by the consulting knowledge is concretized. They boast a stable inner logic and at the same time can be adapted, in a modular and flexible fashion, to changed circumstances. Moreover, they allocate visual evidence in the form of a graphic model that is coherent but cannot be understood as a representation of consulting knowledge. The systematic effects of business activity described therein can be ascribed neither to a referent, nor to an ultimate, infallible level. They are not simplified, flattened visual inscriptions of complex situations. In fact, these visual models themselves *are* the knowledge of consulting.

They are "boundary objects"[16] that are located between different orders of knowledge and seek to form bridges between them. For this reason, they must be capable of being flexibly coupled to different contexts, as well as conveying a specific agenda connected with them. Although they make reference to other knowledge holdings and forms, these are coordinated and do not determine the specific character of consulting knowledge. Consulting models do not possess conclusive, secure insights; rather, they are relational instruments for generating difference. Instead of representing knowledge as a true, well-established proposition, they promote the concept of relational accountability. Consulting knowledge, understood as an epistemological configuration, does not seek to distinguish between the true and the false, but to activate and demonstrate the possible courses of action that are practicable at any given moment.

Consulting knowledge is therefore not only a business service, but an expression of more fundamental transformations. It is part of a new, proto-cybernetic order of knowledge, which can be seen here for the first time, and which, up to the present day, has been a mainstay of managerial conduct. It breaks with the hypotheses of the thermodynamic era, in which the understanding of knowledge as a true, justified opinion predominated. In place of conclusive certainties and laws, as they still tended to manifest themselves in thermodynamic laws of energy conservation, we see the conception of knowledge as a mutable, relational, and process-based property. Managing this extremely precarious and fleeting

---

[15] Tom Peters and Robert H. Waterman, *In Search of Excellence: Lessons from America's Best-Run Companies* (New York: Harper & Row, 1982).
[16] On the concept of "boundary objects," see Susan Leigh Star and James R. Griesemer, "Institutional Ecology, 'Translations' and Boundary Objects: Amateurs and Professionals in Berkeley's Museum of Vertebrate Zoology, 1907–39," *Social Studies of Science* 19 (1989): 387–420.

form of knowledge is the manifest goal of the ascendant branch of consulting. Consulting knowledge is thus not a simplified form of more complex knowledge holdings, or an appendage of other orders of knowledge. It is a self-sufficient knowledge possessing an efficacious structure.

In the sixty years stretching between the Wheel of Motion model and the McKinsey 7-S Framework, business and management have been fundamentally transformed. It is no longer the regulation and administration of a maximum level of labor power that is at the center of production, but questions around the management of innovation processes. The image of the "human motor"[17] has been transformed into the concept of "human capital."[18] It no longer encompasses just thermodynamic energy—pure labor power—but also psychological factors. Creativity and intellectual performance can be neither determined nor quantified with the nineteenth-century laws of thermodynamics.

Nonetheless, consulting knowledge continues to be based on the framework of the Taylorist/Fordist production regime and the forms arising in the visual culture dominant at this time. Whereas Gilbreth sought to open up the terra incognita of physical productivity with his systematization of "therbligs," now "levers" are to achieve similar results for the complex business organizations of the postindustrial era. For his Wheel of Motion, Gilbreth drew on aspects of Hinduism and Buddhism, which were extraordinarily popular between 1900 and 1920. For the first time, anthropological descriptions afforded access to these cultures, and the notions of equilibrium and stability tied to them.[19] The McKinsey 7-S Framework, meanwhile, borrowed not only from the rhetoric of Cicero, but also incorporated Japanese approaches to management.[20] It represents, at least partly, a departure from Western conceptions of rationality, by seeking to adapt certain Zen-Buddhist concepts like the Kaizen to the needs of Western corporations.

Both forms of consulting knowledge described here involve *visual* knowledge, and not, as has been previously suggested, the *visual representation* of

---

[17] Anson Rabinbach, *The Human Motor: Energy, Fatigue, and the Origins of Modernity* (Berkeley: University of California Press, 1992).

[18] Jacob Mincer, "Investment in Human Capital and Personal Income Distribution," *The Journal of Political Economy* 66, no. 4 (1958): 281–302. See also Dirk Baecker, *Postheroisches Management: Ein Vademecum* (Berlin: Merve, 1994); Brigitta Bernet and David Gugerli: '"Sputniks Resonanzen': Der Aufstieg der Humankapitaltheorie im Kalten Krieg," *Historische Anthropologie* 19, no. 3 (2011): 433–46.

[19] See Laurence Waddell, *The Buddhism of Tibet or Lamaism, with Its Mystic Cult, Symbolism and Mythology, and in Its Relation to Indian Buddhism* (London: Allen, 1895).

[20] This model was developed in collaboration with Richard T. Pascale, professor at the Stanford Business School, and Anthony G. Athos, professor at the Harvard Business School. See Richard T. Pascale and Anthony G. Athos, *The Art of Japanese Management: Applications for American Executives* (New York: Simon & Schuster, 1981).

knowledge. Behind the Wheel of Motion model there stands an entire arsenal of various visualization practices utilized for consulting purposes. Gilbreth deployed the most advanced media technologies of the day, such as newly invented charting techniques or filmmaking instruments. The stability of this visual knowledge has been reproduced up to the present day, with models of corporate consulting such as the McKinsey 7-S Framework. Here, too, the model is part of a visual ensemble comprising PowerPoint presentations, flip charts, cluster maps, statistical pie charts, and bar graphs. Consulting no longer assumes the form of written reports; instead, it consists of loosely gathered visual decision-making cues, which are tailored for the fast-paced nature of executive meetings and the decisions made therein.

Since this time, the consulting industry has developed into a knowledge system that is central to the economy. It is a cornerstone of strategic decision making, which often determines the success or failure of a business, and thus has direct effects on society as a whole. At the same time, the principle of consulting (and the science based on it) is essential for the faith put into managerial decisions. Consulting is the *ultima ratio*, the only approach that is still legitimate and practicable, in which commercial enterprises, on account of certain intractable impasses, seem to encounter their limits. It is for this reason that the form of this knowledge, with which I will be occupied in the following analysis, is so decisive. I understand consulting not only as part of the economy, but also as a point of intersection where the boundaries of economic logic and legitimation are on view, one that is newly determined on a constant basis. Consulting is the attempt to integrate the destructive, crisis-prone traits of the capitalist economy into the business itself, and to thus profit, as Schumpeter puts it, from the creative aspect linked to destruction.[21] Corporate consulting is, therefore, not a mere sideshow in the economy as a whole, but a sphere in which the contradictions of this form of society manifest themselves, and are given over to processes of reworking.

In order to reach a better understanding of present-day, self-evident forms of visual business communication, and to place them in their historical context, in what follows I will reconstruct the emergence of visual forms of managerial communication between 1880 and 1930, with an emphasis on the development of consulting knowledge.[22]

---

[21] Joseph Alois Schumpeter, *Capitalism, Socialism and Democracy* (New York: Routledge Chapman Hall, 2005 [1946]); Werner Sombart, *War and Capitalism (European Sociology)* (North Stratford, NH: Ayer, 1975 [1913]).

[22] For a similar perspective, see Adam J. Tooze, "Die Vermessung der Welt: Ansätze zu einer Kulturgeschichte der Wirtschaftsstatistik," in *Wirtschaftsgeschichte als Kulturgeschichte: Dimensionen eines Perspektivenwechsels*, ed. Hartmut Berghoff and Jakob Vogel (Frankfurt a. M.: Campus Verlag, 2004), 325–51.

Media, "Visual Management," and Consulting

The time span of my investigation, from 1880 to 1930, covers three parallel developments, which lead to a fundamental transformation of industrial knowledge structures. First, there is the constitution of an independent form of managerial activity in industry. Second, and at the same time, there is the establishment of the field of corporate consulting. Third, there is the emergence of a series of visualization techniques after 1880, which are at the disposition of the first two spheres, management and corporate consulting.

Managerialism

The notion of the concrete activity of "managing" is relatively young. In around 1830, we can find evidence of distinctly "managerial" practices in commercial and industrial enterprises.[23] The success of the 1832 publication *On the Economy of Machinery and Manufactures* is a paradigmatic example of this.[24] In this book, Charles Babbage recommends defining clear areas of responsibility in a business. Up to 1860, individual practices of corporate control were bundled together to form a corporation-centric, paternalistic, direct managerial practice, which mainly rested on oral communication in the form of direct instructions and commands.[25] From the 1860s on, the constricted relationship between management and the enterprise was progressively dissolved.[26] Firms expanded to become "multiunit business enterprises."[27] The increased need for coordination and growing geographical distances between individual sites of production overtaxed existing direct, oral management practices and led to a "crisis of control."[28] As a reaction to this, practices based on the "written record" were imposed.[29] New media techniques such as the "typewriter, duplicating methods, and filing systems"[30] led to the establishment of a bureaucratic system

---

[23] Sidney Pollard, *The Genesis of Modern Management: A Study of the Industrial Revolution in Great Britain* (Aldershot, UK: Gregg Revivals, 1993).

[24] Charles Babbage, *On the Economy of Machinery and Manufactures* (London: Charles Knight, 1832).

[25] JoAnne Yates, *Control Through Communication: The Rise of System in American Management* (Baltimore: Johns Hopkins University Press, 1989), 3.

[26] Thomas K. McCraw, ed., *Creating Modern Capitalism: How Entrepreneurs, Companies, and Countries Triumphed in Three Industrial Revolutions* (Cambridge, MA: Harvard University Press, 1999), 14; Claude S. George, *The History of Management Thought* (Englewood Cliffs, NJ: Prentice-Hall, 1972), 81.

[27] Alfred Chandler, *The Visible Hand: The Managerial Revolution in American Business*, 16th ed. (Cambridge, MA: Harvard University Press, 2002 [1977]).

[28] James Beniger, *The Control Revolution: Technological and Economic Origins of the Information Society* (Cambridge, MA: Harvard University Press, 1986), 10.

[29] Yates, *Control Through Communication*, 164.

[30] Ibid., 21.

of constant control and readjustment, dubbed "systematic management."[31] At the beginning of the twentieth century, the new medium of film was integrated into this practice.

Consulting

It is certainly no coincidence that the corporate consulting industry emerged at a time when there was a generalized trend toward standardization and bureaucratization in the corporate world. Only a handful of corporate consulting firms, such as Sedgwick (founded in 1858), existed before this period.[32] In 1886, the Arthur D. Little Company was founded. In 1907, Harrington Emerson established his first corporate consulting firm. The pace of this development accelerated in the 1910s.[33] Frank and Lillian Gilbreth created their consultancy Gilbreth, Inc. in 1912; the next year Arthur Anderson came into existence, followed by Booz Allen & Hamilton in 1914.[34] In addition, a number of individual efficiency experts, such as Henry L. Gantt and Carl G. Barth, emerged from the milieu surrounding Frederick W. Taylor. Around 1900, they began to install the Taylorist system of scientific management in different industries.[35] The great majority of these consultants were either engineers or came from the sphere of accounting or business administration.[36] Between 1903 and 1913, the first societies in the consulting industry were founded.[37] In 1912, Harrington Emerson inaugurated the New York Efficiency Society.[38] By this point, the Taylor Society had already been in existence for two years, and Frank B. Gilbreth was a significant participant in its initiation.[39] Beginning in the 1910s, the industry was professionalized. This can be seen, for instance, in the introduction of courses in business administration

[31] Joseph Litterer, *The Emergence of Systematic Management as Shown by the Literature of Management from 1870–1900* (New York: Garland, 1986).

[32] Sugata Biswas and Daryl Twitchell, *Management Consulting: A Complete Guide to the Industry*, 2nd ed. (New York: John Wiley & Sons, 2002), 17–19.

[33] Staffan Canback, "The Logic of Management Consulting: Part 1," *Journal of Management Consulting* 10, no. 2 (1998): 4.

[34] Biswas and Twitchell, *Management Consulting*, 19.

[35] Judith A. Merkle, *Management and Ideology. The Legacy of the International Scientific Management Movement* (Berkeley: University of California Press, 1980), 59.

[36] Biswas and Twitchell, *Management Consulting*, 18.

[37] Matthias Kipping, "Consultancies, Institutions and the Diffusion of Taylorism in Britain, Germany and France, 1920s to 1950s," *Business History* 39, no. 4 (1997): 69.

[38] Horace B. Drury, *Scientific Management: A History and Criticism* (New York: Columbia University Press, 1915), 19.

[39] Daniel Nelson, "Scientific Management, Systematic Management, and Labor, 1880–1915," *The Business History Review* 48, no. 4 (1974): 479–500.

studies in business schools, which had only recently come into existence.[40] These consultancy firms developed their own methods, such as "forecasting," which were no longer tied to efficiency increases on the factory floor. For example, Booz Allen & Hamilton offered a "business research service," which extended its field of activity from corporate consulting to the sphere of strategy and future planning.[41] Frank B. Gilbreth, meanwhile, developed a graphic system for the rationalization of decision-making processes in management.[42] Prior to the outbreak of World War I, therefore, the consulting industry had established itself under the label of "efficiency engineering,"[43] as well as developing and practically experimenting with its first instruments, models, and forms of consulting science.

The Graphic Method

Simultaneous with the professionalization of management and the rise of the corporate consulting industry, the *graphic method media network*[44] was formed, a "heterogeneous ensemble"[45] of technologies, practices, and actors, which were grouped around a modality of media representation. The point of departure for this phenomenon is the development of graphic visualization techniques in

[40] The first business school to be established was the University of Pennsylvania's Wharton School in 1881, which was followed by the UK's Manchester Metropolitan Business School in 1889, the Universität St. Gallen, the University of Chicago School of Business, and the College of Commerce at UC Berkeley in 1898, Dartmouth College's Tuck School of Business in 1900, the Harvard Business School in 1908, and the Columbia University Business School in 1916. See also Rakesh Khurana, *From Higher Aims to Hired Hands: The Social Transformation of American Business Schools and the Unfulfilled Promise of Management as a Profession* (Princeton, NJ: Princeton University Press, 2007).

[41] Canback, "The Logic of Management Consulting: Part I," 4.

[42] Frank B. Gilbreth, "Graphical Control on the Exception Principle for Executives," *The Journal of the American Society of Mechanical Engineers* 39, no. 4 (1917): 311–12.

[43] George, *The History of Management Thought*, 107.

[44] The term used in the original German edition of this book, *Medienverbund*, refers to the work of Friedrich Kittler, who uses the term to describe media technologies that underpin society. *Medienverbund* was translated in the American edition of his writings as "media link." See Friedrich Kittler, *Gramophone, Film, Typewriter*, trans. Geoffrey Winthrop-Young and Michael Wutz (Stanford, CA: Stanford University Press, 1999). Nonetheless, the German word *Verbund* carries other connotations than those associated with the idea of interlinked technologies. It is etymologically derived from the Middle High German word *Bündnis*, a word which not only describes the connections between technological apparatuses or materials, but also alliances of economic organizations. This conscious, strategic usage of "allying oneself" (*sich verbünden*) is lost in the narrowing of the term to the level of mere technological linking between different entities. My praxeological-materialist approach, by contrast, focuses precisely on the level of usage. Hence, *Medienverbund* will be translated with the more broadly conceived term "media network." This also connects to approaches that sought to describe the interrelations of media technologies, culture, and society, such as Alison Griffiths, *Wondrous Difference: Cinema, Anthropology, & Turn-of-the-Century Visual Culture* (New York: Columbia University Press, 2002), where she establishes close ties between film, anthropological research, and the museum institution.

[45] See Michel Foucault, *Power/Knowledge: Selected Interviews & Other Writings 1972–1977*, ed. Colin Gordon (New York: Pantheon Books, 1980), 194–210.

the nineteenth century. In this "golden age" of the graphic method,[46] a variety of innovations in the area of data visualization took place. Taken together, they form a media network that encompasses a wide range of visualization techniques. Graphic methods such as diagrams, pictorial representations of tabular information, or apparatuses for visual recording originally come from scientific disciplines such as mathematics, materials science, statistics, or physiology. Their deployment and development are linked with names like William Playfair, Étienne-Jules Marey, Francis Galton, Charles Lallemand, Jacques Bertillon, and Eadweard Muybridge. By the end of the nineteenth century, stable, proven practices of data visualization had been developed. At the same time, these techniques, and the modes of representation connected with them, were propagated and popularized. They were complemented with innovations such as film. With the aid of various media, data were visualized, calculated, and graphically compared, while previously imperceptible processes were photochemically depicted or graphically registered and modeled.

In the interaction between these three areas—the rise of management, the establishment of the consulting industry, and the possibilities of the graphic method media network—we can observe a visualization drive in the corporate world. This is not, however, simply a managerial fashion[47] with a short shelf-life, but a structurally transformational development that yields new forms of managerial and industrial knowledge. In the following pages, I will dub this new visual "regime"[48] of the economy *visual management*.

Visual Management

Visual management was the initial form taken by an abstract, self-referential system of making and implementing decisions. It is based on a feedback system which was oriented toward the ideal of real-time functioning, and which abstracted all incoming data through the use of visualization processes. With visual management, data could be successfully selected, hierarchized, and interpolated. Data were thus used for the most important aspect of industrial management: making quick decisions that were appropriate for the situation and that could be easily reproduced. This managerial logic, which many

---

[46] Michael Friendly, "The Golden Age of Statistical Graphics," *Statistical Science* 23, no. 4 (2008): 502–35.

[47] See Alfred Kieser, "Rhetoric and Myth in Management Fashion," *Organization* 4, no. 1 (1997): 49–74.

[48] On Rancière's notion of the "regime," see Jacques Rancière, *The Politics of Aesthetics: The Distribution of the Sensible*, trans. Gabriel Rockhill (New York: Continuum International Publishing Group, 2004); Jacques Rancière, *Aesthetics and Its Discontents*, trans. Steven Corcoran (Cambridge: Polity Press, 2009).

writers have related to the rise of cybernetics in the 1940s,[49] was, in the early twentieth-century consulting industry and among its customers (large-scale industrial enterprises), already a progressive, avant-garde anchor orienting further developments in management. Far from merely being a tentative ideal, it is a widespread practice that can be found in managerial literature as well as in the systems of administration and regulation developed by businesses. Located in a transitional phase between thermodynamic and cybernetic managerial practice, visual management is also symptomatic of the crisis of earlier attempts to model commercial activity.

The practices of administration and regulation in the thermodynamic age were still aimed at using clearly defined resources, such as labor power, as efficiently as possible. In contrast, the model of visual management represented the mirror image of this procedure. The administrative doctrine constructed on this basis, taking *temporal* aspects into account, places systemic factors in the foreground. Instead of essentialist notions of clearly defined energy resources underpinning everything, it proposes a relational and temporal understanding of unstable factors mutually influencing each other. In this new situation, hitherto existing oral and written managerial practices, which overwhelmingly served to take stock of resources, proved to be deficient. Unstable systemic effects, constantly in a state of flux, could not be apprehended within this rigid logic of documentation.

The rise of visual management's proto-cybernetic administrative logic is considerably shaped by the consulting industry, the historical situation of industrial and commercial enterprises, and the new availability of visualization techniques. I describe this process as a *medialization drive* in the corporate sector. The sphere of corporate consulting made a significant contribution to this phenomenon. It was here that a certain virtuosity in the handling of visualization practices was developed. Its specific function, the preparation of consulting knowledge, yielded a close symbiosis with the visualization techniques available at the time. Such techniques appear to be particularly well suited for conveying knowledge related to consulting, while the knowledge thus propagated nonetheless remained flexible enough to adapt to the local conditions of each firm. I therefore conceive of consulting as a boundary object, in which disparate epistemological orders encounter one other. From this collision arises a point of difference, which can lead to existing presuppositions appearing in a new light. This recognition is henceforth operationalized as a resource for change. At the same time, the prescribed form of visual presentation forestalls an impression of total capriciousness. The local situation discovered in the course of a consulting exercise is subordinated

<hr />

[49] See Claus Pias, ed., *Cybernetics—Kybernetik: The Macy-Conferences 1946–1953*, Vol. II (Zurich: Diaphanes, 2003).

to a set of methods and devices consisting of graphics, charts, and pictorial representations, and is thus, to a certain extent, visually standardized. The forms of visual knowledge partly coincide with the forms of consulting knowledge. The visual form not only represents the concrete data of the given business situation, but points to and highlights the external character of consulting. In doing so, it creates the point of difference from the everyday production routine needed for an organization to undergo a transformative process. Such a form is responsible for this point of difference being discerned and becoming subject to description and comparisons. In this way, consulting gains in authority and thus the capacity to implement its recommendations.

A Media History of Consulting

One of the points of departure for this book is the observation that disciplinary perspectives strongly determine methodological access to the overlapping spheres of media, economics, and business. On the one side, there are approaches drawing on film studies, media studies, and cultural studies, with their primarily aesthetic or media-technological perspectives, which only peripherally grapple with the field of business.[50] On the other side, there are methods taken from economic history and organization studies, which question the productivity, stability, and functionality of markets, organizations, and institutions such as corporate consulting.[51] The goal of my methodology is to consider these two perspectives in conjunction with one another, in order to pursue the epistemological ramifications of the film and media studies approach in economic contexts.[52] Until now, the interaction of these two registers—corporate institutions and commercial rationality, on the one hand, and the specific logic

[50] Exemplary, in this regard, is Marta Braun, *Picturing Time: The Work of Etienne-Jules Marey (1830–1904)* (Chicago: University of Chicago Press, 1992); and Kittler, *Gramophone, Film, Typewriter.*

[51] Christopher McKenna, *The World's Newest Profession: Management Consulting in the Twentieth Century* (Cambridge, MA: Cambridge University Press, 2006); Thomas Armbrüster, *The Economics and Sociology of Management Consulting* (Cambridge, MA: Cambridge University Press, 2006); Thomas Armbrüster, *Management and Organization in Germany* (Hampshire, UK: Ashgate, 2005); Matthias Kipping and Lars Engwall, *Management Consulting: Emergence and Dynamics of a Knowledge Industry* (Oxford: Oxford University Press, 2001); Matthias Kipping, "Consultancies, Institutions and the Diffusion of Taylorism in Britain, Germany and France, 1920s to 1950s," *Business History* 39, no. 4 (1997): 67–83; Matthias Kipping, *Management Consultancies in Germany, Britain and France: 1900–60* (University of Reading, Discussion Papers in Economics and Management, Series A, 1996).

[52] For a transdisciplinary perspective on business history, see Hartmut Berghoff and Jakob Vogel, "Wirtschaftsgeschichte als Kulturgeschichte: Ansätze zur Bergung transdisziplinärer Synergiepotentiale," in *Wirtschaftsgeschichte als Kulturgeschichte: Dimensionen eines Perspektivenwechsels*, ed. Hartmut Berghoff and Jakob Vogel (Frankfurt a.M.: Campus Verlag, 2004), 9–41.

of media aesthetics and technology, on the other hand—is far from having been adequately understood. At the crux of these approaches stands the question of how strategic managerial decisions in the corporate sphere are defined and co-determined by media.[53] The resulting work aims to open the consulting industry up to perspectives from both film and media studies *and* economic history, and that also represents an experimental methodological bridge between two disciplines that heretofore have functioned rather autonomously from one another.[54]

In the spirit of this bridge-building exercise, and, perhaps, rather unusually for a media history of corporate consulting, I will begin my book with a cursory summary of the approaches to consulting found in the field of economic history—approaches which implicitly and explicitly grapple with systems of communication and coordination in industrial contexts. It is on this basis that the new field of research opened up by the connection I propose will become apparent.

Media and Economic History

The time frame of my research, from 1880 to 1920, corresponds with that of Alfred Chandler's study *The Visible Hand*, which describes the formation of the modern "multiunit business enterprise" in the mid-nineteenth century, and the consequent need for coordination and communication.[55] Chandler diagnoses a "communication revolution" unleashed by the advent of the postal system, the telegraph, and the telephone. As he puts it, communication media are part of general technological developments, in which management replaces older, inefficient technologies with new communication media.[56] Chandler operates with a concept of media which, on the one hand, is restricted to the sphere of communication technologies and, on the other hand, displays an instrumentalist character. Communication media appear as part of "latent pattern maintenance"[57] in order to maintain or bolster existing structures and modes of functioning.[58] But

[53] For a perspective toward a shift in the understanding of media in organizational research, see Florian Hoof and Sebastian K. Boell, "Culture, Technology, and Process in 'Media Theories': Towards a Shift in the Understanding of Media in Organizational Research," *Organization* 26, no. 4 (2019): 636–654.

[54] For arguments toward a historic turn in organization studies, see Peter Clark, "The Treatment of History in Organisation Studies: Towards an 'Historic Turn'?" *Business History* 46, no. 3 (2004): 331–52; Roy Stager Jacques, "History, Historiography and Organization Studies: The Challenge and the Potential," *Management & Organizational History* 1, no. 1 (2006): 31–49.

[55] Alfred D. Chandler Jr., *The Visible Hand: The Managerial Revolution in American Business* (Cambridge, MA: Harvard University Press, 2002)

[56] Ibid., 195.

[57] Talcott Parsons and Neil J. Smelser, *Economy and Society: A Study in the Integration of Economic and Social Theory* (London: Routledge and Kegan Paul, 1956), 18–19.

[58] For a critique of Chandler's approach, see Neil Fligstein, *The Transformation of Corporate Control* (Cambridge, MA: Harvard University Press, 1990).

he does not ascribe them with a specific efficacy. He ignores the epistemological character of media in favor of a functional interpretation.

In contrast, Marxist approaches focus less on management's changing conceptions of control, and more on the constant battle for power and influence between workers and corporate power structures. Here, there can even be a focus on film and media techniques, such as the time-and-motion studies that Frank and Lillian Gilbreth carried out with the aid of photographic and cinematic procedures. From a Marxist perspective, these practices mainly play the role of enabling management to accumulate and monopolize business and production knowledge.[59] This perspective has been criticized for excessively focusing on one specific type of control.[60] Moreover, it does not give consideration to the fact that normative management approaches such as Taylorism were not unconditionally successful in the past,[61] nor does it help to explain the specific form taken by the particular conception of management that finally prevails.

Drawing on this critique, Richard Edwards has pointed to the central role of asymmetrical forms of implicit experiential knowledge in the perpetuation of an undisrupted fostering of performance.[62] Total control is impossible, because management is always dependent on the cooperation of workers. From this observation, Edwards draws the plausible conclusion that managerial control must be investigated in the context of the available "social media of control."[63]

Nonetheless, such macro-theoretically constructed approaches in economic history, whether Chandler's evolutionist-universalist approach[64] or Braverman's and Edwards' (neo-) Marxist perspectives, tend to consider processes of communication and mediation as historical details with no ability to affect the process as a whole. They understand the specificity of communication and media technologies only to a very limited degree.

More recent studies have attempted to fill this gap. James Beniger's *The Control Revolution*, for example, describes the establishment, from the 1840s on, of new communication technologies such as feedback processes, time-and-motion

---

[59] See Harry Braverman, *Labor and Monopoly Capital: The Degradation of Work in the Twentieth Century* (New York: Monthly Review Press, 1974), 120–21.

[60] Niels Beckenbach, *Industriesoziologie* (Berlin: Walter de Gruyter 1991), 166.

[61] Richard Edwards, *Contested Terrain: The Transformation of the Workplace in the Twentieth Century* (New York: Basic Books, 1979), 110.

[62] Ibid.

[63] Beckenbach, *Industriesoziologie*, 169.

[64] See Charles Booth and Michael Rowlinson, "Management and Organizational History: Prospects," *Management & Organizational History* 1, no. 1 (2006): 6; Roy Stager Jacques, *Manufacturing the Employee: Management Knowledge from the 19th to 21st Centuries* (London: Sage, 1996), 14; Simon Down, "Knowledge Sharing Review the Use of History in Business and Management, and Some Implications for Management Learning," *Management Learning* 32, no. 3 (2001): 402.

studies, advertising strategies, the development of the postal system, the introduction of standard time zones, the rise of modern bureaucracy, and even the invention of punch-card systems.[65] The breadth of his focus has been criticized on
the basis that, despite having thematized the role of technology, Beniger nonetheless did not devote enough specific attention to it.[66] Following on from this
work, JoAnne Yates has developed a perspective that more closely focuses on
the distinct dynamics of new media technologies. Restricting her study to the
period 1850–1920, she explores individual innovations such as storage systems,
the typewriter, and duplication technologies, in order to analyze their immediate
effects on management. Yates sees the real effect of media technologies in the
accompanying written recording of workplace communication.[67] This process
gives rise to new possibilities. For example, written records also allow for the
preservation and replication of workplace processes.[68] Communication acts are
capable of retrospective verification and evaluation. "Formal internal communication" is developed into an effective tool of managerial control.[69] Yates sees
the introduction of media technologies as being linked to the "rise of system"
described by Joseph Litterer.[70] Litterer, for his part, argues that management at
the end of the nineteenth century can be characterized by its systematization
of existing workplace structures and procedures.[71] For Yates, the phenomenon
observed by Litterer forms the backdrop to the implementation of new communication technologies. Without it, the implementation of "systematic management" and the resulting interconnection of organizational hierarchies in
businesses would simply not have been possible.[72] Nonetheless, the notion of
"systematic management," which Yates adopts to describe this transition, encompasses only a part of those function which comprise management. "[It] was basically concerned with the managerial functions of directing and controlling, but
not with other functions such as planning, organizing, or facilitating."[73] What
kind of an influence this medialization drive had on the planning and organization of management remains an open question.

Whereas aspects of control in existing approaches to economic history have
a relatively broad and detailed significance, the genesis of the strategic planning

[65] Beniger, *The Control Revolution*.
[66] Yates, *Control Through Communication*, xvi.
[67] Ibid., 65–77.
[68] Ibid., 56–63.
[69] Ibid., 2.
[70] Ibid., xvi.
[71] See Joseph Litterer, "Systematic Management: The Search for Order and Integration," *The Business History Review* 35, no. 4 (1961): 461–76; Joseph Litterer, *The Emergence of Systematic Management as Shown by the Literature of Management from 1870–1900* (New York: Garland, 1986).
[72] Litterer, "Systematic Management," 469.
[73] Ibid., 476.

competencies of management has not been adequately addressed. I would like to close this gap. Building on Yates's study, and the conclusion that summarizes it: "formal internal communication became a managerial tool for coordination and control,"[74] I seek to interrogate the media-epistemological backdrop of managerial planning and decision-making practices.

In the framework of established written forms of business communication, new forms of data visualization, as my thesis has it, have had a similar, if not greater, influence on managerial *planning and strategy competencies*. Strategic decisions were no longer simply gut decisions based on the values of "subjective" experience. The more rapid accessibility of business data and the possibility of visually representing complex relations gave management new possibilities for discussing the decision-making process at hand and weighing up different scenarios against one another. The visual-graphic regime provided the conditions for the possibility of managerial self-reflection, which lies at the basis of the formation of a distinct methodological canon of strategy planning, as well as the development of the elite function of managerial employees.

In this sense, I will use a broader notion of media, which describes media approaches and apparatuses not only as tools for enabling communication. I do not conceive of them as a technology whose contours are borrowed from mathematical models,[75] thereby producing systematic, linear communication paths. The analytic separation of the functions of *control* and *coordination* from the functions of *planning* and *future anticipation* obscures the epistemic effects of media processes more than it helps to comprehend them. Certainly, media techniques enable communication and are part of the sphere of control and coordination, but they also constitute the conditions with which the content communicated can be represented or modified. This directly flows into the sphere of strategic planning and stands paradigmatically for the overlapping epistemological values of media. From management's point of view, the goal in deploying media may well be clearly formulated, but the resultant effects in the workplace corresponded to this predetermined program only in the rarest of cases.[76] The epistemological structures of the medium are the main reason for this. Such media

---

[74] Yates, *Control Through Communication*, 7. See also JoAnne Yates, "Graphs as a Managerial Tool: A Case Study of Du Pont's Use of Graphs in the Early Twentieth Century," *The Journal of Business Communication* 22, no. 1 (1985): 5–33.

[75] See C. E. Shannon, "A Mathematical Theory of Communication," *The Bell System Technical Journal* 27, nos. 7, 10 (1948): 379–423; 623–56.

[76] Hesse makes a similar argument in his investigation of the contingent effects of postal, telegram, and telephone communication on the economic system as a whole. See Jan-Otmar Hesse, *Im Netz der Kommunikation: Die Reichs-Post- und Telegraphenverwaltung: 1876–1914* (Munich: Beck, 2002), 423.

"specificities" or structures are often at cross-purposes to the desired media effects that have been tacitly assumed by management upon their introduction.

Media Epistemology and Management

From the perspective of the history of knowledge and media, this represents a problem of epistemology.[77] New representational forms for corporate data should not, therefore, be understood exclusively as improved means of communication. Rather, they directly alter the form of corporate knowledge. Visual knowledge exists in a different form from that of written knowledge, for example. It is disseminated, stored, and communicated in different ways. Moreover, through the utilization of media originally used in the sciences, such as film or graphic methods,[78] it can constitute an importation of new knowledge concepts from science to the business world. This coincides with a more fundamental change which transformed the relationship between business and science in the years 1850–1920, which can be roughly described as the scientification of a business's knowledge holdings. Industrial engineers increasingly had recourse to the models and methods of scientific disciplines such as mathematics in order to install more efficient production systems. They replaced and complemented existing forms of implicit experience-based knowledge with scientific expertise. This shift also affected the manner in which such knowledge holdings were processed, conveyed, stored, and circulated. Although implicit forms of experience-based knowledge had always been a part of industry's organization of production, the new forms of explicit knowledge were actively disseminated in the workplace. Thus, the tendency toward visualization that took hold in the 1880s centered not only on the issue of control, but also on the simple and rapid accessibility of knowledge. In the process, industrial engineers, early corporate consultants, and managerial staff had recourse not only to scientifically tested forms of visualization, but also, and more overwhelmingly, to the visual principles of popular culture and its most widely used media. In this sense, the medialization drive led to principles from other fields of media culture having an influence on the newly delineated forms of administrative knowledge. The new communication media not only served to refine techniques of control; they

[77] Gaston Bachelard, *Épistémologie: Textes Choisis* (Paris: PUF, 1971); Georges Canguilhem, *Ideology and Rationality in the History of the Life Sciences*, trans. Arthur Goldhammer (Cambridge, MA: MIT Press, 1988); Georges Canguilhem, ed., *Études d'histoire et de philosophie des sciences concernant les vivants et la vie* (Paris: Vrin, 1968).

[78] Scott Curtis, *The Shape of the Spectatorship: Art, Science, and Early Cinema in Germany* (New York: Columbia University Press, 2015); Oliver Gaycken, *Devices of Curiosity: Early Cinema and Popular Science* (Oxford: Oxford University Press, 2015).

also formed a point of crystallization for innovation processes to become visible in the form of specific media. Hence, they often appeared to defy rational interpretation.

The history of the reciprocal effects of media, economics, and management on each other is reflected in exemplary fashion in the practice of corporate consulting. Here, I will investigate the various circumstances that initially made possible the complex and heterogeneous practice of corporate consulting, shaping it and keeping it stable over a long period of time. The transition in managerial practices that took place during this time is central to the form of visual management. It complements the previously existing forms of *written* and *oral* management. In relation to the knowledge practice of corporate consulting and management, the modus of visual management is of central importance. For a business's managerial layers, this led to immediate changes in the form, structure, and accessibility (via external consultants) of its corporate knowledge.

In the following pages, I will identify the practice of corporate consulting as a significant driving force for the visual media paradigm shift in the business world. However, this neither takes the form of a history of efficiency measures, in which new approaches to management necessarily lead to better forms of administration, nor does it assume the guise of a disciplinary history, in which innovations appear as the continual progress of a constant *dispositif* of control. Instead, a media history of accidents, experiments, and mishaps will emerge,[79] which will seek to clarify the question as to why and in what form these media techniques were implemented, and what effects this change had for management and its related forms of industrial administration, decision making, control, and planning. This complements and completes approaches drawn from economic history, which largely concentrate on the institutional, economic, and juridical conditions of consulting.[80] Not only institutional changes, but also continually changing managerial knowledge practices, exert an influence on consulting. This can be apprehended through an approach based on the history of knowledge and media. With respect to the forms of consulting knowledge that arose between 1880 and 1930, it is possible to write the history "of lapsed knowledge and that

---

[79] On the productive nature of misguided solutions, see Susan Leigh Star, "The Structure of Ill-Structured Solutions: Boundary Objects and Heterogeneous Distributed Problem Solving," in *Distributed Artificial Intelligence vol. II*, ed. Les Gasser and Michael N. Huhns (London: Pitman, 1989), 37–54. See also Erkki Huhtamo and Jussi Parikka, eds., *Media Archaeology: Approaches, Applications, and Implications* (Berkeley: University of California Press, 2011); Charles Acland, ed., *Residual Media* (Minneapolis: University of Minnesota Press, 2007).

[80] See McKenna, *The World's Newest Profession*.

of sanctioned knowledge [. . .] which is still current because still being used."[81] Which forms of consulting knowledge have disappeared into one of history's many dustbins? More important, which forms still characterize the industry of corporate consulting up to the present day?

Structure

This book includes historical case studies that illuminate the different areas of commercial and industrial activity in which visualization techniques were implemented at the beginning of the twentieth century. It is divided into two parts. In the first section, encompassing Chapters 1 and 2, I will use a media-archeological perspective, in which media are understood as the practices and expressions of a historical time span which sheds light on the increasing role played by media techniques in the business sphere at the turn of the twentieth century. I will describe and explore the conditions which favored the drive toward medialization in the economy and follow their development. Chapter 1, "Visualizing 'Everything under the Sun': Mapping Graphic Media Networks," deepens the methodological considerations already broached at the beginning of this book and develops a research program for a praxeological historical epistemology of media. It describes and systematizes the various dimensions of the graphic method media network and traces the popularization of the graphic method in the early 1900s. Chapter 2, "Visual Culture and Consulting: Charting, Simulation, and Calculation Devices," outlines the medialization drive in the sphere of industry and commerce. It gathers together case studies on early visual management systems, apparatuses, and practices with which industrial processes were turned into data and transformed into a graphic-pictorial form. These include Karol Adamiecki's "harmonogram," developed in the late nineteenth century, which was a management system that consisted of a central chart on which the relevant data for steel production were visually rendered in order to manage production disruptions. A few years later, the American engineer Henry L. Gantt, part of Frederick W. Taylor's business consulting team, designed Gantt-Charting, a similar graphic system of control and administration which visually depicted production standards. Red markings ("danger lines") indicated delays that affected the entire factory floor. Using graphic calculations, the Norwegian mathematician Carl Barth similarly developed calculation methods that facilitated the installation and operation of lathe machines. Nomographic tool cards

---

[81] Georges Canguilhem, "The Object of the History of Science," in *Continental Philosophy of Science*, ed. Garry Gutting (Oxford: Blackwell, 2005), 201.

introduced in the German metallurgy industry in the 1910s served the same purpose. Nomographic calculation processes became standard practice in the planning and installation of production machinery.

In the context of the medialization drive described in the first chapters, a three-part case study of the American consulting firm Gilbreth, Inc. forms the conclusion to my study. Chapter 3, "Gilbreth, Inc.: Selling Film to Corporations," describes how, in the 1910s, the consulting firm began to use the latest development in media technology—film—for industrial purposes. In motion-study laboratories, they undertook filmed motion studies in order to improve labor activity. They also built three-dimensional wire models and made pedagogical films, using cinema in order to promote their method of film-based corporate consulting. Chapter 4, "Consulting, Cinematic Utopia, and Organizational Restraints," describes the influence of film culture in the period between early cinema and the first feature-length films on the practices of corporate consulting. This concerns the human image linked to it and the pedagogical approaches of model-based and film-based learnings that were deployed. The book ends with Chapter 5, "Failing in Style: Business Consulting in Wartime Berlin," which reconstructs the progression of a consulting commission in the Berlin-based Auergesellschaft at the beginning of World War I. This was the first consulting project in the world that made extensive use of the visualization techniques of film and the graphic method. It was here that the first forms of visual consulting knowledge manifested themselves. From this experimental phase of knowledge formation, we subsequently turn to the Wheel of Motion, described earlier, as the prototypical form of consulting knowledge.

These case studies show the central importance of media practices for the consulting industry and business management. The medialization drive thus appears less as an abstract movement; instead, it can be contextualized concretely as a process prone to disruption. A common factor in the efforts of both internally employed industrial engineers and external corporate consultants is their recourse to a wide variety of visualization techniques, from film to graphic representation. Here it is less a matter of adopting individual media forms, like film, graphic charts, or photography, *as such*. Due to the simultaneity with which different media forms entered into economic relations in the framework of the projects undertaken by corporate consultants, I consider them from an epistemological and media-historical perspective not as individual mediums, but as a media network. How did the genesis of corporate consulting and the knowledge surrounding it unfold, and what influence did these developments have on the inception of Visual Management? My focus rests on three areas, which mutually overlap and infiltrate each other.

First, I concern myself with the conditions for the emergence of visual consulting knowledge. What visualization techniques did the first corporate consultants rely on? They faced the challenge of having to represent potential but as yet unrealized transformations. How did they operationalize media techniques in order to predict the future for the purpose of corporate consulting?

Second, I focus on the reciprocal effects that consulting knowledge and concrete business management practices had on each other. How was the potential knowledge of the consultancies transformed into practical changes in the workplace, at the end of which stood the media-based forms of visual management?

Third, these forms of economic rational action will be historicized as a part of more general media conditions. Here I insist on the medialization drive as a significant independent factor. Consequently, I will define the visualization techniques utilized as an interrelated media network, with which a new dimension of activity finds its way into the sphere of commercial and industrial activity. Here, I will supplement the existing approaches of economic and management history with a media-history perspective.

1

Visualizing "Everything under the Sun"

Mapping Graphic Media Networks

The corporate drive toward media-oriented forms of "visual management," as I describe it later, rests on a wide range of practices of visual representation, which I call a "graphic method media network." It incorporates visualization techniques for the graphic display of available data, such as bar and line diagrams. To these, we can add graphic calculation techniques such as nomography, as well as graphic means of recording data on kinetic motion processes. Among other things, they include physiological techniques of pulse and muscle analysis, and, later, filmic processes for analyzing body movements. In the course of the nineteenth century, such visualization methods were developed into self-evident, frequently used tools in disciplines like statistics, commercial science, mathematics, engineering, physiology, political science, and macroeconomics. From the 1880s on, management in industrial and commercial firms increasingly made use of these graphic, photographic, and filmic techniques, which could be utilized for obtaining, analyzing, communicating, and processing data. At this point, media networks and business practices represent, to borrow a phrase from George Canguilhem, two roads merging into each other.[1] This connection leads to fundamental changes in business practices, which I will define and describe with the concept of *visual management*.

Discussions of the historical development of visualization processes (available since 1880) generally concentrate on their relevance for individual disciplinary areas, such as statistics.[2] For the 1800s, this may represent an appropriate form of historicizing media devices, but it is easy to overlook the fact that, at the end of this century, the popularity of graphic methods led to the disciplinary spaces of their development and utilization being left behind. From 1880—and at the latest since the publication of Michael G. Mulhall's work, whose title *The Balance*

---

[1] Canguilhem, "The Object of the History of Science."

[2] See Michael Friendly, "The Golden Age of Statistical Graphics," *Statistical Science* 23, no. 4 (2008): 502–35; Ian Spence, "No Humble Pie: The Origins and Usage of a Statistical Chart," *Journal of Educational and Behavioral Statistics* 30, no. 4 (2005): 353–68; Stephen E. Fienberg, "Graphical Methods in Statistics," in *The American Statistician* 33, no. 4 (1979): 165–78; James R. Beniger and Dorothy L. Robyn, "Quantitative Graphics in Statistics," *The American Statistician* 32, no. 1 (1978): 1–11; H. Gray Funkhouser, "Historical Development of the Graphical Representation of Statistical Data," *Osiris* 3 (1937): 269–404.

Angels of Efficiency. Florian Hoof, Oxford University Press (2020) © Oxford University Press.
DOI: 10.1093/oso/9780190886363.003.0001

Sheet of the World,[3] as the author himself maintained, contained the graphic display of "everything under the sun"[4]—the graphic method is developed into a universal mode of representation. Having arisen in the context of scientific disciplines, they ceased to be individual medium isolated from one another once they had become popularized. As a consequence, they came to be deployed in other spheres as processes of data visualization. This also includes the sphere of business management explored in the present volume. Here, the various graphic methods are combined into new, hybrid visualization processes and uniformly characterized by participating actors as a mode of "graphic representation." They form a media ensemble and exhibit all the hallmarks of a media network.

Figures involved in the sphere of consulting, engineering, and business management borrowed visualization processes and adapted them for commercial purposes. The graphic method media network represented, for them, a reservoir for their managerial activity's media conditions of possibility. These apparatuses and practices form part of a transformation process in which industrial management releases itself from a fixation on oral and written forms of communication. This development is considerably driven and consolidated by the branch of business consulting and the booming field of engineering studies. Consultants recognized the potential that the new visualization techniques offered for their business model. Graphic procedures served to convey their disciplinary knowledge. At the same time, the use of these techniques, because they originated in the sciences, lent consulting the veneer of scientific objectivity and exactitude.[5] Engineers saw them as useful techniques for their discipline, situated as it was between theoretical science and practical application. For business management, the hope for decision-making processes that were fast, creative, and intuitive was closely linked with visual surfaces that could be flexibly combined and recombined.

Media Usage: Media as a "Borrowed Enunciative System"

The point of departure for my project to comprehend *science, media,* and *business* in equal measure is, in the first phase, a historical-epistemological research perspective.[6] It is distinguished from a "transparent and fluid" historiography in

---

[3] Michael G. Mulhall, *The Balance Sheet of the World: For Ten Years, 1870–1880* (London: Edward Stanford, 1881); Michael G. Mulhall, *The Progress of the World in Arts, Agriculture, Commerce, Manufactures, Instruction, Railways, and Public Wealth Since the Beginning of the Nineteenth Century* (London: Edward Stanford, 1880).

[4] Funkhouser, "Historical Development of the Graphical Representation of Statistical Data," 346.

[5] Lorraine Daston and Peter Galison, "The Image of Objectivity," *Representations* 132, no. 40 (1992): 81–128.

[6] Cf. Canguilhem, "The Object of the History of Science," 198–207; Georges Canguilhem: "Die Rolle der Epistemologie in der heutigen Historiographie der Wissenschaft," in *Wissenschaftsgeschichte*

that it correlates procedures within a knowledge-generating context "also to non-science, to ideology, to political and social practice."[7] This does not mean, however, that developments observed in parallel, by which similar figures of thought can, for instance, be detected, automatically constitute a discursive context on account of their homologous form, as Georges Canguilhem remarks: "Before putting two journeys end to end on a road, it would first be a good idea to be sure that it is indeed a question of the same road."[8] In this sense, I understand the spheres of "Media" and "Business" as two roads, for which we initially need to prove whether they do, after all, form one and the same trajectory. It is only then that we can speak of a medialization drive.

To this end, I will focus on *media usage*. This includes not only the practical utilization of media, from managerial visualization practices to the processing of business data, but also related epistemological processes: actors not only use media as a practical tool; media also provide discursive channels with which new forms of knowledge are shaped. The aspect of *usage* is, on the one hand, an indicator for a process of adaptation and, on the other hand, an epistemological production process. I thus understand "usage" as an independent sphere, in which the connection of two roads must first show itself. This connection, as my thesis has it, can be described in the concrete form of the graphic method media network.

But what exactly comprises this *graphic method media network*? First, the media network incorporates concrete apparatuses and devices, and the practices linked to them, which can be described in their broader technicality or materiality. In a wide variety of business areas between 1880 and 1930, they evidently represent a sensory addendum to existing commercial practices. Thus, management understood film as a "technological object,"[9] which enabled the pedagogical disciplining of employees. Film recordings could be produced and narrative editing practices were readily available, as was a mature film projection technology. Additionally, there existed an unquestioned definition of the *cinema principle*. Potential spectators had learned how to receive moving images, and

---

und Epistemologie: Gesammelte Aufsätze, ed. Georges Canguilhem (Frankfurt a. M.: Suhrkamp, 1979), 38–58; see also Hans-Jörg Rheinberger, *Experiment, Differenz, Schrift: Zur Geschichte epistemischer Dinge* (Marburg: Basilisken-Presse 1992); Hans-Jörg Rheinberger, "Strukturen des Experimentierens: Zum Umgang mit dem Nicht-Wissen," in *Wissenschaft als kulturelle Praxis, 1750–1900*, ed. Hans Erich Bödeker (Göttingen: Vandenhoeck und Ruprecht, 1999), 415–24; fundamental, too, is Gaston Bachelard, *Épistémologie: Textes Choisis*.

---

[7] Canguilhem, "The Object of the History of Science," 204.
[8] Ibid.
[9] Hans-Jörg Rheinberger, *Toward a History of Epistemic Things: Synthesizing Proteins in the Test Tube* (Stanford, CA: Stanford University Press, 1997).

all the fundamental technological and cultural prerequisites of film were known and described.

At the same time, there are expectations attached with the media network, which move beyond the already recognized technological possibilities of individual apparatuses and modes of representation. Paradigmatic for this difficult-to-grasp level is the virtually fantastic promise of efficiency offered by consultants peddling new graphic methods. The *graphic method media network* thus not only incorporates a technological dimension, but also an epistemological dimension that protrudes into an unknown future. The promises and expectations tied with it feed on the rapid development of these "new media."[10]

The boom in the medium of film during the first decades of the twentieth century, for example, is also based on the technological dimension of the medium. To reduce it to this, however, gives it short shrift and curtails the discursive/cultural dimension of this fundamental medium shift. It is not a goal-oriented revolution that leads to the cinema, but an agglomeration of a variety of perceptual experiments[11] and divergent economic business models. What applies to film also pertains to the entire *graphic method media network*.

It is precisely this intersection between verified and unverifiable knowledge that the media network addresses, and it functions, in this context, as a discursive crystallization point. With the discursive enunciation system of film, the participants communicate via the still inexistent conceptual systems of management. Problems that are produced through a transformation of corporate knowledge find the ability to be articulated in the courses of action instigated by filmic processes. I therefore suggest that we understand the media network in this context as a *borrowed* enunciation system. It can be used as a system of articulation for a great variety of discourses. Considered from this perspective, the question as to whether the courses of action or utopian considerations that have thus arisen are actually successful is a secondary one. After all, even the failure of media processes functions as a *borrowed* enunciation system. In this sense, "dysfunctionality" is revealed as a productive resource and contributes to a better understanding of this context.

The *graphic method media network* has thus influenced the business world in a number of different ways. The euphoria for cinema, which had taken hold of

---

[10] On the aspect of the "newness" of media, see Lisa Gitelman, *Always Already New: Media, History and the Data of Culture* (Cambridge, MA: MIT Press 2006); Wendy Hui Kyong Chun, "Did Somebody Say New Media?," in *New Media Old Media: A History and Theory Reader*, ed. Wendy Hui Kyong Chun and Thomas Keenan (London: Routledge, 2006), 1–10. Lisa Gitelman and Geoffrey B. Pingree, "What's New about New Media?," in *New Media, 1740–1915*, ed. Lisa Gitelman and Geoffrey B. Pingree (Cambridge, MA: MIT Press 2003), xi–xxii. Carolyn Marvin, *When Old Technologies Were New* (Oxford: Oxford University Press, 1988).

[11] Such as, for example, Hugo Münsterberg, *The Photoplay: A Psychological Study* (London: Routledge, 2002 [1916]).

the corporate consultant Frank B. Gilbreth and led him to dream of a utopia of perfect corporate consulting, and with which he subsequently failed in equally grandiose fashion, can be understood as precisely such a negotiation process.[12] It also rests on the technological dimension of film. As a borrowed enunciation system, film is, however, precisely not efficacious in this dimension. Here the film functions as an open, relatively unstable discursive articulation system.[13] It is precisely for this reason that the film medium is in a position to produce differentiation and enable new alliances. This borrowed, blurred character allows for the description of new movements and conceptual figures of the "managerial," and it is predetermined, precisely, by the media network in question.

Usage

These two opposing poles of ideal types of media—the concrete technological media apparatus and the surplus of signification tied to it—are analytically held together through a perspective drawn from media archaeology, which focuses on the *media practices* of the consulting industry.[14] These prove, as a rule, to be "persistent and relatively stable."[15] The consulting field also represents a logic of action, an economic field and an institutional structure, which simultaneously characterizes and propels industry's medialization drive. Modern management and the concept of "consulting" are not the results of a process of diffusing culture. It is not the Owl of Minerva that brings visual consulting, visual management, and other proto-cybernetic approaches to businesses.[16] Rather, it is active actors with concrete, situated interests that propel the medialization drive, simultaneously enabling it and representing it. Their actions, however, are extremely contradictory. The pragmatic adoption of media often passes over seamlessly into utopian ideas. At determined intervals, it seems, they are even brushed by the owl. It was not at dusk, but at the late-night screenings of the first movie theaters that the corporate consultant Frank B. Gilbreth recognized the *cinema principle* as his ideal model for conveying knowledge in business enterprises.

---

[12] See Chapter 4 of this volume, " 'I go to the movies most every night': Cinema and Management."

[13] On the aspect of "uncertain media," see Gitelman and Pingree, "What's New about New Media?," xv.

[14] See Michel Foucault, *The Archaeology of Knowledge and the Discourse on Language*, trans. Sheridan Smith (New York: Pantheon Books, 1972); Siegfried Zielinski, *Deep Time of the Media: Towards an Archaeology of Hearing and Seeing by Technical Means* (Cambridge, MA: MIT Press, 2006). On the aspect of usage, see Peter Geimer, "Was ist kein Bild? Zur 'Störung der Verweisung,'" in *Ordnungen der Sichtbarkeit: Fotografie in Wissenschaft, Kunst und Technologie*, ed. Peter Geimer (Frankfurt am Main: Suhrkamp 2002), 313–41.

[15] James A. Secord, "Knowledge in Transit," *Isis* 95 (2004): 665.

[16] Harold A. Innis, "Minerva's Owl," in *The Bias of Communication* (Toronto: University of Toronto Press, 2008 [1951]), 3.

The use of media, and the practices that resulted from it, are always a hybrid form of rational *and* utopian activities. On the one hand, there are the conditions allowing for media techniques (whether filmic, photographic, or graphic recording and inscription devices), while on the other hand, there are the conditions of corporate and industrial organization and production.[17] In between, there looms the question of how this medialization drive transforms the knowledge practices of management in factories and other workplaces. The concept of the epistemological history of media sketched out here aims to bring together the two levels—the concrete usage of media and the utopian surplus of meaning connected with it—while also clearly separating them from each other on an analytic level.

Business

Business usage contexts thus appear not only as a subordinate space for valorizing scientific knowledge and cultural, media, technological, or aesthetic developments. My perspective focuses, rather, on the processes of usage and adaptation that we can observe herein. This *praxeological* approach,[18] operating close to the object, results in different emphases from that which a history of media technologies[19] or a visually oriented perspective would yield.[20] It extends

[17] For a sociomaterial understanding of industrial organizations, see Wanda J. Orlikowski and Susan V. Scott, "Sociomateriality: Challenging the Separation of Technology, Work and Organization," *Academy of Management Annals* 2, no. 1 (2008): 433–74.

[18] Bourdieu coins the term "praxeological mode of recognition," in order to unite subjectivism and objectivism in a single perspective. With respect to the relationship of knowledge structures and the subjects acting within them, *sens pratique* can be analyzed as the junction between knowledge and the forms of action tied to it. Related to a media theory perspective, this becomes relevant when the focus rests on the transitions between media and economic epistemologies. It thereby becomes possible to understand the usage and coupling processes. See Pierre Bourdieu, *The Logic of Practice*, trans. Richard Nice (Stanford, CA: Stanford University Press, 1990); Pierre Bourdieu, "Structuralism and Theory of Sociological Knowledge," *Social Research* 35, no. 4 (1968): 681–706; Pierre Bourdieu, "Postface à Architecture gothique et pensée scolastique de E. Panofsky," in Erwin Panofsky, *Achitecture gothique et pensée scolastique. Précédé de l'abbé suger de Saint-Denis*, trans. and postface by Pierre Bourdieu (Paris: Les Éditions de Minuit, 1967), pp. 135–67.

[19] See Friedrich Kittler, *Discourse Networks 1800/1900*, trans. Michael Metteer and Chris Cullens (Stanford, CA: Stanford University Press, 1990); Kittler, *Gramophone, Film, Typewriter*; Friedrich Kittler, "Dracula´s Legacy," in *Literature, Media, Information Systems*, ed. John Johnston (New York: Routledge, 2012), 50–84.

[20] See Gottfried Boehm and Maurice Merleau-Ponty, eds., *Was ist ein Bild?* (Munich: Fink, 1994); Uwe Pörksen, *Weltmarkt der Bilder: Eine Philosophie der Visiotype* (Stuttgart: Klett-Cotta, 1997); W. J. T. Mitchell, *Picture Theory* (Chicago: University of Chicago Press, 1995); W. J. T. Mitchell, "Diagrammatology," *Critical Inquiry* 7, no. 3 (1981): 622–33; Horst Bredekamp, "Towards the Iconic Turn," in *Hardware: Kritische Berichte* 1 (1998): 85ff; Stefan Majetschak, "Sichtvermerke: Über Unterschiede zwischen Kunst- und Gebrauchsbildern," in *Bild-Zeichen: Perspektiven einer Wissenschaft vom Bild* (Munich: Fink, 2005), 97–121; Sybille Krämer, "Operative Bildlichkeit: Von der 'Grammatologie' zu einer 'Diagrammatologie'? Reflexionen über erkennendes 'Sehen'," in *Logik des Bildlichen: Zur Kritik der ikonischen Vernunft*, ed. Martina Heßler and Dieter Mersch (Bielefeld: transcript, 2009), 94–122.

approaches that explain business innovation through the diffusion, in corporate contexts, of conceptual figures from the history of ideas. Before new forms of knowledge establish themselves in corporate contexts, however, there is usage and exchange, and finally integration into existing structures. Here, innovations encounter each other at an extremely opaque site of conflict, insofar as corporate knowledge is organized through a vast range of agreed courses of action—or, that is, through the coexistence of heterogeneous social groups which collaborate at close quarters, or through divergent managerial strategies.[21]

The economic historian Richard Edwards describes these different negotiation processes in business contexts with the model of "contested terrain."[22] He uses this concept to apprehend a variety of sites of conflict and long-term processes of displacement and negotiation, such as the shaping of production technologies or transformed balancing processes in business organizations. As I understand it, the term also incorporates the introduction of new media in management and consulting, as well as the visual culture that is thereby produced. In this context, approaches from the perspective of economic history are helpful to better understand the praxeological intertwining of media and business. The graphic method media network should thus be comprehended as a part of these negotiation processes, which contour the latent long-term conflict between and within staff and management. Here, the two roads of "business" and "media" encounter each other—not, however, by combining into a peaceful symbiosis. Rather, they are parts of the contested terrain in which organizational conflicts and negotiation processes play out. This has effects on the forms of knowledge which impose themselves in the business world's medialization drive. At the same time, the media itself changes through the business structures and practices that they encounter. In order to adequately apprehend them, I shall combine the concept of contested terrain with an epistemological perspective. Herewith I take into view the changing relations between knowledge, media, and business organizations.

Epistemology

Originally, historical epistemology was conceptualized in the history of knowledge and scientific research, a field formalized between verification and falsification, in which scientific innovations underpin a constant retrospective dependence on the implicit and explicit rules of the respective scientific

---

[21] Fligstein, *The Transformation of Corporate Control*; Chandler, *The Visible Hand*; Beniger, *The Control Revolution*.
[22] Edwards, *Contested Terrain*.

discipline.[23] Here, we assume that there is an "interessement"[24] with a potential preparedness for cooperation, around which research processes are formed. Even if the fields of science and business followed thoroughly similar organizational routines, there are also significant differences. In contrast to scientific research, commercial activity, to put it concisely, attempts to safeguard existing business models. Enterprises thus seek to reduce any uncertainties that might be tied to research alliances with open-ended results, precisely because they could disrupt routine business.[25] From an analytic perspective, it is therefore preferable to emphasize the improbability and instability of cooperation in business contexts. "Cooperation" under the conditions of a latent lack of interest or coercion necessarily leads to conflicts, which we can describe with the aforementioned concept of "contested terrain."[26] Here, conflicts took place and flowed into technological configurations, which then led to an enduring preference for certain interests while marginalizing others. It is these kinds of media conditions for corporate cooperation and temporary stability that I seek to better understand.

The concept of the "boundary object," as developed by Susan L. Star and James Griesemer,[27] offers the starting point for such a perspective. This concept focuses on the necessary conditions for cooperation or communication to happen in the first place. Moreover, there must exist an environment that guarantees a *compatibility* between the different interests. In the terminology of systems theory, they can also stay disconnected from each other and fail to activate any operations together. This condition is structured through *boundary objects*.

> Boundary objects are objects which are both plastic enough to adapt to local needs and the constraints of the several parties employing them, yet robust

---

[23] Karin Knorr-Cetina, *Epistemic Cultures: How the Sciences Make Knowledge* (Cambridge, MA: Harvard University Press, 1999); Bruno Latour and Steve Woolgar, *Laboratory Life: The Construction of Scientific Facts* (Princeton, NJ: Princeton University Press, 1986); Bruno Latour, *Science in Action: How to Follow Scientists and Engineers through Society* (Cambridge, MA: Harvard University Press, 1994); Michael Lynch and Steve Woolgar, eds., *Representation in Scientific Practice* (Cambridge, MA: MIT Press 1990); Rheinberger, *Experiment, Differenz, Schrift: Zur Geschichte epistemischer Dinge*; Hans-Jörg Rheinberger and Michael Hagner, *Die Experimentalisierung des Lebens: Experimentalsysteme in der biologischen Wissenschaft 1850–1950* (Berlin: Akademie Verlag, 1993). Cornelius Borck, Volker Hess, and Henning Schmidgen, *Maß und Eigensinn: Studien im Anschluß an George Canguilhem* (Munich: Wilhelm Fink, 2005).

[24] See Michel Callon, "Some Elements of a Sociology of Translation: Domestication of the Scallops and the Fisherman of St. Brieuc Bay," in *Power, Action and Belief: A New Sociology of Knowledge*, ed. John Law (London: Routledge & Kegan Paul, 1986), 196–233.

[25] It is for this reason that firms boasted independent, specific structures. For more on this, see Dirk Baecker, *Die Form des Unternehmens* (Frankfurt am Main: Suhrkamp, 1993).

[26] A similar perspective, albeit related to the question of the interplay of technology and science, is provided with the concept of "trading zones." See Peter Galison, *Image & Logic: A Material Culture of Microphysics* (Chicago: University of Chicago Press, 1997).

[27] For more details on the theoretical premises of this, see Florian Hoof, "Ist jetzt alles Netzwerk? Mediale 'Schwellen- und Grenzobjekte'," in *Jenseits des Labors: Labor, Wissen, Transformation*, ed. Florian Hoof, Eva-Maria Jung, and Ulrich Salaschek (Bielefeld: transcript, 2011), 45–62.

enough to maintain a common identity across sites. They are weakly structured in common use, and become strongly structured in individual-site use. These objects may be abstract or concrete. They have different meanings in different social worlds but their structure is common enough to more than one world to make them recognizable, a means of translation.[28]

These include objects that mediate between actors "from different social worlds"[29] because they boast a lower entry threshold for the relevant parties, or they can flexibly adapt to their different sets of interests. It is at this point that an object becomes an overarching entity that enables communication, co-operation, or coexistence between the various reference systems.[30] Film is an excellent example of this. Understood as an educational tool or as a device for motion studies, it can offer to managers and corporate consultants the promise of efficiency and control, while employees may understand film more in the context of cinema culture, and as part of their leisure activities, as the film theorist Siegfried Kracauer discussed with respect to the salaried employee culture of the 1920s.[31] In this light, film is an exemplary boundary object, which brings together contrasting levels of meaning.[32] As my overall thesis has it, this also applies more generally to the status and significance of the graphic method media network, which alongside film also incorporates other media such as graphs and diagrams.

Media Boundary Objects

Taken together, the media contained within the graphic method media network form an underlying structure for processing communication, transmission, and storage.[33] Understood as a "communication medium,"[34] they shape

[28] Star and Griesemer, "Institutional Ecology, 'Translations' and Boundary Objects," 393.

[29] Ibid., 388.

[30] In comparison to concepts like "remediation" or "convergence," they thus emphasize the improbability and instability of media objects. See Jay D. Bolter and Richard A. Grusin, *Remediation: Understanding New Media* (Cambridge, MA: MIT Press, 2000); Henry Jenkins, *Convergence Culture: Where Old and New Media Collide* (New York: New York University Press, 2006).

[31] Siegfried Kracauer, *The Salaried Masses: Duty and Distraction in Weimar Germany*, trans. Quintin Hoare (London: Verso, 1998 [1930]).

[32] For a historical perspective on film as boundary object, see Florian Hoof, "'Have We Seen It All Before?' A Sociomaterial Approach to Film History," in *At the Borders of (Film) History, Temporality, Archaeology*, ed. Alberto Beltrame and Andrea Mariani (Udine: Forum, 2015), 347–57.

[33] To understand media concepts as fundamental structures, see, for example, Harold A. Innis, *Empire and Communications* (Toronto: University of Toronto Press, 1972); Walter J. Ong, *Orality and Literacy: The Technologizing of the Word* (London: Methuen, 1987); and Eric A. Havelock, *The Literate Revolution in Greece and Its Cultural Consequences* (Princeton, NJ: Princeton University Press, 1982).

[34] Geoffrey C. Bowker and Susan Leigh Star, *Sorting Things Out: Classification and Its Consequences* (Cambridge, MA: The MIT Press, 2000), 298.

and steer the "extent and form of human coexistence."[35] But they do not constitute individual media, which become efficacious independently of each other.
While they do indeed exhibit an independent, internal logic, they nonetheless
mutually overlap and stabilize each other. It is not only an object that structures
an area, but "regimes and networks of boundary objects."[36] As a network of
varying media practices, their pertinence and stability can only be explained
if they are understood as "media boundary objects."[37] They correlate with the
concept of the "media network" (*Medienverbund*)[38] or the "discourse network"
(*Aufschreibesystem*)[39] as used in research on the early period of the cinema,
which emphasizes infrastructural and technical factors. On the level of media
aesthetics, parallels to the concept of the "aesthetic regime" can also be drawn.[40]
Furthermore, the concept enables access to a perception of the world that constantly changes its viewpoints and perspectives through the intervention of
media.[41]

In this sense, the graphic method media network enables specific forms of
communication and circulation, while at the same time it prevents them when
they do not correspond to the predetermined structure. Decisive, here, is not
only the way a medium is used, but also its specific materiality. In his investigation of media in bureaucratic structures, Harold Innis has aptly pointed to
this tendency: stone tablets as the bearers of administrative decrees are robust
but heavy to transport, while papyrus, on the other hand, with its easy trans-
portability, enables the opening up of space, but it is also an extremely unstable
medium.[42] Bowker and Star, meanwhile, refer to the example of electronic information systems to argue that the material or technological characteristics of a
medium cannot be considered in isolation from its usage.

> The medium of an information system is not just wires and plugs, bits and
> bytes, but also conventions of representation, information both formal and em-
> pirical. A system becomes a system in design and use, not the one without the
> other. The medium is the message.[43]

---

[35] Marshall McLuhan, *Understanding Media: The Extensions of Men* (London: Routledge Classics, 2001 [1964]), 9.

[36] Bowker and Star, *Sorting Things Out: Classification and Its Consequences*, 313.

[37] See Hoof, "Ist jetzt alles Netzwerk? Mediale 'Schwellen- und Grenzobjekte.'"

[38] See Kittler, *Gramophone, Film, Typewriter*; Griffiths, *Wondrous Difference*.

[39] See Kittler, *Discourse Networks 1800/1900*.

[40] Rancière, *Aesthetics and Its Discontents*.

[41] Fritz Heider, "Thing and Medium," in Fritz Heider, *On Perception, Event, Structure, and Psychological Environment: Selected Papers* (New York: International Universities Press, 1959).

[42] Harold A. Innis (Toronto: University of Toronto Press, 1951), *The Bias of Communication*; Innis, *Empire and Communications*.

[43] Bowker and Star, *Sorting Things Out*, 292.

The interplay of media materiality and usage thus determines the possibility of administrative and organizational control. We could speak in similar terms about the graphic method: specific issues or data can be represented or filmed, while others, which cannot, must be blocked out.[44] It is insufficient, however, to comprehend media boundary objects simply as instruments of cooperation or as "immutable mobiles,"[45] as abstract bearers of network connectivity. Invariably, they can also be tools of ignorance, which hinder communicative acts and come between potential nodal points. They thus keep potential conflicts latent and stabilize fragile systems such as business organizations. Media theory therefore offers access to businesses which otherwise distinguish themselves through highly heterogeneous components. The different parts of such organizations may well be in spatial or temporal proximity, but they are not necessarily connected to one another. Such constellations, which can be frequently observed in the media of bureaucratic and management structures, may be theoretically described as parts of a process or an environment, which, while they might not exhibit any significance, nonetheless *can* appear as factors for future development.[46] Here, the model has links with the core ideas of media archaeology, which concerns itself with the status of "residual media" and technological dead ends—that is, extinct or dysfunctional media developments, which are nonetheless of historical epistemological significance.[47]

From the perspective of media history, the concept of *media boundary objects* offers an initial stopping point on the path toward a description of media processes in corporate contexts. They form part of an epistemological production process. There they are efficacious not only because they (are supposed to) fulfil a specific purpose, but also due to their form. As objects of circulation, they bring together different groups and actors within the economic field, and thus have an influence on the process of constituting business management. Through their circulation, they nonetheless retain their structures and thereby leave their mark on the participating actors: "Something actually *becomes* an object only in the context of action and use; it then becomes as well something that has force to mediate subsequent action."[48] It is from this perspective that the visualization

---

[44] On the aspect of media as decision-making aids, see Florian Hoof, "Medien managerialer Entscheidungen: Decision-Making 'At a Glance,'" *Soziale Systeme: Zeitschrift für soziologische Theorie* 20, no. 1 (2015): 24–25.

[45] Bruno Latour, "Drawing Things Together" in *Representation in Scientific Practice*, ed. Michael Lynch and Steve Woolgar (Cambridge, MA: MIT Press 1990), 26–35.

[46] For a more detailed theoretical critique of the approach of "material semiotics," see Florian Hoof, "The Media Boundary Objects Concept: Theorizing Film and Media," in *Media Matter: The Materiality of Media, Matter as Medium*, ed. Bernd Herzogenrath (New York: Bloomsbury 2015), 180–200.

[47] See Acland, *Residual Media*.

[48] Bowker and Star, *Sorting Things Out*, 298.

techniques analyzed here will be understood as *media boundary objects*. My perspective, drawing on the historical epistemology of media, places particular emphasis on the aspect of media usage. The comprehensive concept of media will be related to concretely observable conditions of usage in this *contested terrain*. As epistemological media processes in corporate contexts, we can view business conflicts and negotiation processes in their praxeological, technical, and aesthetic dimensions.

Dimensions of Media Action

For the area under investigation it is now necessary to connect the relatively extensive approach of media boundary objects with the historical forms of media techniques. How can we understand the media boundary objects of the graphic method media network under discussion here, as well as the consulting knowledge tied to it? What potential courses of action are contained within a film, or the Wheel of Motion developed by Frank B. Gilbreth? In order to answer these questions, the concept will be extended, in a further step, with the *dimension of media action*. Considered thus, the graphic method media network represents a repertoire of action options, which may be adapted for business purposes. I will give an ideal-typical description of these action options as *media types of action*. They represent hybrid forms of coupling, which are constituted from their operationalization in concrete action and usage contexts. Once, in an initial step, the types of action are defined, then in a subsequent step we can understand them as the conditions of possibility of the media network existing in the early twentieth century.

For the graphic method media network, I thus propose a pragmatic categorization in three ideal types.[49] These divide into "static," "kinetic," and "calculative" modes of functioning. Here, the separation of ideal types rests on a usage of media connected with visualization techniques. Before they can be allocated, we must pose the praxeological question as to how, and for what purposes, these techniques are concretely utilized, and which actions are therewith carried out.[50] All three ideal-types can be reduced to a single, fundamental functionality

---

[49] Max Weber, "Die Objektivität sozialwissenschaftlicher und sozialpolitischer Erkenntnis," in Weber, *Gesammelte Aufsätze zur Wissenschaftslehre* (Tübingen: Mohr, 1922), 146–214.

[50] See Pierre Bourdieu, *The Logic of Practice*; Max Weber, "The Social Categories of Economic Action," in *Economy and Society*, ed. Guenther Roth and Claus Wittich (Berkeley: University of California Press, 1978); Pierre Bourdieu, "Structuralism and Theory of Sociological Knowledge"; Pierre Bourdieu, "Postface à Architecture gothique et pensée scolastique de E. Panofsky."

through the "rising of a [. . .] viewpoint."[51] The static mode is based on processes of representation, the kinetic mode on processes of registration, and the calculative mode on processes of calculation. Individual graphic methods can be described as hybrid interconnections between these three ideal types, and as possible *media boundary objects*. The functionalities may be flexibly coupled with each other in the form of concrete visualization techniques, and thus adapt to the requirements of specific enterprises. At the same time, the three modes also have certain preconditions. Data, objects, and procedures must be translated into visual form.[52]

We can thus define the graphic method media network methods arising at the end of the nineteenth century through three types of media action. When taken together, individual courses of action, which can be praxeologically classified into three ideal types of action, form new knowledge structures, which are distinct from what had previously prevailed. With this theoretical model, we can show that it is in the interplay between media techniques and corporate-industrial circumstances that a contextual configuration of knowledge, a media epistemology of corporate situations, arises. In the following pages, the three ideal types (the "static," "kinetic," and "calculative") will be established on the basis of individual historical examples. Nonetheless, this decidedly does not imply any claim to a historically detailed survey of these developments. The examples simply serve to establish a logic of media action.

The "Static" Mode of Graphic Representation

The *static* ideal type is based on the simple principle of the graphic display of data in a defined space. In like fashion to an architecturally static system, every data point occupies a fixed position. They form a relational system, which draws its stability from the static character of the data. Graphical forms such as curves, bars, and points relay their meaning through predetermined scales that define the space. The graphic forms are not defined through descriptions of analytic geometry. They do not represent set mathematical patterns; instead, they are part of a single relation of representation between data and the assignation of values in the predetermined system of coordinates.[53]

---

[51] Weber, "Die Objektivität sozialwissenschaftlicher und sozialpolitischer Erkenntnis," 191.

[52] Types of action are not distinct categorizations that can be derived from their own "materiality" or a logic distinction. They represent an agglomeration of the power of action, which manifests itself in a special media configuration. The type in question offers the actions of various options for using different forms of visualization, inscription, and storage.

[53] Funkhouser, "Historical Development of the Graphical Representation of Statistical Data," 274–77.

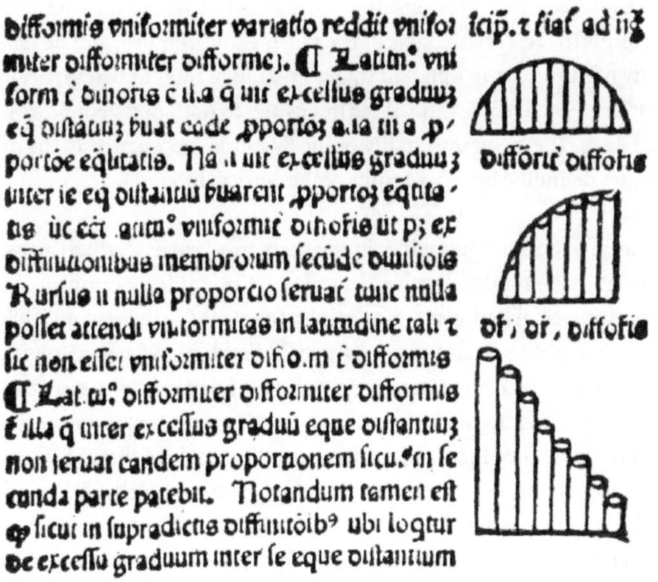
difformis vniformiter variatio reddit vnifor scip.τ fiat ad in
miter difformiter difformem). ¶ Latitu: vni
form e dnionis e illa q inter excessus graduum
eq distantium haet eadem proportione alia in a p
portione equalitatis. Nam si inter excessus graduum
inter se eq distantium haberent proportionem eqnta
tis iter esset latitu: vniformis difformis ut p; ex
diffinitionibus membrorum secunde diuisionis
Rursus si nulla proporcio seruatur tunc nulla
posset attendi vniformitas in latitudine tali τ
sic non esset vniformiter difformis i difformis
¶ Lat.tu: difformiter difformiter difformis
e illa q inter excessus graduum eque distantium
non seruat eandem proportionem sicut in se
cunda parte patebit. Notandum tamen est
q sicut in supradictis diffinitionibus ubi loquitur
de excessu graduum inter se eque distantium

Figure 5 The graphic representation of motion data in a system of coordinates published by Nicole Oresme, from the mid-fourteenth century.

The static ideal type is a system of displaying data that serves the purpose of visualizing available data. As opposed to tabular forms, which can be confusing, these data are translated into graphic displays such as bar charts or line graphs. The goal is to be able to better understand, interpret, and communicate data in visual form. They serve to produce comprehensible relations between different groups of data as patterns or relations of similarity. These are indeed graphic techniques; however, such visualizations derive their legitimacy not through their pictorial aspect, but through the static relationship between data and the graphic display derived from it.

The principle of the static display data can be traced back to the fourteenth-century scientist, theologian, and advisor to the French royal court Nicole Oresme.[54] Although he remained bound to a scholastic understanding of science, Oresme nonetheless devised one of the earliest graphic displays of data, which rested on their relative positions within a system of coordinates.

[54] Ernst Borchert, *Die Lehre von der Bewegung bei Nicolaus Oresme* (Münster: Aschendorffsche Verlagsbuchhandlung, 1934).

He traces the extension (extensio) of the subject or bearer on a base line that corresponds to Descartes' x-axis of the seventeenth century; and he marks the intensity of the bearer in different stages by straight lines drawn vertically from the base line (y-axis). The ratio of the intensities to one another appears in these vertical lines. The changing quality of the bearer is represented in the geometrical figure delimited by the summits of the vertical lines.[55]

In the context of population policy in the early modern era, which arose with the development of the modern nation-state, statistical tables, examples of which included the numerical listings of mortality rates, became increasingly widespread over the course of the seventeenth century.[56] Fields as diverse as physics, meteorology, and early forms of macroeconomics and demography saw the rise of an understanding of empirical data that was based on the expressive power of large quantities of data. Graphic displays were used to analyze these data sets,[57] such as the bar graphs that were published for the first time in Joseph Priestley's 1765 work *A Chart of Biography*.[58]

In 1786, meanwhile, another advisor to the French king, the Scottish engineer and political theorist William Playfair, was the first figure to bring together different techniques of graphic representation, with *The Commercial and Political Atlas and Statistical Breviary* (see Fig. 6).[59] In the framework of his treatise, Playfair developed the fundamental forms of the graphic display of statistical data: the "line graph, circle graph, bar graph, and pie graph."[60] With only minor changes, these can still be found in present-day usage. Playfair characterized the graphic method with the term "linear arithmetic."[61] He did not seek to achieve the most precise representation of the underlying data, but rather to provide the reader with a globally faithful impression.

The advantage proposed, by this method, is not that of giving a more accurate statement than by figures, but it is to give a more simple and permanent idea of the gradual progress and comparative amounts, at different periods, by presenting to the eye a figure.[62]

---

[55] Siegfried Giedion, *Mechanization Takes Command: A Contribution to Anonymous History* (Minneapolis: University of Minnesota Press, 2013 [1948]), 16.

[56] See Michel Foucault, *Security, Territory, Population: Lectures at the Collège de France 1977–1978* (Basingstoke, UK: Palgrave Macmillan, 2009), 67, 99ff.

[57] Funkhouser, "Historical Development of the Graphical Representation of Statistical Data," 278–79.

[58] Joseph Priestley, *A Chart of Biography* (London: 1765).

[59] William Playfair, *The Commercial and Political Atlas and Statistical Breviary* (London: Faksimile, 2005 [1786]).

[60] Funkhouser, "Historical Development of the Graphical Representation of Statistical Data," 280.

[61] Playfair, *The Commercial and Political Atlas and Statistical Breviary*, xx.

[62] Ibid., ix–xii.

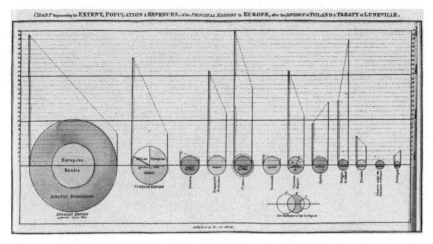

Figure 6 The first use of pie charts in combination with bar graphs for the comparative representation of the national economic data of European states.

The graphic method thus became an accepted technique for representing numerical data.[63] It could be used to quickly and simply represent great quantities of data "at a glance,"[64] and thereby make them easier to process. These advantages overcame the initial skepticism toward the imprecision of graphic representation. Even Louis XVI was impressed by the potential for visualizing national economic data. The difference from traditional techniques of data representation lay in the altered perception of the data depicted.

> Graphs convey comparative information in ways that no tables of numbers or written accounts ever could. Trends, differences, and associations are seen in the blink of an eye. The eye perceives instantly what the brain would take seconds or minutes to infer from a table of numbers and this is what makes graphs so attractive to scientists, business persons, and many others.[65]

The method of displaying statistical data was fundamental for these visual charts. The legitimacy of this form of representation rested on the ineluctable connection between numerical value and the graphic display. Before the publication of his graphic atlas, Playfair was, from 1777 to 1782, active as a collaborator with

---

[63] Fienberg, "Graphical Methods in Statistics," 165.

[64] Ibid., 166.

[65] Ian Spence, "William Playfair and His Graphical Inventions: An Excerpt From the Introduction to the Republication of His Atlas and Statisitcal Breviary," *The American Statistician* 59, no. 3 (2005): 224.

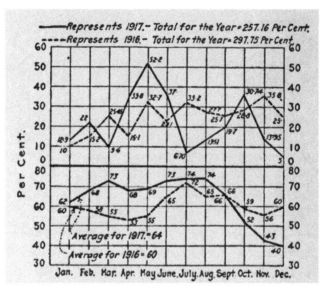

Figure 7 The turnover of a company's department in a multicurve graph.

James Watt in his steam engine factory Boulton & Watt.[66] Playfair discussed his plans with Watt prior to publishing the graphic atlas. Watt was of the opinion that a graphic display of data insufficiently served the needs of scientific exactitude. He convinced Playfair to "include at least some of the original data in tabular form."[67] Playfair did indeed follow this suggestion in the first editions of his publication. As of the third edition, however, he deleted all tabular data from the graphs.[68] There remained the ideal type of statistical data representation: a mode of visualization whose legitimacy was purely derived from the mathematically exact depiction of numerical values in graphic form.

The basic principle of static display allows for a broad field of substitution, but these tables still allowed for the most varied kinds of data processing to be visualized. National economic data, for which Playfair's atlas was initially conceived, was particularly suitable for the possibilities they offered. It allowed, for example, for the comparison and illustration of core economic figures such as trade balances. But it also offered the potential for representing social statistics. In his 1833 work *Essai sur la statistique morale de la France*, A. M. Guery deployed a graphic, color-coded chart of crime rates in relation to particular age groups.[69]

[66] Ian Spence and Howard Wainer, "Who Was Playfair?" *Chance* 10, no. 1 (1997): 35–37.
[67] Ian Spence and Howard Wainer, "Introduction" (2005), in Playfair, *The Commercial and Political Atlas and Statistical Breviary*, 18.
[68] Ibid., 14.
[69] Funkhouser, "Historical Development of the Graphical Representation of Statistical Data," 304.

All these graphic techniques are based on the principle of static display. They constituted graphic tableaux consisting of different forms of data, which were brought together in graphic relationships. The graphic depictions provided the first forms of modern decision-making knowledge. Decision makers pressed for time who had to direct complex systems, such as a state or a religious order, relied on these tables. By the end of the nineteenth century, this form of data visualization also appeared in industrial enterprises and corporations. Curve graphs were particularly useful for depicting wage costs or revenue tendencies (see Fig. 7).[70]

The static techniques of displaying data carried out to this point were based on the graphic form of the curve or the bar. A further step was taken at the end of the nineteenth century by graphic representations of *météorologie économique et sociale* (social and economic meteorology).[71] The continued instrumentalization of the principle of static representation was reflected in the graphic tableaux constructed by Alfred de Foville. These graphs, dubbed barometers,[72] collected varied data sets in a single overarching diagram. The goal was not to reproduce mathematically exact data, but to popularize (*vulgariser*) developments and relay them to the wider population (*la foule*).[73] Graphic barometers were governmental instruments of intervention and control, and were part of the politics of large numbers.[74] The popularization of national economic data was directed toward this end.

The socioeconomic barometer for Paris consisted of data concerning tobacco sales, suicide rates, postal communication, box office earnings of Parisian theaters, coal consumption, or the quantity of goods transported by railway. The tableau modeled both the *social* and the *economic* by relating disparate sources of data to each other. Not only did this data derive from different spheres, but it also exhibited considerable numerical differences. Transferring these heterogeneous data sets into systems of coordinates would simply have been impossible. Foville homogenized the data through a uniform graphic display, and they were no longer given a concrete value. He translated changes of individual data sources into a color code, which consisted of the colors red, pink, white, gray, and black. Here, red stood for positive developments (drawing on the color of the sun), while black (the color of the "*éclipse totale*") stood in for negative developments.[75] These markings rested on concrete values. But when they assumed the

[70] See also Yates, "Graphs as a Managerial Tool. A Case Study of Du Pont's Use of Graphs in the Early Twentieth Century."

[71] A. de Foville, "Essai de météorologie économique et sociale," *Journal de la Société de Statistique de Paris* (1888): 245.

[72] On the development of the principle of the barometer, see Reiner Zwer, "Die statistische Konjunkturforschung in Vergangenheit und Gegenwart," *Statistische Hefte* 4, no. 1 (1963): 38–79.

[73] Foville, "Essai de météorologie économique et sociale," 245.

[74] Alain Desrosières, *The Politics of Large Numbers* (Cambridge, MA: Harvard University Press, 2002).

[75] Foville, "Essai de météorologie économique et sociale," 248.

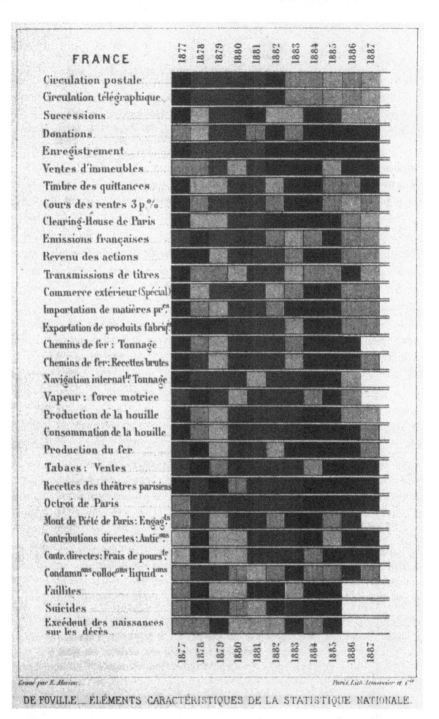

Figure 8 Statistical meteorology: a statistical barometer for Paris published by Foville in 1888. The abrupt changes in the color coding from gray through red to black (in the illustration light gray/dark gray/black) depict the economic crisis in France unfolding after the stock market crash of 1882.

form of the graphic tableau, they became a machine of difference, and the surface became an abstract model of social and economic forces.

> Does the unanimity of these symptoms not prove that, by consulting all of them, we can have a correct idea of the situation at a given moment? Do you not see, right in front of your eyes, when the barometer is right and when it stops being right? Is the long crisis that has cost France so dearly not right there, as if it had been photographed? It seems that we can see it pass, and this image, in its silent language, shows its breadth, duration and intensity?[76]

The form of the graphic barometer served as a heuristic technique for anticipating the future, and it was closely linked to the rising forms of domination in the modern state. These processes were a reaction to the fundamental decision-making dilemma described as early as 1832 by Carl von Clausewitz. According to von Clausewitz, a significant part of the information necessary for any decision always remains "wrapped in a fog of greater or lesser uncertainty."[77] Hence, decisions are always, at least in part, determined by random chance. As von Clausewitz himself suggested by drawing on terminology from the military sphere,[78] graphic barometers could be used for discerning known patterns for economic crisis or omens of social unrest, "*d'un coup d'œil*" (at a glance).[79] They should contribute to sharpening the understanding of decision makers and giving them a "quick and appropriate decision" with a "sense of proportion" under the conditions of uncertainty in "space and time."[80] Alongside simple data visualizations corresponding to the principle of static display, we can also assign diagrams including multiple curve, and graphic barometers with complex surfaces combining different data sets to the *static* type of representation.

The "Kinetic" Mode of Graphic Registration

I have borrowed the term "kinetic" from technical mechanics. According to the basic law of dynamics defined by Newton, mechanical kinetics describes a relation that consists of static (power) and kinematic (acceleration) magnitudes.[81] The common process of mechanics consists of an initial step of undertaking a

[76] Ibid.
[77] Carl von Clausewitz, *On War*, ed. and trans. Michael Howard and Peter Paret (Princeton, NJ: Princeton University Press, 1989), 101.
[78] Ibid., 102.
[79] Foville, "Essai de météorologie économique et sociale," 247.
[80] Clausewitz, *On War*, 102.
[81] See Bruno Assmann, *Technische Mechanik: Kinematik und Kinetik* (Munich: Oldenbourg, 1975).

kinematic analysis of movement. Then a system must be defined. In this segment, a known movement can be mathematically described. The kinematic analysis merely represents a registration, a description of movement through the variables of trajectory, speed, and acceleration.[82] Complex dynamic process can therefore be translated into mathematical calculations, the basis for subsequent kinetic computations. Unlike in the merely descriptive process of registering kinematic movement, we can also find a concern for discerning the causes of movements. The relations of force of a movement can be determined, and the targeted manipulation of a motion system can be realized.

The *kinetic* type of media action described here has a similar goal, albeit with a decisive difference.[83] It follows the logic of kinematic visual registration. This type of action is then deployed when the access to the "inner" laws of dynamic processes is not possible. Graphic media apparatuses of this type make visible things, conditions, or processes which escape the perception of the naked eye, or which are unable to be mathematically decomposed and described on account of their complexity. They produce graphic data, with which, in the sense of kinetic calculation processes, the causes of movements or planned manipulations of the system can be prepared.[84]

Technologies of Regulation

The genesis of kinetic registration systems came about through the direct coupling of a selection technique with a graphic method of inscription. It took place in the heyday of the first industrial revolution.[85] The first mechanism that corresponded to these criteria was a regulation technology developed by James Watt, which served to optimize the performance of steam engines.

---

[82] See Franz Reuleaux, *The Kinematics of Machinery: Outlines of a Theory of Machines* (London: Macmillan, 1876).

[83] See Francis C. Moon, *The Machines of Leonardo Da Vinci and Franz Reuleaux: Kinematics of Machines from the Renaissance to the 20th Century* (Dordrecht, the Netherlands: Springer, 2007).

[84] See, for example, Bericht der Schriftleitung, "Berichte der Schriftleitung: Die Verwendung des 'Arbeitsaufzeichners' zur Feststellung des Wirkungsgrades," *Werkstattstechnik* 10, no. 16 (1916): 341–42; Bericht der Schriftleitung, "Berichte der Schriftleitung: Mechanische Aufzeichnungen der geleisteten Arbeit," *Werkstattstechnik* 10, no. 16 (1916): 337–40; Bericht der Schriftleitung, "Berichte der Schriftleitung: Photographisches Festhalten von Maschineneinrichtungen," *Werkstattstechnik* 17, no. 1 (1923): 24; Fr. Bock, "Versuche mit einem neuen Torsionsmesser," *Werkstattstechnik* 5, no. 1 (1911): 12–17; Gustav Schmaltz, "Über Methoden zur photographischen Registrierung geradliniger Schwingungsbewegungen" *Maschinenbau/Gestaltung* 2, no. 5–6 (1922): 150–60.

[85] On the predecessors of graphic registration, see E. H. Hoff and L. A. Geddes, "Graphic Recording Before Carl Ludwig: An Historical Summary," *Archives internationales d'Histoire des Sciences* 50 (1959): 4–16.

> James Watt [. . .] was the first to devise an automatic registering instrument, known as Watt's indicator by which diagrams showing the relation of the steam pressure in the cylinder to the movement of the piston are automatically drawn.[86]

The "heterogeneous ensemble"[87] of the kinetic system of registration resulted from a problem of economic control and regulation. In order to operate a steam engine, the locomotive driver had to possess comprehensive knowledge about the functioning of its mechanisms. If he did not know the pressure in the water tank, then the stoker could only fire it up according to personal experience. This was seldom efficient, and led to heightened costs for combustion material, as well as raising the risk of an explosion. Neither represented good conditions for an orderly, efficient factory or railway company. There thus arose the necessity of knowing with certainty what the pressure level of the tank was at any given moment. Only thus could the heating be calibrated to the required levels. Spheres of industry which were dependent on steam engines, such as manufacturing and the railways, were directly concerned by this question. The problem of regulating steam engines formed the context for the development of kinetic processes of registration. James Watt constructed an apparatus for this need, which allowed for steam pressure and performance to be graphically depicted, and hence for coal firing in the steam tank to be optimally determined.

> When the manometer was connected to the cylinder, a chart of the pressure throughout an engine-cycle was recorded. From this record the power of the engine was calculated and its reciprocal motions all nicely regulated and tuned to yield maximum performance.[88]

The registration apparatus developed by Watt was intended to be an apparatus for controlling previously invisible aspects of industrial production. The necessary prerequisites for this device were multiple. On the one hand, precise measurements were required, while on the other hand, the results needed to be quickly read by the engine-driver. The combination of the graphic display and the immediate ability to scan the data led to the Watt Steam Engine Indicator. This prototype of the graphic registration process fulfilled these demands:

---

[86] Funkhouser, "Historical Development of the Graphical Representation of Statistical Data," 289.

[87] Michel Foucault, *Power/Knowledge: Selected Interviews and Other Writings 1972-1977*, ed. Colin Gordon (New York: Pantheon, 1980), 194.

[88] Hoff and Geddes, "Graphic Recording Before Carl Ludwig," 17.

practically all of the essential features of the system of graphic registration had been worked out: The paper or other surfaces, be it a cylinder, a roll of paper tape, a rotation disk, a moving grid, or a horizontal sheet of paper, moved by clockwork, was the central feature.[89]

This device registered the pressure conditions in the tank and reproduced it as a curve on the inscription medium. At issue, here, was the form of representation, which also came to be deployed in the static techniques of displaying data. Nonetheless, this curve was not a depiction of data. In the kinetic techniques, the phenomenon recorded (in this case, the changing pressure in a tank) coincided with the resulting graphic form. The generation of data, the visualization of kinetic phenomena, was only possible in graphic form. Outside of the graphic form, there were no other comparative data. It was not a technique of representation, but a technique of registration. It generated data by making it visible.

The introduction of this registration apparatus changed industrial and corporate management as it existed at the time. The earlier status quo of regulating steam engines had to be updated. Without instruments and exact measurement results, engine drivers had to operate the steam engine according to their own experience. To draw any conclusions about the conduct of the engine driver, the only indications for management were the absolute consumption of coal and possible production problems. With spatially distant engine drivers, such as in a train, direct managerial control was absent. The conduct of the train driver could only be reflected in the consumption of coal and any possible delays to the train itself. Any intervention was very restricted and only possible for seriously flawed conduct. Only the introduction of a regulation technology—"self-recording instruments"[90]—enabled this implicit knowledge to be made explicit and to be stored for long periods of time. These instruments allowed railway companies to almost halve their consumption of coal.[91] The kinetic type of action thus had a transformative effect on business structures. It was used by management, therefore, as a control instrument not only for machinery, but also for the workforce.

Registration Apparatuses
A few decades later, registration apparatuses with an identical functioning principle were extended to the realm of physiology. In Europe's numerous

---

[89] Ibid., 12.

[90] Thomas L. Hankins, "Blood, Dirt and Nomograms: A Particular History of Graphs," *Isis* 90, no. 1 (1999): 56.

[91] Hoff and Geddes, "Graphic Recording Before Carl Ludwig," 16.

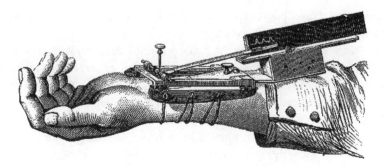

Figure 9 A "spymograph": the pulse is graphically registered on a black surface with a pair of scanning and recording elements.

physiological institutes and laboratories, they were deployed for registering organic movements and making them visible.[92]

As with Watt's invention, the apparatus used here consisted of a device for registering movement. It was accompanied by another device, directly attached to the first, which could graphically record the conditions of movement. This combination paradigmatically finds itself in *spymographs*, which combined reading the pulse with an apparatus for graphic recording (see Fig. 9). Registrations of bodily functions were relayed through an outlet to an attached device used for graphic inscription and then permanently saved. The graphic recording systems used in physiology, such as James Watt's instruments, are heterogeneous ensembles. They combined mechanical devices and graphic inscription processes and applied them to new epistemological objects. The mechanical pulse reading of the spymograph, which did not have a directly attached graphic display, brought no advantages over a doctor feeling the pulse by hand. Only the coupling of a gauging instrument with a graphic registration device functioning as a storage unit transformed the spymograph into a kinetic action type. Many of the physiological apparatuses developed in the nineteenth century were reliant on this principle.

Photochemical Registration

After photochemical processes extended and replaced physically attached graphic registration apparatuses, this situation changed. Initially, this primarily took the form of mechanical devices. The inscription surface consisted of soot-blackened cylinders of paper rolls. A needle or a stylus plotted the registered movements in the form of a curve. In the late eighteenth century, these

---

[92] See Phillipp Sarasin and Jakob Tanner, *Physiologie und industrielle Gesellschaft* (Frankfurt am Main: Suhrkamp, 1998); Braun, *Picturing Time: The Work of Etienne-Jules Marey (1830–1904)*; Anson Rabinbach, *The Human Motor: Energy, Fatigue, and the Origins of Modernity* (Berkeley: University of California Press, 1992).

simple forms of inscription were extended and partly replaced by photographic and filmic techniques of registration.

One of the driving forces for the development of these innovations was the French physiological Étienne-Jules Marey.[93] He implemented photographic processes in order to depict registration processes graphically. The spymograph exhibited an unambiguous separation between the reading and inscription apparatus. This separation became obsolete when Marey began to assemble photographic processes for analyzing physical movement. The photographic images he recorded simultaneously registered the physical conditions and displayed them.

Similar developments also took place in other spheres of scientific research. Their common concern was to establish the production of knowledge with photochemical processes as an objective, scientific instrument. For this usage of photography, the problem was that for the photographic plate "everything was indifferent."[94] Photographic images depicted too much. In order to exist as a process of visualization, an operationalization of the image parameters was necessary. It had to inscribe the "trace of a knowing,"[95] in order to be able to produce useful knowledge through visualization. Through processes like Alphonse Bertillon's "photosynthesis," which consisted of the "fragmented identification of the face,"[96] photography changed from a purely representative process into one capable of generating truth. In those fields of scientific research that made use of photographic techniques, visibility thus achieved "epistemological dominance."[97] It could "tell us in the most exact manner possible about movements that our eye cannot grasp because they are too slow, too fast or too complicated."[98] Through the introduction of the analytic film image, which "takes apart [movements] and puts them back together again,"[99] the movements in question

[93] Apart from Marey, a series of other researchers, including William Henry Fox Talbot, Eadweard Muybridge, Ernst Mach, and Ottomar Anschütz, also worked on similar adaptations of photochemical processes for scientific purposes. Marey serves here as an exemplary instance of this tendency.

[94] Vogel, Die chemischen Wirkungen des Lichts und die Photographie in ihrer Anwendung in Kunst, Wissenschaft und Industrie (1874), 125, cited in Geimer, "Was ist kein Bild? Zur 'Störung der Verweisung,'" 339.

[95] Gunnar Schmidt, Anamorphotische Körper: Medizinische Bilder vom Menschen im 19. Jahrhundert (Cologne: Böhlau, 2001), 27.

[96] Bernd Busch, Belichtete Welt: Eine Wahrnehmungsgeschichte der Fotografie (Frankfurt am Main: Fischer, 1997), 316.

[97] Schmidt, Anamorphotische Körper, 9.

[98] "Renseigne de la façon la plus exacte sur des mouvements que notre œil ne saurait saisir parce qu'ils sont trop lents, trop rapides ou trop compliqués." Étienne-Jules Marey, "La Chronophotographie—Nouvelle Méthode pour analyser le Mouvement dans les Sciences Physiques et Naturelles," Revue Générale des Sciences Pures et Appliquées 21 (November 15, 1891): 690.

[99] Michel Foucault, Discipline and Punish: The Birth of the Prison (London: Penguin Books, 1991), 138.

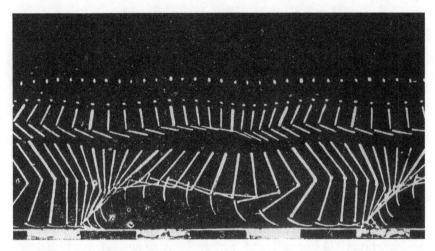

Figure 10 Chronophotographic images replace graphic inscriptions with graphic exposures. "Schematic image of a runner, reduced to a pair of bright lines, which indicates the positions of the limbs."

were temporally permeable. "The image thus obtained gave, with all the precision of a geometric sketch, the two notions of space and time that characterize all movement."[100]

So that the insight gained did not remain limited to what Marey called the mechanical character of a movement, he operationalized the image parameters. Before and after the act of chronophotographic recording, he intervened into the lighting process, in order to expressly reduce visual information. For example, Marey engaged in investigations about the motor activities of runners. To this end, the athletes wore black outfits, on which only the extremities considered relevant were marked with painted white lines. They moved in front of a dark background, and all their other body parties were blackened out. This approach led to an "artificial [. . .] reduction of the surface-extension of the targeted object."[101] He thus made chronophotographs which reduced the body to the details of the act of running that were considered to be relevant (see Fig. 10). The technique transformed the photographic Image into an information surface that no longer corresponded to the criteria of a "natural" representation. Within the image, everything was given a graphic assignation which corresponded to the

---

[100] "L'image ainsi obtenue donnait, avec toute la précision d'une épure gèometrique, les deux notions d'espace et de temps qui caracterisent tout mouvement." Marey, "La Chronophotographie," 691.
[101] Ibid., 692.

Cartesian coordinates of scientific knowledge. The principle was not based on a hermeneutics of the image, but on the measurement and calculation of visible information in the form of graphic inscriptions. The movements of the objects were recorded and made visible in an imagistic equivalent of the Cartesian system of coordinates.

Marey's chronophotographs on a solid plate showed that the kinetic type of media action is not restricted to graphic techniques. Photographic and filmic processes must also be understood as a part of this dimension of media action. The techniques developed by Marey and, later, filmic studies of motion adapted by Frank B. Gilbreth for business purposes can be seen as part of the filmic media network.[102] This transformed itself between 1900 and the 1910s into the cinematicispositive*f*. In relation to the choices of action that these techniques made available, they can, however, also be seen as part of the *graphic method media network*. The principle of the registration apparatus, as James Watt developed it for the regulation of the steam engine, was translated by Frank B. Gilbreth, with the aid of film, into industrial motion studies.[103]

Kinetic Registration

But it is not only apparatuses for controlling machines or physiological techniques for the analysis of dynamic motion processes that fall under the *kinetic* type of media action. There were also developments in the sphere of data representation that corresponded to the *kinetic* ideal type. In contrast, for example, to the spymograph, the connection between data and their graphic form was not defined through the immediacy of the graphic inscription. These processes did not exhibit a direct connection between data and their registration. The data that were deployed here had previously been obtained in a statistical or mathematical fashion, and, in a further step following the logic of the *static* ideal type media, were converted into graphic displays.

Exemplary for this is *Gantt-Charting*, which translated the most varied corporate data into a predetermined graphic tableau (see Fig. 11). The purpose of charting is to depict graphically the complex and dynamic nature of the factory enterprise. The necessary graphic interface consists of the static display of data. The logic of using charts, however, transformed this into the kinetic ideal type of registration.

---

[102] At the same time, Jules Amar proposed to introduce physiological methods into industrial organizations. See Jules Amar, *The Physiology of Industrial Organisation and the Re-employment of the Disabled* (London: The Library Press Limited, 1918).

[103] See Florian Hoof, "The One Best Way: Bildgebende Verfahren der Ökonomie als strukturverändernder Innovationsschub der Managementtheorie ab 1860."

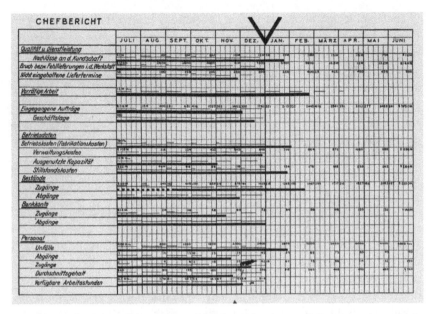

Figure 11 A management report resulting from the system of Gantt charting, which visualizes the firm's planned and actual procedures.

Unlike statistical diagrams, curve records, and similar static forms of presenting facts of the past (Gantt) charts [. . .] are *kinetic*, moving, and project through time the integral elements of service rendered in the past toward the goal in the future.[104]

Similar to Marey's diverse operationalizations of the parameters of the image, Gantt charts consisted of a wide range of data prepared for the purpose in question. In the synopsis, a graphic process arises that belongs not to the static but the kinetic mode of registration. The numerical form of data constitutes a specific visual interface in the graphic form of table. It is no longer determined by the static logic of representation, but by the kinetic logic of registration. It is only in the synopsis of different static data that systematic movements can be recognized. The Gantt charts do not serve the purpose of displaying data, but the modeling and depiction of a complex process. They register it and simultaneously open it up for practices of consulting or management. The process can be analyzed, discussed, and transformed.

[104] Polakov, "Principles of Industrial Philosophy" (1920), cited in Wallace Clark, *The Gantt Chart: A Working Tool of Management* (New York: Ronald Press Company, 1922), 21. Emphasis in the original.

The graphic and filmic inscription apparatuses constructed by James Watt, Étienne-Jules Marey, and Henry L. Gantt are processes of registration and correspond to the logic of action of the *kinetic* ideal type of media. The visualizations gained through kinetic processes have no data referent. They engender graphic inscriptions that are simultaneously the data and their display in one. The graphic apparatuses are directly coupled with the respective data object and represent them in graphic form, or, as in the case of Gantt charts, they order static data in a manner which changes their numerical character and allows them to be transformed into the markers of a kinetic registration (or modeling) process.

The "Calculative" Mode of Graphic Calculation

The static mode of displaying data rests on the direct correlation of numerical data and their graphic depiction in a system of coordinates. In the kinetic mode of representation, there is a direct connection between the registration of motion (or processes) and the output of these transformations in graphic form. The calculative ideal type shifts away from this. Here there is also a correlation between graphic displays and data. But they represent mathematical calculations translated into graphic equivalents. Calculation operations in analytic geometry can either be carried out with recourse to graphic calculation or with a system of numerical equivalence. Beyond that, there are calculation processes which are specially tailored for the graphic form of calculation. In this case, the graphic interface becomes the actual space of mathematical calculation. On the level of representation, solution pathways and calculation steps can be carried out, which correspond not only to the logic of a system of numerical equivalence, but also to the specific qualities of graphic display.

Logarithmic Scales
Exemplary for the calculative type of action embodied herein is the development of nomography. In 1891, the French mathematician Maurice D'Ocagne published his description of this type of graphic calculation,[105] which was followed in 1899 by a detailed treatise on the same subject.[106] The goal of nomography was to radically simplify existing methods of graphic calculation. The previously used approaches for graphically reproducing systems of equivalence involved producing a geometric drawing for every individual case, which delivered the desired result at the end of the process. Alongside millimeter paper (or special logarithmic

---

[105] Maurice D'Ocagne, *Nomographie: Les Calculs usuels effectués au moyen des abaques: Essai d'une théorie générale* (Paris: Gauthier-Villars, 1891).
[106] Maurice D'Ocagne, *Traité de nomographie* (Paris: Gauthier-Villars, 1899).

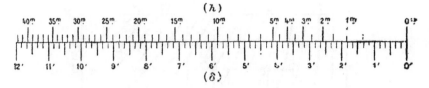

Figure 12 A simple function scale, consisting of two plotted curve functions.

paper), a compass was usually also necessary, as well as (it goes without saying) a knowledge of the mathematical basis of graphic calculation.[107]

In order to decrease the effort required for these kinds of calculations, mathematicians soon developed general calculation tables, and these allowed for frequently required calculation operations to be carried out quickly. Graphic displays had the form of logarithmic scales, such as the Gunter Scale from the seventeenth century. In the early eighteenth century, Louis-Ezéchiel Puchet introduced graphic charts into his publication *Arithmétique linéaire* (see Fig. 12).[108] These were based on the principle of reducing two-dimensional curve functions to one-dimensional function scales. The curve was dissolved into individual points and then aligned with a straight line. This opened the possibility of straightforwardly adding these reshaped curve functions to one another. Without this technique, equivalences which consisted of multiple curve functions could only be produced in a laborious process of multiplication. Tables resting on the principle of intersecting curves were thus replaced by illustrations which exhibited cumulative data points only in the function scales. With this step, equivalences between two variables in a calculation table could be graphically displayed with "unified scales" (*abaques à échelles accolées*). Here, both values of the variables were entered onto a single scale. The reader was now able to comprehend the respective correlating values.

Cartesian Calculation Tables

Equivalences with two known variables in the form $(x1 \times x2 = x3)$ could also be made through the use of "Cartesian calculation tables" (*abaques cartésiens*). Here, too, the function in question could be entered into a two-dimensional system of coordinates. This form of the Cartesian calculation table could be extended to three variables through the function being recorded in the system of

[107] Ludwig Bieberbach, "Über Nomographie," *Die Naturwissenschaften* 10, no. 36 (1922): 775.
[108] Louis-Ezéchiel Pouchet, *Arithmétique linéaire* (Rouen: 1795); Louis-Ezéchiel Pouchet, *Tableau des nouveaux: Poids, mesures et monnoies de la République française* (Rouen: 1796).

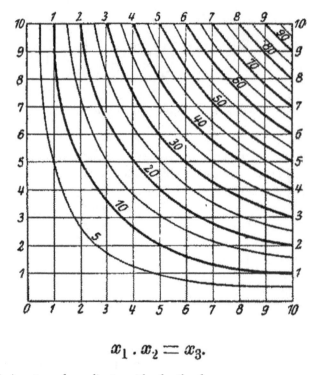

$$x_1 \cdot x_2 = x_3.$$

Figure 13 A system of coordinates with a family of curves.

coordinates not as an individual function curve, but as a family of curves (see Fig. 13). The table thus consisted not only of the values $x1$ and $x2$, but also of another, changing value that could be discerned through the family of curves: $x3$. Nonetheless, the effort required to produce such tables was considerable. In the end, as the earlier example shows, the complicated form of the hyperbola had to be drawn. In order to avoid this, recourse was made to "changing the principle of the table,"[109] as can be seen in Fig. 14.

Here, the scaling of the values on the vertical $x2$-axis was changed. This allowed the production of tables in which an alteration of scales enabled straight lines rather than curves to be drawn. Through the use of logarithmic scales, curves were reduced to the form of straight lines. This simplified the production of tables and the ability to discern the values depicted. And yet, independently of the level of precision required for understanding the information that the graph

---

[109] Bieberbach, "Über Nomographie," 776.

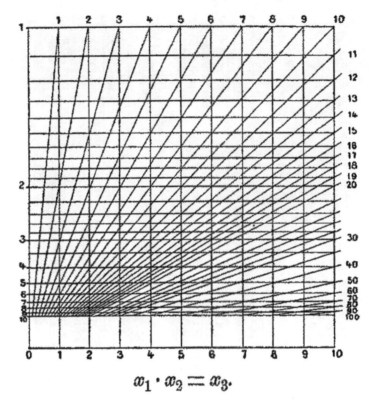

$$\mathcal{x}_1 \cdot \mathcal{x}_2 = \mathcal{x}_3.$$

Figure 14 Through the conversion of the y-values, the curve function can be depicted with lines.

sought to portray, this led to a "tangle of lines"[110] and once again made the comprehension of the graph more difficult (see Fig. 15).

The disadvantages of the processes of graphic representation conceived until this point lay, on the one hand, in their restriction to a maximum of three variables and, on the other hand, in the ever-present problem of the precise and error-free interpretation of the data depicted. It was precisely in the sphere of applied mathematics—for example, in the calculation of the flight path of artillery fire in the military or in road construction—that these techniques were simply not practicable. Here, as a rule, the calculation process was determined by more than three factors. Little wonder, then, that it was precisely these areas that were among the pioneers of nomographic calculation, since their very fortunes

[110] Ibid.

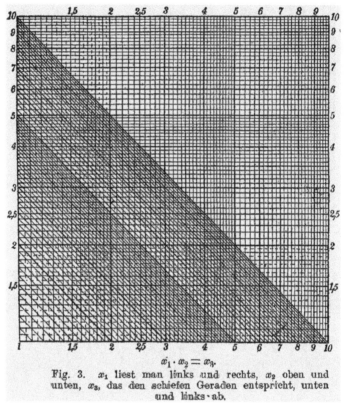

Fig. 3. x_1 liest man links und rechts, x_2 oben und unten, x_3, das den schiefen Geraden entspricht, unten und links·ab,

$$x_1 \cdot x_2 = x_3.$$

Figure 15 At the same time, limits are set to the representability and interpretability of Cartesian calculation tables.

were dependent on the advances of a technique that allowed complex systems of equivalence to be translated in an easy-to-interpret graphic form.

Nomograms allowed complex systems of equivalence to be solved, without the graphic functions in question having to be redrawn every single time. It sufficed to draw a line or place a ruler on the nomogram in order to interpret the results. The nomograms could thus be deployed in combat situations,[111] for example, or in the planning and design of highways.[112] D'Ocagne described the specific differences of nomography with standard graphic calculation and

[111] See A. Witting, *Soldaten—Mathematik* (Berlin: Teubner, 1916); Maurice D'Ocagne, *Principes usuels de nomographie: Avec application à divers problèmes concernant l'artillerie et l'aviation* (Paris: Gauthier-Villars, 1920).

[112] See J. Gysin, *Tafeln zum Abstecken von Eisenbahn- und Strassen-Kurven: In neuer Teilung (Centesimal-Teilung)* (Liestal: Lüdin, 1885).

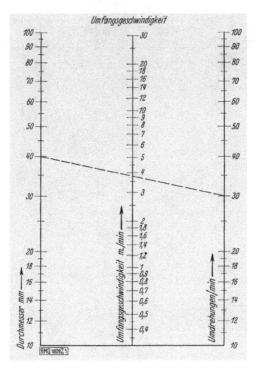

Figure 16 A nomogram with three function scales for determining the circumferential speed of a lathe dependent on a workpiece diameter and rotational speed.

other forms of structured data processing (such as the table or the chart) in the following manner:

> Suppose that we have an equation in several variables and that we set up a system in which various graphical elements, upon which we have marked graduated scales, are designed so that there is a simple graphical relationship, immediately perceived by the eye, between those graphical elements that represent a solution to the equation. We shall then have produced a graphical representation of the equation with which, if we are given the values of all but one of the variables, we can find the remaining value by simply reading it from one of the graduated scales. This construction gives us, in some sense, an image of the algebraic mathematical law expressed by the equation, which we may describe by the name nomogram, which is a combination of the two Greek words for law and I draw.[113]

[113] Maurice D'Ocagne, *Le Calcul Simplifié: Graphical and Mechanical Methods for Simplifying Calculation*, trans. J. Howlett and M. R. Williams (Cambridge, MA: MIT Press, 1986), 83.

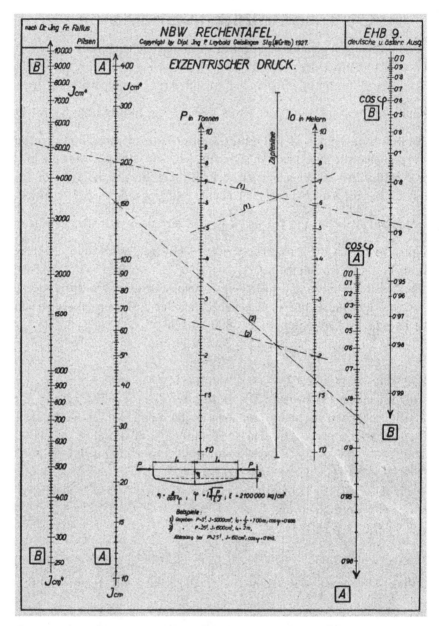

Figure 17 Several combined nomograms for determining complex and unusual pressure relations for iron construction.

With nomography, even complex mathematical systems of equivalence could be prepared graphically in such a way that the results of the calculation could be immediately discerned. The level of visualization became the ineluctable basis of mathematical calculations, or, as D'Ocagne dubbed it, "visual interpolation."

> Their graphical form, however, gives them inestimable advantages over ordinary numerical tables: great reduction in the time needed for their construction, much less space occupied, and great ease of visual interpolation.[114]

In addition to time savings, the nomogram offered other advantages. Once constructed for a specific purpose, other people without a mathematical background could also carry out calculations (see Fig. 16). Moreover, nomograms allowed "the number of variables to be easily increased, almost without limit."[115] The previous limit of three variables had become obsolete. Moreover, D'Ocagne departed from some of the tenets of conventional graphic calculation. The nomographic tables contained at least three function scales. Through the inscription of a straight line, which cut across all three scales, an unknown value in an equation could be ascertained from two given values. Depending on the form of the mathematical equation, in principle an infinite amount of variables could, in combination with multiple nomograms, be added to the table (see Fig. 17).

In contrast to the Cartesian charts, this was not a form of graphic calculation in the original sense. The interface of the nomograms no longer contained representations of graphic functions, but function scales. They depicted the derived approximate values rather than exact values. Nomography followed the principle of rough calculation, and no longer that of the universally usable calculation principle of the graphic method. Hence, in nomography the necessity arose for designing a new nomogram for every purpose, which kept available a set calculation method for the solution of a mathematical equation.

The calculative type of action is held together by an external, mathematical logic. It incorporates techniques of graphic calculation, whose primary goal is not the depiction but the allocation of data. Here, the act of visualization contributes to an acceleration and a considerable simplification of calculation processes. Data were graphically assigned, following a mathematical ratio, in order to be reshaped in the next step with the aid of graphic relations. This type of action boasts its own calculative reality. It is not based on a written, mathematical form, but on a graphic-visual interface. It is not only mathematical forms of calculation that are linked to it. At the same time, it is capable of making connections with other forms of graphic visualization. For decision-making processes, it is a mathematical

114 Ibid.
115 Ibid.

process of calculation, but also a visual layout on which calculation methods and results can be directly displayed in graphic relations. This type of action allows calculation processes to be linked to other forms of *visual management.*

The action dimensions of the media network in use in the late nineteenth century consist of the three aforementioned types of action: the *static, kinetic,* and *calculative.* Individual graphic techniques can be described as hybrid types coupling these three ideal types. In this vein, Gantt charting is a particularly illuminating example. Here, graphic displays are fundamental for creating a specific, kinetic reality, which will subsequently lead to, for example, the visualization of complex industrial processes. In this context, a visual reality of managerial knowledge once again arises, which does not boast a direct representation but is linked to a dynamic kinetic process.

These three modes define the potential of the media network and determine it as the media preconditions of managerial activity. They form the basis for the acceptance of the media network in business contexts. The functionalities can be flexibly coupled with one another in the form of concrete visualization processes and thus adapted to the specific requirements of enterprises. At the same time, these three modes also determine their own conditions. Data, objects, and processes must be translated into a visual form, in order to be part of the graphic-visual reality of management.

The Popularization of the "Graphic Method Media Network"

The media network of the graphic method and the accompanying courses of action had been differentiated by the end of the nineteenth century. Calculative, static, and kinetic techniques were available for the most varied purposes and could be adapted to case-specific hybrid relations. From the 1910s, a number of organizations from the science and business worlds (as well as state institutions) began to standardize the forms of graphic techniques. This was intended to give rise to a generally valid norm—a grammar of the graphic method.[116] The graphic method was recognized as a central practice by the most important actors and institutions in science, business, and society as a whole. It was no longer an

---

[116] In the United States, the Joint Committee on Standards for Graphic Presentation was founded in 1914. There, the most important scientific societies and state institutions were represented, in order to work on a unified standardization of graphic displays: the American Society of Mechanical Engineers, American Statistical Association, American Institute of Electrical Engineers, American Association for the Advancement of Science, American Academy of Political and Social Science, American Genetic Association, American Economic Association, American Society of Naturalists, American Mathematical Society, United States Census Bureau, United States Bureau of Standards, American Association of Public Accountants, Society for the Promotion of Engineering Education, American Chemical Society, American Institute of Mining Engineers, Actuarial Society of America, and the American Psychological Association. The goal was to design a "grammar" of the graphic method, in order to prevent erroneous interpretations and ensure the compatibility of methods across disciplinary boundaries.

innovation, a still unstable and ill-defined development, but a self-evident part of scientific, government, and corporate routines.

Funkhouser and Friendly chart the changes in the epistemological status of the graphic method in the early twentieth century.[117] Prior to that point, during the "golden age of graphics" (roughly between 1860 and 1890),[118] a whole array of new visualization processes had arisen. In the early twentieth century, this dynamic and innovative period came to an end. At this point, it was no longer new developments, but the popularization and adaptation of the graphic method for other spheres that assumed the greatest importance. In the United States, France, and Germany, publications appeared whose object was either the "graphic method" or "graphic representation." These included, among others, comparative diagrams, statistical graphs, visual charts, and nomography, but also instruments for registering motion. This amply illustrated introductory literature is a symptom of the popularity of graphic methods.[119] It is not only

[117] Funkhouser, "Historical Development of the Graphical Representation of Statistical Data," 330; Friendly, "The Golden Age of Statistical Graphics," 502–504.

[118] Funkhouser, "Historical Development of the Graphical Representation of Statistical Data," 330.

[119] See Friedrich Schilling, *Graphische Darstellungen zur Psychologie* (Leipzig: Ernst Wunderlich, 1901); Robert J. Aley, *Graphs* (New York: C. Heath & Co., 1902); John B. Peddle, *The Construction of Graphical Charts* (New York: McGraw-Hill, 1910); Franz Schaaps, "Statistik und graphische Darstellung im Dienste des Kaufmanns," *Zeitschrift für Handelswissenschaft und Handelspraxis* 3, no. 4 (1910): 125–28; V. Michel, "Die graphische Darstellung in der Geschäftsstatistik," *Zeitschrift für Handelswissenschaft und Handelspraxis* 4, no. 3 (1911): 102–4. Felix Auerbach, "Die graphische Darstellung," *Die Naturwissenschaften* 6, no. 7 (1913): 139–45, 159–64; Felix Auerbach, *Die graphische Darstellung: Eine allgemeinverständliche, durch zahlreiche Beispiele aus allen Gebieten der Wissenschaft und Praxis erläuterte Einführung in den Sinn und den Gebrauch der Methode* (Leipzig: Teubner 1914); Marcello von Pirani, *Graphische Darstellung in Wissenschaft und Technik* (Berlin: Göschen 1914); Walter G. Waffenschmidt, "Graphische Methode in der theoretischen Oekonomie, dargestellt in Anlehnung an das Tauschproblem," *Archiv für Sozialwissenschaft und Sozialpolitik* 39 (1915): 438–81, 795–818; Frank J. Warne, *Warne's Book of Charts: A Special Feature of Warne's Elementary Course in Chartography* (Washington, DC: 1916); S. Gilman, *Graphic Charts for the Business Man* (Chicago: La Salle Extension University, 1917); Leonard Porter Ayres, *The War with Germany: A Statistic Summary* (Washington, DC: U.S. Government Printing Office, 1919); Willard C. Brinton, *Graphic Methods for Presenting Facts* (Washington, DC: U.S. Government Printing Office, 1919); Oskar Freund, "Über die Anwendbarkeit graphischer Darstellungsweisen in industriellen Betrieben," *Werkstattstechnik* 13, no. 1 (1919): 5–9; Allan C. Haskell, *How to Make and Use Graphic Charts* (New York: Codex, 1919); Clark, *The Gantt Chart*; Roland Falkner, "Uses and Perils of Business Graphics," *Administration: The Journal of Business Analysis* 3, no. 1 (1922): 52–56; Fritz Krauss, *Die Nomographie oder Fluchtlinienkunst* (Berlin: Springer, 1922); C. v. Dobbeler, "Grundlagen der Nomographie," *Maschinenbau/Gestaltung* 3, no. 4 (1923): 99–107; B. M. Konorski, *Die Grundlagen der Nomographie* (Berlin: Springer, 1923); Otto Lacmann, *Die Herstellung gezeichneter Rechentafel: Ein Lehrbuch der Nomographie* (Berlin: Springer, 1923); A. Leyensetter, "Die Graphische Darstellung als Hilfsmittel zur Regelung und Überwachung der Produktion," *Maschinenbau/Betrieb* 5, no. 19 (1923): 765–67; K. G. Karsten, *Charts and Graphs: An Introduction to Graphic Methods in the Control and Analysis of Statistics* (New York: Prentice-Hall, 1925); Hans Linnenbrügge, *Über eine neue graphische Methode zur Untersuchung der Schiffsschaufelräder* (Sondershausen: Eupel, 1925); Percy A. Bivins, *The Ratio Chart in Business* (New York: Codex, 1926); J. R. Riggleman, *Graphic Methods for Presenting Business Statistics* (New York: McGraw-Hill, 1926); A. R. Palmer, *The Use of Graphs in Commerce and Industry* (London: G. Bell & Sons 1921); T. G. Rose, *Business Charts: A Clear Explanation of the Various Types of Charts Used in Business and of the Principles Governing the Correct Presentation of Facts by Graphical Methods* (London: Sir Isaac Pitman

directed at theoretical, "pure" science, but also relates to the development of "applied" science. In the wake of these developments, the graphic method was also implemented in the sphere of business and industry.[120] These publications are part of contemporary discourse, from which we can discern how highly these techniques were valued during this period and what practical advantages and hopes were linked with the graphic method. Moreover, they indicate that graphic techniques had begun to detach themselves from their previous usage in the fields of mathematics, engineering, statistics, and physiology.

At the same time, we can discern a certain fascination for visualization processes, which translated scientific results into visible lines, curves, and diagrams,[121] thereby rendering them easily comprehensible. The boom in the graphic method, however, not only followed concretely set goals. The aesthetic of a new graphic visuality linked to it also contributed to this mode of representation finding purchase. Graphic displays became a widely used instrument for preparing complex sets of facts for the broader, nonspecialist public. Along with the dissemination of scientific knowledge and models, and the field of workplace accident prevention, this also affected the era's discourse on hygiene.[122] In New York, for instance, parades were held that presented graphic statistics on hygienic issues (see Fig. 18).

These parades sought to draw attention to targeted progress and goals yet to be attained in the sphere of health care: "Many very large charts, curves and other statistical displays were mounted on wagons in such a manner that interpretation was possible from either side of the street."[123] Statistics parades may very well be an exceptional incident in the visibility of graphic techniques among the broader public. But the lonely statistic tables mounted on an ornament-laden wagon pulled by a horse through driving rain nonetheless attest to the high value given to graphic displays at this time. High expectations were attached to them, and they were considered as one of the most advanced forms of visual communication. They allowed for dry numerical data to be transformed into visual evidence. The fact that crowds of people braved the weather points to the fact that

& Sons, 1930); Karl W. Henning, "Zur graphischen Darstellung organisatorischer Arbeitsabläufe," *Zeitschrift für Organisation* 4, no. 1 (1930): 12–17. For publications on nomography, see Chapter 2, n70, of this volume.

[120] This visualization drive can also be inferred from the specialist magazines I have consulted. See Chapter 2, n66, of this volume.

[121] On the special aspect of the curve, see Stefan Rieger, *Schall und Rauch: Eine Mediengeschichte der Kurve* (Frankfurt am Main: Suhrkamp, 2009).

[122] See Philipp Sarasin, *Reizbare Maschinen: Eine Geschichte des Körpers (1765–1914)* (Frankfurt am Main: Suhrkamp, 2001).

[123] Willard C. Brinton, *Graphic Methods for Presenting Facts* (New York: The Engineering Magazine Co., 1914), 343.

Figure 18 The "graphic method" enters the public sphere. A view of a statistic parade held by employees of the City of New York on May 17, 1913.

the expectations for these graphic displays were not entirely unjustified.[124] From a historical perspective, we might object that publications of graphic techniques in the early twentieth century were in no way something new. After all, more than a century earlier, William Playfair had already published *The Commercial and Political Atlas and Statistical Breviary*,[125] which included various techniques for visualizing data.[126] But there was a decisive difference with the publications of the early twentieth century. Playfair used his representational methods as tools for accurately depicting national economic data, such as the external trade deficit between England and Norway. His selection of the different techniques of graphic display rested purely on the goal he was pursuing, which was the visualization of special data sets, and so his focus lay on economic data and not the methods of representation he was using.

This contrasts markedly with the publications put out in the early 1900s, which followed a fundamentally different conception. Visualization techniques were no

[124] Ibid.
[125] Playfair, *The Commercial and Political Atlas and Statistical Breviary* (2005 [1786]).
[126] See in this Chapter of this volume, "The 'Static' Mode of Graphic Representation."

Figure 19 "Mechanical Bar Chart for Popular Display of Statistical Facts." A display apparatus from the Bureau of Foreign and Domestic Commerce used for the public presentation of statistical data.

longer a means to the end of illustrating the trajectory of negative visualization techniques. Rather, they shifted the focus to the various visualization techniques as independent, universally utilizable methods of graphic representation. These publications thus attest to a nascent exchange between business and nonbusiness knowledge practices. Apparatuses and practices originally developed for scientific research came to be increasingly deployed in applied research and nonscientific spheres (see Fig. 19). The professional backgrounds of the authors of these synoptic charts are also pertinent. They frequently came from industrial-scientific research. They felt called to directly work at the interface between theoretical discovery and the commodity form of practical implementation. Outside the precision of the research, the transmission and application of the discoveries gained in other areas was of prime importance.

The exchanges between the scientific and industrial worlds were not an unproblematic undertaking. Both areas depended partly on basic assumptions and orientations for their activity that were exceptionally counterposed to one another. On the one side stood scientists who "seek to know"[127]; on the other side were the implementation-oriented technicians who "seek [. . .] to do."[128] If interest focused on the formation of theory, and not its practical application, then technicians mainly concentrated on practically solving existing problems. Whether theoretical assumptions played a role or not was a secondary issue. The pure theoretician thus enjoyed just as little recognition in the business world as the practically oriented scientist did in the academic sphere.[129] From this, fundamental differences in the actual method proved to be pertinent.[130] Thus, application-related research[131] was connected "by a tendency away from analytical solutions, a reliance on approximations, and, to some extent, a lessening of mathematical rigor."[132] Theoretical research, by contrast, adhered closely to the objective scientific criteria of mathematical precision. This difference became particularly clear with the example of graphic calculation techniques like nomography. The new graphic calculation techniques resting on the principle of rough estimates opened entirely new possibilities for applied industrial research. For scientific research, which adhered closely to a rigid system of mathematical precision, these techniques were not practicable. They were simply not exact enough.[133]

It was thus necessary to adapt the graphic method for each specific purpose. It was for this reason that, alongside aspects which concerned the practical usage of graphic techniques, these publications also contained additional considerations on the relationship between theory and practice, as well as on an understanding

---

[127] Edwin Layton, "Mirror-Image Twins: The Communities of Science and Technology in 19th-Century America," *Technology and Culture* 12, no. 4 (1971): 576.

[128] Ibid.

[129] Ibid., 575–77.

[130] See also Gerald D. Nash, "The Conflict Between Pure and Applied Science in Nineteenth-Century Public Policy: The California State Geological Survey, 1860–1874," *Isis* 54, no. 176 (1963): 217–28. The disjunction or simultaneity of "applied" and "pure" research has, for the relevant time period, not yet been been treated in adequate detail. Initial attempts can be found in Florian Hoof, Eva-Maria Jung, and Ulrich Salaschek, eds., *Jenseits des Labors: Labor, Wissen, Transformation* (Bielefeld: transcript, 2011), and in particular Lea Haller, "Angewandte Forschung? Cortison zwischen Hochschule, Industrie und Klinik."

[131] For a more detailed discussion of the rise of applied engineering science and polytechnics in the late nineteenth century and their comprehension of science and research, see Chapter 2 of this volume, "Nomography and Applied Engineering Science."

[132] Layton, "Mirror-Image Twins," 575.

[133] On this field of tension, see Chapter 2 of this volume, "(Proto-)Nomographic Production Processes."

of research and science that oscillated between exactitude, pragmatism, and the questioning of metrological objectivity. Which forms of mediation and scientific exactitude should be considered, if the level of pure abstraction and theory are to be left behind and so-called *applied* sciences are to be established? Are graphic techniques at all suitable for this? It is the unique media characteristics linked to it that are under focus. Which advantages are connected with the processes of visual display in contrast to standard modes of representation, such as tables or indexical systems like lists? In this view, these publications on the graphic method are precisely a discourse on the possibilities of media techniques. What do visualization techniques achieve in contrast to the previous written and oral practices of communication, calculation, analysis, and decision making? The discourse is also an indication of a new, not-yet-established mode of graphic representation and perception. The form and definition of this innovation were, at this point in time, still indeterminate, and it had to run through a process of discursive consolidation.

The Graphic-Visual Punctum

In 1914, Felix Auerbach, a mathematician and physicist who specialized in experimental physics, published the survey volume: *Die graphische Darstellung: Eine allgemeinverständliche, durch zahlreiche Beispiele aus allen Gebieten der Wissenschaft und Praxis erläuterte Einführung in den Sinn und den Gebrauch der Methode*,[134] which was reprinted in a second edition in 1918. In contrast to the aforementioned publications by Playfair, Auerbach's work focuses less on a thematic goal and more on an interest in epistemological questions. He concerns himself here with the graphic method in and of itself. He seeks to use the new possibilities of visualizing data for the refinement of analytic principles. At the same time, he sees the potential for what was, from his perspective, a necessary opening up of scientific knowledge. The graphic method would allow for findings from different spheres of science to be comprehensible even to nonspecialists. In this sense, they are part of the Enlightenment project of making scientific knowledge generally accessible.[135] In addition, he argues, graphic displays make

---

[134] Felix Auerbach, *Die graphische Darstellung: Eine allgemeinverständliche, durch zahlreiche Beispiele aus allen Gebieten der Wissenschaft und Praxis erläuterte Einführung in den Sinn und den Gebrauch der Methode* (Leipzig: Teubner, 1914). The title translates as *Graphic Representation: A Generally Comprehensible Introduction to the Meaning and Usage of the Method, Illustrated with Numerous Examples from All Areas of Science and Practice*. A year earlier, Auerbach published a series of articles on the same issue. See Auerbach, "Die graphische Darstellung."

[135] See also Felix Auerbach, *Die Furcht vor der Mathematik und ihre Überwindung* (Jena: Fischer, 1924).

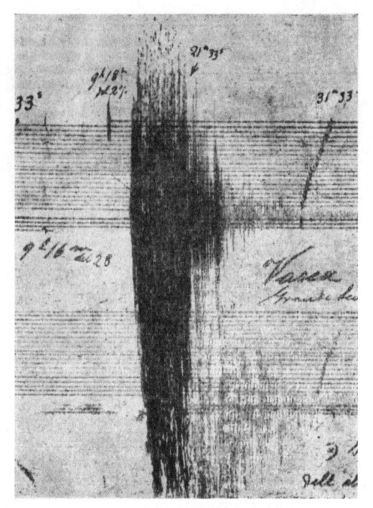

Figure 20 The visual surface of the 1908 Messina earthquake.

a further contribution. They can be used to reduce to distinct graphic forms phenomena that may appear difficult to fathom. Auerbach illustrates his argument with a curve graph of the seismic activities of the 1908 Messina earthquake (see Fig. 20). The worst natural catastrophe in twentieth-century Europe, as far as the number of fatalities is concerned, can thus appear as an explicable and intelligible phenomenon.

Photographs of the destruction or detailed written or oral accounts of suffering and loss were replaced by the graphically domesticated cause. The nonindexical

Figure 21 A photographic image of the destruction after the earthquake and tsunami in the city of Messina, with over 100,000 fatalities.

surfeit of significance, the *punctum* of photography,[136] here retreated behind the sober visualization of the cause. The seismic curve can be measured, placed in graphic relations, and, as in the case of an earthquake, perhaps not be mastered, but at least retrospectively explained and analyzed.

For Auerbach, the graphic method, which extends visuality to invisible rules and phenomena, is contrasted with illustrations that are restricted to the depiction of spatial, directly visible objects. With their perspectival centralization, photographs are capable of depicting the surface details of the destruction wrought by an earthquake, as well as the local luminaries posing in front of them (see Fig. 21). But they do not contribute to a deeper understanding of the disaster. In this sense, the simple graphic inscription of seismic activity shows considerably more. And yet this graphic visualization technique does not rest on the conventions of centralized perspective, but on the scientific conventions of the

---

[136] See Roland Barthes, *Camera Lucida*, trans. Richard Howard (New York: Hill and Wang, 1981).

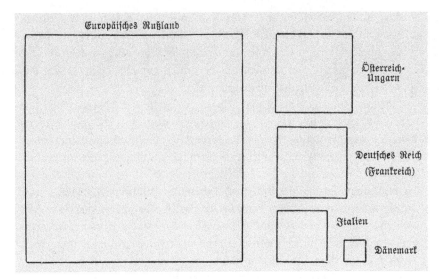

Figure 22 Area sizes of different European nations. Comparability and clarity of mathematical magnitudes through graphic forms.

two-dimensional system of Cartesian coordinates. Auerbach defines the graphic method as a process of making visible that rests on the basic laws of mathematical relations.

> For all the spatial objects in the world, we have, thanks to the organization of our eyes, an absolutely incomparable method of recording them: the production of images. [. . .] What if, in the future, we should want to remedy this natural lack, what if we should resolve to capture and graphically depict the non-spatial, that is, the temporal, and beyond this, everything, everything that relates to temperature and electricity, lightness and color, materiality and spiritual quantity and quality, and hundreds of other types of perception? [. . .] This is the fundamental genetic and disciplinary idea of what we presently call the method of graphic representation.[137]

Producing visibility with the aid of graphic displays has, according to Auerbach, two main advantages. In scientific research, existing mathematical models of knowledge acquisition can be enriched through aspects of *intuition*. Researchers can depart from the factual character of the "iron language" of mathematical

---

[137] Auerbach, "Die graphische Darstellung," 3.

numbers, and thereby forge new paths of discovery. For data from experiments and observations, in particular, the graphic method enables a more playful, more variable approach, from which we can "naturally draw other conclusions (see Fig. 22). Such possibilities immediately become impossible once we introduce every concept as a 'mathematical magnitude.'"[138]

At the same time, graphic displays also allow for the visual preparation of scientific data. In addition to discipline-specific reasons, it is the overt evidence inherent to representation that leads Auerbach to emphasize the media automatism of the availability and transmissibility of the knowledge expressed within.

> [Graphic representation] is a method of presenting known phenomena, facts, truths in such a way that they immediately speak for themselves; that everyone who has learnt to understand the language of representation, can independently and autonomously comprehend it and work with what they are presented with. It is, therefore, a practical method [. . .] even if recognition and action, analysis and synthesis are most intimately connected with each other everywhere in the world.[139]

Auerbach was a staunch advocate of progressive modernity,[140] and he sympathized with reform projects like the Bauhaus in Weimar. Notably, Walter Gropius designed the Villa Auerbach for him, the first residential building for a private citizen that was built according to the construction kit principle of *Neues Bauen*. With this background, Auerbach conceived of graphic techniques as a method to successfully combat what he saw as problematic developments within science. In his view, these developments included the tendency toward scientific discourse detaching itself from the needs of everyday life. He rejected theory for its own sake and instead demanded the return of an ostensibly lost connection between theory and practice. Graphic representation, moreover, could be of use not only within existing business structures. Rather, Auerbach insists that they will have specific effects. For him, the medium is the message. He affirms that the process of illustrating scientific combinations has the potential to once again bring theory and practice closer to each other.

---

[138] Ibid., 96.

[139] Ibid., 1.

[140] He also published a description of the Zeiss plant in Jena, reworked across several editions. Zeiss was considered a progressive model business which even trialed communal models of worker participation. See Felix Auerbach, *Das Zeisswerk und die Carl-Zeiss-Stiftung in Jena: Ihre wissenschaftliche, technische und soziale Entwicklung und Bedeutung* (Jena: Fischer, 1903). For Auerbach's proximity to artistic modernism, see Karin Leonhard, "Bild und Zahl: Das Diagramm in Kunst und Naturwissenschaft am Beispiel Wassily Kandinsky und Felix Auerbachs," in Anja Zimmermann, ed., *Sichtbarkeit und Medium: Austausch, verknüpfung und Differenz naturwissenschaftlicher und ästhetischer Bildstrategien* (Hamburg: Hamburg University Press 2005), 231–45.

It is no wonder that graphic representation, whose earlier neglect is precisely explicable through the oppressive tyranny of a predilection for abstract thought, has embarked on a veritable triumphant march through all areas of scientific research, beginning with the precise natural sciences and disciplines using static national economic data, and gradually conquering the most far-flung terrain.[141]

As opposed to the existing categories and definitions of a theory-based mode of thinking, which aims for the utmost logical clarity, the graphic method offers researchers the possibility for playfulness, inspiration, and creativity with respect to existing fields of knowledge. Of course, it is, as Auerbach argues:

> the most unassuming of arts, since it provides the eye with nothing other than lines and clusters of lines and still more lines, as well as the occasional surface and, very rarely, spatial, model-like figures. But for those who can read this language, it is, in its own way, more eloquent that any other; it relays an incredible amount of information in a very small space; since we can, so to speak, read this text forwards and backwards, up and down, analytically and synthetically, and every time we obtain the same discovery in a new form, a new context, a new genesis, and in the end this discovery is, over and over again, a new one.[142]

The visualizations brought about through graphic techniques are not dead forms or simplified derivations of complex combinations, since "with time these symbols will gain life."[143] They give, to transpose Marshall McLuhan's discussion of Cubist painting to the graphic method, "the inside and outside, the top, bottom, back, and front and the rest, in two dimensions" and thereby drop "the illusion of perspective in favor of instant sensory awareness of the whole."[144] They are, in other words, in a position to create their own sphere of knowledge. The graphic method assumes two forms: on the one hand, it is a scientific method for analyzing and displaying available data, while on the other hand it is a system for ordering an intuitive, creative thinking in order to see things afresh and recognize new aspects to them. The compatibility of the graphic mode provides a framework for markedly different sets of knowledge to be combined with each other and complement each other. The ensuing multidimensionality, the juxtaposition of varying factors in the compatible form of a graphic chart, takes the place of spatially structured illustrations.

---

[141] Auerbach, "Die graphische Darstellung," 4.
[142] Ibid., 4.
[143] Ibid., 97.
[144] McLuhan, *Understanding Media*, 13.

The visualization possibilities of spatial representations, such as photography, are determined by a large number of factors. They are underpinned by conventions of perception, such as centralized perspective, or are oriented toward the ideal of a direct, realistic portrayal. The graphic method, by contrast, is an abstract machine for making connections with almost unlimited utility.[145] The graphic form allows for the relational connection of objects, even if the objects in question have no inherent commonalities with each other. Transformed into the form of a graph, even supposedly arbitrary data points can be brought into relation with one another. It is in this way that the specific logic of the graphic method is established, which has effects that are independent of the data that are inputted into them.

Applied Industrial Research

In the same year in which Auerbach's introductory volume appeared, Marcello von Pirani also published an introduction to the "graphic method," with his *Graphische Darstellung in Wissenschaft und Technik.*[146] Like Auerbach, von Pirani was a mathematician, but he was mostly active in industrial research. Whereas Auerbach came from a classical academic scientific background, von Pirani worked at the intersection between science and industry. From 1904 to 1918, he directed the laboratory at the Siemens & Halske AG lightbulb factory. In 1919, Siemens & Halske, Deutsche Gasglühlicht AG/Auergesellschaft,[147] and AEG merged to form Osram AG. For the new corporation, von Pirani presided over the science and technology bureau in the electric lighting branch, until his emigration in 1936.[148] While in exile in Britain, he was active in the research laboratory of the General Electric Co. Ltd. in the London suburb of Wembley.

Von Pirani's interest in graphic displays grew from his activity in the field of applied industrial research. It is with this background that his publication, one of

---

[145] Gilles Deleuze and Félix Guattari, *A Thousand Plateaus: Capitalism and Schizophrenia*, vol. II, trans. Brian Massumi (London: Bloomsbury Academic, 2013). See also Alexandros-Andreas Kyrtsis, "Diagrammatic Rhetoric in Business and Architecture," lecture at "Imagining Business Oxford University Said Business School" conference, June 26–27, 2008, p. 6.

[146] Von Pirani, *Graphische Darstellung in Wissenschaft und Technik*. The title translates as *Graphic Representation in Science and Technology*.

[147] This happened three years after the discontinuation of the consulting project of the corporate consultancy firm Gilbreth, Inc., analyzed in Chapter 5 of this volume.

[148] Renate Tobies, "Zur Position von Mathematik und Mathematiker/innen in der Industrieforschung vor 1945," *NTM: Zeitschrift für Geschichte der Wissenschaft, Technik und Medizin* 15, no. 4 (2007): 243–45.

the first guides to be derived from practical experience, should be understood. How are techniques of scientific origin adapted to the logic of commercial action? In mathematical research, for instance, the time required for a given calculation plays a secondary role; it is the precision of the result that has priority. With calculations in commercial or industrial organization, by contrast, it is speed rather than precision that is generally the most important factor. Reaching approximate values through rough estimates is often sufficient for these purposes. Furthermore, the calculations to be carried out need to be as simple as possible. After all, the personnel of corporations, in contrast to the academic milieu, are generally not made up of specialists in mathematics. Graphic approaches were an attempt to bridge this gap. At the very least, they would allow for incompatible forms of knowledge to be indirectly brought into proximity to one another. This is the context in which von Pirani describes graphic representation as a possibility for ordering data and information in a targeted fashion, thereby making them more conspicuous:

> Graphic representation pursues the goal of summarizing connections that have been acquired experimentally or theoretically and reproduced in the form of observation results or mathematical formulae, in such a way that the totality of the connected values of relevant sizes is presented to the eye in a clear fashion.[149]

Techniques of graphic representation can be used to translate large and complex sets of data into more easily legible forms of presentation. They no longer exist in heterogeneous forms of data but can be reduced to a single level through the principle of abstract graphic representation. The eye can perceive the relevant facts of the graphic interface "at a glance,"[150] without having to navigate through the depths of assorted data information (see Fig. 23). This accelerates the actual operation of data processing and, according to von Pirani, expedites the decisions dependent on this information.

With this description of the knowledge sets formed by the *graphic method*, von Pirani finds himself in good company. A few years later, American management literature, in particular, described the advantages of the rapid and direct

---

[149] Von Pirani, *Graphische Darstellung in Wissenschaft und Technik*, 5.

[150] The same turn of phrase can be found in, among others, Henry L. Gantt, "A Graphical Daily Balance in Manufacture," *Transactions of the American Society of Mechanical Engineers* (henceforth given as *Transactions ASME*) 24 (1903): 1325; Frank B. Gilbreth, *Field System* (New York: The Myron C. Clark Publishing Co., 1908), 6; Haskell, *How to Make and Use Graphic Charts*, 80; Falkner, "Uses and Perils of Business Graphics," 52.

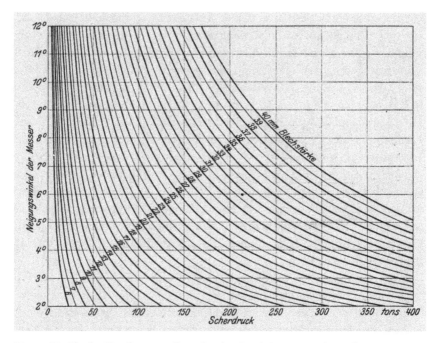

Figure 23 The family of curves allows for the simple interpretations of cutting pressure for sheet metal work. The underlying mathematical data are no longer necessary for interpreting graphic charts.

comprehension of graphic visualizations in almost stereotypical fashion. They offered the reader information "at a glance," thereby allowing decisions to be rapidly made. The term "at a glance" in American usage refers not only to the act of perception, but also the prevailing reception situation. Perception is only successful when the object perceived, in this case graphic visualizations, boasts a suitable interface. The arrangement of data, and the ensuing clarity that is attained, is accompanied by a necessary relativization of the actual precision of the data depicted.

In contrast to a table, graphic representation can only ever work with a numerical precision limited by the size of the graph, but it has the advantage over the table of being able to be consulted continuously, and therefore it retains the possibility of interpreting values between the observed or calculated values.[151]

[151] Von Pirani, *Graphische Darstellung in Wissenschaft und Technik*, 5.

The tables still contain exact values. Furthermore, there is still a direct correlation between the visual representations and the tabular values from which they are derived. But the values have turned into imprecise points in a chart. They gain relevance not from a reference to an exact number, but by dint of being part of a more comprehensive, graphically depicted mass of data. The epistemological status of this data has changed. It is now based on the ideal type of the *static* display of data. But it is no longer dependent on mathematical calculation models. Rather, a specific data sphere is created. The "graphic path," with the help of the graphic interpolation between observed vales and the extrapolation of values "beyond the observed values,"[152] opens up new possibilities for acquiring and operationalizing data. Knowledge sets, which appear in the form of graphic displays, can be placed into new groupings. Future developments can similarly be derived from the existing data sets. Auerbach himself had pointed to this when describing it as the intuitive-creative moment of the graphic method.

Alongside possibilities for visual interpolation and extrapolation, the graphic form facilitates the comparability and control of data. Whereas the number columns of tabular values are only comparable to each other after a great deal of detailed work, graphic methods allow for the immediate verification of errors in their very system of representation (see Figs. 24 and 25). Numerical values that unexpectedly depart too far from anticipated trends are immediately visible. This new functionality of visual data was particularly advantageous for business purposes, such as the control of production processes. The criterion of data precision is here of only secondary significance. It is much more important to recognize major deviations and react promptly to them, since the most effective response to business disruptions does not consist in an exact reaction but one that is as rapid as possible.

In contrast to Auerbach, however, von Pirani is also critical of some aspects of the graphic method. He highlights the danger of erroneous visual interpretations due to the graphic reduction of knowledge. Precisely when data are projected into the future through extrapolation, the graphic form of knowledge can lead to a deceptive "feeling of constancy," resulting in conclusions that "depart from the objective situation on the ground."[153] Indeed, for the period's theoretical scientists, the graphic method is synonymous with provocation. It relativizes the criterion of precision in favor of the simple accessibility of knowledge. By departing from some of science's central criteria of objectivity, applied research had succeeded in adapting the graphic method for practical problems.

[152] Ibid., 16.
[153] Ibid., 17.

Volt	Ampere
5,0	0,51
5,3	0,52
5,6	0,531
5,85	0,539
6,02	0,548
6,2	0,553
6,4	0,565
6,75	0,579
7,0	0,591
7,2	0,60

Figure 24 Tabulated form of data showing the relationship between electric current strength and tension.

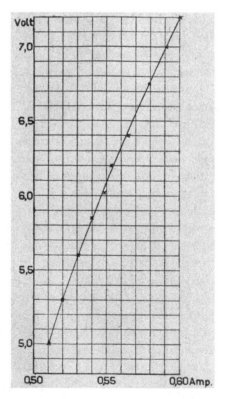

Figure 25 Interpolation and extrapolation of the tabulated form of data as a graphic means for visualizing physical laws. The relationship between electric current strength and tension as a law proceeding from slightly deviating measurements.

Originally, the graphic method had been developed in disciplines like material engineering and physiology. Eventually it was also implemented in other spheres.

> The usability of graphic representation is, it need hardly be stressed, just as universal as, if not more universal than, that of the tabular mode of representation. It is not restricted to the precise sciences, but has also found purchase in areas which are quite distant from them, such as in commercial enterprises.[154]

The adaptive, universal character necessary for this nonetheless initially consisted in the abandonment of core scientific criteria. The graphic method changed from a primarily scientific practice to a visualization process.

The "Graphic Method" Media Network

Auerbach's and von Pirani's publications are part of a popularization drive, which also defines the principle of the graphic method. Under the rubric of visibility and visualization, they collected graphic techniques from different areas, from statistics and physiology to material engineering. They then defined these techniques as belonging to a common, coherent media network.

Nomography, statistical evaluations, curve diagrams, and graphic charts have, in their original spheres of usage, initially very little in common, but they are all techniques which developed under the influence of differentiating methods and disciplinary problems. As argued at the beginning of this chapter, identical ideal types of media (static, kinetic, calculative) can be discerned in different areas. This systematic definition of the media network describes media's latently present conditions of possibility. Hence, it still says essentially nothing about whether the different techniques can also function as a unit, as a homologous and therefore universally utilizable mode of usage. Étienne-Jules Marey coined the term "graphic method" in his 1878 publication of the same name.[155] And yet, here it was not a question of the descriptive approaches seeking to position graphic methods as a universally implementable mode of visualization. After all, Marey's publication, as part of a physiological-medical discourse, still stood in the tradition of the mechanical objectivity of graphic techniques and recording devices.[156] Like Playfair's visualizations of national economies, they

---

[154] Ibid., 5.
[155] See Étienne-Jules Marey, *La Méthode graphique dans les sciences expérimentales et principalement en physiologie et en médecine* (Paris: 1878)
[156] See Lorraine Daston and Peter Gallison, "The Image of Objectivity," *Representations* 40 (1992): 81–128.

were designed to display the arsenal of graphic possibilities for a specific branch of science: physiology.[157]

In contrast, the descriptions and the discursive address of the graphic methods discussed by Auerbach and von Pirani were designed in an entirely different fashion. The original application purposes of individual graphic techniques still only had an illustrative character. Instead, the immanent media characteristics were returned to the foreground. In place of the description of individual functionalities of the graphic method, we see considerations on aspects of visibility, perception, vision, mediation, and intuition. In other words, the graphic method and the possibilities of visualization tied to it are grasped in an implicitly epistemological perspective, which clearly demarcates itself from an instrumental mode of consideration. In the wake of the renewed constitution of these practices, a pertinent media theory discourse on the conditions of possibility of media techniques was developed. This arose in the context of tensions between applied and theoretical research, but it also represented a reaction to the processes of bureaucratization and standardization underway in various social spheres. In contrast, the graphic method appeared as an escape route from the rigid patterns of thought that usually accompany these processes. It was even granted the power of prognostication and was ascribed its own autonomous power, which distanced it from tendencies toward normalization and standardization. Although closely linked with forms of standardization such as *Scientific Management*, such techniques were described in contemporary discourse as a mode of intuitive and creative thinking. The graphic method is part of a more general social discourse that, on the one hand, celebrates rationalization measures such as standardization and, on the other hand, illuminates the dark side of overly stringent formalization and rule setting. The discourse on the possibilities of graphic techniques illustrated this dichotomy. The coupling of graphic techniques (described in contemporary discourse as a creative thought environment) with Scientific Management facilitated the plausibility of this rigid management system. It did indeed primarily consist of a hierarchy differentiated by function, but within this system, corporate management could make creative decisions with the help of the graphic method. Visual management combined the certainty of standardized processes with the flexibility of techniques of graphic representation.

Auerbach and von Pirani see three great advantages to the graphic method in comparison to standard methods of data processing such as the table, the written report, or the mathematic formula: it offered a clear depiction of the data and thus a direct time savings. This corresponds to the *static* ideal type of media. It

---

[157] See Braun, *Picturing Time.*

also extended the possible sphere of implementation of graphic techniques beyond the scientific sphere. It simplified the circulation of knowledge between different disciplinary areas and allowed a common ordering of knowledge in graphic form. This corresponds to the *calculative* ideal type of media.

The third and most important point is the observation that graphic visualizations are also instruments of thought and reflection. This corresponds to the *kinetic* ideal type. Their graphic-visual form admits of an intuitive momentum in decision-making processes. Written or oral forms of communications do not possess this quality due to the lack of an aesthetic, imagistic level. This creative moment of visual thought—the positive, productive, *punctative* moment of the graphic method—is precisely possible through its radically reductionist character, which translates everything into lines and strokes. This is precisely how unintended possibilities of comparison can appear, which, while they may not be ascribed to the original data, seem to function excellently as a *dispositif* of decision making and control. The graphic method possesses a user interface that facilitates making quick judgements on a given course of action. From this perspective, it is primarily a formalized technique of control and decision making rather than a representational tool subordinated to the data. In place of a theoretically infinite mass of data, there is a graphic decision environment that ought to minimize contingencies.[158] Being combined with the graphic method allows the data to be transformed into a technique for control and decision-making, which draws its legitimacy through accompanying graphic techniques.

At issue here is the bureaucratization of managing business processes and the subsequent strategic planning for the future. The technique rests on the three types of media action: *static, kinetic,* and *calculative*. The commercial visionaries of the nineteenth century reappear in the formalized techniques used for anticipating the future. These techniques, however, should be understood not as a part of a process of formalization, but as the possibility of an intuitive, creative mode of thinking.

---

[158] For the visual culture of decision making, see Florian Hoof, "Decision|Culture: Das Ornament der Finanzkrise," in *Spekulantenwahn: Zwischen ökonomischer Rationalität und medialer Imagination,* ed. Christina Braun and Dorothea Dorn (Berlin: Neofelis, 2015), 111–34.

2

Visual Culture and Consulting

Charting, Simulation, and Calculation Devices

The works by Auerbach and von Pirani formed part of what was already, at the time of their publication in the 1910s, a lengthy process of spreading graphic techniques in business management. This visualization drive was not propelled by a movement in the history of ideas, but by the dynamic of a new branch of industry: corporate consulting. In the early twentieth century, this branch successfully developed a lucrative business model from the scientific transformation of industrial organization and production structures.[1] That these companies incorporated graphic techniques as central components of their consultancy knowledge is hardly surprising. Due to its scientific origins, the graphic method media network offered the necessary evidence of its methodology. Consultants and managers made use of the advantages of the graphic-visual mode as described by Auerbach and von Pirani. They had recourse to the media network and its related static, kinetic, and calculative action options, which were used to develop suitable solutions for business management.

As I will outline in detail in the following three case studies on visual charting, simulation devices, and calculation devices, the consultants installed planning and charting rooms—that is, centralized spaces in which business data were collated. It was here that visualization techniques like charting and other forms of graphic simulation tables allowed for the relevant data from the mass of surrounding information to "stand graphically plotted in plain view [of the factory management]."[2] This form of visual management enabled a fast reaction to production disruptions, which needed to be facilitated in planning processes and accounting. With nomography, it is precisely in everyday planning and calculation in commercial departments that graphic calculation techniques are implemented which allowed imprecise but rapid calculations and a visual representation of the results. With this, different scenarios could be devised, graphically compared,

---

[1] For the most part, the first corporate consultants had their origins in the new field of mechanical engineering. This profession was the dominant force in the industry between 1880 and 1920. See Edwin Layton, *The Revolt of the Engineers: Social Responsibility and the American Engineering Profession* (Baltimore: The Johns Hopkins University Press, 1986), 1–24, 134–53.

[2] A. Leyensetter, "Graphische Darstellung als Hilfsmittel zur Regelung und Überwachung," *Maschinenbau/Betrieb* 5, no. 19 (1923): 765.

Angels of Efficiency. Florian Hoof, Oxford University Press (2020) © Oxford University Press.
DOI: 10.1093/oso/9780190886363.003.0001

and interpolated into the future. Corporate consultants were not only present for the introduction of such methods, but also were considerably involved in their development. In this context, the consultant Harrington Emerson designed and described the fundamental methods of accounting. In production, Frederick W. Taylor refined manufacturing norms on the factory floor and tried to implement them with new graphic-calculating aids. Visual aids such as logarithmic slide rules and nomographic machine cards became standard practice in the regulation of machines in factory-floor production routines. Gantt charts facilitated the coordination of interlinked production processes.

Consultants used the whole arsenal of visualization methods to implement corporate restructurings. At the same time, the mediums they used functioned as bearers of their consulting knowledge. With their help, abstract expertise could be conveyed into concrete visual evidence. Forms of visualization made consulting knowledge visible, as well as valorized the basic idea of corporate consulting. The consultants were no longer limited to offering their long-term experience or particularly plausible systems in corporate restructures. With visual techniques, they could convey their models and strategies in the form of concrete displays. Knowledge about corporate control and planning was given distinct and unambiguous contours. Subsequently, visual consulting knowledge could be discussed and debated.

The graphic visualization produced by consultants was also part of a transformation in contemporary aesthetic discourse.[3] In art, this encompassed the upheavals beginning in the nineteenth century that brought about the shift from perspectival aesthetics to the aesthetics of abstraction. Objective representation is replaced by the "grid."[4] The new aesthetic no longer has the simple representation of things as its object, but instead thematizes the "representation of representation."[5] With cubism at the latest, the "systematic play of difference"[6] is implemented as the epistemological framework of the production of visual images.

In this context a media network was established in the business world that not only promised to be able to select, save, and communicate managerial knowledge, but also open new discursive channels of thinking and reflecting on the very concept of "management."

[3] See Sharon Corwin, "Picturing Efficiency: Precisionism, Scientific Management, and the Effacement of Labor," *Representations* 84 (2003): 139–64.

[4] Rosalind Krauss, *The Originality of the Avant-Garde and Other Modernist Myths* (Cambridge, MA: MIT Press, 1989), 8–22.

[5] Ibid., 37.

[6] Ibid., 35.

"Charting": Corporate Management Through
Visual Routines

Charting is one of the first systematic adaptations of the graphic method in a business context. This technique for visually representing processes and data was developed by the corporate consultant Henry L. Gantt. In 1903, he described the Gantt charting procedure named after him for the first time in the article "A Graphical Daily Balance in Manufacture,"[7] which appeared in the journal *Transactions of the American Society of Mechanical Engineers*. This formed a kind of prelude to an article published immediately afterward, "Shop Management" by Frederick W. Taylor, which now ranks as one of the seminal texts of Scientific Management.[8] This was no coincidence, since Gantt and Taylor, both graduates of the Stevens Institute of Technology, worked closely together.[9] In the years that followed, Gantt charting traced a triumphant path through Western industrial societies. In contrast to Scientific Management, which was to remain a short-lived managerial fashion, it became a widespread technique for controlling and planning production.[10]

Gantt developed an initial version of his system while still working for Taylor's consultancy firm. He was part of the consulting team that from 1898 to 1901 was commissioned to restructure the Bethlehem Steel Company following the principles of Scientific Management. Subsequently, he broadened his method through successive consultancy commissions for the American Locomotive Company in Schenectady, New York, in 1902 and Joseph Bancroft & Sons in Wilmington, Delaware, in the years 1908–1909.

Gantt's system consisted of different types of charts serving to graphically visualize industrial processes. On the one hand, with the "man's record" charts,[11] Gantt sought to comprehend "the most difficulty commodity we have"[12] (as he put it): the labor performance of the workforce. On the other hand, the "daily balance of work" chart was used to display production data and progress for the purposes of general planning and administrative tasks in the firm.[13]

---

[7] Henry L. Gantt, "A Graphical Daily Balance in Manufacture," *Transactions of the American Society of Mechanical Engineers* 24 (1903): 1322–36.

[8] Frederick W. Taylor, "Shop Management," *Transactions of the American Society of Mechanical Engineers* 24 (1903): 1337–480.

[9] Horace B. Drury, *Scientific Management: A History and Criticism* (New York: Columbia University Press, 1915), 89–92.

[10] See Robert Grimshaw, "Aus dem Merkbuch eines Organisators," *Werkstattstechnik* 8, no. 7 (1914): 200–202; Clark, *The Gantt Chart*; P. B. Peterson, "The Evolution of the Gantt Chart," *Proceedings of the Academy of Management* (1988); James M. Wilson, "Gantt Charts: A Centenary Appreciation," *European Journal of Operational Research* 149 (2003): 430–37.

[11] Gantt, "A Graphical Daily Balance in Manufacture," 1323.

[12] Ibid., 1327.

[13] Ibid., 1323.

"Man's Record" Charts: Graphic Human Direction

The "man's record" charts formed the basis for the performance-related "task and bonus wage system"[14] which Gantt used to replace the earlier standard of the unit-wage system.[15] The charts captured and documented the labor performance of individual employees.[16] If they attained a predetermined workload, they were paid a bonus in addition to their base wage.

The days they attained the bonus were marked in black; if they missed out, the days were marked in red. Absent days and relocations were also noted. From this data, visualization could produce individual parameters, such as the productivity curve contained in Plate 1. These charts greatly facilitated the work of labor inspectors. They could now, at a single glance, perceive and evaluate a situation in its individual production departments. Beyond this, charts offered further possibilities for data assessment, which were originally linked with their graphic form. It was not only industrial data in the narrower sense that could be discerned from these graphic tables, but also more complex individual and collective behavioral patterns among the employees, as can be seen in Plate 2. It documents the productivity of workers in a cotton mill, where the pattern of the "slack Saturday habit" was noticed.[17] Workers tended to reach the bonus on Mondays through Fridays, but they regularly missed it on Saturdays. In this case, the charting system of business management aided in providing insight into internalized, deeply ingrained modes of behavior among staff.[18] In this example, the measures taken by management seem to have been effective.

The pattern of the "slack Saturday habit" disappeared within the time span recorded on the chart—a period of eight months. With the graphic method, management could influence social practices developed within factories. But for this a first step was necessary: making this pattern visible in the first place through chart analysis and enabling it to be recognized as such.

These charts originally had the purpose of documenting individual labor performances for the bonus-wage system. With time, it became apparent that they offered entirely different possibilities for corporate management. It was not

[14] In contrast to Frederick W. Taylor's "piece-rate system," which was based on sanctions, Gantt relied on a positive rewards system. See Henry L. Gantt, *Work, Wages, and Profits* (New York: The Engineering Magazine, 1919 [1910]).

[15] This approach was akin to the changes that Frank B. Gilbreth introduced into the construction industry. See Chapter 3 of this volume, "'Lay Some Brick...': From Businessman to Consultant."

[16] The data necessary for these charts derived from the work-slip system, which prescribed the workload and the work phases to be accomplished for each individual worker. The work slips contained a precise statistical itemization of the performance capacity of all the firm's employees.

[17] Gantt, *Work, Wages, and Profits*, 190–91.

[18] Before the introduction of Gantt charting, these group-dynamics processes were familiar to the factory foremen. Management, for its part, only had access to the production figures of departments as a whole.

only business data that they recorded, conveying a *static* ideal-typical function of data representation. Rather, the visual patterns generated were precisely those which designated a surplus of meaning, thereby becoming new management tools. The form of the graphic tableau virtually leant itself to using the individual performance parameters grouped within as a barometer of the mood in the social situation in the respective production divisions.[19] *Static* representations were thus transformed into a *kinetic* tableau. The arrangement of the data recorded therein changed the visual surface into a mediated depiction of a dynamic process. The display could no longer be reduced to its underlying data but was based on the form of the visual management system used by Gantt charting. It was only here that administrative knowledge, as a fusion of different data under the conditions of graphic visualization, existed.

With this kinetic tableau, management possessed a graphic early warning system that showed when a possible problem occurred on the factory floor. They could now react very differently to difficulties—such as those provoked by union-organized workers. Strikes or a targeted slowdown of the work tempo could previously only be perceived as a diffuse consequence of union agitation. Management had no access to more precise data. This situation changed with the advent of Gantt charts, which enabled "the superintendent to know each day what was done the day previous, who did it, and what the expense of it was."[20] They delivered concrete data for every individual worker. Hostile conduct could now be personalized. It had now become easier to identify particular active departments and introduce corresponding measures.[21]

In addition, the graphic form of the Gantt chart served management as a medium of visual communication and control. With the help of these charts, workers could be shown their own labor performance, even when they could not speak English, which in a high-immigration nation like the United States in the early twentieth century was not unusual. Exemplary for this is the situation described by Gantt between Greek workers and their Polish foreman in an American cotton mill. "They were all Greeks, speaking almost no English. The instructor, Samtak, is a Pole, whose English is not very good, and who could make himself intelligible to the Greeks only by Sign."[22] Language (whether in spoken and written form) did not, in these cases, aid comprehension. Graphic

---

[19] On the early use of graphic techniques for representing social conditions, see A. Foville, "Essai de Meteorologie Economique et Social."

[20] Gantt, *Work, Wages, and Profits*, 270.

[21] In 1912, a steelworks managed with the aid of Gantt charts was able to fend off a strike organized by the Industrial Workers of the World union. Management succeeded in quickly replacing the striking workers with new workers, because the charts gave them easy access to production data. See Gantt, *Work, Wages, and Profits*, 191–92, 199.

[22] Ibid., 178.

systems of visual display represented the only possibility for establishing systematic communication within the factory.

Even foremen, who stood a level higher than simple workers in the corporate hierarchy, profited from the charts. Their main task was guaranteeing the correct and prompt carrying out of the labor process and restructuring the labor process during disruptions, such as from a damaged piece of machinery. Unlike the workers, they perceived simple tasks of management on the lowest level.

> Here is where the graphical schedule comes to his assistance, for he can see at a glance just what is behind or what should come next.[23] [...] Its graphical form is so easily read that both foreman and superintendents find it of great value.[24]

As far as the logistical coordination activities of foremen were concerned, charting represented an easing of their burden. It gave them more time to grapple with the meaningful structuring of the work process. They could intervene in advance and could, for example, give preference to certain labor procedures if they complied with the workflow of other departments.[25] Previously, as "the most overworked people" in the whole factory,[26] they simply had no time for such considerations.

It was precisely for the corporate consultants and managers that the new graphic forms of business knowledge would prove to be extremely useful. They not only created new areas of visibility for management, but also facilitated communication between business leaders. Abstract aspects of industrial control could be analyzed in the form of graphic displays. These charts could subsequently be discussed and debated. Chart analyses aided in the articulation and clarification of managerial decision making. In this context, graphic techniques served to bolster the self-confidence of the rising professional category of the salaried manager, an occupation which did not have a particularly good reputation or social standing in the late nineteenth and early twentieth centuries.[27] Through the use of graphic charts, managers possessed, for the first time, the possibility of representing their work, even if it was divided between different spheres of activity. Graphic techniques represented "managerialism"—that is, administrative knowledge, and promoted the self-understanding of a profession that was still in the process of establishing itself. The graphic displays of the Gantt charts

---

[23] Gantt, "A Graphical Daily Balance in Manufacture," 1326.
[24] Ibid., 1325.
[25] Gantt, Work, Wages, and Profits, 274–75.
[26] Gantt, "A Graphical Daily Balance in Manufacture," 1326.
[27] See Jürgen Kocka, "Management in der Industrialisierung: Die Entstehung und Entwicklung des klassischen Musters," Zeitschrift für Unternehmensgeschichte 44, no. 1 (1999): 135–49.

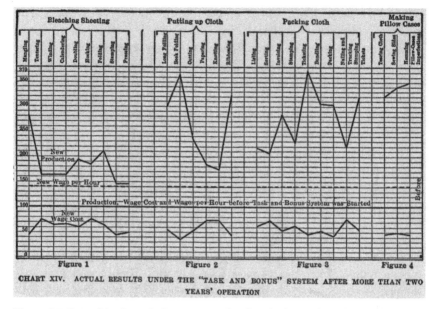

CHART XIV.   ACTUAL RESULTS UNDER THE "TASK AND BONUS" SYSTEM AFTER MORE THAN TWO YEARS' OPERATION

Figure 26 Consulting knowledge is materialized in the form of graphic tableaux.

translated the heterogeneous fields of management into a loose visual coupling, thereby legitimating managerial activity.

As a rule, corporate consultants were responsible for the introduction of these visual management systems in business. In charts, as bearers of their consultancy knowledge, their consulting concepts were materialized and made tangible. These charts served as analytical tools, as well as a proof of the consultant's own activity.[28] As can be seen in Figure 26, they were also suited for illustrating the advantages and progress of their own consulting model, and thus formed the basis for legitimizing their actual consulting activity.

"Daily Balance of Work Charts": Graphic Factory Direction

If the "man's record" charts targeted human labor power, the "daily balance of work" charts were adopted for the planning, coordination, and direction of the factory. These were graphic sequencing plans, which covered two different aspects. They contained the anticipated production details and thus aided in the planning of the production process. Additionally, they could be used to

---

[28] An outline of this approach with the example of the Gilbreth, Inc. consultancy can be found in Chapter 5 of this Volume, "Visual Consulting Knowledge."

continually compare the predetermined production goals with the actual productive output. This served the purpose of controlling production.

The first Gantt charts, published in 1903, displayed major similarities with the form of the table. Already in the 1890s, such tabular Gantt charts were deployed in the consultancy commissions in the steel industry (Plate 3). The data placed along the X-axis contain the various labor phases arranged in a linear manner. Moreover, the necessary quantity of individual components, as well as the planned beginning and end of the production process, are also recorded. This time span is marked with two red lines, the so-called danger lines.[29] The Y-axis corresponds to a time line subdivided into different days. The actual charting takes places in the table's middle section. Here, the various production data are promptly entered into the graph. Two lines per production phase were made available. On the left side ("daily"), the daily production quantity was recorded, while on the right side ("total") the total amount of assembled components was tracked. If unusable components were produced due to an incorrect assembly, then these were also marked on the "daily" line in cursive letters (and usually in red ink). In the planning of production processes with the aid of Gantt charts, the columns of the table were marked with thick lines ("danger lines") in order to denote the anticipated time span.

These markings provided the temporal framework in which the number of pieces contained in the upper part of the chart needed to be assembled. Crossing the lines signified a serious delay or disruption to production. The relevance of the lines is not only related to the production phase that they denoted; it also marked a sphere of temporal tolerance. If this was exceeded, then other phases of production would also be delayed, because they were dependent on the delayed product of the initial production phase. The industrial planners could, at a single glance, without having to go into the details of the data, establish where and in which department the production process had been delayed and react in a corresponding manner. The ascendant mass assembly method required the mastery of complex logistical chains and production processes that were tightly enmeshed with each other. Different spheres of production had to be precisely controlled and coordinated. For an orderly planning of the factory, the "exact knowledge of what is taking place each day [was] absolutely necessary."[30] The need for transparency was not only related to the work performance of employees. It also concerned the quotidian logistics of production processes, which was characterized by disruptions, delays, and variations in production quality.[31] It was necessary to

---

[29] Gantt, *Work, Wages, and Profits,* 274.

[30] Gantt, "Graphical Daily Balance in Manufacture," 1325.

[31] From 1908, for example, Henry L. Gantt received a commission from the Joseph Bancroft & Sons Company

furnish information that management could immediately use in the case of a disruption. A comprehensive reaction by management could reduce, or even avoid, costly production cancelations. Before the introduction of charting, this information was scattered across different storage systems and departments. It required a considerable expenditure of time in order to bring them together when necessary. With Gantt charting, these steps became superfluous and enabled management to make rapid decisions.

> This method makes it unnecessary for the general manager of a manufacturing plant, for instance, to wade through volumes of reports or to go the rounds of his superintendents or foremen in an attempt to find out what work is not progressing satisfactorily.[32]

This required the bundling of all of a business's details into a transparent and rapidly accessible form. Gantt charts were precisely conceived for this purpose.

> The Gantt chart is [...] remarkably compact. Information can be concentrated on a single sheet which would require 37 different sheets if shown on the usual type of curve charts.[33]
>
> Such sheets show at a glance where the delays occur, and indicate what must have our attention in order to keep up the proper output.[34]

By making neuralgic areas of production visible for the first time, it was not only management that was aided in the decision-making process, concerning ongoing factory operations, by this form of charting. Rather, current data about quotidian factory operations could be made available for more far-reaching analytic purposes. Business administrators were placed in a situation of being able to undertake systematic industrial planning on the basis of standardized data. This data no longer existed in tabular or written form, but in a graphic form specifically designed for the purposes of decision making and direction.

A system of the graphic factory report was introduced to provide data for management. At the same time, it also represented a formalized process for routine decision making:

---

[32] Clark, *The Gantt Chart*, 83.
[33] Ibid., 4.
[34] Gantt, "Graphical Daily Balance in Manufacture," 1325.

> The medium of visualization [...] is an automatic machine that takes the raw material of management and converts it into a finished uniform article by the law of transfer of skill, just the same as any other automatic machine.[35]

The conversion of business data into Gantt charts was synonymous with the formation of a fundamental difference: routine data (the steady murmur of everyday activities) were distinguished from data that were relevant for general question to do with longer term managerial needs. Whereas the former was translated into mechanized, bureaucratic procedures, the remaining data formed the basis for strategic decision making by management.[36]

This process of transforming and defining raw business data represented an enormous relief for business management. They no longer needed to be informed of the factory floors on a daily basis in order to keep abreast of the situation. Instead, an administrative body took over the routine activities of capturing and collating information. In this sense, the Gantt charts also formed a part of the professionalization and specialization process of modern management. Everyday routine activities of direction and control in industrial production were delegated to the firm's administration and formalized through bureaucratic techniques.[37] The result was a functional disburdening of corporate management—not to the least because data relevant to strategic planning had been prepared precisely for the purpose of decision-making knowledge. In its graphic form, the managerial logic of decision making was already applied. The lines of distinction were already inscribed; all that needed to be done was to interpret them and transform them into decisions.[38]

> The executive's time is thus saved because each time a figure is received he does not need to compare it with past records and decide whether it is good or bad. He has determined once for all what figures will be satisfactory and has recorded them on the chart. The comparison of the accomplishment with the plan then becomes merely a clerical task and the executive is left free to study the tendencies and take the action indicated by the chart.[39]

Whereas the daily necessities of direction were converted into bureaucratic processes, corporate management could also concentrate on the interpretation of data and the strategic decisions that it impelled.

[35] Chester B. Lord, "Management by Exception," *Transactions of the American Society of Mechanical Engineer* 53 (1931): 49–58.
[36] Hoof, "Medien managerialer Entscheidung," 38.
[37] Niklas Luhmann, *Legitimation durch Verfahren* (Neuwied: Luchterhand, 1969).
[38] Hoof, "Medien managerialer Entscheidung," 34.
[39] Clark, *The Gantt Chart*, 4.

The installation of graphic management systems, generally undertaken under the responsibility of external corporate consultants, accelerated the information flows within an enterprise. Gantt charting placed management in a position of being able to demand systematic data about the whole production situation with a temporal delay of only a few hours.

> It is an entirely feasible thing to know exactly all that has been done in a large plant one day before noon of the next, and to get a complete balance of work in order to lay out THAT AFTERNOON [uppercase in the original] in a logical manner the work for the next day.[40]

At the time, this situation was a novelty for management. The rapid availability of these knowledge sets represented an *epistemological rupture* with the conventional status and concept of documented commercial knowledge. Until then, the recording of industrial knowledge was a process which primarily served the function of retrospectively verifying the production process. It was also used to meet juridical requirements, such as providing revenue statements for shareholders. Through the acceleration of communication flows, the status of commercial knowledge was transformed. On account of its up-to-date nature, it was transformed from an instrument of control into a form of active feedback, and from a resource for ex post facto critique into an active managerial tool, thereby allowing for immediate interventions into production procedures, if this appeared to be opportune. The static representational function of visualizations was transformed into a kinetic method, and it no longer merely presented business data but constituted a specific sphere of managerial knowledge. It depicted dynamic processes, in order to make these useful for administrative decision making. For the individual departments of an enterprise, the effects of these changes were considerable.

This was particularly noticeable in the accounting departments. Their specific task of documenting and controlling monetary and commodity flows previously consisted of verifying production processes that had already been carried out. Additionally, there were pre-established accounting techniques such as double-entry bookkeeping. These aided in the bureaucratic control of the firm and represented a conventionalized intersection of juridical requirements, including the demands of taxation and corporate law. With the acceleration of information flows in this sphere, new possibilities for generating and operationalizing data presented themselves.

---

[40] Gantt, "Graphical Daily Balance in Manufacture," 1330.

By the adoption of the [Gantt-Charting] method [...] the accounting department ceases to be simply a critic of the manufacturing and becomes an active
assistant to every foreman and to the superintendent.[41]

Previously, the entirety of the firm's commercial data was produced, with considerable delay, in the legally binding form of the quarterly report. Now, by contrast,
the data had become available on a permanent basis. This gave management the
possibility of *acting* instead of merely reacting.

The aspects of Gantt charting described earlier primarily concerned regular,
practical aspects and functions of industrial production. Existing techniques of
processing and circulating information were transformed by the introduction of
Gantt charting, which enabled relevant data to be accessed more rapidly. On the
one hand, the data could be rapidly discerned when it appeared in graphic form;
on the other hand, the various data compiled could be directly compared.[42] Its
real potential for innovation lay, however, in an aspect intrinsic to media. This
form of graphic and visual representation opened up new possibilities for con-
templating, analyzing, and interpreting commercial data. This could not be
achieved with previously prevailing techniques.

New approaches to data analysis and synthesis arose precisely through mediation processes and the resulting graphic and visual surfaces. The "filter," the
moment of selection through mediation, increased, in comparison with previous
standard direct and immediate managerial methods, the epistemic potential
of the data that it processed. Face-to-face management, which was previously
widespread, was dependent on the observational talents of the supervisors and
foremen in question.[43] They could provide an "overview" of at most only a few of
the numerous departments or work groups within an enterprise. The overriding
"systematic" problems of coordination remained closed off to this approach of
direct control and error correction. Intervening into systematic aspects was only
possible when they could be made visible successfully. This visualization was
achieved by the Gantt charts, which showed much more than what the eye could
perceive through direct observation.

The value of such a balance [chart] consists in the fact that it makes clear details
that no observer, however keen he may be, can see by inspection. [...] The

---

[41] Ibid., 1336.

[42] Following Yates, this could be conceived of as an improvement of existing techniques of internal
company communication, or, in Chandler's understanding, as a rise in communication efficiency.
See Yates, *Control Through Communication*; Chandler, *The Visible Hand*.

[43] The numerous attempts at reproducing individual observational perspectives by mechanizing
the observational situation, whether through filmed recordings or the use of timing instruments,
may well have objectivized the local gaze, but they did not make visible the systematic aspect of
production.

superintendent sees at a glance what he never could find out by observation or by asking questions.[44]

What can be seen here are new administrative problems that escaped the usual practices of human perception. Immediate perception through the sensory organ of the eye came to be considered as defective in comparison to mediated perceptual processes. The systematic nature of mass production, organizationally divided into multiple departments, could no longer be comprehended on the basis of individual observation alone. It became increasingly important to have recourse to a global knowledge of the enterprise. This would enable managers to make their own evaluation of the systematic characters of the firm.

It is true that there were managerial prescriptions for the organizational status quo as to how a business should be structured and functionally constituted. All too frequently, however, they fell victim to the firm's everyday practice. This was not only due to the willful misapprehension of directives but also to the constant changes to corporate structures. If one department grew particularly strong, then the predetermined structures were normatively transformed. These dynamic, oblique processes did not depict consistent guidelines, or only insufficiently did so. Disruptions to or problems with productions could not be obviated through normative standards.

The new, overlapping, interdependent business structures needed to be encountered. A managerial conception replaced a categorical mode of vision, as was reflected in the Gantt charts. They delivered new, systematic sets of knowledge about the business. From the detailed results visualized in these charts, generalized estimates about the business's situation as a whole could be correspondingly derived. Gantt charting enabled management "to form a definite idea as to whether the plant is being run more or less efficiently."[45] It is not only the comparison and control of normative guidelines that formed the basis of managerial evaluations. The relational knowledge of Gantt charts allowed management to make decisions that no longer rested only on the "iron language"[46] of "naked numbers."[47]

> If management is to direct satisfactorily the operation of our industries under conditions of ever-increasing difficulty, its decisions and its actions must be based not only on carefully proved facts but also on a full appreciation of the importance of the momentum of those facts. The Gantt chart, because of its

---

[44] Gantt, "Graphical Daily Balance in Manufacture," 1330.

[45] Ibid., 1325.

[46] Auerbach, Die graphische Darstellung, 96.

[47] Franz Schaaps, "Statistik und graphische Darstellung im Dienste des Kaufmanns," Zeitschrift für Handelswissenschaft und Handelspraxis 3, no. 4 (1910): 127.

presentation of facts in their relation to time, is the most notable contribution to the art of management made in this generation.[48]

Such graphic combinations allowed an intuitive dimension to enter into the forming of judgements. The perception of visual forms integrated "gut feeling"— the instinct of the executive personnel of the business, which could not be deciphered through facts and statistics—into decision-making processes. If the data were contradictory and could not give rise to a clear decision, the system of visual management allowed managerial staff to take action in conditions of uncertainty. They specified a defined framework, a modeling of the situation which then needed to be innovatively solved. The situation of the structural overtaxing of factory management was not a one-off incident. The bureaucratization of businesses led to an expansion in the scope of business knowledge recorded in writing. With the conventionally formalized processes of reaching a decision, additional necessary data selection could no longer be carried out, since they were not originally devised for such large quantities of data. As Yates writes in her study *Control Through Communication*, the written forms of business communication arose in a situation in which management possessed too little information from the factory workplace.[49] Accordingly, they were geared toward capturing and circulating as much information as possible. The system based on a "written record" was not adjusted to the circumstance that there could be too much information. There was a lack of binding selection criteria, in order to react adequately to a situation. The only possible reaction was to extend the administration and the available storage capacities in the enterprise. These costs, "the horror of extra clerks,"[50] were eschewed by business and could only be implemented with great difficulty. It was precisely this problem that the Gantt charts addressed. In line with visual management, they were not geared toward capturing as much data as possible, but only the relevant data. The technique rested on the visual form of charts, which was simultaneously connected with a selection of data. At the same time, the ensuing visual logic of the graphic tableaux engendered a legitimation of the decision made therein. Gantt charts could be flexibly adapted to the given situation and allowed management to allocate, present, or register business data—not least because data in graphic form represented a combination of *kinetic, calculative*, and *static* ideal types of media.

This data could be used not only for controlling production, but also for the purposes of production planning. Moreover, it was also collected from different

---

[48] Clark, *The Gantt Chart*, 3.

[49] See Yates, *Control Through Communication*.

[50] Yehouda Shenhav, "From Chaos to Systems: The Engineering Foundations of Organization Theory, 1879–1932," *Administrative Science Quarterly* 40 (1995): 565.

spheres of the factory in central planning spaces, where it formed the basis for the future planning of the enterprise.

With the graphic data available, a differentiation process took place within management. It amounts to a separation between the control and direction of routine industrial activities, on the one hand, and strategic planning as the new genuine core of managerial activities, on the other hand.[51] The quotidian necessities of direction are translated into techniques of technical and bureaucratic control.[52] At the same time, graphic methods such as Gantt charting, as a part of visual management, made available a planning and decision-making environment specially conceived for strategic planning. Graphic methods were developed into an intersection between control routines and the short- and long-term planning activities of business administration. Graphic techniques functioned as the basis for scenarios of future anticipation, which served management as the basis for ongoing strategic decisions. "Management is concerned almost entirely with the future. Its task is to decide on policies and to take action in accordance with those policies which will bring about a desired condition."[53] For management, the graphic forms of information represented more than mere representation. Gantt charts became an instrument of formalized future anticipation: "Causes and effects with their relation to time are brought out so clearly that it becomes possible for the executive to foresee future happenings with considerable accuracy."[54] Gantt understood his system of graphically documenting and directing business processes as a significant further development of the Scientific Management introduced by Frederick W. Taylor. Taylor concentrated on the elaboration of concrete norms for steel processing or the determination of standardized times for individual work phases. Gantt built on this prior work, while further securing, with his system, the rapid decision-making capacities of business leadership. This was supposed to bring the business a decisive temporal advantage in competition with other competitors.

> It is the most complete analysis we can make of the working of a plant. [...]
> Such an analysis is far more important than an improved tool steel or a new set
> of piece rates, for it enables those in authority to see each day how their orders
> are being carried out.[55]

[51]   Hoof, "Medien managerialer Entscheidungen," 30.

[52]   Richard Edwards, "Technical Control: An All-Around Adjustor and Equalizer," in *Contested Terrain: The Transformation of the Workplace in the Twentieth Century* (London: Heinemann/Basic Books, 1979), 111–29; Edwards, "Bureaucratic Control: Policy No. 1.1," in *Contested Terrain*, 130–62.

[53]   Clark, *The Gantt Chart*, 3.

[54]   Ibid., 83.

[55]   Gantt, *Work, Wages, and Profits*, 288.

Whereas the exact interpenetration and systematization of the factory's everyday activity conducted by Taylor corresponded to a Cartesian conception of the "one best way," Gantt focused on the flexibility and nimbleness of his administrative system. The knowledge visualized in the Gantt charts takes this equally important temporal aspect of managerial decision making into account. Instead of seeking to completely master the enterprise, Gantt focused on the situational administrative competence of visual management. Within this managerial mode, it is not a question of seeking to know something, but of guiding knowledge itself. The reason that recourse was made to the relational concept of disruption was so that the question concerning a *correct* decision could be expanded to include the aspect of *rapid* decision making. A corridor of tolerance that determined the stability of the system replaced the concept of true and false knowledge. Production processes thus only became relevant for this second level of observation when they exceeded the tolerance corridor and thus, by definition, passed into a condition of disruption. Decisive for visual management, therefore, is the possession of instruments that allow, at any time, a global analysis of the production situation. For the efficiency of a factory it is less the detailed knowledge of individual aspects that is central, and more the temporal component of a rapid reaction to systematic disruptions.

Visualizing, Simulating, and Harmonizing Disruptions

Henry L. Gantt was not the only one who utilized the principle of charting in industrial firms. By 1896, Karol Adamiecki, a Polish engineer and later professor at the Politechnika Warszawska,[56] had implemented a similar system in the steel industry.[57] Born in Dabrowa Gornicza in 1866, Adamiecki accepted a position as an industrial engineer in 1891 in the Huta Bankowa steel mill in his home city, after completing his studies in engineering studies in St. Petersburg. Here, in Poland's first modern steelworks, all the phases of steel production were concentrated in one location, from smelting up to the processing of rolled steel.[58]

From 1896 on, Adamiecki was responsible for supervising the rolling mill train, an area of steel processing which suffered from relatively frequent production disruptions due to the high mechanical and thermal loads involved. In branches with assembly-intensive manufacturing activities, from which sphere

---

[56] Daniel Nelson, "Scientific Management in Retrospect," in *A Mental Revolution: Scientific Management since Taylor*, ed. Daniel Nelson (Columbus: Ohio State University Press, 1992), 5–39.

[57] Edward R. Marsh, "The Harmonogram of Karol Adamiecki," *The Academy of Management Journal* 18, no. 2 (1975): 358.

[58] Zdzislaw Wesolowski, "The Polish Contribution to the Development of Scientific Management," *Proceedings, Academy of Management* (1978), 12.

the majority of rationalization commissions for raising efficiency taken on by Henry L. Gantt and Frank B. Gilbreth were derived, this was less often the case. For raising production efficiency, it was enough to undertake ergonomic changes in assembly and manufacturing and, if necessary, make changes to the production chain. For the steel industry, such rationalization efforts only conditionally came into question. The susceptibility to disruption and the production chain were determined through the raw material of steel. For this reason, Adamiecki did not improve ergonomics but concentrated on disruption management and devised a graphic system of control for this purpose.

In an initial step, he standardized the production chain and attributed a pre-planned time frame to individual manufacturing phases for efficient, normal operation.[59] The greater challenge, however, consisted in countering the frequently arising disruptions to business. Of course, standardization practices and the related close integration of individual production phases increased industrial efficiency in normal business, but in the case of a disruption this switched over into the absolute opposite of business efficiency. In the most unfavorable case, entire production lines could be immobilized within a brief period of time. The consequence was costly production failures. The question arose as to which instruments, beyond normative planning practices, were suitable for integrating the condition of "disruption" into the existing arsenal of leadership, planning, and control practices. It was necessary to overturn the paradox of shaping the contingent aspect of disruption in a plannable and guidable manner. Or, in other words, management needed an environment that facilitated the comprehensive classification and definition of any disruption that arose. Should these occur, there could then be a corresponding reaction to them. In order to maintain the capacity for managerial direction, the systematic effects that a disruption had on production had to be comprehensively representable and visible.

It is in the context of a factory line prone to disruption that Adamiecki developed his theory of "*Harmonizacja pracy*" (work harmonization).[60] The core component of his approach was the insight that every enterprise has to provide its employees with a clearly defined goal. This would serve as an orientation point toward which every employee had to work, even in the event of a disruption.[61] The firm's various work processes had to be subordinated harmoniously to this goal. The term "harmony" thus placed less emphasis on individual

---

[59] See Lyndall Urwick, ed., *The Golden Book of Management: A Historical Record of the Life and Work of Seventy Pioneers* (London: Newman Neame, 1956), 107.

[60] Karol Adamiecki, "Harmonizacja jako jedna z głównych podstaw organizacji naukowej," *Przegl d Techniczny* 49/52/53 (1924).

[61] Seen in this vein, this was an early prototype of the method described by Peter Ducker in the 1950s as "management by objectives."

manufacturing processes; instead, it stressed the importance to a business or organization of interdependent process structures. Considered from the overriding perspective of the enterprise, it was more efficient to do without an individual process optimized to the very last detail. A more robust production system—that is, one more resistant to disruption—could be a more profitable solution. Optimized, seamlessly integrated individual processes may well have guaranteed the highest levels of efficiency when production was running smoothly, but they directly led to higher losses when disruptions occurred. To achieve the ideal of industrial harmony, the optimal relation between the efficiency and the robustness of the process, it was imperative to possess a transparent industrial organization. This was ensured through instruments such as graphic flow charts, which visualized the interdependencies between the different levels of the production process. As Adamiecki realized, however, this transparency could not be attained through standard managerial methods:

> Steel mills were constructed by managers who were unable to determine how each particular mechanism functioned and incapable of visualizing the entire mill as a collective body or as a total system.[62]

For the required visualization of production processes, Adamiecki developed the *harmonograph*, a large table in which factory processes were displayed in graphic form. The different aspects of the production processes could thus be made visible with this charting system. A view of the harmonograph sufficed to take in the production chain from the micro level of the individual work phases to the macro level of the direction of the entire factory. As Henry L. Gantt did at almost the same point in time, Adamiecki relied upon a static system of data representation.

On the micro level of the individual work phase, the *harmonogram* described the prescribed time span and the labor acts of the workers involved. The normative managerial planning requirements it contained were also used to document graphically the actual, current production data. The lengthy strips of paper on which the harmonogram was inscribed showed the production requirements alongside the actual production situation. Deviations from the planning goals were thus directly visible.

The paper strip that contained the harmonogram also included a header field (Fig. 27). This was needed for arranging the individual harmonograms on the overall table (the harmonograph), in the sequence of the planned production

[62] Karol Adamiecki, "Metoda wykreślna organizowania pracy zbiorowej w walcowniach," *Przegl d Techniczny* 17/18/19/20 (1919). Cited in Wesolowski, "The Polish Contribution to the Development of Scientific Management," 15.

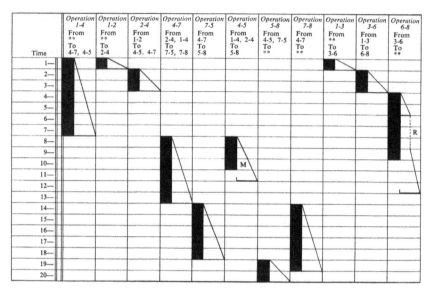

Figure 27 Schematic display of the functioning of a harmonograph.

process. In the header field the concrete work process was given (e.g., "milling" or "drilling") and provided with an unambiguous label (e.g., Operation 4–5). The examples given refer to the central harmonogram in Figure 27. Below this were the requirements for the previous production phases. In this case, the description "From 2–4, 1–4" means that the workpiece required for work phase 4–7 had previously been worked on in the work phases 2–4 and 1–4. The work phases that subsequently needed to be carried out were also provided—in this case, "To 7–5, 7–8." When the workpiece was completed, it had to be forwarded on to these production stations. The numbering determined the relational position of the work phases in the production chain and allowed for flexibility in the display. The table was not only capable of depicting production movements from left to right. With the connection of the graphic tableau and the numbering system in the header fields, even bifurcating or recurring production phases could be represented.

The harmonograms were arranged on a table up to eight meters long (Fig. 28). There, the individual strips of paper were put together and fastened to one another. They contained the labor phases and the time units planned for them. In addition, the position of the work phases in relation to its predecessors and successors in the production chain was displayed. If a production disruption took place, the firm's engineers could use the table to track comprehensively which effects this would have for the whole, integrated process. The length of the processes provided allowed them, with a single glance, to identify the

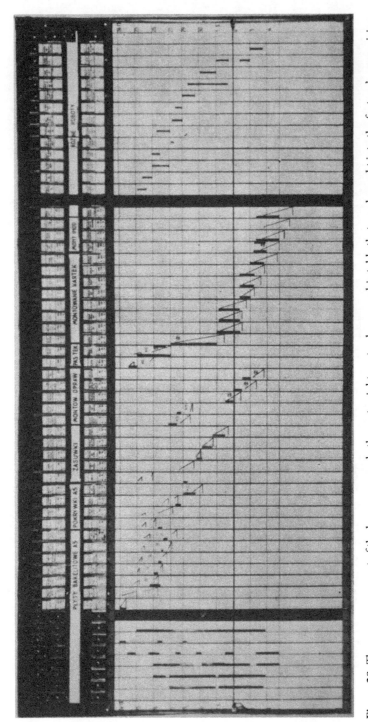

Figure 28 The core component of the harmonograph: the up to eight-meter-long graphic table that was brought into the factory's supervision room. This graphic table shows all relevant production processes.

Figure 29 From planning to simulation: individual harmonograms, realized as mobile paper strips, could be moved around and recombined according to the production situation.

"critical path,"[63] the bottleneck in the production chain. If a disruption took place, and if the bottleneck of the production process was identified, the table was transformed from a device for production planning and control to a simulation tableau.[64]

Because the paper strips of the harmonograph were only fastened together with clips, they could be regrouped and reassembled easily (Fig. 29). In this way, the business executives could attain an optimal reorientation of the production process. The graphic symbols on the surface of the tableau reduced the factory process to an ongoing planning game. Within this model world, the company

---

[63] The "critical path" denotes the "bottleneck" of a production line, which, when it is disrupted, interferes with other areas of production. If two Processes, A (8 time units) and B (5 time units), are dependent on each other to become Product P as a result of Process AB, then A is the "critical path." It requires 3 time units more than B and is directly linked to the Process AB. If there is a delay to Process A, then this immediately disrupts the entire production line.

[64] See also the "route models" described in Chapter 5 of this volume, "Visual Consulting Knowledge."

engineers could play out and discard different scenarios. At the end of these simulations, they could commit to an approach that was appropriate to the situation. Subsequently, all they had to do was convert it from the model world of the harmonograph into business reality. In this case, the system was transformed from a *static* representation of production standards into a system of *kinetic* process modeling. The harmonograph is a system for the graphic inscription of the production flow. It documented its sequence, temporal calibration, and the various production departments involved. Aside from this, Adamiecki's system contained two innovations. With the introduction of the graphic method media network to the business world, another mode of archiving and visualizing commercial data was adopted. Additionally, an entirely new cultural technique of regulation and guidance was established, which was based on graphic-visual knowledge. The graphic visualization also included the case of disruption, that is, the problematic of error-prone processes. The antecedent normative written guides and manuals were only conditionally capable of this. They restricted themselves to the linear arrangement and documentation of production events, and they lacked the potential for a flexible recombination of data and knowledge sets in visual space.

In the late nineteenth century, Adamiecki's graphic control device already contained aspects of systematic control under the conditions of processual contingency. Under the label "PERT (Program Evaluation and Review Technique)"[65] and "critical path,"[66] these enter management theory in the 1950s. Instead of emphasizing the perfection of interlocking individual processes, it sometimes made more sense to conceive of a production line as a robust process. This did not absolutely correspond to Scientific Management's credo of the "one best way," but the scenario of system disruption was taken into account. Through graphic representation, the harmonograph facilitated access to ongoing knowledge sets about the business production process. In this sense, it represented a proto-cybernetic management tool for the coordination, transformation, and direction of an error-prone production process.

[65] A consulting commission that the US Navy gave to the Booz Allen Hamilton consultancy gave rise to the managerial practice known as "PERT," with which the "critical path" of a process could be determined. See D. G. Malcolm, J. H. Roseboom, C. E. Clark, and W. Fazar, "Application of a Technique for Research and Development Program Evaluation," *Operations Research* 7, no. 5 (1959): 646–69.

[66] In parallel, the firms Du Pont and Remmington Rand developed a method similarly oriented toward the principle of the "critical path." See James E. Kelley and Morgan A. Walker, "Critical-Path Planning and Scheduling," *Proceedings of the Eastern Joint Computer Conference* (1959).

Visual Calculation Devices

The graphic methods described up to now, Gantt charting and the harmonograph, deployed external corporate consultants either through restructuring factories and firms or, in the case of Adamiecki, in the context of disruption-prone steel production. They were part of a restructuring process or an exceptional situation.

Visual management was established on the executive level, but also on the level of everyday work practices. This was illustrated by nomography, a technique of graphic calculation. In the following pages, it serves as a paradigmatic example of the increasing significance of visualization processes for industrial knowledge. With nomography, a graphic system of calculation was easy to master, and mathematic/scientific principles were adapted for business purposes. It represented a reaction to more complex knowledge contexts and the "scientification" of industrial knowledge. In this context, nomographic techniques entered the sphere of production and the commercial departments of enterprises. The method did not enable exact calculations, but it did enable rapid ones, even by individuals who could not boast a particularly advanced mathematical education.

This system supplements the medialization drive described earlier with a perspective *from within* the enterprise, which can yield indications as to why corporate consultants found such resonance within businesses for their visual consulting knowledge. In some areas of business, visualization processes and graphic methods had already become widespread, albeit for an entirely different purpose. Using graphic displays for managing the firm thus appeared only as the next logical step.

My analysis rests on the study of trade journals from 1880 to 1930 in the areas of mechanical engineering, organization theory, trade studies, cameral science, material technology, and workplace technology. These were publications in which practical problems or technical innovations in machine construction, accounting, and industrial organization were discussed.[67] These journals did not

---

[67] The corpus of periodicals consists of the following titles and years: *Transactions of the American Society of Mechanical Engineers*, 1880–1930; *American Machinist*, 1880–1930; *Organisation: Zeitschrift für Betriebswissenschaft, Verwaltungspraxis u. Wirtschaftspolitik*, 1898–1925; *Zeitschrift für Betriebswissenschaft, Verwaltungspraxis und Wirtschaftspolitik*, 1898–1925; *Archiv für Sozialwissenschaft und Sozialpolitik*, 1904–1930; *Zeitschrift für handelswissenschaftliche Forschung*, 1906–1930; *Werkstattstechnik*, 1907–1913, 1920–1930; *The Journal of the American Society of Mechanical Engineers*, 1908–1918; *Zeitschrift für Handelswissenschaft und Handelspraxis*, 1908–1930; *Der Betrieb*, 1918–1921; *Zeitschrift für Physik*, 1920–1930; *Maschinenbau: Gestaltung, Betrieb, Wirtschaft*, 1921–1923, published up until 1924 in individual issues as *Maschinenbau/Betrieb, Maschinenbau/Gestaltung*, and *Maschinenbau/Wirtschaft*; *AWF-Nachrichten (Ausschuss für wirtschaftliche Fertigung)*, published as a supplement to *Maschinenbau; Gestaltung, Betrieb, Wirtschaft; Zeitschrift für angewandte Mathematik und Mechanik*, 1921–1930; *Betriebswirtschaftliche Rundschau und Archiv für das Revisions und Treuhandwesen*, 1924–1928; *ZfürO (Zeitschrift für Organisation)*, 1927–1934.

boast an explicitly theoretical or scientific character, but rather, they reflected the contradictory nature of "applied sciences" as a whole. The articles they published ranged from texts that attempted to translate scientific considerations to business contexts, to the simplest pragmatic guides for solving acute problems. It is for this reason that the corpus offers insight into the situation at the time and the discourse over the usage of visualization techniques in industrial enterprises. Here, control and direction difficulties were articulated as an expression of inadequate leadership models in the mid- and upper-level management. These innovative problem aspects, which were also alien to the field, are generally encountered with the introduction of visual techniques: organigrams and flow charts systematize and synchronize opaque production processes. Nomograms enabled flexible calibrations of individual production parameters without any detailed knowledge of mathematics. "Unwieldy" tabular knowledge was brought into a more transparent condition through graphic displays. The first media forms of managerial knowledge resulted from these attempts at managing contingency. In the different orders of business knowledge, from machine construction to account keeping, there arises a specific media form of direction and decision-making knowledge, which boasts close parallels to the visual management systems described earlier: Gantt charting and the harmonograph.

Nomography and Applied Engineering Science

Barely twenty years after the first publication of the principle of nomography by Maurice D'Ocagne, in the 1910s a glut of various nomograms were published.[68] Nomography established itself so massively and rapidly that by 1925 Friedrich Willers, who was an avowed advocate of applied mathematics, spoke almost disparagingly of a new fashion appearing:

> We are almost tempted to speak of nomography as a fashionable trend; we can barely open up a technical journal at random without hitting upon a new kind of calculation table, or at the very least a formula [. . .] tabulated in a new form.[69]

By the end of the 1920s, comprehensive collections of nomographic tables for a wide variety of applications had become available. These stretched from the construction of canal networks, through railway construction, up to the

[68] For a detailed description of nomography, see Chapter 1 of this volume.
[69] Friedrich A. Willers, "Bücherbesprechung: Graphisches Rechnen von K. Giebel," *Werkstattstechnik* 19, no. 22 (1925): 817.

manufacturing and control of technological appliances.[70] In addition, numerous introductory works and articles on the principle and construction of nomographic calculation tables appeared.[71]

D'Ocagne already saw nomography not only as an instrument for scientific research, but also as an effective tool for areas in which applied mathematics played a major role: "there are vast areas of application in which the degree of approximation given by nomograms is broadly sufficient, notably in several branches of engineering science."[72] This was also relevant to engineering science, whose growing influence in the late nineteenth century was characterized by Edwin Layton as a "revolt of the engineers."[73] Between 1880 and 1920, mechanical engineers became one of the most decisive professional groups in the major corporations of industrialized Western nations. Whereas, in 1880, the professional group of engineers consisted of 7,000 individuals, by 1920 it had enlarged by around 2000%, to 136,000 people.[74] It is not least through the Scientific Management movement and their "obsessive concern for social status"[75] that

---

[70] See J. Gysin, *Tafeln zum Abstecken von Eisenbahn- und Strassen-Kurven: In neuer Teilung (Centesimal-Teilung)*; W. Groezinger, *Fluchtlinientafeln zur Berechnung des cos φ* (Berlin: Springer, 1925); Reinhardt Hildebrandt, *Mathematisch-graphische Untersuchungen über die Rentabilitätsverhältnisse des Fabrikbetriebes* (Berlin: Springer, 1925); J. Wachsmann, "Nomogramm für die Dimensionierung von städtischen Kanalnetzen," *Gesundheits-Ingenieur* 48 (1925): 605–607; Franz Faltus, *Fünfzehn Nomogramme für den Eisenbau: Einfache Lösung häufiger Aufgaben des Eisenbaues* (Geislingen an der Steige: NBW Verlag Dipl. Ing. P. Leybold, 1927).

[71] I provide here a small sample of the publications on nomography: D'Ocagne, *Traité de nomographie*; Friedrich Schilling, *Über die Nomographie von M. D'Ocagne* (Leipzig: Teubner, 1900); J. Eugen Mayer, *Das Rechnen in der Technik und seine Hilfsmittel. Rechenschieber, Rechentafeln, Rechenmaschinen usw* (Leipzig: Göschen, 1908); von Pirani, *Graphische Darstellung in Wissenschaft und Technik*; M. Tama, "Graphische Rechentafel," *Werkstattstechnik* 11, no. 1 (1917): 1–4; Joseph Lipka, *Graphical and Mechanical Computation: Part 2: Experimental Data* (New York: Wiley & Sons, 1918); Luckey, *Einführung in die Nomographie, Teil 1: Die Funktionsleiter*; Paul Luckey, *Einführung in die Nomographie, Teil 2: Die Zeichnung als Rechenmaschine* (Leipzig: Teubner, 1920); R. Neuendorff, *Praktische Mathematik* (Leipzig: Teubner 1918 [1911]); S. Brodetsky, *A First Course in Nomography* (G. Bell & Sons, 1920); J. Hak, "Über eine neue Art von Rechentafeln," *Zeitschrift für angewandte Mathematik und Mechanik* 1, no. 2 (1921): 154–57; Bieberbach, "Über Nomographie"; Fritz Krauss, *Die Nomographie oder Fluchtlinienkunst* (Berlin: Springer, 1922); C. v. Dobbeler, "Grundlagen der Nomographie," *Maschinenbau/Gestaltung* 3, no. 4 (1923): 99–107; B. M. Konorski, *Die Grundlagen der Nomographie* (Berlin: Springer, 1923); Otto Lacmann, *Die Herstellung gezeichneter Rechentafel: Ein Lehrbuch der Nomographie* (Berlin: Springer, 1923); Paul Werkmeister, *Das Entwerfen von graphischen Rechentafeln (Nomographie)* (Berlin: Springer, 1923); Hans Schwerdt, *Lehrbuch der Nomographie auf abbildungsgeometrischer Grundlage* (Berlin: Springer, 1924); A. V. Hellborn, "Wie entsteht eine nomographische Netztafel für Gleichungen mit mehreren Veränderlichen?," *Maschinenbau: Gestaltung, Betrieb, Wirtschaft* 5, no. 1 (1926): 1–6; Hans Schwerdt, *Einführung in die praktische Nomographie* (Berlin: Salle, 1927).

[72] Maurice D'Ocagne, *Le Calcul Simplifié: Graphical and Mechanical Methods for Simplifying Calculation*, trans. J. Howlett and M. R. Williams (Cambridge, MA: MIT Press, 1986), 83.

[73] Layton, *The Revolt of the Engineers*. On critical classification, see Peter Meiksins, "The 'Revolt of Engineers' Reconsidered," *Technology and Culture* 29, no. 2 (1988): 219–46.

[74] See Layton, *The Revolt of the Engineers*, 3.

[75] Ibid., 6.

they succeeded in occupying key positions in the corporations that were then emerging. The wave of establishing technical universities that began in the United States, France, and Germany in the late nineteenth century also contributed to this.[76]

Engineering became a disciplinary intersection[77] between scientific aspiration and business necessity.[78] It is thus no surprise that the lion's share of the successful corporate consultants of the 1910s and 1920s boast a background in engineering. "The engineer is both a scientist and a businessman. Engineering is a scientific profession, yet the test of the engineer's work lies not in the laboratory, but in the marketplace."[79] This results in a series of fundamental conflicts about scientificity and the orientation toward application. The increasing transfer of knowledge between science and industrial production connected with it, which culminated in "applied sciences," was, however, far from being a surefire success. It was based on an "irrepressible conflict between science and business."[80] It was precisely the complex calculation bases, which were frequently taken out of the scientific context, that encountered obstacles in everyday business life. Scientific calculation approaches were very labor intensive and time consuming, and were thus no longer practicable for many spheres of industrial production. Moreover, demanding calculation routines also presupposed specially educated personnel with the necessary mathematical grounding. Unlike science, industry rarely required exact calculations. Approximate values were, in most cases, sufficient. In such situations, industrial engineers and sections of corporate personnel relied, for very different reasons, on nomographic calculation processes. Nomography had arrived in industrial enterprises, offering them precisely the advantages that were needed: rapid rather than precise calculation routines. Nomograms, as calculation routines, were boundary objects which could be used without

---

[76] See Mauro F. Guillén, *Models of Management: Work, Authority, and Organization in a Comparative Perspective* (Chicago: University of Chicago Press, 1994), 96–100; Karl-Heinz Manegold, "Geschichte der technischen Hochschulen," in *Technik und Bildung*, ed. Laetitia Boehm and Charlotte Schönbeck (Düsseldorf: VDI Verlag, 1989), 204–34; Wolfgang König, "Spezialisierung und Bildungsanspruch: Zur Geschichte der Technischen Hochschulen im 19. und 20. Jahrhundert," *Berichte zur Wissenschaftsgeschichte* 11, no. 4 (1988): 219–25; Wolfgang König, "Stand und Aufgaben der Forschung zur Geschichte der deutschen Polytechnischen Schulen und Technischen Hochschulen im 19. Jahrhundert," *Technikgeschichte* 48, no. 1 (1981): 47–67; Magali Sarfatti Larson, *The Rise of Professionalism: A Sociological Analysis* (Berkeley: University of California Press, 1977).

[77] See Tom Frank Peters, *Building the Nineteenth Century* (Cambridge, MA: MIT Press, 1996).

[78] See Stephen R. Barley and Gideon Kunda, "Design and Devotion: Surges of Rational and Normative Ideologies of Control in Managerial Discourse," *Administrative Science Quarterly* 37 (1992): 363–99; Walter H. G. Armytage, *A Social History of Engineering* (London: Faber & Faber, 1976); Monte A Calvert, *The Mechanical Engineer in America 1830-1910: Professional Cultures in Conflict* (Baltimore: Johns Hopkins, 1967).

[79] Layton, *The Revolt of the Engineers*, 1.

[80] Ibid.

any significant specialist knowledge, and cooperation between various interest groups within an industrial organization was thereby facilitated.

(Proto-)Nomographic Production Processes

Within industrial production, these forms of calculation routines were initially implemented for the calibration of machines in metalworking. Lathes and planing machines, which were not operated with the correct feed rate or rotation speed, immediately raised production costs. Either the machine needed more time than was actually necessary in order to process a workpiece, or the cutting tools quickly became unusable at such a high speed and had to be unclamped, sharpened, and reclamped. The first system for determining cutting speeds was, however, not based on nomographic approaches, but on empirical experimentation. At the same time, it is a paradigmatic example of the difficulty with which the transfer, or adaptation of scientific knowledge to industry, was developed. After twenty-six years of experimental activity, Frederick W. Taylor, who was also active as an external corporate consultant, had collected enough values for the processing of high-speed steel. With this data set, he was able to set the calibration parameters for metal lathes on a scientific-objective basis.[81] Subsequently, his team of consultants, consisting of the Norwegian mathematician Carl Barth and the aforementioned Henry L. Gantt, transformed the data acquired into a mathematical formula through logarithmic approximation. The consequences of this step for the development of industrial metalworking, the actual backbone of the entire economic dynamism of the early twentieth century, were considerable. In the end, it allowed metal cutting to produce precise round forms, which were the basis for such fundamental workpiece forms as pistons, an indispensable component of mechanical propulsion.

This step was understood in economic history,[82] as well as by representatives of the normalization theorem,[83] as the beginning of Scientific Management. Both

---

[81] Frederick W. Taylor, "On the Art of Cutting Metals," *Transactions of the American Society of Mechanical Engineer* (1906). This text was a 248-page, elaborate special edition with numerous foldable, large-format blueprints, which exhausted the American Society of Mechanical Engineer's publishing budget for several years. In the same year, this treatise also appeared in book form as Frederick W. Taylor, *On the Art of Cutting Metals* (New York: The American Society of Mechanical Engineers, 1906).

[82] Harry Braverman, *Labor and Monopoly Capital: The Degradation of Work in the Twentieth Century* (New York: Monthly Review Press, 1974); Daniel Nelson, *Frederick W. Taylor and the Rise of Scientific Management* (Madison: University of Wisconsin Press, 1980).

[83] Hans Wupper-Tewes, *Rationalisierung als Normalisierung* (Münster: Westfälisches Dampfboot, 1993); Jürgen Link, *Versuch über den Normalismus: Wie Normalität produziert wird* (Opladen: Westdeutscher Verlag, 1997); Herbert Mehrtens and Werner Sohn, eds., *Normalität und Abweichung: Studien zur Theorie und Geschichte der Normalisierungsgesellschaft* (Opladen/Wiesbaden: Westdeutscher Verlag, 1999).

perspectives emphasized the connection of standardization and normalization processes. The standardized norm took the place of the heterogeneous production practices of manual laborers and the implicit knowledge that was related to this. The skilled lathe operator was degraded to someone who followed orders. This perspective follows the negatively expressed theory of a "taut economy." This is the term used by Albert Hirschmann to designate the ideal-typical model of the perfectly efficient economic structure, in contrast to the inefficient, dysfunctional "slack economy."[84] If we are to interpret Scientific Management as a form of "taut economy," then the result ought to be a functioning, frictionless system of control.

These approaches, considered from the perspective of an archaeology of managerial visualization practices, nonetheless can be understood as the first forms of a systematic regime of visualization with which the first corporate consultants approached business restructuring projects. On the one hand, Scientific Management was in no sense a homogeneous movement, but an amorphous label, under which engineering consultants collected a wide variety of philosophies. On the other hand, Scientific Management never, for the most part, took advantage of the effects of a monopolization of knowledge postulated repeatedly by researchers. The approach thus more closely resembled a "slack economy." This was strikingly indicated by the many breakdowns in Taylorist production during this time. The actual difficulty of Scientific Management was not in creating appropriate standards and norms, which were supposed to guarantee optimal results under the conditions of an ideal "taut economy." Much more problematic, in the end, was the implementation of this consulting knowledge on the level of production, which is invariably characterized through elements of the dysfunctional, "slack economy." In order to attain this, the consultants had recourse to new forms of visualizing knowledge, which in turn stabilized the medialization drive within the firm.

The development of universally valid norms for steel production was, as Taylor's multiyear high-speed cutting experiments showed, a significant undertaking. Trial-and-error methods from scientific research could determine valid calculation techniques and tabular values. On the one hand, there arose the possibility of using mathematics to analytically deduce the required values for the calibration of machinery. Another option involved large-scale series of experiments, with which the values derived from the trials could be converted into empirically observable laws of production.[85] Frederick W. Taylor began his

[84] Albert O. Hirschman, *Exit, Voice, and Loyalty: Responses to Decline in Firms, Organizations, and States* (Cambridge, MA: Harvard University Press, 1970), 9–15.

[85] Taylor is part of a widespread engineering movement that strove for the objectivation of planning and construction practices. See David F. Noble, *America by Design: Science, Technology, and the Rise of Corporate Capitalism* (Oxford: Oxford University Press, 1979); Bruce Sinclair, *A Centennial History of the American Society of Mechanical Engineers 1880–1980* (Toronto: University of Toronto Press 1980); Shenhav, "From Chaos to Systems."

$$V = \frac{\text{Constant} \left(1 - \frac{8}{7(32r)}\right)^*}{F^{\frac{2}{5}} + \frac{2.12}{5 + 32r} \left(\frac{48}{32r}D\right)^{\frac{2}{15}} + 0.06 \sqrt{32r + \frac{0.8(32r)}{6(32r) + 48D}}} \qquad [A]$$

Figure 30 The formula for calculating the calibration parameters for lathes.

search for such laws in metal cutting with the goal of developing a purely mathematical solution for the problem. After the first serious setbacks, he nonetheless gave up this approach and concentrated on an empirical-experimental solution pathway. For a mathematical derivation of the parameters, however, too many heterogeneous influencing factors were present, which needed to be taken into account for universally valid laws to be determined. This pragmatic approach, which moves between scientific precision and the needs of application-oriented solutions, is not an isolated incident, but the aforementioned approach of "applied science," as it was embodied in ideal-typical fashion by engineering and, even more so, by the branch of consulting.

At the conclusion of his multiyear research period, encompassing 30,000 individual experiments, Taylor and his team developed a formula that expressed the relationship, decisive for business purposes, of cutting speed to machine wear as a constant C (Fig. 30). The constant C was generated out of up to twelve factors, such as, for example, the type of coolant, the cutting depth, the form of the cutting tool, or the hardness of the material that needs to be processed. The Bethlehem Steel Company, for which Taylor worked at this time as a corporate consultant, displayed the new approach as a pioneering innovation, for the first time in the 1900 Paris World Fair.[86] The basis for this formula was not an exact mathematical deduction, as Taylor strove for at the beginning of his work, but was empirically determined through the experiments he conducted, and only afterward converted into a mathematical formula.

In order to utilize the results of the experimental analysis of materials and cutting techniques in the factory, they had to be adapted, in an ulterior phase, for everyday machine operations. How could the technique be meaningfully integrated into factory procedures? This much became clear: in the form of scientific formulas, such knowledge could not be deployed in a factory setting. It simply took too long to calculate the mathematically exact figures for every individual work process. This led to employees necessarily carrying out work according to

---

[86] Walter Hebeisen, *F. W. Taylor und der Taylorismus: Über das Wirken und die Lehre Taylors und die Kritik am Taylorismus* (Zürich: vdf Verlag, 1999), 58.

commonplace "rules of thumb."[87] Paradoxically, the standards and calculation practices were too exact to serve the goal of efficient production. As a way out of this impasse, the consultants initially converted the individual components of the formula into mathematical function curves on millimeter paper, from which simple tabular diagrams could be generated for every work station. But this too proved to be too time consuming.

It was only with the pragmatic form of the logarithmic slide rule (Fig. 31) that empirical knowledge finally found an application in the business world. This no longer rested, however, on the mathematical formula, but on trial and error and techniques of logarithmic approximation.[88] The display forms previously utilized for the calibration parameters, such as tabular lists (Fig. 32), met their limits with a formula that contained up to twelve variables. With the slide rule it was relatively quick to determine the necessary machine parameters for a given work phase. By offsetting the different function scales against one another, variables like the diameter of the workpiece, the quality of the metal, or the cutting tool used can be taken into account. Likewise, factors like the cooling of the workpiece can also be considered. Tabular charts and logarithmic papers for determining cutting speed no longer needed to be used.

Slide rules were not used by the turners working at the machines but by so-called function officials. Alongside a strategic concern for not burdening the workers with additional "brain work," practical reasons also supported this move:

> The slide rules cannot be left at the lathe to be banged about by the machinist. They must be used by a man with reasonably clean hands, and at a table or desk, and this man must write his instructions as to speed, feed, depth of cut, etc., and send them to the machinist well in advance of the time that the work is to be done.[89]

Autonomous from the actual work process, the functional foremen investigated the different machine parameters with slide rules and then entered their results into "work order slips," which were handed out to workers before the beginning of their shift. On the level of the factory floor, these detailed prescriptions aimed to control the production process and break the power of the foremen, whose experience-based knowledge about their respective departments was replaced by predetermined production requirements. As a result, they had to forfeit their position as a direct dialogue partner of the corporate leadership.

---

[87] Robert Kanigel, *The One Best Way: Frederick Winslow Taylor and the Enigma of Efficiency* (London: Abacus, 2000), 237.

[88] Taylor, *On the Art of Cutting Metals*, 246–48.

[89] Ibid., 25.

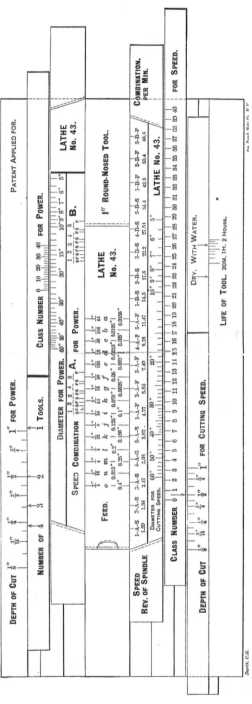

Figure 31 The slide rule patented in 1904 and developed by Carl Barth, a Norwegian mathematician and corporate consultant, together with Frederick W. Taylor and Henry L. Gantt. With this tool, the calibration parameters for metalworking lathes could be investigated.

TABLE 153

Practical Table of Cutting Speeds
Cast Iron

Corresponding to different depths of cut and thickness of feed on Soft, Medium and Hard Cast Iron, when best modern high speed tools are used of steel like tool No. 1, Folder 20, Table 138. See paragraph 751. Tools to be reground every 1 hour and 30 minutes

For accurate laws and formulæ representing the effect of feed and depth of cut on cutting speed, see Folder 19, also see paragraphs 795 to 814

STANDARD $\frac{5}{8}''$ TOOL

DEPTH OF CUT IN INCHES	FEED IN INCHES	CUTTING SPEED, IN FEET PER MINUTE FOR A TOOL WHICH IS TO LAST 1 HOUR AND 30 MINUTES BEFORE REGRINDING		
		SOFT CAST IRON	MEDIUM CAST IRON	HARD CAST IRON
$\frac{3}{32}$		216	108	63.0
		160	80.0	46.6
		110	55.0	32.2
		88.4	44.2	25.8
		75.4	37.7	22.0
$\frac{1}{8}$		200	100	58.6
		148	74.0	43.3
		104	51.8	30.2
		82.6	41.3	24.1
		69.6	34.8	20.3
$\frac{3}{16}$		183	91.6	68.0
		135	67.5	39.4
		94.0	47.0	27.4
		75.4	37.7	22.0
		64.3	32.2	18.8
$\frac{1}{4}$		171	85.7	50.1
		126	63.2	36.9
		87.8	43.9	25.6
		70.4	35.2	20.6
$\frac{3}{8}$		156	77.8	45.4
		116	57.8	33.8
		79.7	39.9	23.3

TABLE 154

Practical Table of Cutting Speeds
Cast Iron

Corresponding to different depths of cut and thickness of feed on Soft, Medium and Hard Cast Iron, when best modern high speed tools are used of steel like tool No. 1, Folder 20, Table 138. See paragraph 751. Tools to be reground every 1 hour and 30 minutes

For accurate laws and formulæ representing the effect of feed and depth of cut on cutting speed, see Folder 19, also see paragraphs 795 to 814

STANDARD $\frac{1}{2}''$ TOOL

DEPTH OF CUT INCHES	FEED IN INCHES	CUTTING SPEED, IN FEET PER MINUTE, FOR A TOOL WHICH IS TO LAST 1 HOUR AND 30 MINUTES BEFORE REGRINDING		
		SOFT CAST IRON	MEDIUM CAST IRON	HARD CAST IRON
$\frac{3}{32}$		206	103	60.0
		147	73.3	42.8
		97.5	48.8	28.5
		76.0	38.0	22.2
		64.1	32.1	18.7
$\frac{1}{8}$		194	97.0	56.7
		138	69.3	40.4
		93.1	46.5	27.2
		72.1	36.1	21.3
		41.8	20.9	12.2
$\frac{3}{16}$		182	91.0	53.0
		128	64.0	37.7
		86.1	43.1	25.1
		67.4	33.7	19.6
$\frac{1}{4}$		173	86.3	50.4
		122	61.0	35.7
		81.9	41.0	23.9

Figure 32 Tabular display of cutting speeds for two cutting tools. In contrast to the slide rule, here only the three variables of cutting depth, feeding speed, and the material hardness of the work piece are considered.

The knowledge of the foremen now stood in competition with Frederick W. Taylor's prescriptions, which were based on objective empirical study. The calculable requirements not only, however, unleashed changes on the level of production. They provided corporate executives with a more precise global planning of individual production processes. It was for this purpose that Carl Barth developed a slide rule that could be used to find out the labor time necessary for a work phase from machine parameters that had previously been calculated with a slide rule, which enabled a rapid calculation of item costs (Fig. 33).[90] These data were not intended for the factory floor but formed the basis for general planning and administrative decisions in the leadership levels of the firm. Management could establish a mathematical correlation of the nature of individual workpieces, up to and including the expected production time. Planning processes were considerably simplified. The system excluded the factor of implicit production knowledge (at least in theory) from the calculation and reduced it to a constant factor in a mathematical formula.

It was precisely because the slide rule was part of a hermetic function system that there were considerable problems in implementing this radical form of the division of labor into everyday factory practice. The first attempts of the corporate consulting team led by Frederick W. Taylor at the Bethlehem Steel Company did not have very positive results.

Although it was one of the most important publications in the sphere of machine construction during the second industrial revolution, or, to use Reinhart Koselleck's term, the second "saddle period,"[91] the attempt to implement these findings on high-speed steel cutting within the Bethlehem Steel Company was a failure.

Taylor's organizational philosophy, which followed the abstract ideal of the separation of mental and manual labor, could not be applied to the factory floor. On the one hand, his attempts at a radical reconstruction of the company met with resistance from its workers. On the other hand, his system was based on a fundamental misjudgment. He worked on the supposition that he had finally succeeded in bringing all necessary knowledge about the production process into a formalized, explicit form. This was not the case, however, since, in spite of the highly detailed prescriptions produced, there was still the need for more certain experiential values, in order for metalworking processes to be carried out. In other words, his attempt to conceive of human labor power as a mechanical

---

[90] Carl G. Barth, "Slide Rules as Part of the Taylor System," *Transactions of the American Society of Mechanical Engineers* 25 (1904): 49–62.

[91] Reinhart Koselleck, *Futures Past: On the Semantics of Historical Time*, trans. Keith Tribe (New York: Columbia University Press, 2004).

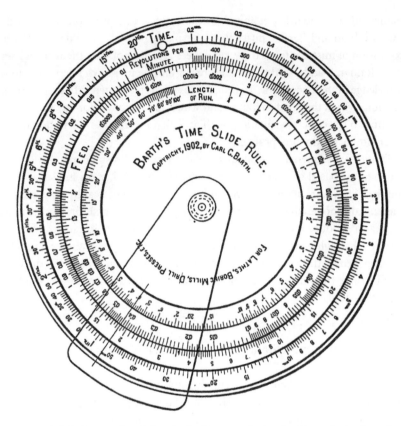

Figure 33 With the circular slide rule, feeding speeds that had been derived on the basis of a slide rule could be determined in order to figure out the required labor time for the production phase in question. This tool formed the basis for planning production processes that were independent of one another. The times ascertained were then entered into the Gantt charts as labor time guidelines.

machine was a mistake. Despite the advanced programming tool of the slide rule, the employees were incapable of operating it in a totally error-free manner.

Although Taylor's colleagues had given the mathematical formula the practicable form of the slide rule, the anticipated transfer of knowledge from the engineering experiments to the factory floor did not take place. The project failed and the commission was withdrawn from the consulting team. This was also causally related with the program followed by Taylorism. The workers were precisely not supposed to be involved in the process. The slide rule, which was kept in a central position for calculating machine times, was more closely oriented to the principle of a universal machine, which had to allow the most precise calculation of mathematical standards possible. For the workers, this principle did not offer low-threshold and flexible possibilities for participation. The slide rule was an expression of mistrust toward the employees and did not offer them any advantages. Rather, it addressed the phantasms of management, who *desired* a global knowledge of their company. The employees were confronted with prepared calculations which they had to follow, and which did not allow for any flexible adaptation to the concrete situation, such as with a mechanical disruption or any other kind of production problem.

Taylor's experiments and calculations produced valid standards; his system, after all, was based on empirical experimentation and thus on statistical probabilities. However, statistical probabilities that did not feature any real-life referents did not enable production to take place. In the end, the workstations needed to produce a concrete item, rather than a mediated, statistically probable metal conglomerate.[92] Nevertheless, Taylor's pioneering studies on metalworking formed the basis for a universal machine grammar, which described, for the first time, the various correlations between the hardness of the material and the cutting tools.

Nomography: A Standard for Industrial Machine Operation

If Taylor had great difficulties in actually implementing his system in factories, nomography did achieve this barely two decades later. Nomography could be used to adapt the basic calculations for metal cutting for numerous spheres of industrial production. Nomograms were cheap to manufacture, could be duplicated any number of times, and did not have to be retained at a central location, as Taylor's slide rules did. In contrast to the slide-rule system, the nomographic tables were conceived of as a supplementary calculation aid for employees. Should a calculation not lead to the desired results, then there was always the possibility of making immediate corrections, which was not the case with rigid, centralized standards. The simple access to the nomograms and the practical advantages and time savings that resulted from this enabled them to become a widely accepted *boundary object*.

Alongside a better inclusion of employees, nomography contributed to further simplifying the calculation of calibration parameters for production machinery. Taylor's high-speed steel system was transferred to metal cutting with lathes. Nomography also enabled company engineers to adapt the system for machines that deviated from the principle of the lathe. The

---

[92] For a historical perspective on the complex relations between production and precision, see Peter Jeffrey Booker, *A History of Engineering Drawing* (London: Northgate, 1979), 187.

values for processing different kinds of metal investigated by Taylor could be transferred to planing machines, milling machines and other specialized equipment.[93] Moreover, new slide rules did not have to be constructed; it sufficed to carry out the necessary mathematical conversions for the nomogram required.

Nomographic calculation was apt for all the production scenarios in which "a great number of similar calculation operations of different sizes [had to be] repeatedly carried out."[94] This applied to almost all production phases organized according to the principle of mass assembly. Unlike in the previous system of manual assembly,[95] a much larger quantity of identical workpieces had to be manufactured. If this production phase was completed, then new calibrations for the next work phase could, with the help of nomographic tables, be identified. The "time-consuming and costly conversions and stoppages for the machines and the workers"[96] could not be entirely eliminated but were significantly reduced. Moreover, an average understanding of mathematical calculations was sufficient, since "nomography uses [...] extremely simple instruments, and the deployment of almost all known nomograms can be undertaken by means of the most elementary geometric skills."[97] It was precisely through using machines which presupposed complex calibration parameters that nomography enabled the foremen to actually adopt the more precise calibration routines. The simple and rapid access prevented them from resorting, out of comfort, to imprecise values from their own experience. Lathes were particularly apt for this, since the nomograms used for them only had to depict the correlation between the circumferential speed, the diameter of the workpiece, and the rotational frequency

[93] See H. Winkel, *Selbstanfertigung von Rechentafeln: 4. Der Ausbau der Leitertafeln* (Berlin: Beuth, 1925), 7–9; Karl Hoffmann, "Anwendung der Nomographie zur Ermittlung der Schnittzeit für geradlinig spanabhebende Werkzeugmaschinen," *Maschinenbau/Gestaltung* 3, no. 4/5 (1923): 109–10; F. Braun, "Die nomographische Berechnung der Laufzeit bei Arbeiten auf der Bilgram-Kegelhobelmaschine," *Werkstattstechnik* 21, no. 10 (1927): 284.

[94] Dobbeler, "Grundlagen der Nomographie," 99.

[95] The shift from an artisanal organization of production to the system of mass production took place in Germany in the 1920s. Depending on the industry, the time span nonetheless starkly varied. See Anita Kugler, "Von der Werkstatt zum Fließband: Etappen der frühen Automobilproduktion in Deutschland," *Geschichte und Gesellschaft: Zeitschrift für historische Sozialwissenschaft* 13 (1987): 304–39; Anita Kugler, *Arbeitsorganisation und Produktionstechnologie der Adam-Opel-Werke (von 1900 bis 1929)* (Berlin: Wissenschaftszentrum Berlin, 1985); Jürgen Bönig, *Die Einführung von Fließbandarbeit in Deutschland bis 1933* (Münster: Lit Verlag 1993); Michael Stahlmann, "Vom Handwerk zur Fließbandarbeit: Die erste Revolution der Arbeitsorganisation bei Opel und Daimler-Benz," *WSI Mitteilungen* (October 1995): 646–53; Michael Stahlmann, *Die erste Revolution in der Autoindustrie: Management und Arbeitspolitik von 1900–1940* (Frankfurt am Main: Campus Verlag, 1993); Matthias Hillecke, "Arbeitsplatzgestaltung in den Gießereien der DaimlerChrysler AG. Ein historischer Rückblick," *Zeitschrift für Arbeitswissenschaft* 59 (2005): 353–59.

[96] Otto Schulz-Mehrin, *Die industrielle Spezialisierung, Wesen, Wirkung, Durchführungsmöglichkeiten und Grenzen: Auf Grund der Untersuchungen des Ausschusses für Wirtschaftliche Fertigung* (Berlin: VDI Verlag, 1920), 12.

[97] Dobbeler, "Grundlagen der Nomographie," 99.

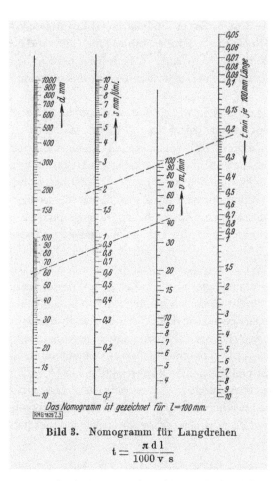

Bild 3.   Nomogramm für Langdrehen

$$t = \frac{\pi\, d\, l}{1000\, v\, s}$$

Figure 34 A nomogram for determining the calibration values of the lathe.

of the machine. Such nomograms could be quickly constructed, and even more simply deciphered.

Figure 34 shows a classical nomogram for longitudinal turning. It contains an illustrative example recorded with two dotted lines. In order to calculate the desired parameters, two steps were necessary: initially, the diameter of the workpiece (60 mm) on the left function scale had to be linked by a straight line with the value of the infeed speed of 40 meters per minute on the second scale from the left. The slope of the straight line thus produced had, in a second step, to be shifted to be parallel with the value of the cutting depth (in this case 2 mm per turn) on the second scale from the left. Subsequently, the time a machine required for a 100 mm long workpiece could be deciphered on the function scale on the right.

This led to the replacement of earlier practices of machine calibration. The previously standard, imprecise mode of external observation with a stopwatch could be replaced with routine calculations. Nomograms allowed the specialized worker or foreman to calibrate the machine more precisely. The more interesting aspect from the company's point of view, however, was the precise synchronization of the planning prescriptions with the actual production times. Nomography enabled the time prescriptions assumed by the company's executives to be verified on the basis of the extent to which there was an "accord with the work-stations" and the "rapid proof [about the] correctness of the computed time" to be carried out.[98] That this proof could be made was central to the question concerning the robustness of the production process, which was already pertinent in Karol Adamiecki's work. It was only when management possessed exact precalculations of the production phases that they could closely align the individual phases with one another. This coordinative control over the whole process raised productivity far more than the philosophy followed by Taylor, which temporally determined every work phase in an almost pedantic manner. Now management was in the position to define realistic time buffers between the individual processes. The robustness of the production process became a workplace setscrew of managerial action.

In the 1920s, the nomographic method established itself as a standard in the calculation of machine parameters. The pioneers in this respect were external experts and consultants from the Ausschuss für wirtschaftliche Fertigung (Committee for Economical Manufacturing, AWF) and the Reichskuratorium für Wirtschaftlichkeit (Imperial Advisory Board for Economic Efficiency, RKW). The two institutions were the essential authorities for German industry when it came to questions of production rationalization and efficient production.[99] The AWF began with the publication of "calculation tables which have been developed for specific tasks" and with the "publication of pamphlets which guide the self-production of such tables."[100] These pamphlets[101] were also intended to

[98] Braun, "Die nomographische Berechnung der Laufzeit bei Arbeiten auf der Bilgram-Kegelhobelmaschine," 284.
[99] The RKW was established on June 10, 1921, by the Reichswirtschaftsministerium (Imperial Ministry for the Economy), the Deutscher Verband Technisch-Wissenschaftlicher Vereine (German Association of Technical-Scientific Societies), and a number of corporations as the "Reichskuratorium für Wirtschaftlichkeit in Industrie und Handwerk" (Imperial Committee for Economic Efficiency in Industry and Manufacturing). The context for its founding was what the Reichswirtschaftsministerium saw as the worrisome state of Germany industry. This situation was to be ameliorated through the introduction of rationalization measures in production. The RKW was to play both an organizational and a communicative role. Additionally, it published documents on the topic of "rationalization," such as the "Handbuch der Rationalisierung" in 1928. See Manfred Pohl, *Die Geschichte der Rationalisierung: Das RKW 1921 bis 1996* (2001), http://www.rkw.de/rkwportrait/d_rkw_geschichte/aufsatz.pdf.
[100] Winkel, *Selbstanfertigung von Rechentafeln*, 3.
[101] Pohl, *Die Geschichte der Rationalisierung*.

show "the advantages of nomography to even the most mathematically uneducated reader."[102] The RKW set up the Ausschuss für graphische Rechenverfahren
(Committee for Graphic Calculation Techniques), which held monthly meetings
from 1922 on. New nomograms for particularly frequent formula were discussed
there and subsequently published. In early 1922, 30 nomograms had already
been published and another 114 were in planning.[103] The calculation tables were
distributed by the AWF from 1922 under the label of *AWF-Maschinenkarten*
(AWF Machine Cards).[104]

With one of the preassembled machine cards, the calibration of a production
machine went from being a challenging task to being a simple activity of deduction. The explicit prescriptions of the AWF supplemented the implicit experiential knowledge of the specialized workers, but—unlike in the case of slide rules
developed by Taylor and Barth—they did not replace it. We can therefore assume
that the plethora of new approaches in the AWF's canon of management literature was coterminous with their nationwide implementation. This is also denoted by the promptly introduced efforts to integrate nomography enduringly
into the educational curriculum of company engineers.[105] Their lasting implementation in the workplace was an aspiration on the part of both the government and the corporate sector, since the "use of nomographic techniques [was]
not so much a matter of mathematics, but much rather a matter of business."[106]

In contrast to the consulting strategy pursued by Taylor a good twenty years
earlier, the introduction of nomography was initially supposed to represent an
additional relief for specialized workers, and thus to indirectly raise productivity. With machine tables, it was not a question of clearly defined components
of a hermetic production system for the transformation of existing business
structures. Nomograms could be implemented, but they did not have to be. On
the one hand, corresponding to the demands of consulting knowledge, they were
modular and flexible. This was advantageous for their acceptance. They were
not, however, perceived as an attack on the status of the specialized worker, but

---

[102] The AWF published the following volumes in the series *Selbstanfertigung von Rechentafeln*: 1.
Das Rechnen mit Teilungen (1924), 2. *Anwendung des logarithmischen Linien-Netzes auf die
Maschinenkarten des AWF* (1924); 3. *Der Aufbau der Leiterntafeln* (1925); 4. *Der Ausbau der
Leitertafeln* (1925).

[103] This can be seen in the issues of the monthly *Mitteilungen des AWF* from 1922 to 1925, which
were published in the journal *Maschinenbau: Gestaltung, Betrieb und Wirtschaft*.

[104] K. Hegner, "Maschinenkarten," *Maschinenbau. Gestaltung, Betrieb, Wirtschaft* 5, no. 13/14
(1923): 575–78.

[105] Maurice D'Ocagne, *Cours de géométrie pure et appliquée de l'Ecole polytechnique*
(Paris: Gauthier-Villars, 1917/1918).

[106] Rudolf Rothe, "Die Nomographie als Gegenstand der Ingenieurausbildung an den Technischen
Hochschulen," *Maschinenbau/Wirtschaft* 3, no. 5 (1923), 113–14.

as a useful instrument.[107] On the other hand, they boasted a stable inner logic, with which the rationalization of the business could be fostered in indirect ways, without risking open conflicts with trade unions. This approach can be characterized as a form of *Dingpolitik* (object politics), which operates less with direct force than with the provision of new options. The rigid command structures of the thermodynamic age were replaced by decision objects loosely coupled with one another, which granted more autonomy to the respective hierarchy levels. Corporate executives received more precise figures for future planning processes, the company engineers reached a constantly high assembly quality and an optimal utilization of the machines, and the tables brought the workers time savings when calibrating machinery. Due to this multilayered application and simultaneous with the lower entry threshold, since it did not call for any specialized mathematical knowledge, the establishment of nomography in the business world was relatively free of problems. As a boundary object, nomography facilitated a coexistence of the actors with entirely different action orientations. But at the same time, they were also subordinated to the inalterable inner logic of nomography, which can be ascribed to the calculative media ideal type. Unlike Taylor and Barth's centrally organized slide-rule system, nomograms offered additional options for action. They could be utilized, but they did not have to be. The scientific knowledge transferred to the business was *compatible* with the already existing experiential knowledge of the workers. According to the situation, the nomograms could be connected with the (implicit) experiential knowledge of the employees. Existing knowledge and action structures were not questioned, but merely amplified.

Nomography in the Commercial Sphere

Outside of industrial production, in the calibration of production machines, the nomographic method was established in commercial departments, whose fundamental accounting techniques can also be attributed to a corporate consultant: Harrington Emerson. For this sphere, nomograms were devised for the purposes of business administration. Here, too, the visualization potential of nomograms offered advantages over the traditional methods of mathematical calculation.

It is known that raw numbers—namely with longer and changing usage, especially when a conception of size is invariably linked with it—have an immensely

---

[107] In the corpus of the trade journals assessed, there are a large number of critical articles about Taylorism. Not a single one, by contrast, describes the deployment of nomography as problematic.

tiring effect on the mind, and, when repeatedly dealt with inside a short period of time, either impair a correct estimation or make it entirely impossible, not to mention the fact that it is in and of itself difficult to mentally picture the correct size relations on the basis of numerical figures. As said, graphic displays effectively counteracted this shortcoming, and their application finds a continuously growing diffusion for general statistical purposes.[108]

If nomographic methods had successfully established themselves in the technical spheres of corporations, such as construction departments, as well as, as shown earlier, in the control of machines in the production process, in commercial departments their implementation required a great deal of convincing:

> While in technical areas nomography [. . .] finds extensive application, the commercial sphere made sparse usage of this instrument. This is all the more regrettable, since the nomographic calculation method boasts several advantages over traditional methods, which are not to be underestimated.[109]

One of the reasons for this was the goal pursued with mathematical calculations. With technical calculations, absolute precision was not so decisive. Frequently, it was only a question of tolerance ranges, which could be determined through rough estimates. Exact values were not absolutely necessary. It was a different case entirely with keeping balanced accounts. Here, mathematical tools and the calculation operations that were carried out with them coincided. Workplace calculation was based on entire numbers. Wage, material, and production costs had unambiguous valuations as part of the reciprocal circulation of commodities, which were expressed in the form of the medium of money, and they could be seamlessly converted into mathematical calculation routines. In short, in commercial departments, for verification systems like double-entry bookkeeping, the exact calculation phase was a basic prerequisite for the legitimacy of the accounting techniques that were carried out. Thus considered, nomography was a striking backward step, since this form of graphical calculation deviated from the precision of prior mathematical methods.[110] Nomography was imprecise. Thus a similar problematic appeared in the commercial sphere, as it existed in the discipline of engineering studies in the conflict between "applied" and "pure" research.

---

[108] Schaaps, "Statistik und graphische Darstellung im Dienste des Kaufmanns," 127.
[109] K. H. Schmidt, "Über einige Anwendungsmöglichkeiten der Nomographie in der Betriebswirtschaft," *Zeitschrift für Handelswissenschaft und Handelspraxis* 19, no. 11 (1926): 257
[110] See also the discussion on the precision of the graphic method in Chapter 1 of this volume, "Applied Industrial Research."

Nomography became of interest for commercial concerns and the consultants preoccupied with them, at the the point in time when accounting's sphere of tasks expanded.[111] Company expansions led to problems of control in the standard forms of accounting.[112] In the 1850s and 1860s, the fundamental practices of accounting were constituted.[113] They encompassed "financial, capital and cost accounting."[114] In the 1880s, these forms of accounting became a widespread standard in commerce and industry.[115] Their sphere of tasks was restricted to the documentation of *direct* costs, which chiefly consisted of labor and material costs.[116] With the ascent of Scientific Management, this narrow definition of accounting practice was broadened. Now, *indirect* costs, such as idle time (the losses incurred through inactive machines or worker shortages), were also taken into account.[117] These were costs that no longer had a direct counterpart but rested on the systemic factors in a factory. In accounting, abstract, "managerial" indicators made their entry. Indirect costs—that is, costs without any direct equivalence—were only comprehensible and usable in the context of a superordinate management, as part of systematic leadership knowledge. Additionally, there was an increasingly functional difference drawn between a cost system internal to the company (cost accounting) and an externally oriented accounting system (financial accounting).[118] An important innovator in this area was the corporate consultant Harrington Emerson, who described basic accounting practices in a series of articles.[119]

From 1900 on, these new forms of accounting knowledge fulfilled new, prognostic functions. As part of double-entry bookkeeping, the commercial techniques no longer only served the direct financial control of the business. They were newly discovered as a resource for making strategic planning decisions.[120] Statistical methods like *breakeven charts* expanded accounting's

[111] On the historical development of accounting around 1900, see Charles W. Wootton and Barbara E. Kemmerer, "The Emergence of Mechanical Accounting in the U.S., 1880–1930," *Accounting Historians Journal* 34, no. 1 (2007): 91–124; Robert N. Anthony, "Management Accounting: A Personal History," *Journal of Management Accounting Research* 15 (2003): 249–53; Richard K. Fleischman and Thomas N. Tyson, "Cost Accounting During the Industrial Revolution: The Present State of Historical Knowledge," *Economic History Review* 46, no. 3 (1993): 503–17; G. A. Lee, "The Concept of Profit in British Accounting, 1760–1900," *The Business History Review* 49, no. 1 (1975): 6–36; Percival F. Brundage, "Milestones on the Path of Accounting," *Harvard Business Review* 29, no. 4 (1951): 71–81.
[112] See Lee, "The Concept of Profit in British Accounting, 1760–1900," 7.
[113] See Chandler, *The Visible Hand*, 109–20.
[114] Ibid., 109.
[115] Ibid., 121.
[116] Kaplan, "The Evolution of Management Accounting," 392.
[117] Chandler, *The Visible Hand*, 278ff.
[118] Kaplan, "The Evolution of Management Accounting," 396.
[119] Ibid., 394.
[120] Ibid., 395–96.

role in the sphere of strategic management.[121] Corporate consultants like Booz Allen & Hamilton specialized in developing perfectly apposite consulting services, like "forecasting" or specially commissioned "business research services."[122] It did not, however, eventuate in a valorization of existing accounting departments. On the contrary, the bookkeepers previously responsible for this task were replaced with clerks, staff with a lower competency level.[123] They were now tasked with delivering the relevant data to the management they reported, who retained the actual decision-making competencies.

In the context of this change, as the thesis posited here has it, nomographic techniques gained significance in the commercial sector. For the prognostic deployment of accounting data, the absolute precision of the data was no longer decisive. It was no longer the clarity of the calculation techniques, but their ability to quickly and straightforwardly process data, that became relevant. The concomitant imprecisions were tolerated, because they simultaneously allowed a rapid reaction to changes. Decisions were now no longer irrevocable after they had been made. On the contrary, their effects could be constantly verified and, if necessary, corrected or adapted. Imprecision no longer meant merely a lack of exactitude, but also opened up room for maneuvering by management, to influence and guide an ongoing process. The sets of data of commercial knowledge available could be used with such calculation methods as managerial knowledge for strategic planning decisions.

Nomography represented one such calculation method. It could be used to establish calculation tables with which the most varied production and operation scenarios could be modeled and calculated. The nomographic calculation tables not only offered the possibility for a rapid and simple calculation. They enabled a wide variety of calculation scenarios to be graphically plotted. Subsequently, the differences on the nomographic tables could be visually compared. Individual factors could be transformed and the immediate effects on the total process resulting from them could be observed. Transformations of outcome parameters were no longer represented merely as numerical deviations, but also as a graphic relation. The mathematical relationship of numerical outcome values to each other became a visual decision-making surface. Due to the

---

[121] This development can also be seen in the fact that the Harvard Business School, for instance, merged the departments of "statistics" and "accounting" (a measure which was in any case not overly successful). See Anthony, "Management Accounting: A Persosnal History," 250ff.

[122] Canback, "The Logic of Management Consulting," 4.

[123] Wootton and Kemmerer, "The Emergence of Mechanical Accounting in the U.S., 1880–1930," 102ff.

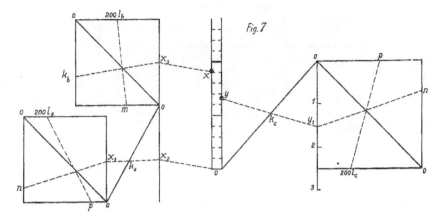

Figure 35 Nomographic calculation tables for economic efficiency comparisons.

visualization of graphic relations, nomography, as an ideal-typical calculative technique, was also a *kinetic* technique, which defined a scenario and allowed different scenarios to be compared. It could be used by corporate consultants to show their clients the effects of different restructuring strategies right before their eyes. At the same time, a visual culture was stabilized among the factory management, which the consultants in turn referred back to in order to promote their special services.

Nomographic Boundary Cost Calculations

Nomograms were exemplary for this and allowed the comparison of various modes of organizing production. With the ascent of automated machines, which could replace manual work phases, the question was frequently posed as to the profitability of such a changeover. The wage costs of manual techniques stood in opposition to the investment and operating costs for automation. Equally, the cost structure of both approaches differed when the assignment volume changed for the respective production phase. The manual performance of a task by a worker could be flexibly adapted to different assignment volumes. If the assignment level was low, the employees could be shifted to another branch of the company or dismissed. With the mechanical performance of the same task, the purchase of a new machine was necessary if demand was high. If demand was low, the existing machinery had to be operated at a reduced load factor. The fixed costs, however, unlike with the manual performance of the task, could not be altered. This kind of comparative boundary cost calculation could be carried out with nomography.

Doppel-Z-Tafel	Einfache Z-Tafel	Addition	Übertragung	Ver-gleichs-skala
$\dfrac{p \cdot n}{200\, l_a} = x_1$ $\quad$ $\dfrac{m \cdot k_b}{200\, l_b} = x_3$	$x_1 \cdot k_a = x_2$ $\quad$ x_3	$\left.\begin{array}{c}\text{Direkte}\\\text{lineare}\\\text{Addition}\\\text{auf Grund}\\\text{des}\\\text{gemein-}\\\text{samen}\\\text{Null-}\\\text{punktes}\end{array}\right\} = x$	$\left\{\begin{array}{c}\text{Über-}\\\text{tragung}\\\text{auf die}\\\text{Vergleichs-}\\\text{skala}\\\text{durch}\\\text{Parallel-}\\\text{projektion}\end{array}\right\} x'$	x
$\dfrac{p \cdot n}{200\, l_c} = y_1$	$y_1 \cdot k_e = y$			y

Figure 36 The mathematical calculation formulas that formed the basis for the nomographic tables.

The nomogram in Figure 35 is an example of such a calculation routine. It enabled the calculation of the performance capability of two work techniques for letter delivery, which were deployed in addressing letters and sorting mail in an advertising department.[124] The nomogram compared two such scenarios: one mainly based on manual labor, and the other that was mostly automated. On the one hand, mail was sorted by hand and addressing was done with the *adrema* (an addressing machine), while on the other hand sorting and addressing were done with the *adressograph*, a machine that carried out both processes mechanically.

On the left side, in two double-Z-tables, the operating costs of the adrema machine were graphically plotted in the upper chart, and the costs for manual sorting in the lower chart. The two formulas depicted there could be found in the tabular list contained in Figure 36 and denoted with the variable $x1$ and $x2$. These values can be converted to the value x in the function scale located in the middle, which gives the respective performances of the two techniques. In the lower part of the table the calculation formula for the double-Z-table ($y1$) can be found on the right side of the nomogram. With it, the performance capability of the variant with the adressograph could be calculated and converted to the value y in the middle function scale.

This technique enabled the direct graphic comparison of the performance capabilities of different scenarios, depending on the operating costs that resulted. It was likewise relatively simple to follow which effects were produced

---

[124] Since it was an exemplary visualization model, this nomographic model was lacking in all units and values, apart from the y-scale on the right-hand side, which provided the load factor as a percentage of the number of machines in use.

from the performance capability of the entire system, when individual variables, like workers' wages, were altered. The graphic relations depicted were not only the basis of the calculation, but also created the possibility of a visual comparison. Numerical values contained graphic equivalents, which could influence decision-making. Similar calculation techniques were also deployed in the self-calculation of costs.[125] Whereas "their results do not possess the absolute precision of numerical calculations,"[126] these were not overly necessary in a rough calculation of general production factors. It was merely a matter of determining a trend which was then supposed to serve as an aid to decision making for possible executive interventions into the production process.

Nomograms facilitated the circulation of relevant data in two ways: on the level of production and on the level of commercial planning. The factory-floor machines that were more precisely calibrated with the aid of nomograms boasted less wear and tire, a more even assembly quality, and thus lower total production costs. On the level of business planning, nomographic calculations allowed for the exact pre-calculation of work processes. This was not only useful in the planning and coordination of business procedures, and in the appraisal of production capacities. It was of equal importance for the acquisition of assignments. It allowed a more precise determination of the production costs for a product that did not yet exist. These possibilities allowed for the calculative "playing out" of production scenarios in advance. Subsequently, the decision could be made whether the assembly of such a product could be economically "calculated." Was there even a market for this product at this price? Could the existing price level of a competing product be undercut? At the same time, such tables represented calculation routines which could be transferred to other areas. Even employees who had no mathematical knowledge could use them. In this sense, nomographic calculation tables involved a decision-making object (a *boundary object*) that was transferable and had a low access threshold, and that circulated between different actors within the company. Nomography, together with the graphic tables and diagrams of the Gantt charts and the harmonographic tables for business administration, was, after all, part of a new visual culture of decision making, calculating, and directing.

[125] F. Eisner, "Die Nomographie, ein Hilfsmittel wirtschaftlicher Gestaltung und schärfster Selbstkostenermittlung," *Maschinenbau/Gestaltung* 1, no. 1 (1922): 11–20.

[126] A. Winkel, "Das Nomogramm in der Selbstkostenberechnung," *Werkstattstechnik* 17, no. 1 (1923): 13.

The Visual Culture of Managerial Consulting

With graphic registration apparatuses, process maps and flow charts, nomographic models for simulation and calculation, and film, visual management was established between 1880 and 1930 as a potent, essential media tool in business contexts. In the graphic method media network, business knowledge was collected and packaged for managerial decision-making processes:

> Graphic representation was particularly appropriate here, since a decision can be made more quickly and more correctly, when all necessary factors are graphically plotted in plain view, than when they first have to be apprehended and compiled by the brain.[127]

A new, "tabulated"[128] order of knowledge of media visuality was formed. The visualization of business knowledge facilitated the exchange of information between previously isolated corporate spheres, such as the mathematical and engineering branches of industry. Apart from the necessary circulation of knowledge for daily business, even more complex strategic-systematic considerations for other corporate spheres could be repurposed. In addition to these direct effects on the quotidian process of carrying out tasks, the new visuality of knowledge also facilitated the previously sparse exchange between science and business. The first forms of managerial knowledge arose: the basis for this new "pragmatic-simulatory" approach were techniques of graphic-medial visualization. Whether they concerned precalculation processes in accounting or the calibration of production machines, the visualization processes used were identical.

The management systems of Adamiecki and Gantt, much like the nomographic calculation tables, were more than mere appendages to the company's systematic internal communication, based on the "written record"[129] and established in the late nineteenth century. While the latter served the documentation and circulation of business data, graphic techniques were aligned with the active selection and visual representation of data. The form of visual preparation did not follow the conventions and necessities of written communication. It anticipated, as became clear in Adamiecki's consideration of disruptive events, aspects of managerial direction and regulation. They were not instruments that management could seize when needed, but were an inseparable part of managerial reality. The new graphic media technologies

[127] Leyensetter, "Graphische Darstellung als Hilfsmittel zur Regelung und Überwachung," 765.
[128] Willers, "Bücherbesprechung," 817.
[129] Yates, *Control Through Communication*.

vehemently changed the practices of corporate administration and planning. The same can be said for nomographic calculation tables. They generated a space which did indeed serve the purpose of calculation, but also a visual space allocated for modeling kinetic processes.

The Image Space of "Visual Management"

Sixteen years after the first introduction of his technique, Gantt compared his system with another media revolution, which took place in parallel with the spread of Gantt charts.

> we shall show a system of progress charts, which bear the same relation to the statistical reports which are so common, that a moving picture film bears to a photograph.[130]

With this analogy, Gantt described, in 1919, the paradigm shift that took place with his graphic management system in commerce and industry. His comparison with film makes clear that his system is more than a mere representation system for existing written knowledge sets within companies. It is not an uninterrupted continuation of internal business communication through other means. As far as the influence that his visualization techniques for company knowledge and the corporate management that was built on was concerned, he was entirely correct. Just as a film cannot be sufficiently explained by pointing to the individual photographic images that constitute them, the graphic knowledge of the charting revolution cannot be understood as a mere visual representation of available data. Both film and charting are, above all, *kinetic* rather than *static* mediums.

While still photography was influenced by other factors, such as its proximity to painting, and is often attributed with the most faithful depiction of reality possible,[131] the projected film images projected with a frequency of 16 to 24 frames per second followed entirely different parameters. Instead of a fixed image space with a centralized perspective, film offered new possibilities, such as montage, which formed a completely transformed media form through the interaction of individual images.[132] Aside from the underlying materiality of the image, which

---

[130] Gantt, *Organizing for Work* (New York: Harcourt, Brace and Howe), 17.

[131] William Mills Ivins, *Prints and Visual Communication* (Cambridge, MA: MIT Press, 1978), 135–57.

[132] Pierre Francastel makes a similar argument. For him, film operates from the very start in the imaginary domain, whereas painting, beginning with Cezanne, turns away from the representative mode of centralized perspective and opens up to new forms of visual depiction. See Pierre Francastel, *Etudes de Sociologie de l'art* (Paris: Gallimard, 1989); Pierre Francastel, *Art & Technology in the Nineteenth and Twentieth Centuries* (New York: Zone Books, 2000).

is based on identical chemical processes, film and photography exhibit very few common characteristics.

A similar relation exists between the surface of graphic charts and their "individual images," the underlying columns of statistical numbers from storage costs, purchasing prices, illness rates, sales numbers, or machine running times. Indisputably, charts are founded on the corporate statistical figures. However—and here the reason for the comparison drawn by Gantt between photography and film becomes clear—charts are, like films, more than a mere compilation of data or individual photographs. With up to 24 images per second, the film does not depict a photographic "reality," but produces its own forms of narration, aesthetics, and economic constraints. The same applies for Gantt charts and Adamiecki's harmonograms. The data visualized there are not a statistical representation of the "reality" of a company. Rather, they are a "selection of schematic abstractions,"[133] which forms a visual surface for decision making. This model is also based on the representation of figures, but more on the representational guidelines and forms of the graphic method. Film transforms human perception through narrative and aesthetic innovations. The same applies to the *graphic method media network*. Harmonographs and Gantt charts revolutionized the perception of business management. Rigid, static processes of data representation were replaced by the kinetic modeling of dynamic yet error-prone processes. With the development of visual knowledge, and the dynamic it unleashed, an imaginary space was formed which contained practices of simulation, play, systematic analysis, and decision making. "The chart itself becomes the moving force for action."[134] A system was established which through its self-evident, practical nature almost invisibly coalesces with the business, but without which modern industry management would not be possible.

Through techniques of montage, film transforms spectatorial perception. It yields a type of spectator who is not so much seized by film images, but regards them, with distracted attention, as an "examiner."[135] The visual surfaces of graphic techniques and the linked practices of the perception, processing, and circulation alter the perception management had for the business. "Unlike statistical diagrams, curve records, and similar static forms of presenting facts of the past [Gantt] charts [. . .] are kinetic, moving."[136] Harmonograph and Gantt charts are not only simple means of representation corresponding to the *static* ideal type. They formed their own sphere of influence, whose attention no longer

[133] See Ivins, *Prints and Visual Communication*, 137.

[134] Clark, *The Gantt Chart*, 5.

[135] Walter Benjamin, "The Work of Art in the Age of Mechanical Reproduction," in *Illuminations: Essays and Reflections*, ed. Hannah Ahrendt and trans. Harry Zohn (New York: Schocken, 1969), 217–52.

[136] Polakov, "Principles of Industrial Philosophy" (1920), cited in Clark, *The Gantt Chart*, 21.

pertains to special, partial aspects, but turns toward reality as a "total field."[137] For systematic aspects of leadership, like dealing with disruptions, management was placed on the same level with practices of *visual* management. Thus, "graphic solutions to production problems"[138] could be generated. These visual solutions do not form a visual logic of the "image." An image does not take action or have agency. They are based on three media action types (static, calculative, kinetic) that are constituted on the basis of visuality and the actors dealing with them. The recombination of these action possibilities establishes an ordered yet flexible process, so as to respond to the demands of management. It was not yet, as Gantt formulated it, a "self-perpetuating system of management,"[139] but the first systematic concretions that hinted at it could be recognized. Of course, visual management did not contain a defined feedback logic in the sense of second-order cybernetics, and yet epistemic processes can be seen which aim at precisely this mode of functioning.

For present-day forms of knowledge management, Scientific Management no longer plays a major role. Yet the visualization techniques that arose in the historical context of this managerial doctrine—harmonographic tables for factory administration, nomographic calculation tables, Gantt charts—have proven to be more enduring. Their concrete advantages and lower entry threshold allowed them to become *media boundary objects*. They thus shaped a new action context of visual knowledge, which in turn became the basis for new forms of business management. Beyond this, they gave legitimacy to managerial decisions and made a considerable contribution to the development process of the occupation of the modern manager. Graphic techniques of visual management took on a legitimizing and identificatory role not only for management, but also for the branch of corporate consultants. They enabled the articulation of abstract administrative knowledge and for the consultants formed the basis of their business model, while managers began to identify themselves as a social group.

This survey of visual management case studies has documented its early forms, first on the basis of their concrete usage in industrial and commercial structures, and second, from the perspective of media history, under the angle of the media understanding tied with them. Visual management, which established itself after 1880, not only contained new forms of managerial decision-making practices, it was part of a visual culture that was used by corporate consultants in a targeted fashion, in

---

137 McLuhan, *Understanding Media*, 13.
138 Marsh, "The Harmonogram of Karol Adamiecki," 358.
139 Gantt, *Work, Wages, and Profits*, 249.

order to promote their consultancy services. They can be ascribed to a reciprocal relationship between the introduction of visual techniques by corporate consultants and a nascent sensitivity in business for visual forms, aesthetics, and practices.

In what follows, this perspective, focused on structures, will be supplemented by a more action-centered approach, with the example of the corporate consultancy Gilbreth, Inc. At the center of this are the concrete advantages and the influence of visualization techniques for the branch of corporate consulting. The focus, here, underscores my thesis that the practices of corporate consultants made a considerable contribution to the stabilization and shaping of the medialization process in business described in this book. The connection with the techniques of visual management, graphic factory administration, and nomography outlined earlier arises on the basis of a homologous procedure and almost identical visualization practices. Copies of a number of the articles cited from German and American trade journals on the theme of visualization can be found in the archives of Frank and Lillian Gilbreth in the Purdue University Library's "Archives and Special Collections." During the establishment of the visualization drive I describe, there also arose a lively exchange of the participating actors concerning innovations of graphic factory management.

3

Gilbreth, Inc.

Selling Film to Corporations

My case study on Gilbreth, Inc. is divided into historically distinct halves. I will begin by outlining Frank B. Gilbreth's origins in the construction industry in the 1890s. It was here that he developed the basic management methods and systems that he would later, after 1911, put into practice as a corporate consultant. His managerial philosophy of "systematic management" was constituted in the early phase of his activity, entirely without the influence of media techniques like film or photography. Instead, it arose in the context of the practical problems he was confronted with in the construction industry. It was only when he left the field of construction and became an independent corporate consultant with his wife, Lillian Gilbreth, that he concertedly introduced media techniques.

In the second section, I will analyze the influence that the structures of the corporate consulting branch had on the Gilbreths' use of media techniques. In comparison with other corporate consultants and their specific consulting models, it is clear that the Gilbreths used media techniques as their consulting firm's central unique selling proposition. They communicated this in a broadly conceived marketing campaign, which in turn has relevance for the development of management theory wider expert audience.

"Lay some brick . . . " From Businessman to Consultant

Born in 1868 in Fairfield, Maine, Frank B. Gilbreth brought his knowledge and the experiences from the construction industry, in which he was involved between 1885 and 1912, to the activity of engineering consulting.

Short-term financial difficulties after the death of his father prevented Gilbreth from pursuing his studies, despite already passing the entrance exam for the Massachusetts Institute of Technology (MIT).[1] As an alternative, he

---

[1] Judith Merkle, *Management and Ideology: The Legacy of the International Scientific Management Movement* (Berkeley: University of California Press, 1980), 46; Helen Q. Schroyer, "Contributions of the Gilbreths to the Development of Management Thought," *Academy of Management Proceedings* 1 (1975): 1–9.

Angels of Efficiency. Florian Hoof, Oxford University Press (2020) © Oxford University Press.
DOI: 10.1093/oso/9780190886363.003.0001

Figure 37 Using the height-adjustable construction device on one of Frank B. Gilbreth's building sites.

decided upon a practical training in the building trade, and in 1885 he began an apprenticeship as a bricklayer with Whidden and Company, a Boston construction company.[2] During this time, he joined the local Bricklayers' Union.[3] After the completion of his apprenticeship, he spent half a year as a foreman and then as a superintendent, and after 1890 he bore responsibility as the general superintendent for different projects in the company.[4] Parallel to his activity for Whidden and Company, on his free Sundays, Gilbreth began to work on devices and techniques for facilitating and accelerating labor processes. His first invention was a variable bricklaying scaffold that could be adjusted in alignment with the labor process (Gilbreth Scaffold), which brought him an award at the Boston Mechanics' Fair in 1892.[5] The contraption had the advantage that the work no longer had to be interrupted for lengthy periods due to readjustment, when a certain height of a wall was reached, since Gilbreth's invention could be continuously adapted to the height of the wall (Fig. 37).

The Gilbreth scaffold also brought about an ergonomic advance, because the necessary construction materials could always be found on the same level as the workers. The bricklayers no longer had to bend down to reach them, which

[2] Price, "One Best Way," 13.
[3] Edna Yost, *Frank and Lillian Gilbreth: Partners for Life* (New York: Van Rees Press, 1949), 49.
[4] Price, "One Best Way," 14.
[5] Ibid., 15.

Figure 38 Building materials ergonomically positioned on the construction device. So-called packs were placed between the wall and the worker. These consisted of eighteen bricks, stacked on two strips of wood in order to facilitate their handling by the worker.

considerably relieved the work procedure and reduced fatigue. With his new scaffold, Gilbreth aimed for a significant increase in labor productivity. While a bricklayer was previously capable of laying around 125 bricks per hour, his new method increased this rate to nearly 350 bricks per hour. The merit of his system also consisted in being able to measure productivity in the first place. Gilbreth sought to quantify production processes for the first time by abandoning the previously standard practice of tossing the brick supplies into big piles. Instead, eighteen bricks were bundled together into easily transported "packs,"[6] which also facilitated the transport and disposal of the bricks (Fig. 38). More important, "this system enables a genuine control of the daily brick usage and thus of the daily work progress."[7] Through the number of "packs" used at the end of the day, the individual work performance of every single worker could be ascertained.

Behind the superficial ergonomic improvements, there also lay the possibility of gaining new data and figures about the production process. Gilbreth installed an early feedback system that was predicated on the informational unit of the "packs." This in turn enabled the introduction of new compensation models. This

---

[6] Frank B. Gilbreth, *Motion Study: A Method for Increasing the Efficiency of the Workman* (New York: D. Van Nostrand Company, 1921), 10.

[7] Frank B. Gilbreth, *Bewegungsstudien: Vorschläge zur Steigerung der Leistungsfähigkeit des Arbeiters* (Berlin: Springer, 1921), 3.

new "differential piece-rate system" was no longer based on the principle of equal pay. Now, the wage could be calculated specifically according to the respective labor performance of the individual worker.

In 1895, Gilbreth left Whidden and Company and founded his own construction company. With his bricklaying scaffold, registered as a patent in 1896,[8] he wanted to establish his company as a rapid construction firm. In order to realize the "speed work"[9] necessary for this, he used mechanical instruments, such as the Gilbreth Scaffold discussed earlier.[10] Moreover, he implemented a compartmentalized labor process. If the bricklayers were previously responsible for their own construction material supplies, this was now the task of specially hired, unqualified auxiliary workers.

Additionally, Gilbreth had recourse to psychological strategies in order to motivate the workers in their labor. Thus, he organized construction sites as sporting events, in which the Star-Spangled Banner[11] was publicly awarded to the fastest bricklaying gang.[12] Moreover, he brought together workers, mostly immigrants from different nationalities, into work groups according to very specific attributes. In Gilbreth's view, forming nationally uniform work groups was ideal, because it was through the possibility of linguistic comprehensibility that a competition between individual workers *within* each group was possible. As a side effect, the competitions *between* groups also became contests between nations, such as Irish, Italian, or Greek immigrants. Thus, Gilbreth adroitly used still existing national roots as an identification space in an environment that was new and strange to the migrant laborers.[13]

Ergonomic improvements and the targeted usage of work incentives complemented a management system which enabled the simultaneous control and supervision over different construction sites from a central location.[14] This system consisted of written chains of command, which replaced previously standard oral orders. The goal of raising efficiency not only related to the labor process on construction, but also included the level of administration from the very beginning, in which all decisions had to be reliably documented. Errors and inefficiencies on construction sites, as well as on the managerial level, thus became visible and retrospectively rectifiable. With this business strategy, Gilbreth had

[8] US-Pat. No. 554.024, submitted on June 4, 1894, patented on February 4, 1896, Patent Label: Scaffold.

[9] Gilbreth, *Field System*, 13.

[10] Further improvements ensued, including the development of simple and flexible concrete mixers. See Gilbreth, *Field System*, 99–101.

[11] See the photograph of a bricklaying gang adorned with the Star-Spangled Banner in February 1909, Gilbreth LOM, SPCOLL, Purdue University Libraries, NF11/0031-1, No. A49-239.

[12] Gilbreth, *Field System*, 17–20.

[13] On the concept of the nation as a space of identification, see Benedict Anderson, *Imagined Communities: Reflections of the Origin and Spread of Nationalism* (London: Verso, 1991).

[14] See Price, "One Best Way," 14.

great success and also acquired the reputation of a "dynamic systematic man-ager."[15] "By the time he was twenty-seven he had offices in New York, Boston and London. He had a yacht, smoked cigars, and had the reputation of a snappy dresser."[16] Finally, he made it to MIT—not, as planned, as a student, but as the building contractor responsible for the construction of the Lowell Laboratory. His rapid construction system allowed him to have the building ready six weeks before the planned completion date, which for the construction industry at the time was a small sensation.

The Consulting Business Model: Selling Rather Than Using Knowledge

Gilbreth's withdrawal from the building trade coincided with the devastating earthquake in San Francisco in the year 1906. Here, Gilbreth saw a chance to extend his construction activity to the West Coast, having been previously concentrated on the East Coast. He wanted to profit on a grand scale from the structural restoration of the 28,000 buildings destroyed in the Bay Area. For his systematic approach, it was advantageous not only to acquire individual building commissions, but also to snap up as many parallel contracts as pos-sible. Then he could show off the cost advantages of his systematic admin-istration and construction control. As a consequence, he took on a series of contracts, in the private and the public sphere, as part of the city's reconstruc-tion. The economic crisis that gripped the United States a year later brought a spate of his customers into repayment difficulties. At the same time, local construction companies—which, since they used conventional construction techniques, could not compete with the lower rates offered by Gilbreth—were able to manifestly disrupt the provision of building materials to his construc-tion sites. These disruptions led to an explosion of construction costs. It was evident that Gilbreth possessed an efficient and rapid construction system, but the higher wages paid and the concomitant higher fixed costs made the system prone to disruptions.[17] Since he could not exert control over the external

---

[15] Ibid.

[16] See Frank B. Gilbreth and E. G. Gilbreth-Carey, *Cheaper by the Dozen* (New York: T.Y. Crowell Co., 1948), chapter 5.

[17] Ironically, the production system developed by Gilbreth was superior to the usual systems used in major industrial firms. But as a construction company owner, he could not take the next logical step and transform his company into an integrated "multiunit business enterprise," as was standard practice in the steel and mining industries. Here, the dependency on external suppliers was reduced through integrating them into a single enterprise. Since the construction industry did not possess a solid local anchoring and suffered from significant conjunctural vacillations, this development was impossible. For a detailed description of his production system, see Frank B. Gilbreth, *Bricklaying System* (New York: The Myron C. Clark Publishing Co., 1909).

material flows of the local construction material dealers, and his company only had modest financial reserves, the persistent disruptions of delivery logistics brought his firm to the edge of collapse. It was only through the contribution of outside banks to his business that insolvency could be averted. His company was unable to recover from this setback.[18]

Inarguably, in 1907 Gilbreth saved his business from bankruptcy, but the following economic uncertainty in the winter of 1911 finally brought his company to an irreversible financial decline. Although the company survived, and Gilbreth was still nominally active in a leading position, the creditor banks had taken power over the company. Subsequently they forced Gilbreth to restructure the company. He therefore lost interest in the company and was barely concerned with the company's contract acquisition.[19] Instead, he increasingly began to turn his labor system away from the construction industry and toward a universally applicable model for management consulting.

Possibly, however, he also saw that his business model, which was based on the efficient mastery of the labor-intensive activity of bricklaying, was put at risk through the introduction of precast elements in the construction business.[20] The trend toward precast elements devalued the advantages of his management system in the construction industry, which relied on the efficient structuring of the labor-intensive activity of bricklaying. Gilbreth thus turned his attention toward assembly-intensive industrial labor. There it was suggested that he could achieve significant success with his methodology.

Furthermore, in the last two years of Gilbreth's time in the construction industry, strikes increasingly impacted his building sites. These generally targeted his wage and labor system.[21] The craftsmen, originally organized in the form of craft guilds, were opposed to their work performances being measured and documented, as well as to the hollowing out of the basic principle of equal pay. Through the individual measurement of work performance, Gilbreth had introduced a new flexible compensation system that was oriented to the actual work carried out. It was in this context that union-organized and unorganized workers were increasingly in solidarity with one another,[22] which forced Gilbreth in certain cases to back away from his method and return to paying workers equally regardless of the individual performance of each worker. Sticking with his system

[18] Price, "One Best Way," 39.

[19] See Yost, *Frank and Lillian Gilbreth*, 206.

[20] See Frank B. Gilbreth and L. M. Gilbreth, *Applied Motion Study: A Collection of Papers on the Efficient Method to Industrial Preparedness* (New York: Sturgis & Walton Company, 1917), 55.

[21] Price, "One Best Way," 84–89.

[22] As a former union member, Gilbreth was aware of the influence of trade unions and used it for his own purposes, by systematically playing the union members he preferred off against unorganized workers. See Gilbreth, *Field System*, 23.

would have acutely endangered the construction of building and led to high con-
tractual penalties for his company.[23]

Already during the first crisis of his construction business in the year 1907,
Gilbreth began preparing the ground for publicizing his system of administering
and directing business. He published a summary of his methods for the construction industry in 1908 under the title *The Field System*.[24] This represented
a detailed description of his systematic approach to construction. This was an
unusual step insofar as it represented a revelation of his own business secrets to
potential competitors. Copies of the book that circulated within his company
before its publication, in order to convey the system to his foremen and project
managers, were protected by Gilbreth through a range of mechanisms:

> Only a limited number of copies of the volume [*Field System*] were in exist-
> ence, each being numbered, and the possessor of each being accountable for
> its return even to the extent of being bonded in a small sum to cover its loss.
> Notwithstanding such precautions, unscrupulous competitors sought in many
> ways to obtain the information contained in this volume. Office boys were
> bribed, certain pages were photographed, and discharged superintendents
> in one or two instances carried the book with them. However, its publication
> makes such attempts no longer necessary, and shows a most broad-minded and
> generous spirit on the part of the contractor as well.[25]

Field System exclusively treated the construction business, but it also marked
Gilbreth's conclusive departure from this area. With the publication of his
system, he took the first step away from his previous status as a direct participant
in the business processes of the construction industry.

His new position was that of a publicly available corporate consultant, whose
business model rested on the preparation and sale of expertise in industrial and
commercial businesses. The appearance of *Field System* was thus not so much an
open-minded, generous gesture toward Gilbreth's competitors in the construction industry, and more the beginning of an unparalleled image and marketing
campaign. It allowed Gilbreth to become the emblem of the modern business
and management consulting industry within barely five years.

Field System was not a standard academic publication but a form of "indirect advertising." Gilbreth deliberately integrated into the book "a few pages of

---

[23]   Due to strikes, Gilbreth had to abandon his system in 1908 in Gardner, Massachusetts, and in 1911
in Glen Fall, New York, and replace the bonus award system with a unified wage system. See Price, "Frank
and Lillian Gilbreth and the Motion Study Controversy: 1907–1930," in *A Mental Revolution: Scientific
Management Since Taylor*, ed. Daniel Nelson (Columbus: Ohio State University Press, 1992), 59.

[24]   See Gilbreth, *Field System*. With "Office System" and "Concrete System," further publications
appeared that applied his management philosophy to office work and concrete construction.

[25]   Gilbreth, *Field System*, 5.

advertisements [. . .] to show that the book is not advertising."[26] In fact, advertising his new business model was the only purpose that this publication was intended to fulfill. In this sense, *Field System* is a prototype for all of Gilbreth's later publications, which were less oriented toward furnishing evidence for a scientifically exact approach toward waste elimination. Instead, these publications were supposed to promote the model of media-supported corporate consulting and form the basis for attracting clients.

Media Brand Strategies in the Construction Industry

During Gilbreth's time in the construction industry, media like film and photography were still very remote from the central role that they would later play in the method he developed. Until his new beginning as a corporate consultant, they only played a secondary role in the systematic guidance and control system he had developed. It is true that, in 1908 and 1911, he had already instated a "betterman room" in the Glen Fall and Gardner construction projects, in which he paid workers to be filmed on the job. But these were merely experiments, which were not designed to be directly implemented on building sites. It was only in 1912 that he used filming techniques in a systematically applied way, for the New England Butt Company in Providence, Rhode Island, for his first major contract as a corporate consultant.[27]

Field System made mention only of photography and only for its potential to save time and expense through the documentation of construction progress or the absence of building materials. That the use of photographic cameras was still not self-evident and required a precise explanation can be seen in the section of several pages length that gave a detailed description of problematic camera angles and advice on avoiding over- or underexposed images.[28] Here already, as with his later filmed motion studies, Gilbreth was aware of the specific potential of media visualizations. Alongside technical-functional details, the references to photography also contained an early form of corporate branding policy.

On all the photos, Gilbreth's name (which was also the name of his company) was visible. For this purpose, he included specially made signs, which were photographed together with the actual object depicted (Fig. 39).[29]

[26] Frank B. Gilbreth, Diary, 1909, vol. 5, 45, Frank and Lillian Gilbreth Papers, SPCOLL, Purdue University Libraries, AS/3.
[27] See Price, "Frank and Lillian Gilbreth and the Motion Study Controversy: 1907–1930," 61.
[28] Gilbreth, *Field System*, 37–41.
[29] If the name "Gilbreth" could not be seen on the photographs, it was retroactively added to them. This was the case, for example, when Georg Schlesinger required slides for use in training engineers in Germany. See Lindstrom, "Science and Management," 181.

Figure 39 The Gilbreth brand. An example of consistent company branding from the year 1915 in the depiction of an ergonomically adjustable chair.

> It being desirable that the sign "*Frank B. Gilbreth*" appear on all photographs, it will be necessary for every job to be provided with a portable sign which can be moved from place to place when taking photographs.[30]

The effects of this persistent strategy can still be seen today: Frank B. Gilbreth is the only construction company owner whose name can be identified in the photographs of the reconstruction of San Francisco exhibited in the city's Cable Car Museum.

Gilbreth went further in this direction by exposing his name onto the negatives in advance, so that it would be automatically included on all the positive prints, such as the contractually distributed glass slides. This had the advantage that the name could no longer be later removed.[31] But aside from

[30] Gilbreth, *Field System*, 38.
[31] See F. B. Gilbreth, letter to L. M. Gilbreth, September 21, 1914, Gilbreth LOM, SPCOLL, Purdue University Libraries, NF 92/813-5.

this usage of photographic technology, *Field System* was chiefly an approach that sought to replace oral communication forms and practices through their written equivalents. Gilbreth was thus initially a conventional representative of "systematic management," which Joseph Litterer characterized in the following terms: "Systematic management was basically concerned with making sure that the work which had to be done would be accomplished on time, and with as little duplication of effort or confusion as possible."[32] And the simplest path to reach this was, as it was put in point two of the "general outlines" of *Field System*: "TO AVOID REPEATING ORALLY [caps in the original], by putting in writing, all those instructions from which there are no exceptions."[33] Gilbreth's methodology was coterminous with the central approach of "systematic management," the introduction of the "written record."[34] The high relevance of the written mode, in contrast to its media-assisted motion studies were not only restricted to the construction industry, but was also the distinctive hallmark of his activities as a corporate consultant. All the same, Gilbreth is even today considered to be the outstanding representative of a film and media-assisted variant of management, although he had only implemented these techniques into his practice to a limited extent. Edna Yost commented somewhat confusedly on this inapt description in her detailed study of Frank and Lillian Gilbreth. "Contrary to the belief of some, Gilbreth did not use micromotion methods unless they were really needed."[35] At bottom, Gilbreth was, aside from his use of filmed motion studies, an orthodox representative of "systematic management," which during his lifetime was also designated in modified form as *Scientific Management* or *Taylorism*.

Frank B. Gilbreth: Corporate Consultant

The Emergence of the Consulting Industry

After Frank B. Gilbreth had left the construction industry and sought a new beginning as a corporate consultant, "the world's newest profession"[36] was still in its early days. Around the turn of the century, pioneers like Arthur D. Little and Harrington Emerson founded the first institutionalized consulting firms. This development accelerated in the 1910s as a wave of new corporate consultancies

[32] Litterer, *Systematic Management*, 476.
[33] Gilbreth, *Field System*, 13.
[34] Yates, *Control Through Communication*.
[35] Yost, *Frank and Lillian Gilbreth: Partners for Life*, 260.
[36] McKenna, *The World's Newest Profession*.

was formed.[37] In the consulting industry, a brisk competition thus arose among smaller, owner-operated consulting offices, which included Gilbreth himself. The industry preferred to have recourse, here, to individually profiled and fa-mous personalities such as Frederick W. Taylor, Henry L. Gantt, and Harrington Emerson. To a great extent, corporate consulting was, due to the minimal experi-ence in collaboration within this still young industry, a matter of trust. Specialist competency was closely tied with individual, often prominent figures. This was also due to the fact that the method of Scientific Management was not a con-solidated system.[38] Rather, it incorporated diverse attempts at organization and rationalization, which often boast a more experimental than stringent, repro-ducible character. There were neither binding standards as to what corporate consulting nor was there a structural-formal network of those working in this area. As a consequence, there is no homogeneous methodological canon on the shape that consulting of companies should take.

This contingent condition began to change in the 1910s.[39] Something that we can characterize as the emergence of the industry took place. In 1910, the existence of corporate consultancies, in the framework of the so-called Eastern Rates Cases, became known to a broader public. This consisted of a legal con-flict between US railway and shipping companies about the appropriate level of freight tariffs. The railway companies insisted on a rise in tariffs, which they justified with a necessary raise in wages, while the shipping companies rejected this justification for higher prices. As a result, under the aegis of the Interstate Commerce Commission, an investigation was held into the rectitude of the dif-ferent demands, which consisted of a series of public hearings. In these hearings, Louis D. Brandeis, the chief advocate for the shipping companies, argued for a suggestion that could apparently accommodate all interests. Through the intro-duction of a system with the label "Scientific Management," it was possible to raise the salaries of employees while also reducing operating costs. The proposal was taken on by the Interstate Commerce Commission and discussed in a "cross-examination hearing."[40] As witnesses, the most high-profile corporate consult-ants at the time, such as Harrington Emerson, were invited.

Scientific Management itself was not a specialized system, but a collective term that strategically brought together existing methods for rationalization

---

[37] Canback, "The Logic of Management Consulting," 3–11.

[38] Certainly, trust is also associated with individual people in the contemporary consulting in-dustry. Nonetheless, this trust has, through the professionalization of the industry, shifted to the individual firms and their representatives. Hence, the choice to select a consulting firm McKinsey & Company or the Boston Consulting Group was also the choice to opt for a specific consulting philosophy.

[39] Canback, "The Logic of Management Consulting," 3–11.

[40] Horace B. Drury, *Scientific Management: A History and Criticism* (New York: Columbia University, 1915), 18.

and increasing efficiency. It was only on the evening before the first hearing that the term arose, in a convivial meeting of the leading engineering consultants in Henry L. Gantt's New York apartment. Along with the representative of the shipping companies, Louis D. Brandeis, Frank B. Gilbreth was among those present. After a lively discussion, they settled on the term "Scientific Management," not so much due to the actual meaning of the word, since the methods for increasing efficiency among those present were too different, but due to the lack of alternatives. It represented the lowest common denominator, one which could gather different consulting approaches under amorphous terminology.

In retrospect, the invention of this term was a one-off serendipity for the consulting industry. It was thus that, for the first time, Scientific Management became anchored as a synonym for a process of regulated industrial rationalization among the American public. If, earlier, these approaches were known to a small, specialized public, they were perceived by the broader public through the considerable press attention received by the hearings. The legal decision over wage rises and freight tariffs had far-reaching consequences; it reached them through the basic question concerning the legitimate level of American wages as a whole. The hearings thus became a nationwide event and developed into a heated clash over the value of human work. We should also add that the proposal for the introduction of scientific business management played no de facto role in the subsequent conclusion of the hearings. The rise in freight tariffs demanded was disallowed, because in the past, excessive dividend payouts to the shareholders of railway companies had been made.[41] But there was no let-up to the development of the consulting industry. There followed the establishment of the first associations of "efficiency consultants." In 1912, Harrington Emerson founded the New York Efficiency Society.[42] Already two years earlier, the Taylor Society had been inaugurated, in which Gilbreth was a major participant,[43] and which itself pursued the promotion of Scientific Management. The increasing networking of these actors and the growing renown and acceptance of their approaches led, in the following years, to the nationwide introduction of courses on scientific business management in American universities and, particularly, in the newly established business schools.[44]

Under the label of Scientific Management, numerous different consulting models and philosophies were collected. Although they were all drawn together under the rubric of "scientific," the existing competition between the individual corporate consultants accounted for the development of distinct consulting

---

[41] Ibid., 21.
[42] Ibid., 19.
[43] Nelson, "Scientific Management, Systematic Management, and Labor, 1880–1915," 479–500.
[44] See n40 in the Introduction.

models. This resulted in a differentiation of the methods in which everyone solicited customers with their own particularly original and credible system of corporate consulting. Corporate consultants developed their methods into distinguishing features that helped differentiate them from the competition. These could be technical innovation, patented techniques, or special consulting philosophies.

Early Models of Hybrid Consulting Knowledge

One of the most successful actors in the rising consulting industry was Harrington Emerson. He paradigmatically stood for the structures required in this industry. In order to be successful, it was necessary to develop an unmistakable consulting philosophy. This formed the basis for a concomitant service product: a concrete consulting model that could be marketed and sold. Emerson was not only an exemplar of the then developing structures of consulting knowledge, but also of the increasing influence which corporate consulting exerted in the business world. In the 1910s, there was hardly a single major business that did without the services of external corporate consultants.

Much like Frank B. Gilbreth, Emerson was not educated as an engineer and could look back on a diverse professional curriculum vitae. He was initially employed as a university professor in Nebraska and then in a real estate business. He later worked as a troubleshooter for the Union Pacific and Burlington & Missouri railroads. During the gold rush, he managed a lucrative ferry service between Seattle and Alaska. After he held a leading position in a glass factory for two years, he became self-employed at the beginning of the 1900s and founded the consulting firm Shop Betterment. Between 1907 and 1910, his firm advised more than 200 companies and brought in revenue of $25 million. In terms of revenue and size, his consultancy firm was one of the era's most successful. In the 1920s, between forty and fifty consultants worked for his outfit.[45]

As a pioneer of this branch, he recognized that special branding, developing an unmistakable consulting philosophy, was central to corporate consulting. He called his method "efficiency engineering,"[46] which later established itself as a synonym for the whole consulting industry. Under this label, Emerson developed a particular form and method of management consulting. This was based less on genuine engineering science methods than on a mix of different influences. For Emerson, the major prototypes of his consulting model were the organic cycles of nature. These cycles, which in his view were the most efficient forms

---

[45] Drury, *Scientific Management*, 114.
[46] George, *The History of Management Thought*, 107.

of natural organization, were far removed from organizational forms devised by humans. He explicitly excluded, however, military models of organization from this verdict.[47] It is thus little surprise that his methodology initially rested on the adaptation of military structures and practices for business. As a particularly successful example, he repeatedly invoked the military strategies of the Prussian army. More specifically, the Prussian wars against France between 1866 and 1870, under the command of Helmuth Karl Bernhard von Moltke, served him as a prototype for effective industrial organization.[48] He reduced these different influences to twelve principles that described his approach to a successful industrial rationalization,[49] and in which he borrowed liberally from the principles of conducting war outlined by Carl von Clausewitz. The connection to natural cycles and the coupling of his ideas with successful military structures of the past generated the necessary self-evidence of his consulting model. At the same time, they functioned as the unique selling point of the service he offered. Whoever gave Emerson a commission for rationalizing their business received a distinctive and clearly defined consulting service, which consisted of elements of military history and the logic of organic-biological processes, with which they were also legitimized.

Apart from the public representation of his methods in analogies with the military and the cycles of nature, Emerson's approach differed little from that of other engineering consultants. Once he had received a consulting commission, he introduced written bookkeeping and systematized written processes on the factory floor. Like Frederick W. Taylor, Henry L. Gantt, and Frank B. Gilbreth, he followed the principle of "systematic management."

The branch of corporate consultants in the 1910s distinguished itself through a dual structure. On the one hand, every consulting company cultivated its own distinctive profile. Hence, Harrington Emerson championed the von Moltke Principle of military forms of organization and valor, Frederick W. Taylor advocated a scientific, systematic approach to business management, and Henry L. Gantt was known for implementing innovative charting techniques. On the other hand, each of the concretely applied tools and techniques often boasted only marginal differences with its competitors.

The biggest source of contracts for the consulting industry were major corporations whose organizational structures had become opaque due to a crisis of control, and which thus needed to be restructured. The day-to-day production processes, as well as the ill-defined communication structures in the businesses,

---

[47] See Gareth Morgan, *Images of Organization* (London: Sage, 1997), 15–16.
[48] Harrington Emerson, *Efficiency as a Basis for Operation and Wages* (New York: The Engineering Magazine Co., 1911), 49, 65–66, 96–97.
[49] Harrington Emerson, *The Twelve Principles of Efficiency* (New York: The Engineering Magazine Co., 1913).

had to be standardized or newly implemented. Here, in their concrete usage within enterprises, the different consulting philosophies were more than merely the external shell of a sales strategy. If a consultation model could be particularly well communicated, this helped in the implementation of the planned changes in the factory. A credible model was the prerequisite for new structures to actually be implemented on location. In the end, there was resistance to the proposed changes not only on the part of the unions and workers, but also among staff in middle management.

Gilbreth, Inc.: Media-Assisted Corporate Consulting

With his entry into the sphere of corporate consulting, Gilbreth also had to position himself within this system, if he wanted enduring success in the field. His starting conditions were thus not particularly favorable. Gilbreth was not among the inner circle of successful corporate consultants. He had no academic reputation and could only look back on a crisis-riddled career as a building contractor. Hence, from the beginning he lived under a particular pressure to raise the reputation and renown of his newly founded corporate consultancy. If Emerson's unique selling proposition was his consulting philosophy rooted in military organizational structures and biological explanatory models, Gilbreth focused on the ostensibly objective filmic techniques of analysis as a distinctive way to anchor his approach in the public's eye.

Gilbreth's media approach owed little to the need for using scientifically exact instruments. Rather, it was part of a campaign, which was aligned toward positioning the unique selling proposition of a media-assisted consulting technique within the industry (Fig. 40). The great advantage of his method was the direct visual evidence allied with the media method. If Emerson or Taylor had a comprehensive philosophy, which they revealed in extensive writings, Gilbreth was able to present the images and film footage produced in his analyses directly for public consumption. He did not have to elucidate an abstract system but could visualize his method and make it manifest with photography and film. With that, he combined the activity of the corporate consultant with the rising medium of film and the contemporary fascination for this new media technology. A new form of management supplemented itself through new forms of media perception.

Whereas Emerson still had recourse to categorical thinking in *militaristic* and *naturalistic* terms, Gilbreth went past the limits of this mode of thinking. The actual *objects* of management gained, in the truest sense of the word, center stage, by placing them in the focus of his media techniques. His approach represented a pragmatic, object-centered form of problem solving. For this it was necessary

Figure 40 "This is a cyclegraph." Media representation as an end in itself; visual evidence and data generation as inseparable components of Gilbreth's media-based corporate consulting.

to visualize segments of the labor and production process, and open them up to further analysis. Categorical thinking was replaced by process-oriented optimization thinking, which no longer could be affixed to the dispositions of human subjects, as Taylor did with reference to the laziness of workers.[50] For Gilbreth, the only thing that counted was the concrete proposal for improvement, which could be represented with the media-hardened surface of his consulting style. The actual activity of managing was, with the help of media techniques, justified on its own terms. By analytically fragmenting production processes and then reunifying them as a process consisting of distinct individual components, Gilbreth pursued an approach that in its fundamental principles was in accord with the forms of corporate consulting that have been widespread up to the present day. His approach was distinguished by the fact that data only gained in relevance if it was utilized for improvements.[51] This concerned not only the practical implementation on the factory floor but was already addressed in the acquisition of contracts. His method could not only be implemented; it could also be simply communicated in advance. The concentration on visual forms, such as film, helped him to reduce a complex approach to an easily comprehensible concept of film-aided consulting.

---

[50] Taylor, *The Principles of Scientific Management*, 19.
[51] This did not include the amorphous concept of laziness, which was unable to be investigated. Only fatigue as a physiological condition could be pragmatically approached.

Laboratory Knowledge Versus Experiential Knowledge

The greatest difference with Frederick W. Taylor and other advocates of Scientific Management consisted of its particular consideration for the ergonomic and psychic dispositions of the work process. His early successes as a building contractor not only rested on new technical instruments and the principle of the division of labor. He also began to improve the bricklaying labor process *itself*. Additionally, he modified conventional motion processes in such a way that they were both faster and less straining for the workers to carry out. With this method ("motion studies"), he analytically fragmented movement in individual micro-segments of motion, in order to recombine them again through the viewpoint of their ergonomic aspects. The goal of motion studies was to eliminate *unnecessary* movements of a work process and generate from a *convoluted* movement a simplified and thus more efficient movement. He had already developed the principle of motion studies during his time as a building contractor, even though he was not yet using filming techniques. In the construction industry, he used "rough investigation methods"[52] of observation and photographic snapshots.[53]

This compartmentalized and laboriously detailed approach competed against Taylorism, which had become popular in corporate circles at the time. Orthodox Taylorism, as a concept of corporate consulting, was also successful because, with its approach, it seemed to speak to the diffuse feeling of every factory owner that all workers were lazy and work-shy as soon as the boss turned his back on them. Correspondingly, raising efficiency was only a question of heightening discipline and control over the workers. These pithy demands for control met with open ears among potential customers in industry. Frank and Lillian Gilbreth, by contrast (and not least due to Lillian's background in industrial psychology), had a thoroughly different image of the work process, since it incorporated ideas about ergonomic and psychological dispositions. The problem arose as to how this complex model could best coexist with the evident demand for discipline and control. A distinctive depiction of his model appeared to promise little success, since research into labor psychology was only in its earliest phases. From this side, the Gilbreths could only hope for a modicum of understanding. Added to this as a complicating factor was the fact that demands for ergonomic improvements always amounted to an implicit critique of predetermined structures of workplaces on the factory floor. Workplace layout was the responsibility of factory management. The Gilbreths' approach thus always demanded a certain amount of self-reflection among the factory managers themselves. Due to this,

---

[52] Kaminsky, *Arbeitsablauf- und Bewegungsstudien*, 13.

[53] Even without filmic recording possibilities, he aimed for enormous increases in bricklaying productivity. The original seventeen different motion forms which a bricklayer carried out were reduced through the transformation of the motion process and the workplace to only four different forms of movement. See Gilbreth, *Motion Study*, 88–89.

they required a consulting model that promised more than simply applying the largely untested findings of psychology and physiology to a factory setting. They also required arguments with which they generated evidence and could convince dubious corporate managers of their method.

The core of Gilbreth's success in acquiring contracts lay in the utilization of visual media techniques and their imaginary worlds. On the one hand, Gilbreth carried out concrete investigations on raising efficiency in business, but on the other hand, they were also part of a public marketing campaign (Fig. 41). This had the goal of scientifically justifying his consulting method, as well as representing it in a particularly practically oriented fashion. In this way, he sought to demarcate himself from his competitors in the consulting industry. Indicative of this were the filmic techniques and various methods of data visualization that Gilbreth deployed. This ensemble of different visualization techniques was grouped around his own unique selling proposition: *lab-based consulting* (Fig. 42). With this, he combined the promises of mechanical media objectivity with the spatial form of the laboratory, in which he carried out motion studies.

The consulting service that Gilbreth offered his customers was a motion analysis laboratory equipped with the latest available media technology. He was able,

Figure 41 "The man with the camera." Frank B Gilbreth poses for the film camera in front of a motion study laboratory, his unique selling proposition for the efficient, scientific rationalization of industry.

Figure 42 Lab-based consulting. The clients also enjoyed visiting the film set in the motion study laboratory. New media technologies and the direct experience of the motion studies produced film-based consulting's atmosphere of evidence-based scientificity.

as the previous chapter outlined, to instrumentalize the medialization drive taking place in business for his own purposes. He seized the widespread culture of graphic visualizations and integrated it into his approach.[54] The consulting method he offered appeared to be equipped with the latest technology. Within the laboratory, the sought-after changes took the shape of experimental and analytic pathways. Because the laboratory was directly installed in the company, the suggestions for improvement that arose there were trialed in parallel with the factory under realistic conditions. Thus, pragmatic improvements arose which were based on the methodical precision of a laboratory study and the applicability of a realistic production situation.

Between 1912 and 1924, Frank and Lillian Gilbreth were able to attract a series of consulting contracts in the American steel, automotive, and packing industries for their company Gilbreth, Inc. These included, among others, Cluett Peabody, Pierce Arrow, U.S. Rubber, Eastman Kodak, Remington Typewriter Company, New England Butt Company, and Ball Brothers. Their field of activity

---

[54] On this, see the medialization drive, and the visual management media network aligned with it, as described in detail in Chapter 1 of this volume.

was, however, not restricted to the American market. They also maintained business relations with Georg Schlesinger, one of Germany's leading rationalization experts.[55] Through Schlesinger, contacts were established with two German corporations, Carl Zeiss Jena and the Berlin-based Auergesellschaft (predecessor to Osram). Indeed, it is in the acquisition of contracts in Germany that available archival documents allow detailed insight into how adroitly Gilbreth implemented media techniques as promotional and marketing instruments. For instance, Gilbreth could arouse great interest for his model while on an overseas trip as part of a delegation from the American Society of Mechanical Engineers (ASME), during a meeting with the Verein deutscher Ingenieure (Society of German Engineers, VDI), by promoting his method of the "One Best Way to Do Work" with the screening of a film. He thereby convinced Schlesinger, a keen advocate of the Taylor system in Germany, to provide him with a commission for rationalizing the Auergesellschaft.[56] This company was at the time the world's biggest business ever to be transformed following the principles of Scientific Management. At this time, Gilbreth still did not have any experiences in rationalization projects in Europe, and even in the United States he still had not successfully carried out a major rationalization project. The use of media functioned as a unique selling point that distinguished him from the other competitors present in the consulting industry. Whereas other consultants possessed many years of experience in the consulting business, Gilbreth replaced this through the self-evident nature of media images. He substituted experienced experts with experts from lab-based consulting (Fig. 43). The lack of experience did not appear problematic, since he only worked with scientifically exact data from the laboratory. The previous decision making based on experiential values no longer appeared appropriate for the times. Gilbreth conflated the laboratory space with the factory space into a fiction of total control. With his method, he suggested, it would now be possible to solve, through scientific precision, the problems of the companies affected by the crisis of control.

On the one hand, his approach was in a position to generate methodologically direct evidence, because the use of media and its representation in the public imagination were indistinguishable; on the other hand, the new apparatuses of media technology also promised a new, better, more scientific, more precise strategy.

As far as the representational potentialities of their own consulting models were concerned, Gilbreth's competitors largely restricted themselves to the

---

[55] See Georg Schlesinger, "Die Entwicklung der deutschen Organisationswissenschaft für industrielle Betriebe," *Werkstattstechnik* 17, no. 5 (1923): 152–54; Georg Schlesinger, "Brennende Probleme der Betriebsorganisation und ihre natürliche Lösung," *Werkstattstechnik* 18, no. 10 (1924): 269–72.

[56] See Price, "One Best Way," 238.

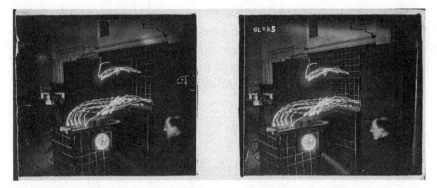

Figure 43 Media embellishment of nonmedia findings. Retroactively prepared stereochronocyclegraphs of the bricklaying technique developed by Gilbreth. He had devised this without any filmic motion studies.

possibilities offered by written publication. Gilbreth himself, meanwhile, had recourse to visualizations that, to say nothing of the fascination with images, were also embedded in contemporary aesthetic discourse. In art, this encompassed the shift, beginning in the early nineteenth century, from a perspectival aesthetic to an aesthetic of abstraction.[57] Objective representations were replaced by the "grid."[58] There arose collage techniques and with them a "metalanguage of the visual."[59] The new aesthetic no longer aimed for the simple representation of objects, but thematized the "representation of representation."[60] With cubism, at the latest, the "playful play of difference"[61] was established as the epistemological framework for reproducing the visual image. For Rancière, this aesthetic regime was characterized by the "blurring of the borders between the logic of facts and the logic of fiction."[62] The aesthetic difference between fact and fiction disappeared. The surface was converted from a representation of perspectival viewpoints determined by strict conventions to a grid: a surface that visually enabled evidence to be generated. This evidence followed the logic of the visual, which was precisely constituted through the blurred boundaries between fact and fiction. Visual discourse departed from the existing conventions of perception and became a form of pure, visual representation.

[57] See Florian Hoof, "Between Recognition and Abstraction: Early Vocational Training Film," in *The Image in Early Cinema: Form and Material*, ed. Scott Curtis, Philippe Gauthier, Tom Gunning, and Joshua Yumibe (Bloomington: Indiana University Press, 2018), 111–19.

[58] See Krauss, *The Originality of the Avant-Garde and Other Modernist Myths*, 8–22.

[59] Ibid., 37.

[60] Ibid., 37.

[61] Ibid., 35.

[62] Rancière, *The Politics of Aesthetics*, 36.

In parallel, Gilbreth began, five years after the first cubist paintings by Picasso and Braque, to produce his representations of abstract chronocyclegraphic curves and lines. Moreover, these representations form part of corporate visual culture, as was outlined in the previous chapter with the examples of Gantt charting, the harmonograph, and nomography. In this context, Gilbreth had recourse to his media network, consisting of filmic and graphic procedures, thereby gaining an advantage in the competition for consulting contracts.

Filmed Motion Studies

The core component of his laboratory motion studies was the cyclegraph, a film apparatus conceived specifically for this purpose. It served to register work processes and movements, so that the film sequences could be used for analysis. At the same time, the filmic procedures should replace the previously instated work inspectors, who as a rule used a stopwatch to ascertain the required duration of the work phases carried out. The subjective impression of the moment supported by time measurements should be replaced by the mechanical objectivity of filmic registration. With this, Gilbreth distinguished himself from the apparently omnipotent father of Scientific Management, Frederick W. Taylor, who relied on the manual registration of work phases through the "stopwatch men." Cyclegraphs recorded only the details and data necessary for motion studies. In the year 1912, he introduced the process for the first time in the framework of his consulting activity for the New England Butt Company and presented it that same year to the annual conference of the American Society of Mechanical Engineering.[63] Fundamentally, it consisted of a biometric recording apparatus, which captured work movements on a photographic plate or film. Gilbreth realized this in the following manner: "In order to depict the moving image in a schematically clear manner, we affix to the hand of the worker a small electric lightbulb, which plotted the movement as a bright line on the plate"[64] (Fig. 44).

The recording of light traces was carried out either through a long exposure on a photographic plate or through being filmed. In either case, however, the workplace had to be darkened, so that the light traces from the surroundings would be eliminated. The resulting studies (Fig. 45) showed a reduced level of information that was aimed at the rationalization of movement. Only the movements of the workers' extremities that needed to be improved could thus be seen in the

    [63] Gilbreth, "The Present State of the Art of Industrial Management, Gilbreth Discussion Contribution," Transactions of the American Society of Mechanical Engineering 34 (1912): 1224–26.
    [64] Colin Ross, "Das Wesen der wissenschaftlichen Betriebsführung," in Frank Gilbreth, Das ABC der wissenschaftlichen Betriebsführung, trans. and ed. Colin Ross (Berlin: Springer 1917), 5.

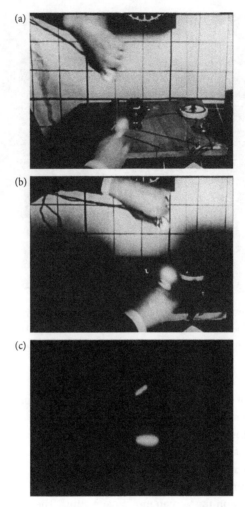

Figure 44 Demonstration of the principle of the cyclegraph with two light bulbs attached to the hands.

recorded footage. Everything else was masked out. On the level of knowledge, there was a "separation of movement from the body."[65] Pure movement flows could subsequently be subjected to processes of optimization. In order to be able to recognize the differences of various movement flows, the movements were only "measured [and] studied [by the] best of all workers."[66]

---

[65] Giedion, *Mechanization Takes Command*, 103.
[66] Gilbreth, *Das ABC der wissenschaftlichen Betriebsführung*, 56.

Figure 45 Cyclegraph of the experienced worker Bakoski. In the United States of the 1910s, the name could only be found in the resident's registry in Providence. The images thus must have come from the New England Butt Company, Providence, Rhode Island.

On the basis of this visual data, in the next phase the motion recordings were investigated and synthesized into a new motion sequence. The goal, here, was to generate the most fluid possible workflow. If, in Figure 46, the motion lines recorded were distinguished through jerky discharge movements and abrupt, sharp changes in direction, these movements, recognized as unfavorable, were replaced through more smooth-flowing motions (Fig. 47). This was supposed to reduce the burden on the human motion apparatus. The rounded curves of the new ergonomic movements capped the loading peaks and ensured an equitable workload for employees.

As a result, the work tempo could be increased without significantly raising the workload felt by staff. Gilbreth saw this as the royal path toward minimizing the appearance of fatigue among workers while also improving labor efficiency. After the failure of physiology's search for the cause of fatigue within the human body, it was clear that there was not something like a vaccine serum against the supposed disease of "fatigue." Attempts to stimulate workers through chemical substances could not be realized in the dangerous environment of the factory. Gilbreth found a pragmatic answer for examining the entire system of labor and transforming it, with the goal of minimizing fatigue. It was not through invasive approaches, like a vaccine serum or chemical substances, but through the

Figure 46 Cyclegraphic motion studies on the left, the conventional, crooked, nonoptimized motion process; on the right, the already optimized, rounded motion.

Figure 47 Cyclegraphic motion studies on the left, the conventional, crooked, nonoptimized motion process; on the right, the already optimized, rounded motion.

complete detection and control of the environment that cases of fatigue could be avoided. Fatigue would no longer be completely conquered, but located and tendentially minimized.

In the first motion studies in the construction industry, Gilbreth was still aware of the insufficiencies of conventional movements from his own experience as a bricklayer. With the cyclegraph, he now possessed a set of instruments with which he could systematically record, analyze, and subsequently synthesize totally different movements less known to him. The cyclegraph first created the problem of inefficiency by recording it and making it visible. At the same time, the visual recordings arising from this legitimized the intervention into business practices necessary for change.

If the cyclegraph could register the direction and forms of movements, its further development, the chronocyclegraph, was in a position to carry out a temporal synchronization of this movement:

> In the illuminated circle [of the cyclegraph], an interrupter is introduced, so that the light shines according to established intervals that are as small as possible. The moving image thus does not represent an uninterrupted line of light, but a line made out of points of light, from whose number the temporal duration of the movement can be immediately determined.[67]

With the chronocyclegraph, the evaluation of moving images not only found the direction and form of movements, but also the time necessary for consideration (Fig. 48). Individual motion segments, like changing direction or persevering in a given position, could be precisely tested for the necessary time. This allowed the corporate consultants to calculate alternative motion scenarios and compare their advantages and disadvantages.

The chronocyclegraph created its own sphere of labor analysis, which no longer referred to the practical verification of ideas and transformations on the factory floor. The system of chronocyclegraphy was a self-referential recording and calculation system. Sought-after improvements to the workflows were achieved, in that the data gained through media techniques were restricted and synthesized.

Knowledge Transfer Through Motion Awareness

If the optimal motion form, the so-called One Best Way, was to be found from the existing work practices through analysis and synthesis, the latter had to be adapted for the respective activities in the industry. In order to guarantee the

---

[67] Ross, "Das Wesen der wissenschaftlichen Betriebsführung," 4.

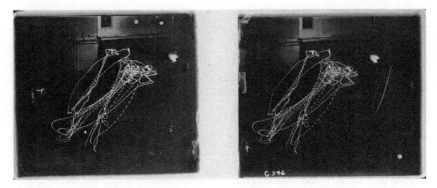

Figure 48 Stereoscopic image of a chronocyclegraph.

necessary knowledge transfer in industry, Gilbreth initially relied on media visualizations in the most varied forms. Instructive, evidence-generating images were required because Gilbreth, like the entire movement of Scientific Management, was faced with the specific challenge of implementing a new orientation of business activity against a still existing order of knowledge in the company. Due to Gilbreth's specific method, this possessed a particular relevance, but it was also a general problem of Scientific Management. On the one hand, there was the scientific recognition of the best method:

> This one best method and best implement can only be discovered or developed through a scientific study and analysis of all of the methods and implements in use, together with accurate, minute, motion and time study. This involves the gradual substitution of science for rule of thumb throughout the mechanic arts.[68]

On the other hand, a substitution of the standard rule of thumb practices had to be carried out. Because the differences between the new and the old methods appeared minimal, the improvements were hard to communicate. This also had to do with the fact that Scientific Management sought to strictly separate mental from manual work. The employer did not need to understand the logic behind Taylor's viewpoint (which Gilbreth shared). The global context, the *system*, was from this perspective not relevant for the workers, who only had to carry out reduced movements. This disposition led to a situation where the new principles developed through motion studies "appear to be so self-evident that many men think it almost childish to state them."[69]

[68] Taylor, *The Principles of Scientific Management*, 25.
[69] Ibid., 13.

Figure 49 Spatial representation of three-dimensional wire model through stereography.

As such, various visualization techniques had the task of highlighting the meaningfulness of the new doctrine on motion, in order to facilitate the implementation of new managerial methods. Gilbreth's method was distinct from orthodox Taylorism, which introduced labor instruction cards, a written form of work training. They contained a short description of the work phases that needed to be carried out, the quantity of the parts that needed to be assembled, and the anticipated time frame for this. However, they were not conceived for improving a work phase, but for controlling the worker. In contrast to this, Gilbreth began to implement media-assisted staff lessons. The labor instruction cards were an integral component of production control, in order to react to deviations from the predetermined work phases. Gilbreth's visualizations were supposed to offer the employees an aid for learning new work processes or improving existing ones. In this he was significantly influenced by Maria Montessori's pedagogical concept, which was predicated on the idea that knowledge transfers could be optimally enabled through illustrative models. Gilbreth followed this concept and translated it into his reduced motion footage with three-dimensional wire models (Fig. 49).[70]

Geometric deductions, arranged in a stylized system of coordinates, served to make the workers "motion minded."[71] "Thus the workman can be taught which of his gestures are right and which are wrong."[72] After all, "the light curves and the wire models reveal the motion in full plasticity. Motion acquires a form of its own and a life of its own."[73]

---

[70] For more details on the connection between Gilbreth and Montessori, see Chapter 4 of this volume, "Media and Montessori: Senses—Nerves—Motoricity."

[71] Giedion, *Mechanization Takes Command*, 103–104; see also L. Gilbreth and Gilbreth, *Applied Motion Studies*.

[72] Ibid., 103.

[73] Ibid., 104.

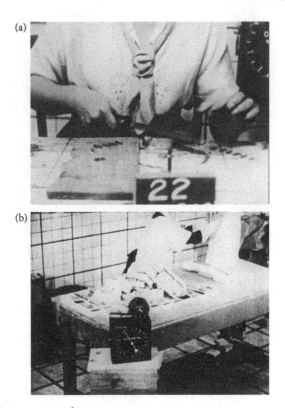

Figure 50 Motion-centered image extract.

Apart from wire models, Gilbreth also introduced work study films. He visualized the advantages of the new, transformed motion processes with respect to the original motion process. The work study films were distinguished by the fact that the camera perspective in most examples was static and focused on movement. The camera field only captured that part of the labor process required for carrying out motion studies (Fig. 50). Everything else lay outside the camera's visual field. Background and work space were arranged as a system of coordinates with a square, rigidly defined frame, in order to draw conclusions on the length and position of the movements. This system of motion registration could also be integrated within the camera lens (Fig. 51). The film stock used here was already pre-exposed with the desired grid structure before any footage was taken.

The challenge of precision in the visual surface was supplemented on the temporal level with the Gilbreth Clock, which could "measure the millionth fraction of an hour with absolute precision. This clock is [. . .] consistently included, alongside, for the purpose of controlling it, a normal clock."[74] Due to the

[74] Ross, "Das Wesen der wissenschaftlichen Betriebsführung," 4.

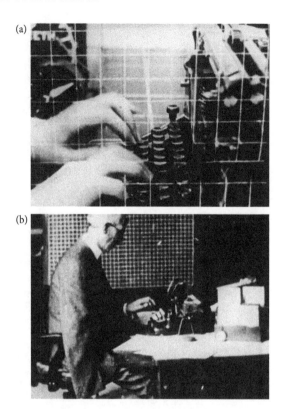

Figure 51 Gridding in front of and behind the camera as a visualization strategy.

imprecision of the recording operator in the activation of the recording device's crank, one should "only in emergency cases assume that 16 images reproduce the events of a full second." More exact results corresponding to the idea of a scientific "film measurement technique," were "achieved through including the measurement clock in the photograph."[75]

Alongside the technical prerequisites for a clear and exact geometrically comprehensible image, there were also operationalizations that could be recognized with respect to the objects under examination. For the work study films, only the best and most skilled workers were sought out. This was to guarantee that only "ideal" movements were recorded, although the film material was thought of as visual material for less skillful workers.

Apart from the purposes of motion recording and analysis, the films were also supposed to be deployed as educational devices. In this framework, Gilbreth

[75] Arthur Lassally, *Bild und Film im Dienst der Technik: 2. Teil: Betriebskinematographie* (Halle: Verlag Wilhelm Knapp, 1919), 12–13.

supplemented the aforementioned filmic techniques of scientific precision with "cinema techniques [. . .] including progressions from distant shots to close-ups."[76] With that, he wanted to convince the workers of the changes on the factory floor that, from his viewpoint, were required, and give them the instructions necessary for it.

The equally applied personal education of individual workers could not be extended to the staff as a whole. Film screenings offered, in this context, a more economic way to simultaneously educate a greater number of employees. As screening devices, he set up projectors, like the Kinox I and later the Kinox II from the Ernemann firm.[77] These projectors were relatively faint, but they were small, affordable, and easy to transport. The main reason for this film technology, however, was the projector lamps built into them. They were operated at only 6 volts and correspondingly boasted a modest generation of heat. This allowed interventions into the film's unspooling, which with larger and more light-intensive projectors unavoidably led to the self-combustion of the film stock. It thus became possible to spontaneously pause a film, using it as a quasi-photographic still image, or rewind important scenes several times over, or even run it in slow motion.[78] For this, Gilbreth partly made recourse to high-speed cameras. The films were to be screened in factories as part of an educational offensive and paused at important moments, repeated, and discussed in detail by the labor engineers, who also functioned as the film projectionists. If the workers had any questions, they could then be answered and discussed with the aid of the relevant film material.

While Gilbreth had settled on the medium of film, he also fundamentally changed the technology for his own purposes. By introducing fast-forward and rewind as a constitutive feature of the work study film, he broke with a media technology in the sense that it represented the cinematic *dispositif*. It was not continuous narration that formed the focus for him, but the fragmentation of filmic information in discrete units. Film was used by Gilbreth as the bearer of a data stream, to which one could have recourse at any moment with the aid of the film transport. In this usage, the aspects of a continuous flux of images connected with film were placed in the background. The use of work study films more closely resembled the graphs emerging at this time and the use of visualization

[76] Anne G. Shaw, *The Purpose and Practice of Motion Study* (Manchester: Columbine Press, 1960), 101.

[77] See F. B. Gilbreth, letter to L. M. Gilbreth, May 4, 1914, and May 6, 1914, Gilbreth LOM, SPCOLL, Purdue University Libraries, NF 91/813-6; Peter Göllner, *Ernemann Camera: Die Geschichte des Dresdner Photo-Kino-Werks* (Hückelhoven: Wittig, 1995), 244.

[78] "Technical War Films and Vocational Training," lecture manuscript, F. B. Gilbreth American Society of Mechanical Engineers Meeting, June 4–7, 1918, Gilbreth LOM, SPCOLL, Purdue University Libraries, NF 126/887.

Figure 52 Frank B Gilbreth, sitting behind the film projector, led a film-based group training session: "Executives and workmen's theatre for viewing and criticizing micromotion films and simultaneous motion cycle charts of best workers demonstrating the One Best Way to do work."

models.[79] In this sense, it was a form of the filmically animated graphic method and, with it, the medialization drive and media network belonging to it, as discussed in the previous chapters. Constitutive for the functionality of film-based worker education was the interruption of the film transport. It was only in this way that film was suitable as a graphic representation technique for industrial education purposes. Much like in individual education, it was also possible for the observing work instructors, during the screening of films for entire departments, to go into individual details through fast-forwarding or rewinding. Nonetheless, the size of the educational group was limited. As can be seen in Figure 52, even at a short projection distance, the film had to be protected from disruptive light dispersal by a box, in order to receive a clear image. The faintness of the projectors did not allow for greater projection distances.

With this coherent technique of media-assisted corporate consulting, as discussed earlier, there was nonetheless a problem: it was almost never applied in practice. In particular, the potential of the education of workers with media was in many cases not realized and in many cases, media techniques made no inroads

---

[79] See, for instance, "AWF-Getriebefilme: Vollständiges Verzeichnis der Trickfilme," *AWF-Mitteilungen* (1927), 250–51.

Figure 53 Work study analysis with an Ernemann Kinox projector, made by middle management at the Auergesellschaft in Berlin on April 20, 1915.

among the workers on the factory floor. The film screenings, actually previewed for the corporate education of employees, were initially introduced for educating management. There, in the framework of presentations accompanying the films, they were directed at upper management, in order to familiarize them with the systems and implementation of new management models. Likewise, Gilbreth focused his use of different visualization techniques in the acquisition of contracts. In the framework of consultancy commissions, such as that with the Auergesellschaft, they served to legitimate his own approach with his clients, thereby preventing a premature abrogation of the consulting commission.[80] The epistemological relevance of his media techniques thus primarily concerned the elapsing production process of modern industrial and commercial management. As an instrument of worker education and discipline, film was, however, very seldom utilized. What Gilbreth sketched out in his publications was above all a program, an ideal-typical model for the corporate knowledge transfer

---

[80] A detailed discussion of these circumstances is given in Chapter 5 of this volume, "Failed Consulting in Berlin: Auergesellschaft."

through the education of employees. It was a model, nonetheless, that as a rule failed to fulfil its promise. Film was therefore, for Gilbreth, not an instrument of discipline, but part of his activity as a corporate consultant and the consulting knowledge connected with it.

Branding of Media-Assisted Corporate Consulting

The film and media apparatuses developed by Gilbreth were doubtless suited for motion analysis and worker education. The more important addressees of his media network were, however, not the simple company employees, but his potential customers: company owners, managers, and the supervisory boards of shareholding societies. Gilbreth's media usage thus always proceeded on two levels. On the one hand, the media apparatuses and images were instruments of labor rationalization. On the other hand, they were a visible part of his public marketing campaign. The same film material could be used for the purposes of education and analysis, as well as being suitable for promoting his model of corporate consulting. With this, Gilbreth was able to quickly establish himself as a successful corporate consultant.

Media-Mechanical Objectivity

From the beginning, Frederick W. Taylor, who was at this time the most successful advocate of systematic industrial rationalization, showed great interest in Gilbreth's method. Although Gilbreth did not possess a particularly good reputation, since his very pragmatic approach was not always in accord with the customs of academic methodology, Taylor worked together with him.[81] Taylor had already published his system of Scientific Management as early as 1903,[82] but he lacked a compelling case proving that his system would also be enduringly successful in practice. In this sense, the barely fifteen years of experience that Gilbreth could boast of in the construction industry was one of the most impressive proofs of the superiority of Taylorism, or the systematic, Scientific Management. For this is how Taylor understood Gilbreth's approach. Between their methods, there were, alongside several commonalities, just as many serious

---

[81] Gilbreth had, among other things, become involved in a legal dispute with the publisher McGraw-Hill, whose corporate headquarters he had built when still a running a construction company. The charged nature of this legal dispute consisted in the fact that McGraw-Hill was at this time one of the most influential and important publishers specializing in business publications and managerial literature.

[82] Taylor, "Shop Management."

differences.[83] Their close early collaboration primarily represented a marriage of convenience.[84] Taylor needed a persuasive example for the practical suitability of Scientific Management, and Gilbreth sought recognition in the field of corporate consulting. Gilbreth had the best practice example of Scientific Management, while Taylor had the connections and networks that Gilbreth needed for his entry into the field of consulting. It was for this reason, too, that Gilbreth positioned himself at the beginning of his time as a consultant as a supporter of Taylorism, but less out of conviction than due to the dominant structures in the consulting industry. It was simply impossible for Gilbreth to establish his own method in the area without Taylor's support.

After Gilbreth gained his first successes as a corporate consultant, he began to criticize Taylor's time studies as not precise enough and thus unscientific. Whereas Taylor's method rested on the stopwatch as an instrument for measuring time, and the observational talents of the work inspectors, Gilbreth argued that only the laboratory situation and the objective recording undertaken with film sufficed for a scientific standard.

> The element of a movement, sometimes encompassing a time of less than a thousandth of a minute and thus barely visible to the eye, can not be perceived by an observer, even if he is equipped with an extremely rapid reaction time and the best stop-watch in the world.[85]

Gilbreth expressed himself more clearly in 1920 with respect to a lecture at the Taylor Society in the United States, in which he postulated that, while the stopwatch may well have been the most precise technique at the time of its introduction in 1903, the situation had changed with technical progress:

> Today, the stop-watch, in contrast to a [filmic] technique, which both measures and records the existing movements and the surrounding relations, should be considered as substandard [. . .] since it is not the best technique available for recording and preservation.[86]

---

[83] See Philipp Sarasin, "Die Rationalisierung des Körpers: Über 'Scientific Management' und 'biologische Rationalisierung,'" in Geschichtswissenschaft und Diskuranalyse, ed. Philipp Sarasin (Frankfurt am Main: Suhrkamp, 2003), 61–99.

[84] This was in no way a teacher–pupil relationship, as von Herrmann erroneously presents it. See Christian von Herrmann, "Pensum—Spur—Code: Register der Arbeitswissenschaft bei Taylor, Gilbreth und Bernstein," in Anthropologie der Arbeit, ed. Ulrich Bröckling and Eva Horn (Tübingen: Narr, 2002), 197–98.

[85] Irene Witte, Kritik des Zeitstudienverfahrens: Eine Untersuchung der Ursachen, die zu einem Mißerfolg des Zeitstudiums führen (Berlin: Springer, 1921), 25.

[86] F. Gilbreth lecture, cited in Witte, Kritik des Zeitstudienverfahrens, 26.

Discrediting the stopwatch technique as unscientific due to its imprecision was of a purely strategic nature. Gilbreth himself in no way carried out his work studies exclusively in the laboratory. He too used normal observation studies with a stopwatch. Many of his films and chronocyclegraphs were produced after the conclusion of the respective work study.[87] They were only manufactured for the purposes of their public image and in order to preserve the illusion of scientific precision. But he did not justified the scientific nature of his method by soley stressing the contrast between the stopwatch and film. Film was not recognized as a scientific instrument per se. Finally, entertainment cinema was established at the beginning of the twentieth century, which at the latest through the cinema reform movements and the concomitant controversies over moral standards concerning film was extremely controversial.[88] Consequently, Gilbreth coupled the film with the controlled environment of the laboratory, that turned film into a scientifically relevant, objective recording apparatus. For this, Gilbreth fabricated a series of filmic and photographic recordings, which were supposed to demonstrate the superiority of the coupling of film and the laboratory.

The stills stemming from a motion study film, as seen in Figure 54, show a typist in a Micro-Motion Analysis Laboratory. Even with this footage, its scientific-analytic aptness can be brought into question. The slightly askew film axis corresponded to the attempt to assemble a representative, totalizing image of the situation. For the geometrical-relational classifiability of the motion sequences, the 90-degree angle was certainly a must.[89]

Alongside the representative motion study recordings, Gilbreth also made photographs of the same work processes (Fig. 55). Of course, they showed the same laboratory setting as the motion study film, albeit with a few decisive compositing corrections. Through an open window and the person positioned askew in front of it, Gilbreth had changed the lighting set-up. The lighting elements were shifted toward the foreground, and the graphic background panels intensified the plasticity and depth effect of the image. This ensured a dramatization of the lighting situation and lent the intrinsically objective atmosphere of the laboratory a sheen of glamour and extravagance. The laboratory became a popularizable representation of scientific evidence, by, paradoxically, withdrawing all functional elements of scientific visuality from it.

The scientific character of the laboratory was in turn underscored by Gilbreth with stereoscopies (Fig. 56), in which only the representation of objective precision was

---

[87] Price, "One Best Way," 196.

[88] See Lee Grieveson, *Policing Cinema: Movies and Censorship in Early-Twentieth-Century America* (Berkeley: University of California Press, 2004); Shelley Stamp Lindsey, "'Oil upon the Flames of Vice': The Battle over White Slave Films in New York City," *Film History* 9, no. 4 (1997): 351–64.

[89] With this, prerequisites would be available for retroactively surveying the film image, almost in the sense of a filmic system of coordinates, thereby allowing for movements to be spatially determined.

Figure 54 Stills from the film *Training of a Champion Typist*.

Figure 55 "Glamorizing the Lab." Melodramatic staging of a motion study in evening dress.

Figure 56 Stereographic representation of a laboratory situation. The laboratory as a guarantee of scientific objectivity.

foregrounded. Measuring devices, geometric tables, the supervisory laboratory, and the test person visualized, in their interplay with the three-dimensional perspectival effect of stereography,[90] the superiority of laboratory space as a space of knowledge.

The Expert from the Laboratory

Further references to the intertwining of media techniques with the model of corporate consulting from the laboratory delivered filmic and photographic self-representations of Gilbreth and his colleagues. A number of photos showed neither scientific results nor details of analysis and synthesis techniques, but the experts from the laboratory. These photographs were neither chance snapshots, nor were they the result of private enthusiasm for photography. Finally, they were almost all stereographically recorded, in order to be shown in public. Additionally, Gilbreth enumerated all the photographs and developed a storage system specifically for this purpose, in order to rapidly access the photographs. From the very beginning they were designed to be presented in public contexts.

Stereographic Laboratory Space

Here, three topoi were conflated with each other into a representation of lab-based consulting: the figure of the all-knowing experts and scientists, the spatial config-uration of the laboratory, and the media technology exhibited within it, which primarily consisted of (chrono-)cyclegraphic inscriptions. With this constellation Gilbreth promoted his media-assisted approach to corporate consulting, as well as popularizing, within the specialized public and beyond, a concept of management that was based on central information spaces and practices of data visualization.

The stereographs here had different forms and usage purposes. Gilbreth used self-stylizations, like the cyclegraph in Figure 57, as printed postcards. For Christmas or similar events, he sent them—even partly personalized—to friends and business partners.[91] As a rule, these greeting cards showed Gilbreth and the cyclegraphically exposed greeting in the spaces of the motion study laboratories. He had recourse to the medium of the postcard, which enjoyed increasing pop-ularity from 1900 on,[92] and combined it with the equally popular mass medium

[90] Rosalind Krauss, *Le Photographique: Pour une théorie des écarts* (Paris: Editions Macula, 1990), 42.

[91] Gilbreth sent one of these greeting cards, for instance, as a birthday message to Herman Remané, the director of the Auergesellschaft in Berlin. See F. B. Gilbreth, letter to L. M. Gilbreth, December 6, 1914. Gilbreth LOM, SPCOLL, Purdue University Libraries, NF 92/813-5.

[92] From 1900, sending postcards became a worldwide phenomenon and a mass medium. In Germany and France, the mass delivery of postcards led to the breakdown of the postal system,

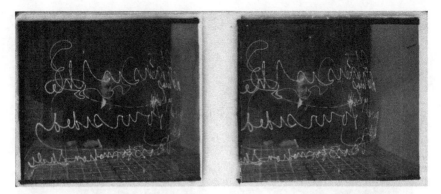

Figure 57 Experts, laboratories, visual inscriptions. Frank and Lillian Gilbreth sent Christmas cards with cyclegraphic writing to business partners and friends.

of stereographic photographs.[93] Furthermore, he manufactured glass slides from the stereographs.

In personal meetings with potential customers or at industrial fairs and exhibitions, Gilbreth illustrated the superiority of his scientific media method. In these settings, he generally tended to use a stereoscope, through which the laboratory space could be spatially experienced.

That this was a matter of photographic montages fabricated with a great deal of effort can be seen in Figure 58. Here, a long-exposure cyclegraph in a darkened room was combined with a daylight exposure at the end. The result was a stereoscope, which on the one hand contained cyclegraphic inscriptions (in this case, the reach radius of an employee working at an office desk) and, on the other hand, the crisp portrait photograph of Russ Allen, one of Gilbreth's closest collaborators. Here, too, the expert, the laboratory, and the image-producing processes that were used merged into a constructed emblem of lab-based consulting. This example was almost an early form of the pictogram. It was not without reason that the effect of stereoscopy, the required scanning of the visual space by the viewer, was comparable to the reception situation in a painting gallery.[94] Through stereoscopy, the viewer is subjected to the mechanical compulsion to concentrate "all attention on the object present."[95] Such a reception situation is not dissimilar to

because the standard structures were overloaded with the quantity of postcards. See Tom Phillips, *The Postcard Century: 2000 Cards and their Messages* (London: Thames & Hudson, 2000).

[93] Rosalind Krauss, *Le Photographique*, 43–44; Edward W. Earle, Howard Saul Becker, Thomas W. Southall, and Harvey Green, eds., *Points of View: The Stereograph in America: A Cultural History* (Rochester, NY: Visual Studies Workshop Press, 1979); Walter Böttger, "Stereoskop-Bilder," *Film und Lichtbild* 1, no. 5 (1912): 56–61.

[94] Krauss, *Le Photographique*, 43–44.

[95] Ibid., 42.

Figure 58 Laboratory knowledge as symbolic pictogram. Russ Allen demonstrates the maximum reach radius at a work desk.

that of the cinema.[96] In this case, the functioning of stereoscopy and the object complemented each other in ideal fashion. For, in the strict sense, there was no object. It was the space, the space of the laboratory, that was to be represented (Fig. 59). The viewer could apprehend this nonobject precisely through scanning the stereoscopic effect of space. The mechanisms of stereoscopy merged with the object and allowed it to be experienced with "muscular micro-efforts."[97]

Alongside stereoscopy, Gilbreth also manufactured photographs. They offered a photographic-documentary access to the laboratory situation but contained very similar effects. Thus, Figure 60 showed a laboratory situation, which along with the laboratory expert integrated into the image with a similar procedure as that in the previous example now also contained the actual object of investigation. This object, Dr. Myrtelle M. Canvan, demonstrated "the One Best Way to transfer cultures in a pathological laboratory."[98] The person under investigation appears blurry, such as would also be expected in the previous image with Russ Allen. It was, after all, a motion study and not a photographic portrait. But here, too, the laboratory setting is supplemented by the razor-sharp laboratory and efficiency expert, in this case Dr. Elmer E. Southard, professor of neuropathology in the Harvard Medical School. That this was a scientific laboratory was made clear in the square background and the recording apparatus shown in the foreground.

These images did not have a scientific value in the sense of a visualization of previously invisible movement flows. They were promotional images for the Gilbreth method of laboratory-based corporate consulting. Thus, it was

---

[96] Ibid., 43.
[97] Ibid., 42.
[98] Image description, Gilbreth LOM, SPCOLL, Purdue University Libraries, NF 56/0299-12.

Figure 59 The experts Lillian and, to her right, Frank B. Gilbreth, the laboratory, and their seated object of research.

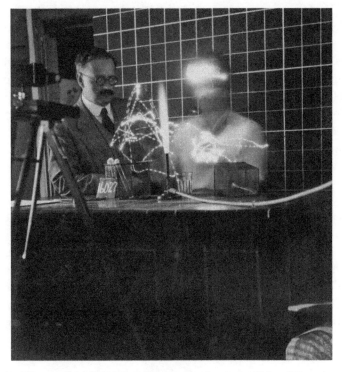

Figure 60 The expert and his object. Rationalization in medicine. "Note the complete absence of hesitation, indecision and fumbling."

suggested, the possibility of a direct, unfeigned, scientific access to human resources arose.

Laboratory Films

A similar tendency can also be perceived in the film fragments that have been preserved. The sequences not only showed work studies and detail shots of workplace performances. Images of the workers were also regularly made, which were grouped around the symbol of the scientific media technique of recording. The images were not restricted to delivering simple filmic views from the laboratory, as, for instance, the "cinema of attractions" offered a few years earlier.[99] Nor did the film images resemble the documentary short films about science and technology common at the time. Rather, they appeared more as films with highly composed imagery. The workers themselves interacted with the camera and followed the patterns of behavior before the camera that were widespread in amateur films at the time.[100] The form allows us to conclude that these "spontaneous" jokes and movement derived less from the mood of the workers, but rather followed a strategy of representing the motion studies in a form that was filmically as attractive as possible. These films were not mere photographic footage, which would bring the laboratory, much like nature documentaries, closer to the public as an exotic, unreachable location. They combined the scientific quality of the laboratory with the gumption of the expert. This resulted in a model that promised a smooth transition from the precise knowledge of the laboratory to an industrial setting.

In Figure 61, a group of motion experts, including Frank and Lillian Gilbreth, can be seen in a motion study laboratory. Punctually, at the beginning of the footage, the staged merriment in the laboratory starts with a small gesture for the camera. And of course it is not Frank B. Gilbreth himself who waves. He can still be seen in the first frame, sovereignly standing on the outer left part of the image, observing his colleagues and his wife, Lillian, who stands to the right of the man waving. The footage is not of a piece with the home movies widespread at the time, in which the father of the family tries to attract attention through a "winking compulsion."[101] It was the depiction of the workers of a consultancy firm, which demonstrated *sovereign* mastery of the filmic medium.[102] Nonetheless, they are partly subordinated to the convention of scenic self-representation through gestures.

[99] Tom Gunning, "Before Documentary: Early Nonfiction Films and the 'View' Aesthetic," in *Uncharted Territory: Essays on Early Nonfiction Film*, ed. Daan Hertogs and Nico de Klerk (Amsterdam: Stichting Nederlands Filmmuseum, 1997), 9–24.

[100] Alexandra Schneider, *Die Stars sind wir: Heimkino als filmische Praxis* (Marburg: Schüren, 2004), 119–78.

[101] Ibid., 161.

[102] See also Figure 41, in which Gilbreth is shown with the camera in the pose of a film director.

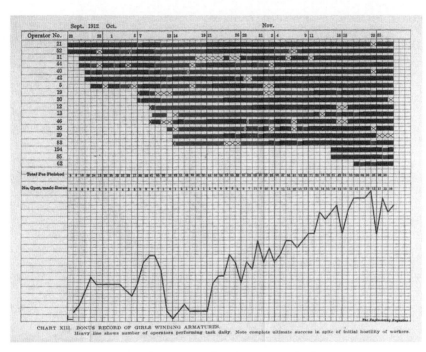

Plate 1 Gantt, Henry L. *Work, Wages, and Profits.* New York: The Engineering Magazine Co., 1919, 202–203. First published 1910.

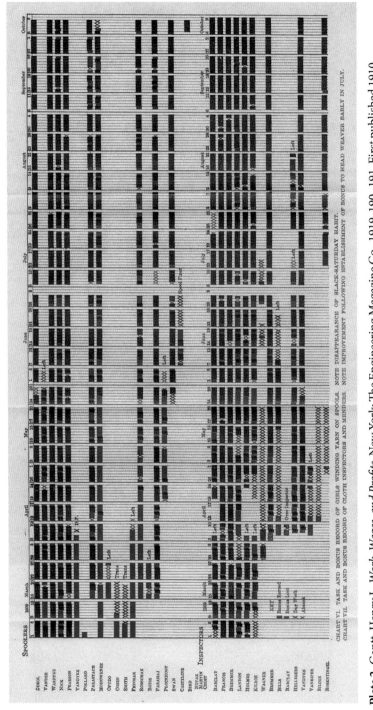

Plate 2 Gantt, Henry L. *Work, Wages, and Profits*. New York: The Engineering Magazine Co., 1919, 190–191. First published 1910.

FOUNDRY PRODUCTION SHEET A. L. CO. SCHENECTADY WORKS		ORDER NO. 83 8 ENGINES D.L.& W.																					
PART		BELL STAND		EXHAUST PIPE		TENDER FRAME CENTER PIN		ENGINE TRUCK SWING BOLSTER		GRATE BAR		GRATE SIDE		GRATE SIDE		ASH PAN END		ASH PAN SIDE		GRATE FRAME SUPPORT		GRATE BAR	
PATTERN NO.		17,212		17,939		16,927		16,907		19,458		18,953		18,954		21,343		21,341		18,959		18,961	
PATTERN DUE		2-2		2-2		2-2		2-2		2-2		2-2		2-2		2-2		2-2		2-2		2-2	
PATTERN REC'D.		1-22		1-22		2-6		2-4		2-9		2-10		2-10		2-10		2-10		2-14		2-14	
NO. WANTED PER DAY		1		1		1		1		8		2		2		1		1		1		1	
TOTAL NO. WANTED		8		8		8		8		64		16		16		8		8		8		8	
NUMBER MOULDED		Daily	Total	Daily	Total	Daily	Total	Daily	Total	Daily	Total	Daily	Total	Daily	Total	Daily	Total	Daily	Total	Daily	Total	Daily	Total
1903 FEB.	2																						
	3			1	1																		
	4			2	3																		
	5			2	5			1	1														
	6																						
	7	7		I 1	5																		
	9			2	7	2	2	1	2	P													
	10							1	3	3	3	1 P	1	1 P	1	P		P					
	11	4	4					1	4	I 8	10	2	3	2	3	1	1						
	12	I 2	5	1	8	2	4	1	5	7 2	5	1	4	1	4	2	3						
	13					3	7	1	6			2	6	2	6		2	3	3				
	14	1	6					1	7	8	13	1	7	1	7					P		P	
	16	2	8			1	8	1	8	I 5	17	1	8	1	8	2	4	1	4	3	6	2	2
	17									I 8	24	1	9	1	9	2	6			4	7	2	4
	18									2 8	30	1	10	1	10	2	8	2	6	1	8	I 2	5
	19									I 8	37	2	12	2	12			2	8			I 1	5
	20									8	45	2	14	2	14								
	21									8	53	2	16	2	16								
	23									I 7	59											1	6
	24									5	64											1	7
	25																					1	8
	26																						

Begin moulding not later than date opposite upper red line
Finish " " " " " " lower " "

Plate 3 Gantt, Henry L. *Work, Wages, and Profits.* New York: The Engineering Magazine Co., 1919, 273. First published 1910. Figure first published in Gantt, Henry L. "Graphical Daily Balance in Manufacture." *Transactions ASME* 24 (1903): 1322–1336, figure 289.

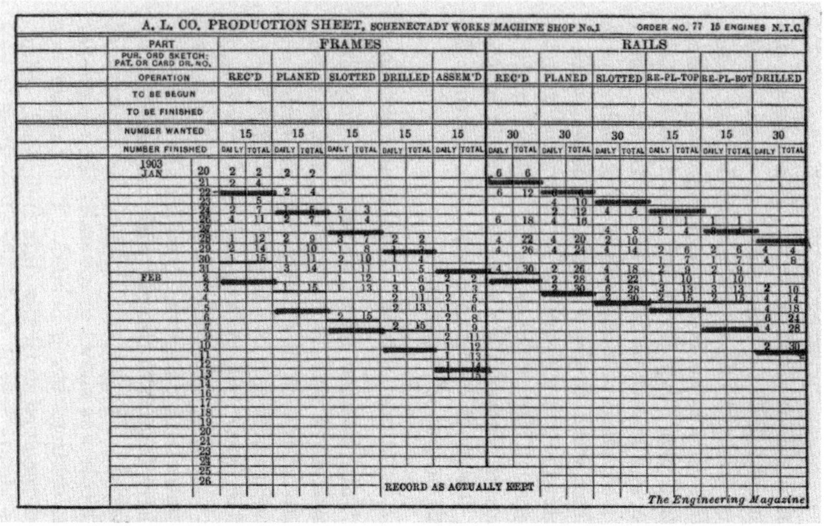

Plate 4 Gantt, Henry L. *Work, Wages, and Profits.* New York: The Engineering Magazine Co., 1919, 276. First published 1910.

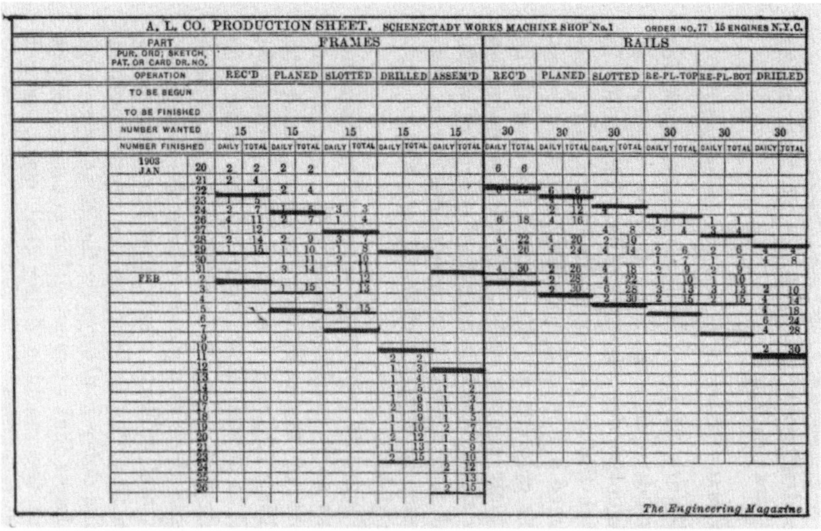

Plate 5 Gantt, Henry L. *Work, Wages, and Profits.* New York: The Engineering Magazine Co., 1919, 277. First published 1910.

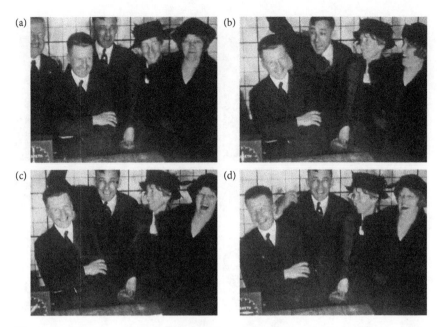

Figure 61 Confidence in the laboratory. Staged cheerfulness in front of the camera.

Figure 62 The duplicated gaze of the camera. A camera films a camera. The media technology of film as a guarantee of scientific precision.

This was possibly due to the fact that it represented an introduced pattern, which helped, in short scenes, to avoid a laborious narrative preparation of the scenes.

The next example (Figs. 62 and 63) shows even more clearly that this was a systematic visual strategy. The two men had taken footage of regatta rowers on the Hudson River, and now pose before the Gilbreth clock and a film camera, symbols of scientific precision. Two things can be perceived in the footage. The first aspect is the fact that the scene was filmed with two cameras. The first

Figure 63 Gilbreth's workers as sovereign and media-based film and rationalization experts.

camera (Fig. 62) is installed for the actual motion study, while the second camera (Fig. 63) only has the purpose of filming the first camera and the participating workers as they were being filmed. Or, to use Gilbreth's own words: "We do one film of me doing a film."[103] At the same time as the actual work study film, the film about the method and practice of the motion study is shot for promotional purposes. Here too, as in the first example, we can see a staged interaction with the camera—in this case, doffing a hat and greeting the camera. From the film fragments we can see that there were several attempts to film the gesture with the hat. The first attempt was perhaps not expressive enough for the camera man and therefore had to be repeated.

Gilbreth's ascent in the field of corporate consulting was tied with a potent discourse representing practices of visualization as an adequate approach to prepare business data for management. At the same time, the laboratory was located as the central space of knowledge for modern management and progressive corporate consulting. It thus complements the medialization drive that could be

[103] F. B. Gilbreth, letter to L. M. Gilbreth, November 5, 1914, Gilbreth LOM, SPCOLL, Purdue University Libraries, NF 92/813-5.

observed since 1880, and the developing visual culture in commercial and industrial contexts.

Media as Containers of Diffuse Legal Claims

Gilbreth not only deployed media devices as marketing instruments, but he also
used them to generate genuine unique selling propositions.

In 1913, he registered a patent with the title *Method and Apparatus for the
Study and Correction of Motions* (Fig. 64). The patent application that described
the cyclegraph and the laboratory setting of his method of analysis was deposited
in 1916.[104] Whereas Frederick W. Taylor's rather unspecific concept of "time and
motion studies"[105] could not be patented, Gilbreth was able to legally protect his
Micro-Motion Analysis Laboratory, even if the principle behind it was just as unspecific as Taylor's methods.

Media techniques not only allowed Gilbreth to develop a successful public image.
He was also able to privatize generally available knowledge, by simply patenting it
as part of his media technologies. In Germany, however, he learned that his right
to patent his filmic procedures was not recognized everywhere in equal measure.
Here, too, he sought to register a patent, but this was rejected with the justification
that important core components of his media apparatus could not be patented. They
did not represent an innovation, since they had long been known about and in use.
This not only applied to the cyclegraph, but also to the Gilbreth clock, which served
him to arrange his film footage along an exact time axis. Gilbreth always insisted
that this procedure was his basic invention, but in Germany it was assessed as already being sufficiently known.

> With movements that very quickly succeed each other, and which are of an
> intertwined nature, there was a turn to using the cinematograph, in which the
> direction can automatically be seen, but the time measurement has to be expe-
> rienced through a specially constructed clock which is included in every image.
> This type of measurement is doubtless well-known, notably through Marey-
> France, Fuchs-Germany, Fuchs-Brno and many others.[106]

---

[104] US-Pat. No. 1.199.980, submitted on May 23, 1913, patented on October 3, 1916, Patent
Label: "Method and Apparatus for the Study and Correction of Motions."

[105] Taylor's time studies were based on the control of the workers through work inspectors, who
measured the time necessary for an individual work phase with the aid of a stopwatch. The main goal
was to combat "soldiering," that is, the willful slowing down of the work tempo. See Taylor, "Shop
Management," 1903, in *Transactions American Society of Mechanical Engineers,* 1337–480.

[106] Response to Gilbreth's application for claiming patent protection in Germany for the
chronocyclegraph, Gilbreth LOM, SPCOLL, Purdue University Libraries, NF 94/816-20.

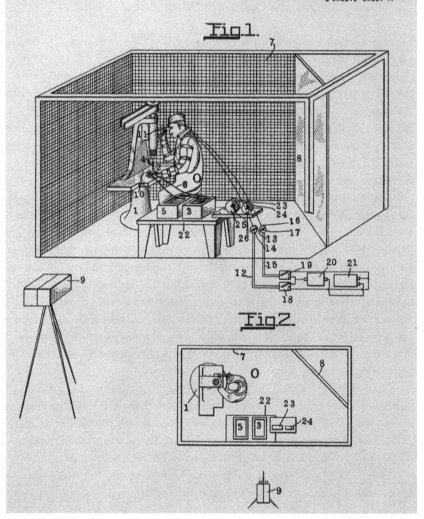

F. B. GILBRETH.
METHOD AND APPARATUS FOR THE STUDY AND CORRECTION OF MOTIONS.
APPLICATION FILED MAY 23, 1913.

1,199,980.

Patented Oct. 3, 1916.
2 SHEETS—SHEET 1.

Figure 64 Aerial view and an oblique-angled view of the Micro-Motion Analysis Laboratory from Frank B. Gilbreth's patent application.

The only thing that was new in his method, the evaluation report continued, was its application to the factory space. The media technology, by contrast, was based on already existing devices and practices. As a result, the patent application in Germany was refused.

In the United States and Canada, Gilbreth's patent applications were much more successful. Here, Gilbreth deliberately employed media apparatuses so as to legally protect his combination of methods. Although individual parts of his method were, on the whole, already known, he could patent their combination into a coherent method.[107] In 1914, shortly before the outbreak of World War I, Gilbreth visited the Institut Marey in Paris and met with Dr. Dupuy, one of the leaders of the institute at the time (Fig. 65). It was in this context that Gilbreth referred to Marey's experiments: "[Marey] got all his ideas from Muybridge."[108] Furthermore, Marey had not, according to Gilbreth, appropriately cited the ideas he borrowed from Muybridge. That Gilbreth highlighted this aspect in particular may have been because his own ideas on the use of media were not too different from those of Marey. Gilbreth was all too keen to hear that Marey himself had resorted to previously available techniques and used this for his own purposes without proper citation.

If his own patents were infringed upon, Gilbreth nonetheless reacted very harshly—after all, plagiarism put his business model at risk. He thundered against the publications of other efficiency experts in Germany, who offered or made public similar processes of filmic analysis. This happened, for instance, to Eduard Michel's publication *Wie macht man Zeitstudien?*,[109] published by the VDI Verlag in 1920, and Karl A. Tramm's *Psychotechnik und Taylorsystem*, which appeared in 1921.[110] Michel, in particular, was a competitor who had to be taken seriously, since he had successfully started his own consulting company.[111] In a letter to Irene Witte, his then colleague in Germany, Gilbreth spoke in indignant and abusive terms about the competing consultants he found in the country:

---

[107] In conjunction with the precarious status of his patent registration, there was also an irregularity in the Frank and Lillian Gilbreth archives. For the years leading up to the patenting of the cyclegraph, a gap in the documentation arises, even though Gilbreth's archive is generally characterized by a very thorough documentation of all archive materials (including a large quantity of secondary texts on diverse topics). Nonetheless, there are no documents giving information on the development of this patent. Moreover, the entire archive contains none of the writings of Étienne-Jules Marey or other pioneers of filmic motion studies, which at the very least is rather unusual.

[108] F. B. Gilbreth, letter to L. M. Gilbreth, May 15, 1914, Gilbreth LOM, SPCOLL, Purdue University Libraries, NF 91/813-6.

[109] Eduard Michel, *Wie macht man Zeitstudien?* (Berlin: Verlag des Vereins deutscher Ingenieure, 1920).

[110] Karl A. Tramm, *Psychotechnik und Taylor-System* (Berlin: Springer, 1921).

[111] See Kipping, "Consultancies, Institutions and the Diffusion of Taylorism in Britain, Germany and France 1920s to 1950s," 70.

Figure 65 The cyclegraph as a genuine invention by Frank B. Gilbreth? Frank B. Gilbreth and Lucien Bull, assistant and successor to Étienne-Jules Marey, pose before the Institut Marey in Paris.

> I think that it is no longer a joke that our stuff is stolen without credit. [. . .] [Karl Tramm] has stolen without credit the cyclegraph method and the chronocyclegraph method and on page 89 and page 90, he has shown pictures taken in 1912 at the New England Butt Company and has given credit to the Deutsche Forschungsgesellschaft für Luftfahrt.[112]

But without any patent protection in Germany, all he could do was take umbrage at the theft of his American patents.

> I never laughed so much in my life as when I saw the picture of the scaffold reproduced in the reprint, which you sent me. [. . .] I think that you should take this author to task and point out the supreme ignorance and ridiculousness of such a sketch. Surely no practical man would have any respect for any engineer who would recommend any such idiotic arrangement as the scaffold as shown.[113]

Due to Gilbreth's perception of the widespread misuse of his intellectual property, he even questioned the value of future activities in Germany. After photos of his consultancy circulated without his name being attached to them, he decided to stop sending photos to Germany: "we will be forced to refrain from sending any more of our pictures to Germany until they are first fully

---

[112] F. B. Gilbreth, letter to I. Witte, July 29, 1921, TECHNOSEUM, Witte Nachlass, Sig. 992, No. 1/3-24.
[113] F. B. Gilbreth, letter to I. Witte, TECHNOSEUM, Witte Nachlass, Sig. 992, No. 1/2-17.

copyrighted and protected in Germany."[114] The extent to which Gilbreth was the lawful originator of his methods may be significant to nationally oriented research projects in corporate management or film history, but it is of no importance for the argumentation I pursue later. The only thing that is relevant is the circumstance that Gilbreth's use of media technologies to claim a patent for knowledge that was, in part, already commonly available resulted in a thoroughly unclear situation. In the United States and Canada he could use his duly certified patent to promote his consulting approach as "lab-based" and thus as scientific. The patent also allowed him to forestall any unwanted competition. He may have seen Thomas Alva Edison's successful monopolization of the American film industry through the Motion Pictures Patents Company's film patents as a model and sought to establish a similar strategy in the sphere of corporate consulting.

After Gilbreth attained a patent for his motion study laboratory, he no longer felt bound to the conventions of the scientific community. During his collaboration with Taylor, he was still prepared to do this and regularly presented his innovations to scientific congresses. Now he declared his method to be a trade secret and was no longer content to make the results of his laboratory studies transparent and therefore replicable. His motion laboratory became a black box of content, at the same time as it formed the central argument of his PR strategy, which promoted his approach as "The One Best Way to Do Work (Fig. 66)."[115]

To this end he used classical communication channels like magazines and newspapers,[116] in which he placed numerous editorial articles about the superiority of the laboratory as a space for knowledge and discovery. He regularly organized crash courses under the title, "The One Best Way to Do Work" at American universities and the newly established business schools.[117] He likewise presented his method at important industry fairs (Fig. 67).[118] Moreover, he conceived a mobile exhibition on the topic of unnecessary fatigue and inefficiency, which he also sought to distribute to the major museums of technology, as a 1913 letter to the Deutsches Museum München on this matter shows (Fig. 68).[119] As

[114] F. B. Gilbreth, letter to I. Witte, July 29, 1921, TECHNOSEUM, Witte Nachlass, Sig. 992, No. 1/3-24.
[115] See the information brochures, "The One Best Way to Do Work," TECHNOSEUM, Witte Nachlass, Sig. 996, No. 2/1-116.
[116] See "Now You Can Map a Motion," *Providence Sunday Journal*, June 15, 1913, TECHNOSEUM, Witte Nachlass, Sig. 996, No. 2/7-35.
[117] F. B. Gilbreth, letter to I. Witte, TECHNOSEUM, Witte Nachlass, Sig. 992, No. 2/1-11; L. M. Gilbreth, letter to I. Witte, TECHNOSEUM, Witte Nachlass, Sig. 992, No. 2/1-20.
[118] I. Witte, letter to W. Hellmich, February 18, 1921, TECHNOSEUM, Witte Nachlass, Sig. 996, No. 6/13-129.
[119] F. B. Gilbreth, letter to Deutsches Museum München, October 10, 1913, Gilbreth LOM, SPCOLL, Purdue University Libraries, NF 97/816-6a.

Figure 66 View of a motion laboratory set up and operated by Gilbreth.

We are copying the form of "Research Narratives" edited by our friend Mr. Alfred D. Flinn.

King George V. Queen Mary and Princess Mary at the Gilbreth motion study laboratory for finding The One Best Way to Do Work.

Figure 67 Extract from the regularly published Information brochure *Gilbreth's The One Best Way to Do Work*. As part of the firm's publicity strategy, it reported on the innovations and successes of lab-based consulting.

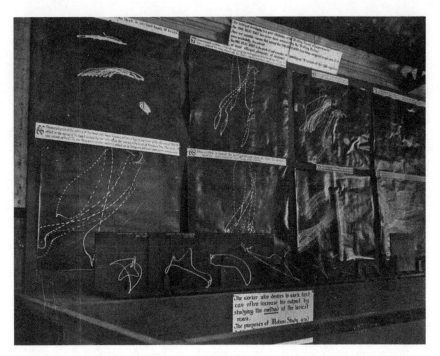

Figure 68 The profile of lab-based consulting in the public sphere. Image of a touring exhibition conceived by Gilbreth on the topic of avoiding fatigue through scientific and media techniques.

a consequence of his media network strategy, laboratory-derived visual knowledge became a synonym for science within business structures. Gilbreth had succeeded in publicly anchoring film-based laboratory studies as the most appropriate pathway to industrial rationalization.

Unlike Taylor's systematic approaches, which presupposed a complete restructuring of the entire business, the laboratory promised a pragmatic, visible, and thus comprehensible change. By situating the laboratory inside the business in question, it was possible to adapt to local circumstances and react directly to production processes without rigid prescriptions, as Gilbreth outlines:

All instruments necessary for the performance of labor and the measurement of motion are available to the observer, and the data gleaned from the individual workers are more precise and more reliable, than if the investigation had been carried out in workshop conditions and the distractions that are prevalent there. As soon as the best type of labor operation is ascertained with the aid of the tools available in the laboratory, the labor conditions required for achieving this result in the workshop are changed until they match those that prevail in the laboratory.[120]

In the laboratory, improvements could be experimentally verified and adjusted before their implementation, without any risk to the firm's ongoing operations. At the same time, the laboratory setting guaranteed the impression of scientific precision, which was intended to facilitate its later adaptation in industrial production.

Gilbreth's pragmatic approach, oriented to concrete problems, also imposed itself because competing corporate consultants had significant difficulties in introducing Scientific Management through purely systematic argumentation. Even Taylor suffered a series of setbacks in his attempts at industrial rationalization. Additionally, considerable differences arose between the Taylor System he espoused and the reality that its introduction in a business yielded. As a result, Taylor's rather rigid system was also held responsible for the breakdown of previously functional corporate cultures, as could be seen in the 1913 strikes at Bosch and Renault.[121] In 1928, Irene Witte gave the following overview of Taylor's lack of success: "His system, however, was introduced and recognized in this country [Germany], but not anywhere else, not even in America."[122] Barely thirty years later, Adam Abruzzi summarized the relevance of the scientific method for industry:

> There are many fields, including classical industrial engineering, in which writers and practitioners alike seem compelled to claim that what they are doing is scientific. The most popular method of proving this claim is to make liberal use of the label "scientific" in either the "regular" or the "king" size.[123]

Apart from the assertion of its scientific nature, little remained of this approach in the industrial sphere. "A laboratory investigation, for example, can hardly be expected to reveal much about the performance characteristics of workers

---

[120] Frank B. Gilbreth and Lillian Gilbreth, *Angewandte Bewegungsstudien: Neun Vorträge aus der Praxis der wissenschaftlichen Betriebsführung* (Berlin: VDI Verlag, 1920), 8.

[121] Heidrun Homburg, "Anfänge des Taylorsystems in Deutschland vor dem ersten Weltkrieg: Eine Problemskizze unter besonderer Berücksichtigung der Arbeitskämpfe bei Bosch 1913," *Geschichte und Gesellschaft: Zeitschrift für historische Sozialwissenschaft* 4, no. 1 (1978): 170–94.

[122] Irene Witte, *F. W. Taylor: Der Vater wirtschaftlicher Betriebsführung* (Stuttgart: Poeschel Verlag, 1928).

[123] Adam Abruzzi, *Work, Workers and Work Measurement* (New York: Columbia University Press, 1956), 3.

in a factory environment."[124] It was not so simple to transfer the principle of scientific inquiry to the completely different area of industrial production. It was true that a series of problems materialized in Gilbreth's practice, but he was, in the end, able to produce a media façade behind which such setbacks remained invisible.

[124] Ibid., 9.

4

Consulting, Cinematic Utopia, and Organizational Restraints

In this chapter, I will shed light on Frank and Lillian Gilbreth's understanding of media and the attempts at implementing their consulting model in the business world. In the context of the problems that arose with Taylorist approaches, their media-based method of corporate consulting appeared as a logical, modular, and coherent solution for tackling the crisis of corporate control. This approach was at least successful in positioning itself in the public sphere. For the Gilbreths, media technology was, however, more than a mere useful instrument for corporate consulting. They associated the new media of this period, and above all film, with utopian ideas about the efficacy of these new visual forms of representation. In the corporate reality of a consulting project, these ideas could only be realized to a limited degree. The Gilbreths were not alone in their desire to expose to new influences models of business leadership and administration that found themselves outmoded and crisis ridden. Their approach, which was considerably influenced by Lillian Gilbreth's background in industrial psychology, was part of a whole series of other reform-oriented attempts that were introduced in what was at the time a corporate environment receptive to innovation.

Despite being bereft of a clear, unambiguous solution to the growing social unrest and economic crisis, there arose a series of experiments and trial models for securing lasting corporate peace.[1] A certain disorientation prevailed with respect to how the new political and economic challenges could be dealt with. Alongside representatives like Frederick W. Taylor, whose techniques were the driving force behind the restoration of factory discipline in the nineteenth century, other figures sought progressive, reform-oriented concepts. Central, here, was less an intensification of the disciplinary regime than a transformed conception of everyday corporate life, which simultaneously posed the underlying question

---

[1] Exemplary for this was the Daimler motor company's project of "workshop resettlement." Alongside experiments with decentralized labor structures, this projected also incorporated an ambitious educational program for its workforce, which included a regular series of films and lectures, such as that given by the anthroposopher Rudolf Steiner with the title "What and How Should Be Socialized." See "Betr. Film-Vorträge: Einteilung der Vortragstage," Anschlag No. 26b, Werk Untertürkheim, July 20, 1920, Mercedes-Benz Archive, DMG 33; Eugen Rosenstock-Huessy, *Werkstattaussiedlung: Untersuchungen über den Lebensraum des Industriearbeiters* (Berlin: Springer, 1922).

Angels of Efficiency. Florian Hoof, Oxford University Press (2020) © Oxford University Press.
DOI: 10.1093/oso/9780190886363.003.0001

concerning the restructuring of the business chain of value creation. The employees were to be integrated through sociopolitical educational programs and an augmented participation in corporate decision making. The business logic and the approaches of corporate management opened themselves up to external influences, which partly boasted a groping, uncertain, if not utopian character.

Frank and Lillian Gilbreth's adaptation and introduction of film in an industrial context, as part of a broader media network of graphic methods, was part of this process of opening up the logic of corporate organization and production. They based it on what they saw as the still embryonic potential of media techniques, and above all that of the ascendant medium of film. The public campaign, mainly driven by Frank Gilbreth, to make the consulting approach well-known and self-evident, can first be discerned by the fact that it was dependent on a scientific-instrumental understanding of media. For him, film seemed to have the purpose of generating corporate knowledge and establishing it as an instrument of education and discipline. With the concrete implementation of their media-based consulting techniques, however, the Gilbreths were not very successful. This may lead us to doubt whether their media techniques still fall under the definition of a scientific apparatus.

Gilbreth had enormous success in situating his method in the public eye and attracting commissions. At the same time, problems arose in carrying out their consulting method in practice, much as he programmatically portrayed it in public. This, as my thesis would have it, was less an expression of an inadequate implementation, poor personnel planning, or other external circumstances.[2] Rather, this paradoxical situation arose through the collision of two knowledge cultures. In integrating the laboratory as a part of the process of scientific discovery in the sphere of commerce and industry, Gilbreth attempted to combine the knowledge of the factory space with that of the laboratory space (Fig. 69).

This was a risky undertaking. After all, Gilbreth had to replace the knowledge structures that he encountered in businesses with those produced in the laboratory. Existing knowledge structures centered on the routines and necessities of everyday factory life, and they had persisted over a long period of time. For the most part this was a matter of tacit knowledge,[3] which was inaccessible to outsiders. Gilbreth wanted to complement this knowledge through explicit laboratory knowledge, which adhered to analytic-scientific principles. He took the risk of replacing existing, implicit knowledge structures with a new explicit form of corporate knowledge, largely because he himself was gripped by the media

[2] This is the opinion, for instance, of Brian Price, who ascribes Gilbreth's failure to restructure the Auergesellschaft to an insufficient integration of on-site management and inconsistencies in the administrative personnel within the consulting team. See Price, "One Best Way: Frank and Lillian Gilbreth's Transformation of Scientific Management, 1885–1940."

[3] Michael Polanyi, *The Tacit Dimension* (Chicago: The University of Chicago Press, 1966).

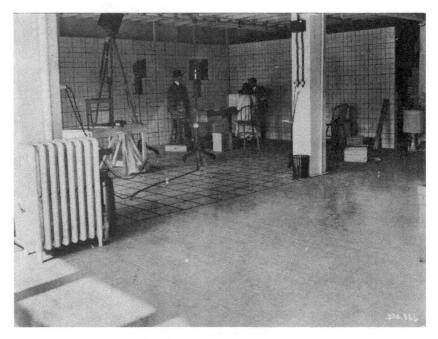

Figure 69 Laboratory on the left, factory on the right. A demarcated, modular laboratory space within the factory. View of a motion study laboratory on a Lever Brothers Company factory floor, from the year 1921.

euphoria that existed at this time. He was convinced that the knowledge transfer this required would succeed through deploying the media that stood at his disposal. With film, in particular, he saw enormous potential for industrial management, which went far beyond the filmic techniques and practices available at the time. New forms of filmic montage techniques and the possibilities of the feature-length film would enable the advantages of scientific methods to be made evident. As his vision had it, the forms of visual language developed in the ascendant film industry simply had to be repurposed for the correct pedagogical purposes. As such, new scientific discoveries could be conveyed to employees and adapted for industrial needs.[4]

---

[4] See L. Gilbreth and F. Gilbreth, *Modern Methods of Transferring Skill*, illustrated by Military Films. Undated Booklet, ca. 1921–22, Gilbreth LOM, SPCOLL, Purdue University Libraries, VT 2/ 0019.

"I go to the movies most every night": Cinema and Management

Gilbreth was not exclusively a pragmatic Taylorist who saw film as a useful rationalization tool, with which he could promote his consulting firm and scientifically restructure basic work processes. He was also a passionate filmgoer who was fascinated by the possibilities of film, which had a considerable effect on his activities as a corporate consultant.[5]

In the years 1914–1916, Gilbreth carried out a fundamental change in the orientation of his method of management consulting.[6] He departed from the narrow ideas of Taylorism, or scientific business management, and cultivated his own profile as a corporate consultant. In significant areas, he deviated from the doctrines of orthodox Taylorism and instead propagated his method of *lab-based consulting*. He placed the ergonomic aspect of his method in the foreground and presented his approach as a participatory training system for employees. Until now, this turn has primarily been explained through the dispute between Gilbreth and Taylor that broke out during the former's stay in Berlin.[7] But this is not a plausible reason for why he should see the future of industrial rationalization in the technology of film and in a much more participatory approach. His enthusiasm for the cinema better explains this shift.

During his stay in Berlin, Gilbreth fell prey to an almost obsessive passion for cinema. This sheds light on the media and cultural circumstances which contributed to a change of his management method. At the same time, the epistemological potential of film in the 1910s, as well as its general influence on the sphere of business administration and personnel management, could be seen in exemplary fashion. Gilbreth dared to take this risky step and departed from the conventional forms of industrial rationalization. This decision was notably bolstered by the impressions that he gained during his many visits to the cinema. The cinema *dispositif* had a lasting effect on his understanding of management.

Central to this was the turn away from a mechanistic concept of labor power. Instead of understanding the factory workers as mere *human motors*,[8] Gilbreth saw them as social beings. Linked to this turn was another address to

---

[5] In this he was not alone. See, for instance, Münsterberg, "Why We Go to the Movies."

[6] See Jane Lancaster, *Making Time: Lillian Moller Gilbreth, A Life Beyond "Cheaper by the Dozen"* (Beirut: Northeastern University Press, 2004); Price, "One Best Way: Frank and Lillian Gilbreth's Transformation of Scientific Management, 1885–1940"; Yost, *Frank and Lillian Gilbreth*; Witte, *Taylor, Gilbreth, Ford.*

[7] See Price, "Frank and Lillian Gilbreth and the Motion Study Controversy: 1907–1930"; Milton J. Nadworny, "Frederick Taylor and Frank Gilbreth: Competition in Scientific Management," *The Business History Review* 31, no. 1 (1957): 23–34.

[8] See Anson Rabinbach, *The Human Motor: Energy, Fatigue, and the Origins of Modernity* (Berkeley: University of California Press, 1992).

the employees. Disciplinary order, the "programming" of the human motor, was replaced by the participatory inclusion of workers. But why did the cinema come to play a decisive role in this context?

In contrast to the factory floors in which Gilbreth was active as a corporate consultant, in the movie theaters he encountered workers in an entirely different situation. There they responded enthusiastically to the films, were emotionally moved, and let themselves be carried away by the storyline. At the same time, they appeared less as a threatening, ungovernable, anonymous mass.[9] In the end, all filmgoers submitted to the principle of the cinema *dispositif*. They were captivated as they watched the screen and anticipated what would happen. In this situation, the workers appeared as being capable of being influenced and thus governed, if only recourse could be made to the right tools, in this case film. For Gilbreth, this may have functioned as an unhoped-for utopia of corporate consulting. With cinema, he thought, there would be no problem in training workers and convincing them of the advantages of his consulting method. If even mediocre films were capable of emotionally moving the spectator, then in this reception situation they would also be susceptible to his filmic-rational arguments.[10]

Differences Between the American and European Film Industries

Why Gilbreth was gripped by a cinema frenzy in Berlin can be explained by the different cinema and film structures in Germany and the United States, as well as by the local cinema situation in Berlin. At this time, Berlin had the world's most diverse cinema landscape. It would be hard to conceive of a more extreme contrast than that between the German capital and Gilbreth's home city, Providence, a fast-growing, barely urbanized industrial town on the American East Coast. His stay in Berlin was not only marked by the challenge of carrying the world's then biggest organizational experiment in a company's ongoing production process. Gilbreth also experienced the visual shock of the cinema. He became aware of the possibilities that film contained, beyond its use as an instrument for scientific recording. His stay in Berlin was akin to an abrupt leap forward in time, which immediately propelled him, without any transition, into the formative period of classical narrative cinema and the era of glamorous picture palaces.[11] He

---

[9] On the contemporaneous notion of the "mass," see the treatment by Gustav Le Bon, first published in 1895 and translated into English in 1896, *The Crowd: A Study of the Popular Mind* (New York: MacMillan, 1896).

[10] See Gilbreth and Gilbreth, *Modern Methods of Transferring Skill*.

[11] For an overview on the Berlin picture palaces, see Paul Zucker, *Theater und Lichtspielhäuser* (Berlin: Ernst Wasmuth, 1926); Paul Zucker, *Lichtspielhäuser: Tonfilmtheater* (Berlin: Ernst Wasmuth, 1931); Fritz Wilms, *Lichtspieltheaterbauten* (Berlin: Friedrich Ernst Hübsch Verlag, 1928).

was confronted with the forms of the cinema film and the infrastructure linked to it, which in the United States in the year 1913 did not yet exist in this form. The differences with the situation in the United States were considerable, and they concerned the length of films, camera movements, and shot sizes, as well as the expense and size of the sets and props used.[12] The picture palace, which markedly differed from the simpler form of the American Nickelodeon, had also established itself in Berlin.[13] Across Germany, the new screening venues, much like the feature-length films they screened, were more firmly considered part of legitimate culture, rather than being stigmatized as mere amusement. Moreover, the cinema landscape in Germany had introduced the format of the documentary short preceding the feature, which offered short overviews of different aspects of industry, science, and technology. It was not shown as part of a randomly assembled program of films in front of the half-empty rows of a rundown Nickelodeon, but in fully occupied, magnificent, architecturally designed, purpose-built picture palaces. Gilbreth's enthusiasm for this kind of cinema had an effect on the conception of his model of corporate consulting. In the context of the apparently infinite possibilities of film for training and influencing workers, participatory approaches appeared as a realistic alternative to the existing approaches of workplace discipline advocated by Taylorism. But how did these significant differences between the cinema landscape in the United States and Germany (especially Berlin) arise?

In Germany there had been, since 1906, a veritable boom in founding neighborhood movie theaters in the simple form of the *Kintopp* or the *Schaubude*. For the most part, they were former inns and corner stores that had fallen on hard times.[14] The films shown there were no longer than fifteen minutes and showed simple, immobile views of a few minutes duration.[15] From 1909, basic forms of montage and narration were already in existence.[16] Since a part of the film was

[12] Eileen Bowser, *History of the American Cinema, Vol. II: The Transformation of Cinema, 1907–1915* (New York: MacMillan, 1990), 249–51.

[13] On the Situation of the Nickelodeon in general, see Brian Singer, "Manhattan Nickelodeons: New Data on Audiences and Exhibitors," *Cinema Journal* 34, no. 3 (1995): 5–35; Brian Singer, *Melodrama and Modernity: Early Sensational Cinema and Its Context* (New York: Columbia University Press, 2001); Lee Grieveson, "Fighting Films: Race, Morality, and the Governing of Cinema, 1912–1915," in *The Silent Cinema Reader*, ed. Lee Grieveson and Peter Krämer (London: Routledge, 2004), 169–86; Lee Grieveson, "Feature Films and Cinema Program," in Grieveson amd Krämer, *The Silent Cinema Reader*, 187–95; Dan Streible, *Fight Pictures: A History of Boxing and Early Cinema* (Berkeley: University of California Press, 2008).

[14] Joseph Garncarz, "Über die Entstehung der Kinos in Deutschland 1896–1914," *KINtop. Jahrbuch zur Erforschung des frühen Films* 11 (2002): 152.

[15] See Tom Gunning, "Before Documentary: Early Nonfiction Films and the 'View' Aesthetic," in *Uncharted Territory: Essays on Early Nonfiction Film*, ed. Daan Hertogs and Nico de Klerk (Amsterdam: Stichting Nederlands Filmmuseum, 1997), 9–24.

[16] Within this time frame, Tom Gunning differentiates between the "system of monstrative attractions" (1895–1908) and the "system of narrative integration" (1909–1914). See Tom Gunning, *D. W. Griffith and the Origins of American Narrative Film: The Early Years at Biograph* (Urbana: University of Illinois Press, 1991).

based on the explicit depiction of sex and violence, the early storefront cinemas had a poor reputation as cheap entertainment for the working class. Up until this point, developments in early cinema in the United States and Germany were relatively similar. In the United States, vaudeville theaters and Nickelodeons also went through a boom that resembled the German *Kintopp* and *Schaubude* with respect to their programming and public perception.[17]

From 1908, the situation in the United States fundamentally changed with the founding of the Motion Pictures Patents Company (MPPC). The merger of the major American film companies and the bundling of their film technology patents in the MPPC created a monopolistic structure, by means of which they controlled more than 60% of the American film market by 1913.[18] In essence, this system conserved the programming structure of a succession of short films of a few minutes in duration that had been standard until 1908. In Europe, by contrast, a much more heterogeneous and diverse film market arose. Thus, by 1910, "a veritable film length frenzy"[19] had taken over Germany, one which was inconceivable in the United States due to the rigid programming schema that prevailed there. Short films were replaced by the new format of the feature film, which consisted of several reels of film and could thus reach running times of more than two hours. In contrast to the United States, in Germany there were no restrictions on importing films, no major disputes over patent rights, or even any monopolistic structures. Within Germany, Berlin acquired a special status as a film city. Freed of government restrictions and profiting from its central location between the film industries of France, Italy, Denmark, and Sweden, the city saw the development of a fierce competition between the major film firms. A verified tool for prevailing within the hotly contested film market was the production of spectacular, and ever more costly, feature-length films.

Feature films changed not only the viewing habits of filmgoers, but also the structures of the screening venues themselves. Risky big-budget productions had to be heavily promoted in order to be profitable. The public visibility this resulted in overturned the poor image that the small storefront cinemas had been saddled with. Moreover, the middle class was now sought after as film patrons. Otherwise, the high costs could not be refinanced. Film had to be transformed into a legitimate cultural commodity; otherwise the business of feature film production could not be made profitable. The major French studios, Gaumont and

---

[17] As far as New York, the cinema capital of the United States, was concerned, in the borough of Manhattan alone there were 315 Nickelodeons in 1908. See Singer, "Manhattan Nickelodeons," 7.

[18] Janet Staiger, "Combination and Litigation: Structures of US Film Distribution, 1896–1917," in Thomas Elsaesser, ed., *Early Cinema: Space, Frame, Narrative* (London: BFI, 1990), 191.

[19] Corinna Müller, "Variationen des Kinoprogramms: Filmform und Filmgeschichte," in *Die Modellierung des Kinofilms: Zur Geschichte des Kinoprogramms zwischen Kurzfilm und Langfilm 1905/06–1918*, ed. Corinna Müller and Harro Segeberg (Munich: Fink, 1998), 61.

Eclair, the Italian Cines, and the German Union Theater Gruppe (UT) reacted to this situation by building imposing picture palaces. These no longer took their place in the lineage of the fairground attractions like the *Kintopps* but were associated with established forms of built culture such as theater and opera. The pioneering work in this sphere was carried out by the UT: "In 1908 already, the first UT was established in Alexanderplatz, and thus the path from the *Kintopp* or the *Schaubude* to the *Palast* was traversed in an extremely short period of time."[20]

By the end of 1913, there were already ten premiere cinemas in Berlin, which distinguished themselves in the urban domain through their imposing architecture, boasting capacities of between 900 and 1,600 seats.[21] This transformation of the cinema landscape brought about a valorization of film itself. Cinema became culture: film premieres were now major social events, which had very little in common with the cheap working-class entertainment of the *Kintopp*. The situation in the United States was somewhat different. Here, the first genuine picture palace, The Strand on Broadway in New York City, was only opened in April 1914.[22] As far as the development of the massive picture palaces and the spread of the narrative feature film was concerned, Europe—and Berlin in particular—had a head start of several years over the United States.

Gilbreth as Berlin Filmgoer

With his stay in Berlin, Gilbreth made a leap from the one-reel films that were still the norm in the United States, with a length of up to seventeen minutes, to the European standard of the "multireel film," which had a running time of up to three hours.[23] But it was not only the length of these films that impressed Gilbreth. The more narrative-oriented film language they possessed[24] also gave him insight into film's previously unknown aesthetic possibilities.

Between January 1914 and mid-June 1915, Gilbreth stayed in Berlin almost continuously, apart from two trips back home to the United States. He mostly lived in the Hotel Fürstenhof, a luxury hotel on Potsdamer Platz equipped for business travelers. Across the street from the hotel was the Kammerlichtspiele, a picture palace with 1,200 seats, which Gilbreth frequented. Upon discovering

---

[20] "Bereits 1908 wurde das erste U.T. am Alexanderplatz gegründet, so daß der Weg vom 'Kientopp' oder der 'Schaubude' bis zum 'Palast' in ganz kurzer Zeit zurückgelegt wurde." Alexander Jason, *Der Film in Ziffern und Zahlen: 1895–1925* (Berlin: Deutsches Druck- und Verlagshaus, 1925), 31.

[21] Jeanpaul Goergen, "Cinema in the Spotlight: The Lichtspiel-Theaters and the Newspapers in Berlin, September 1913: A Case Study," in *Kinoöffentlichkeit (1895–1920): Entstehung. Etablierung. Differenzierung*, ed. Corinna Müller and Harro Segeberg (Marburg: Schüren, 2008), 66–86.

[22] "New Stand Opens; Biggest of Movies," *New York Times*, April 12, 1914.

[23] Bowser, *History of the American Cinema, vol. II*, 185.

[24] Müller, "Variationen des Kinoprogramms," 64.

Figure 70 Berlin's film landscape in the year 1914. The cinemas regularly visited by Gilbreth are marked. How many of the nearly 300 Berlin Kintopps he visited cannot be determined from the archive.

Berlin's cinema scene, he became a passionate filmgoer, who visited one of the inner-city theaters shown in Figure 70 almost every evening.[25] Occasionally, he also visited the Variétés, whose programs mixed theatrical performances with films. But for the most part he disparaged this form of popular entertainment, which was in his opinion rudimentary and without any future prospects.[26] As a rule, he preferred to watch the feature-length films with "cultural aspirations," which were screened in the impressive picture palaces.[27]

Exemplary for the enthusiasm that Gilbreth felt for the new cinematic possibilities of the feature film and the advanced techniques of editing, montage, shot size, and mise-en-scène[28] are his reactions to *Judith of Bethulia*,[29] the first feature-length film by D. W. Griffith (Fig. 71).[30]

---

[25] "I go to the movies most every night." F. B. Gilbreth, letter to L. M. Gilbreth, April 4, 1914, Gilbreth LOM, SPCOLL, Purdue University Libraries, NF 91/813-6.

[26] F. B. Gilbreth, letter to L. M. Gilbreth, April 5, 1914, Gilbreth LOM, SPCOLL, Purdue University Libraries, NF 91/813-6.

[27] In 1914, for instance, the Cines-Palast in Nollendorf showed the 120-minute Italian epic *Quo Vadis*.

[28] The correspondence between Frank and Lillian Gilbreth features numerous enthusiastic descriptions of films, particularly French films.

[29] *Judith of Bethulia* (titled *Judith von Bethulien* in the German release) premiered on March 8, 1914.

[30] For details on Griffith, see Gunning, *D. W. Griffith and the Origins of American Narrative Film*.

Figure 71 Frame enlargements from *Judith of Bethulia*, the first feature-length film by D.W. Griffith. It was the techniques of filmic narration that particularly fascinated Gilbreth. Elaborate action scenes, the use of different focal lengths, including close-ups, and an unprecedented use of depth of field characterized the film, which was still shot with a static camera.

> Don't let anyone ever tell you that moving pictures are N.G. [no good] I've just come from Judith, and believe me it is so far ahead of any play that I ever saw that they are piffle. Some people do not realize that any part of a play or the movie that is not first class is out out [*sic!*] and they do it over again and again. This play is a wonder and not a dry eye in the house. I'm studying movies now as never before [. . .].[31]

The film was four-and-one-half reels long and had a running time of around sixty-five minutes. It may have been screened as a Bible-themed cinema event during the Easter holidays. *Variety*'s review of the film was enthusiastic, describing it as a "genuine masterpiece of craftsmanship," and praising it for its "marvellous lighting effects! And the general detail! Really you must see it all for yourself in order to get any comprehensive idea of the presentment."[32] The

---

[31] F. B. Gilbreth, letter to L. M. Gilbreth, April 9, 1914, Gilbreth LOM, SPCOLL, Purdue University Libraries, NF 91/813-6.
[32] "*Judith of Bethulia*," *Variety*, March 27, 1914.

drama and action scenes, extremely innovative for the time, as well as the narrative techniques of parallel montage, close-ups for dramatic effect, and an unprecedented use of deep focus showed Gilbreth the (pedagogical) potential that film could have for conveying ideas and concepts in the workplace.

Gilbreth's enthusiasm for cinema was not restricted to individual film events. It reached the point where he spent his free Sundays, such as October 4, 1914, almost entirely in the cinema. In the afternoon he visited the UT's Lichtspiele Unter den Linden and in the evening the Cines-Palast in Nollendorfplatz.

> Today is Sunday and I celebrated by staying in bed till 2 P.M. Then I wandered out. I walked over to Unter den Linden. Lost my way as usual, but finally found it—went to a movie, had supper and lost my way again coming back. Tonight I went to the movie in Nollendorf Platz and they showed some lantern slides of the war. The cities look exactly like San Francisco.[33]

During the week he frequently attended late-night film screenings after the end of his workday at the Auergesellschaft. The night-time visit to the cinema appeared to have become such a habit that he was even known to fall asleep during a screening:

> Last night I went to the movies, and I dropped to sleep for a minute, I thought, but I think it must have been longer, because when I woke up, people [...] were all looking at me and laughing heartily. I guess I must have been doing one of my record-breaking snoring contests. It was really very embarrassing, so much so that I sneaked out during the last film.[34]

Gilbreth was interested not only in the visual and narrative possibilities of the cinema, but also the developments in projector technology. Accompanied by his colleague S. E. Whitaker, the manager responsible for his corporate consulting team in the Auergesellschaft, Gilbreth went to a screening of a three-dimensional film in April 1914, when the Palast Theater am Zoo was showing *"Fantomo" der plastische Film* (Fig. 72).

The film was promoted as an "attention-grabbing invention" and as a "total transformation of cinematography." The projected figures, as the promotional blurb put it, "have the visual appearance of living actors in a freely lit stage space."[35]

[33] F. B. Gilbreth, letter to L. M. Gilbreth, October 4, 1914, Gilbreth LOM, SPCOLL, Purdue University Libraries, NF 92/813-5.

[34] F. B. Gilbreth, letter to L. M. Gilbreth, November 7, 1914, Gilbreth LOM, SPCOLL, Purdue University Libraries, NF 92/813-5.

[35] Program announcement for the Palast Theater am Zoo, *Berliner Tagblatt*, April 17, 1914, morning edition.

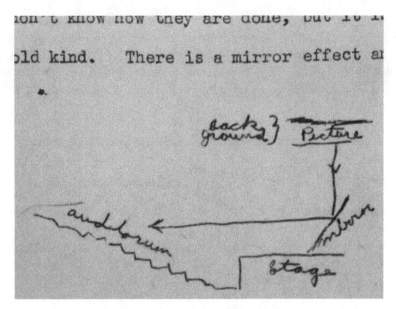

Figure 72 Sketch for a three-dimensional projection technique in the Palast Theater am Zoo, from Frank Gilbreth's correspondence with his wife, Lillian.

> This evening Whitaker and I went to the Palace theatre and [we] saw a variety show including also some new movies. They are semi-stereoscopic [*sic!*] I don't know how they are done, but it is very novel, but not so pleasing as the old kind. There is a mirror effect and apparently the pictures are on a screen, thru which you see the background.[36]

Gilbreth drew up his own sketch of the projection technique used. After all, as a corporate consultant, the flat surface of film projection posed a problem. For training purposes, film was not suited for use in his motion studies. The filmic motion recordings thus had to be conveyed in purpose-built, three-dimensional motion models from wire, so that they could represent the spatial character of a given movement. A three-dimensional projection technology would have made this superfluous. With the medium of film, motion training would have been directly possible without any increased effort. He subsequently sought to practically implement the project of three-dimensional film, and he later sought to acquire the camera technology necessary for this. "I've also bought two very small motion pictures cameras and they are so made that we can take stereoscopic

[36] F. B. Gilbreth, letter to L. M. Gilbreth, April 29, 1914, Gilbreth LOM, SPCOLL, Purdue University Libraries, NF 91/813-6.

motion pictures by simply attaching them together."[37] Particularly in the sphere of pedagogy, Gilbreth was certain, "my stereoscopic movies will make a sensation."[38] Although, in the Auergesellschaft, he was confronted with problems surrounding the practical implementation of filmic consulting services,[39] he saw film as a realistic option for beginning a new chapter in the method of factory rationalization.[40]

> I've just come from the movies with Whitaker. I'm having lots of fun with them [. . .]. I can just see those bricklaying films on the screens. The public doesn't know it, but they need it and it is only a question of time.[41]

Before the fiction feature film, the program usually consisted of nonfiction documentary shorts. Alongside newsreels, this part of the program was frequently occupied by documentary footage of industry, science, and technology. These were precisely the kind of films that Gilbreth himself had produced since 1912. Here in Germany, he thought, there was a need for his films.

> The more I see of movies the more I am convinced that it is the greatest game in the world. It is not for us to tackle drama nor comedy but "teaching" and "efficiency" and motion study. I say we do one film anyway even if we can't sell it. I say we do one film of me doing a film and use it for college lectures and if we can sell it or even get an ad out of it, let's do it.[42]

His thoughts of emerging as a film producer were shattered, at least as far as the German market was concerned, by the introduction of censorship rules after the outbreak of World War I. Various problems with importing and exporting exposed and unexposed film material brought a swift end to his plans.[43] A whole series of preserved film fragments lead us to conclude that even after his return

---

[37] F. B. Gilbreth, letter to L. M. Gilbreth, April 29, 1915, Gilbreth LOM, SPCOLL, Purdue University Libraries, NF 92/813-5.

[38] F. B. Gilbreth, letter to L. M. Gilbreth, May 23, 1915, Gilbreth LOM, SPCOLL, Purdue University Libraries, NF 92/813-5.

[39] For details on the issues facing the Auergesellschaft, see Chapter 5 of this volume.

[40] F. B. Gilbreth, letter to L. M. Gilbreth, April 29, 1914, Gilbreth LOM, SPCOLL, Purdue University Libraries, NF 91/813-6.

[41] F. B. Gilbreth, letter to L. M. Gilbreth, April 29, 1914, Gilbreth LOM, SPCOLL, Purdue University Libraries, NF 91/813-6.

[42] F. B. Gilbreth, letter to L. M. Gilbreth, November 5, 1914, Gilbreth LOM, SPCOLL, Purdue University Libraries, NF 92/813-5.

[43] On this censorship regime, see Wolfgang Mühl-Benninghaus, "German Film Censorship During World War I," *Film History* 9, no. 1 (1997): 71–94.

to the United States, Gilbreth had continued to work on his career as a film producer.[44]

What remains is the strong impression that the cinema left on Gilbreth in the years 1914–1915. As a regular filmgoer, he was confronted with the already further advanced development of entertainment cinema in Europe. Hence his recognition that film, which he had until then only used as a recording instrument, also possessed a significant pedagogical potential. Problems of communication, which Gilbreth knew from his earlier activities in the construction industry as well as in his role as a corporate consultant, could, he thought, be solved in the future with the aid of film. Film and its associated pedagogical possibilities led Gilbreth to dream of an alternative form of industrial rationalization which was less systematic than it was communicative. And as could be expected, the pragmatic businessman that Gilbreth was also saw film as another potential source of profit, as his films could be reused by third parties in the popular newsreel programs.

The media devices developed and used by Gilbreth were an expression of a comprehensive conception of media, which was not restricted to its "instrumental" character. In combination with the pedagogical discourse of this time, Gilbreth ascribed it with potential which should be seen more as a media promise of the future than as something arising from the workplace reality of the factory floor. Media is not only an expression of the technology available at this time, and the options for action that it gave rise to, like the possibility for recording and communicating new sets of knowledge. It also formed a crystallization point in a newly constituted epistemological field of management and consulting knowledge. Media devices and practices became the vehicles for a surfeit of meaning, which helped the future epistemological figures of management to imagine. In essence, Gilbreth's starting point was that film would open entirely new pedagogical possibilities for rationalizing industry. It would thus be conceivable to avoid existing problems of "change management," as they appeared in particular in Taylorist approaches. A more humane work environment, conditioned through the new forms of filmic analysis and the newly available forms of visual communication knowledge sharing, would place the coexistence of employees and managers on a new level. It was less the diverging interests and more the commonalities that would be emphasized through the use of new media techniques.[45] This mixture of media euphoria and social utopia was laconically commented

---

[44] Gilbreth's films, *Odds and Ends #3*, Gilbreth Library of Management Videos, SPCOLL, Purdue University Libraries.

[45] To reduce Gilbreth's consulting concept to a form of behaviorism, as Claude S. George does, therefore does not do it justice. See George, *The History of Management Thought*, 149.

on by a worker for the New England Butt Company after his experiences with Gilbreth's method: "Visionary—impractical."[46]

Media and Montessori: Senses—Nerves—Motoricity

How, then, did it come about that a Calvinist efficiency expert ascribed such power to the medium of film, which seemed to derive less from contemporary rational calculation than it did from a kind of transcendental belief in media?

At its core, Gilbreth's method was based on a trust in the new possibilities of communicating workplace knowledge through film. Behind this, however, stood the concepts of pedagogical reform vigorously promoted by Maria Montessori, whose writings outlined the possibilities for a systematic social education beginning in childhood. Instead of discipline techniques, Montessori felt that the free development of the individual should be at the center of child-rearing. These two developments—the technical and aesthetic advances of film, on the one hand, and on the other hand, the new theories of pedagogy, which emphasized the positive malleability of humans—formed the basis for Gilbreth's fundamental conception of media.

Frank and Lillian Gilbreth verifiably came into contact with Montessori's pedagogy in late 1911–early 1912 through a series of articles published in *McClure's Magazine*.[47] Lillian Gilbreth explicitly made reference to Maria Montessori in her dissertation *The Psychology of Management*, completed in 1914.[48] In an undated note,[49] Frank B. Gilbreth described his own motion models, which he manufactured from the chronocyclegraph recordings, in analogy to the principle of the Montessori models. In 1909 already, three years earlier, the English translation of her magnum opus *The Montessori Method* had been released,[50] and we can assume that, as an industrial and organizational psychologist, Lillian Gilbreth knew of this publication. A December 1913 book tour through the United States by Maria Montessori, who was according to the *New York Tribune* "the most interesting woman of Europe"[51] at this time, generated even more popular attention for her method. Her approach to pedagogical reform met with great

---

[46] Yost, *Frank and Lillian Gilbreth*, 250.

[47] The series of articles appeared in the May 1911, December 1911, and January 1912 issues of *McClure's Magazine*.

[48] Lillian M. Gilbreth, *The Psychology of Management: The Function of the Mind in Determining, Teaching and Installing Methods of Least Waste* (New York: Sturgis & Walton Company, 1914), 231.

[49] "FBG's Notes," undated, Gilbreth LOM, SPCOLL, Purdue University Libraries, NF 50-292-1.

[50] Maria Montessori, *The Montessori Method: Scientific Pedagogy as Applied to Child Education in "The Children's Houses"* (New York: Frederick A. Stokes Company, 1912).

[51] Cited in Robert H. Beck, "Kilpatrick's Critique of Montessori's Method and Theory," *Studies in Philosophy and Education* 1, no. 4/5 (1961): 153.

enthusiasm. In New York she even gave a lecture at Carnegie Hall, which due to popular demand was followed by a hastily organized additional appearance, since more than 1,000 people were locked out of her first engagement.[52]

Between Montessori's and Gilbreth's approaches, there was a striking similarity, which impels us to conclude that Frank and Lillian Gilbreth, particularly when it came to their motion models, were at the very least inspired by Montessori. Similarities between the two methods concern not only the actual methodological approach and the concomitant concentration on raising awareness of motion processes, but also the fixation on combating social "inefficiency." The thrust of Montessori's and Gilbreth's ideas, as well as their discourse, are in this respect nearly identical. Montessori wrote in 1915:

> Another natural law concerns instead the individual worker, and is the law of least effort by which man seeks to produce the most he can, working as little as he can. This law is of very great importance not because of the existence of the wish to work as little as possible but because, by following it, production is increased with less expenditure of energy.[53]

Like the Gilbreths, Montessori also rejected the idea that the main problem of inefficient activity lay in the inability or "laziness" of the individual. Rather, inefficient work practices arose due to a lack of understanding or insufficient training. They were thus a *pedagogical* problem rather than a problem of an absence of discipline. Whereas Gilbreth was primarily concerned with the training of industrial workers, Montessori applied an identical approach to the education of children.

Methodologically, Montessori stood for the scientification of pedagogy. Her approach represented a rejection of the "conservatism and mystical obscurantism" of standard educational methods.[54] Instead of traditional wisdom around child-rearing, she relied on empirical techniques of experimental educational science. Her form of pedagogy consisted of a laboratory-like spatial situation, in which children had the freedom to choose from different learning materials. Additionally, Montessori developed a learning box that contained different *play* elements (Fig. 73). These were all tested and statistically verified in various control groups for their suitability as learning material. These elements would enable children to learn body movements and then subsequently translate them from the symbolic model environment to the "real" world. An article from

[52] "Dr. Montessori's Aim: She Tells Great Audience That She Seeks Perfection of the Race," *New York Times*, December 9, 1913.

[53] Maria Montessori, *The Secret of Childhood* (London: Sangam Books, 1983), 202–203.

[54] William Heard Kilpatrick, *The Montessori System Examined* (Cambridge, MA: The Riverside Press, 1914), 5.

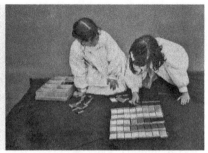

Figure 73 Learning with Montessori objects. In the image on the left, a girl learns a letter's shape by touching a model of the letter. The child is to recognize objects by their weight while blindfolded. The photograph on the right shows children ordering blocks by color.

the *New York Times* about the *Casa dei bambini*, Montessori's model school in Rome, illustrated this principle with the example of a child:

> He has been allowed to hold and handle objects devised for this special purpose [. . .]. He has trained his little fingers and hands in lacing and tying and buttoning and putting things together and taking them apart [. . .].[55]

Playing with learning materials was to encourage the ability of the child to think abstractly, and train the interaction of the nervous system and the perceptual organs with the motoric center. Following the premises of sensualism,[56] the sensory organs were separated from each other and individually stimulated, in order to train them in the most effective manner possible.

As can be seen in Figures 73–75, Montessori and Gilbreth both had recourse to a highly pragmatic reception of the idea postulated by Jean-Jacques Rousseau of training the senses through stimulus reduction:

> Why, then, are we not given practice at walking as the blind do in darkness, to know the bodies we may happen to come upon, to judge the objects which surround us—in a word, to do at night without light all that they do by day without eyes?[57]

---

[55] A. Reno Margulies, "How to Teach Mothers the Montessori of Child Control," *New York Times*, November 24, 1912.

[56] See Heinz Rhyn, "Sinnlichkeit/Sensualismus," in *Historisches Wörterbuch der Pädagogik*, ed. Dietrich Benner and Jürgen Oelkers (Weinheim: Beltz, 2004), 866–85.

[57] Jean-Jacques Rousseau, *Émile or on Education*, trans. and ed. Allan Bloom (New York: Basic Books, 1979), 133.

Figure 74 Frank B. Gilbreth watches motion sequences of typewriting being practiced.

Figure 75 Frank B. Gilbreth here follows the principle advocated by Montessori of initially practicing movements with models while "blind," so that they could be transferred from the model world to the real world.

Montessori would cover children's eyes with a cloth, while Gilbreth made his test subjects (and himself) wear darkened protective glasses. Both of them thus simulated the night imagined by Rousseau, in order to bolster the impressions of the individual senses, in this case touch.

At the same time, the required movement processes were to be imitated as perfectly as possible and thereby learned. In Montessori's discourse, after all, "playing" did not mean *free* but *correct* playing under constant observation:

> Behind this apparent and real liberty is the watchful eye of the teacher, seeing without seeming to see, and without giving to the children direction of which

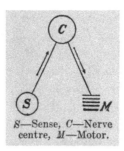

Figure 76 Maria Montessori's physiological model. Playing with specially made learning materials in a controlled learning environment is supposed to ensure the passage of the learning effect from sensory organs through the nervous system to the motor center.

they can rely. But she is ready with an unobtrusive word of suggestion whenever it is necessary.[58]

The ideal of efficient living lay at the basis of pedagogy.[59] Montessori's perspective saw infancy as already important for raising individuals to be socially efficient human beings. Similar to Gilbreth's workers, who were to become aware of their own movements and thereby internalize the "one best way," *correct playing* was at the center of Montessori's method. Correct playing would be assured through the use of special playing materials and the constant observation of the children. The goal was to introduce a process of self-reflection whose goal was the optimal interconnection of perceptual organs, the nervous system, and the motoric center (Fig. 76).

It is a long work, for the child, seeing the model, must follow the movements necessary to reproduce it, while there is no direct correspondence between the visual sensation and the movements which he must make.[60]

The motion awareness that was striven for could not be achieved through discipline and obedience. Rather, a form of guided self-reflection was necessary for

[58] Margulies, "How to Teach Mothers the Montessori of Child Control."

[59] On the social spread of efficiency movement, see Mary Nolan, *Visions of Modernity: American Business and the Modernization of Germany* (Oxford: Oxford University Press, 1994); Daniel Nelson, *A Mental Revolution: Scientific Management Since Taylor* (Columbus: Ohio State University Press, 1992); Judith A. Merkle, *Management and Ideology: The Legacy of the International Scientific Management Movement* (Berkeley: University of California Press, 1980); David F. Noble, *America by Design: Science, Technology, and the Rise of Corporate Capitalism* (Oxford: Oxford University Press, 1979).

[60] Montessori, *The Montessori Method*, 295.

this process, in which the individual was not prevented from reaching an understanding of his or her own abilities through external pressure. The learning process had to be given so much playing space that the sensory organs, the nervous system, and the motoric center could be combined into a triad of optimal movement.

An externally exerted disciplinary force would only disrupt the internal psychological-physiological system and hinder the success of the learning process. In the planning and conception of new factories, Gilbreth utilized a similar principle. He provided the managers with "route models," which were miniature wooden models of the factory space. The managers could play with these models in order to find out the optimal structure for setting up the production process.[61]

Montessori stood in the tradition of Jean-Jacques Rousseau, Johann Heinrich Pestalozzi, and Friedrich Fröbel,[62] who all argued that education was a process that worked from the interior to the exterior and should thus not be disrupted by external interventions. As in the seed of a plant, all personality traits and abilities already lay in every individual from birth. All that needed to be done was to encourage these abilities, by organizing the education process in as free and playful a way as possible. For Rousseau, the three basic elements of education—"nature," "men," and "things"—should be conveyed in as undistorted a way as possible when educating a given individual. With these ideals, Montessori formed her pragmatic model based on learning materials. Another reason why she had such great success was because she placed particular focus on the dimension of things: "The use that we are taught to make of this development is the education of men. And what we acquire from our own experience about the objects which affect us is the education of things."[63] In this endeavor, she had recourse to the earlier work of Jean Itard[64] and Édouard Séguin,[65] who were the first to develop learning objects like shadowboxes and pinboards, in order to systematically use the pedagogical potential of the object-world for educational purposes.[66] One of the reasons for Montessori's success may have been the immediacy of her objects. She translated a pedagogical philosophy first developed by Rousseau into concrete, tangible objects. Her learning materials represented the promise

---

[61] See also Chapter 5 of this volume.

[62] Kilpatrick, *The Montessori System Examined*, 7.

[63] Rousseau, *Émile or On Education*, 38.

[64] Volker Ladenthin, "Zur Pädagogik Jean Itards und zu Aspekten ihrer Rezeption bei Maria Montessori," *Pädagogische Rundschau* 51 (1997): 499–515; Joseph L. French, "Itard, Jean-Marie-Gaspard," in *Encyclopedia of Psychology*, ed. E.A. Kazdin (Washington, DC: American Psychological Association, 2000).

[65] Édouard Séguin, *Traitement Moral, Hygiène et Éducation des Idiots* (Paris: Bailliere, 1846).

[66] Wolfgang Beudels, "'Ich fühle was du nicht hörst und das schmeckt rot': Wahrnehmung, Wahrnehmungsstörungen und Wahrnehmungsförderung in der Montessori-Pädagogik und der Psychomotorik," in *Montessori-Pädagogik und frühe Kindheit—Eine Revolution in der Erziehung?*, ed. Reinhard Fischer, Christian Fischer, and Harald Ludwig (Münster: Lit Verlag, 2004), 77.

of successfully applying the amorphous ideals of developmental pedagogy into the scientifically verified environment of her playing spaces.

Film as a System for Motivation and Training

The film camera represented for Gilbreth what the learning materials, whose colors, shapes, and material were precisely determined, and the external observers were for Montessori. The camera could simultaneously observe, pick up on errors, and deliver pedagogical viewing material in the form of film loops and chronocyclegraph views. "The moving film in the ordinary camera will give stretched-out cyclegraphs, just as though we made a Montessori model and then pulled it out."[67] Furthermore, there was also the possibility of producing motion models out of wire from the chronocyclegraph footage, which, as Montessori demanded, required an abstraction between the world of the model and the real world (Fig. 77).[68]

For Frank and Lillian Gilbreth, film recordings were thus part of an ambitious pedagogical project, which was largely based on a conviction inspired by pedagogical reform that was similar to the methods prescribed by Montessori. The training potential of visual models and film recordings would make the workers aware of their movements. For the Gilbreths, "motion awareness" did not so much signify the coalescence of manual and intellectual labor, as it did a process of pragmatic-behaviorist fine-tuning. It sufficed for the eye to be synchronized with the motoric apparatus. Brain and nerves were, in their view, communicative channels that were to be stimulated through visual stimuli in order to produce more motion-aware and thus efficient workers.

For this purpose, images and models offered a further advantage over written instructions. A significant proportion of the employees of assembly-line industries in the United States, for whom Gilbreth primarily worked, consisted of immigrants with a limited ability to read and write English. For the most part, instructions in written form were simply not understood. In her dissertation, Lillian Gilbreth argued that images and models presented a universally comprehensible form of sharing knowledge.[69]

Similar to Montessori's scientific setup, Frank Gilbreth also saw the primacy of scientific precision as indispensable for his film-based worker training. The

---

[67] "FBG's Notes," undated, Gilbreth LOM, SPCOLL, Purdue University Libraries, NF 50-292-1.

[68] In this, Gilbreth was not alone. Later, other business training regimes also made recourse to visualization models. See, for example, AWF-Mitteilungen, "Stereoskopische Aufnahmen von Getriebemodellen," *AWF-Mitteilungen* 6, no. 5 (1927): 251–52; AWF-Mitteilungen, "Getriebefilme und stereoskopische Aufnahmen von Getriebemodellen," *AWF-Mitteilungen* 6, no. 18 (1927): 923.

[69] L. Gilbreth, *The Psychology of Management*, 227.

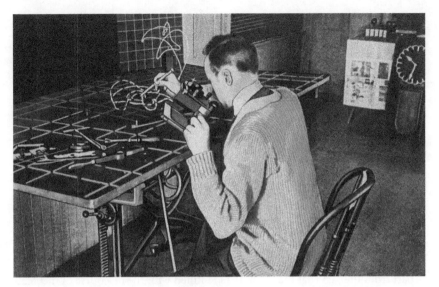

Figure 77 The fabrication of a motion model from a chronocyclegraph. The markings of black and gray points on the wire model denote the time and speed required for carrying out the movement.

reason for the introduction of media techniques of image generation in industry lay, according to Gilbreth, in the basic premises of Scientific Management, to which he felt duty-bound: "Scientific management is simply management that is based upon actual measurement."[70] The "scientificity" of this managerial method rested on the precision of the measurements on which the system was based. It was only "by the aid of cinematograph pictures"[71] that Gilbreth saw himself in a position to reach the level of precision he felt was necessary. The time studies carried out by Frederick W. Taylor were based on the simple observation of the worker by a work inspector equipped with a stopwatch and an observational chart. To this, Gilbreth counterposed his film-based motion studies. Media techniques, he argued, would exclude the possibility of erroneous results occurring through the subjective perception of the individual observer. The work inspector was dependent on the fleeting moment of observation. In this moment, a decision had to be made as to which events would be documented (and, at the same time, which ones would *not* be documented). In contrast to this, the motion data recorded on the film material could be saved for a later

---

[70] Frank B. Gilbreth and Lillian M. Gilbreth, *Applied Motion Study: A Collection of Papers on the Efficient Method to Industrial Preparedness* (New York: Sturgis & Walton Company, 1917), 3.
[71] Gilbreth and Gilbreth, *Applied Motion Study*, 36.

detailed analysis. Unlike with the work inspectors, who did not correspond with the ideal of the unprejudiced gaze, "everything [was] indifferent" to the process of media recording.[72] An evaluation of the data gained could then ensue, thereby preventing the imprecisions of human observation. It is possible that this did not lead to major differences in the results, but the evaluation of the media data could be carried out in an accountable fashion. Whereas experiential knowledge, as the basis for the work inspector to make decisions, exhibited an implicit framework, the criteria of a media-based analysis were transparent and accessible at any time. Gilbreth replaced the implicit experience of the work inspectors with the notion of the mechanical objectivity[73] of the explicit, immediate, and unbiased nature of media recording.

Motivation Through Film

Apart from the fact that the Gilbreths identified with the discourse of mechanical objectivity, and positioned their media technique as a more precise technical instrument of recording, their notion of media incorporated still other aspects. They also considered media to be an opportunity to situate science itself as a transparent and accountable process within the setting of the factory floor. These views on the possibilities of these techniques matched those that Felix Auerbach had expressed with respect to graphic techniques. He also saw a potential for transparency in visualizations and graphic displays.[74] In this sense, Auerbach held that the mechanical objectivity of media recordings was not only part of a scientific, laboratory-based arrangement. The use of media devices *themselves* generated a surplus value which the observation of workers through a work inspector could not offer, and which was to be understood through the close description of mechanical objectivity:

> The process of motion study is such as to interest the worker. While undoubtedly some success could be made of motion study through a trained observer merely watching the worker, we find it of utmost importance and mutually advantageous from every standpoint, to gain the full and hearty cooperation of the worker at once, and to enlist him as a co-worker in the motion study from the moment the first investigation is made. Our methods of making motion

---

[72] Jakob Vogel, *Die chemische Wirkung des Lichts und die Photographie in ihrer Anwendung in Kunst, Wissenschaft und Industrie*, 125, cited in Peter Geimer, "Was ist kein Bild? Zur 'Störung der Verweisung'" (Frankfurt am Main: Suhrkamp, 2002), 339.

[73] Lorraine Daston and Peter Gallison, "The Image of Objectivity," *Representations* 40, Special Issue: Seeing Science (1992): 81–128.

[74] See Chapter 1 of this volume, "The Graphic-Visual Punctum."

study are by the use of the micro motion, simultaneous motion cycle chart, and chronocyclegraph methods. All make it imperative that the worker shall understand what is being done and why, and make it most profitable to everyone that the worker shall be able, as well as willing, to help in the work of obtaining methods of least waste by means of motion study.[75]

The Gilbreths positioned themselves against approaches like Taylorism, in which a deep mistrust toward the workers prevailed. Taylorism was based on highly discreet analytic devices, such as the Taylor-Thompson stopwatch, which "guarantees the uninterrupted control of the workers' practical activities"[76] (Fig. 78).

In contrast, the Gilbreths deliberately foregrounded the media technology they used (Figs. 79 and 80). The demonstrative exhibition of the devices used for filmic motion studies was not intended to reduce employees to passive objects of investigation. Workers were to be convinced through a transparent process of meaningful film analysis, which instead of arousing mistrust would actively incorporate them into the investigation process.

In the conception of Lillian Gilbreth, an industrial psychologist, such factory-floor interventions would no longer be perceived as the product of external arbitrary chance, but as part of a scientifically unbiased process made visible.

> We have here nothing hidden or occult or secret, like the working practices of an old-time craft; we have here a science that is the result of accurately recorded, exact investigation.[77]

Workers who recognized this gained the status almost of coequal colleagues. Through the visibility of media techniques that was made available to them, the workers themselves became experts. They could carry out the concrete act of recording and computing the results with the material media devices and recordings that they deployed. The laboratory setting of the "betterman-rooms" and the interconnected devices of the motion laboratories, such as the chronocyclegraph and film and photo cameras, returned as representatives of scientific methodology in the viewing field of employees. The results of scientific techniques, in turn, were not encountered in the form of abstract logic or inaccessible written instructions. They were illustrated representations, like the chronocyclegraph or the labor study film, which were directly visible and boasted an immediate relation to the labor movement in question. The interpenetration

---

[75] Frank B. Gilbreth, "The Effect of Motion Study upon the Workers," *The ANNALS of the American Academy of Political and Social Science* 1000 (1916): 272.

[76] Fritz Giese, *Psychologisches Wörterbuch*, vol. *VII* (Berlin/Leipzig: Teubner, 1928), 159–60.

[77] Gilbreth, *Applied Motion Study*, 3.

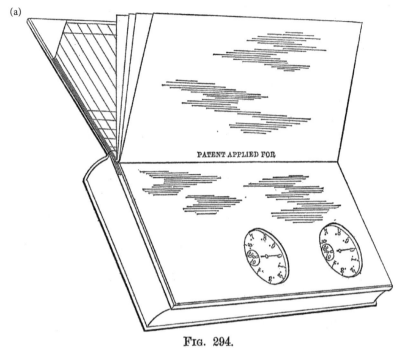

Figure 78 The Taylorist recording apparatus as a panoptic countermodel to Frank B. Gilbreth's participatory management approach. The Taylor-Thomson-stopwatch in a discrete book form and the accompanying observation sheet enabled time studies without the active involvement of the workers, and without the worker necessarily even being aware of being part of a time study.

Figure 79 The conscious exhibition of media techniques and apparatuses as representatives of objective, scientific techniques in the motion study laboratory.

Figure 80 Instead of discreet control through stopwatches, Gilbreth's apparatuses offered to improve performance through the incentive of increasing the worker's personal wage level.

of the laboratory and the factory space not only contained the adaptation of scientifically exact techniques; media devices also represented the principle of the production of scientific knowledge per se. For many factory workers, this may have been the first contact of any kind with technical processes of scientific research.[78]

The Gilbreths' conception of media was not exhausted in the idea of popularizing scientific practices through the introduction of visible media devices and transparent techniques. They ascribe still more efficacy to image-producing technologies. Even the willingness, or at least motivation, to cooperate could be increased with the introduction of media techniques:

> When using the chronocyclegraph device; the worker is not only interested in the electric lights and their various paths and orbits of dots and dashes, but is most anxious that these paths shall be those of the greatest skill and the fewest number of motions possible.[79]

Since the worker was directly tied to the media devices, the Gilbreths believed, the data were particularly faithful and convincing. The immediacy of the media recording and the resulting representations in models, film, and photographs did not permit any "behind." The media surfaces were to coincide with the reality of microeconomic rationality. Disruptive human factors, like that of the potentially hostile or inattentive work inspectors, no longer had any influence on the direct combination of labor motion, media recording, and visual representation. Reflected in the media recording devices, the worker had no choice but to submit to the rationality of this coupling of media and science.

This situation not only drew its efficacy, however, from the belief in an infallibly exact recording. The reason for the additional motivation lay not only in the rather authoritarian gestures of the mechanical objectivity of media processes. On the contrary, Lillian Gilbreth saw its origin in a collective media frenzy which could be exploited for business:

> It is, therefore, not strange that the world's best actors and singers are now grasping the opportunity to make their best efforts permanent through the instrumentality of the motion picture films and the talking machine records.

[78] Certainly, from the mid-eighteenth century, the bourgeois public in Germany developed an interest in the popularization of the (natural) sciences. Belonging to this trend was the "Gesellschaft für Verbreitung von Volksbildung" (Society for the Propagation of Popular Education), which dedicated itself exclusively to workers' education. Nonetheless, these attempts were not very successful and were restricted to the "classical" natural sciences. See Andreas W. Daum, *Wissenschaftspopularisierung im 19. Jahrhundert: Bürgerliche Kultur, naturwissenschaftliche Bildung und die deutsche Öffentlichkeit, 1848–1914* (Munich: Oldenbourg, 1998), 168–78.

[79] Gilbreth, "The Effect of Motion Study upon the Workers," 273.

This same feeling, minus the glow of enthusiasm that at least attends the actor during the work, is present in more or less degree in the mind of the worker.[80]

If the workers were filmed, then they themselves became film protagonists. This would itself unleash additional stores of motivation. Linked with this was the assumption of a surfeit of signification from the parallel field of the film entertainment industry. Lillian Gilbreth speculated that the film recordings for scientific purposes would be associated with the glamour and identification potential of the silent film and its star cults. The workers filmed would subsequently become part of a star system within industrial cinema. After all, their image was projected onto an oversized screen, much like those of the early stars of the silent film era. Together with the immediacy of the medium and the associated transparency of its process, Gilbreth wanted to create the kind of cooperative atmosphere indispensable for his method.

Typing Faster

The scope of this media training system can be paradigmatically understood with the example of a commission that the Gilbreths carried out for the Remington Typewriter Company.[81] With its newly introduced typewriter, the Remington Standard 10, the firm competed at the time against the Underwood No. 5 model, made by the Underwood Typewriter Company. In this competition between the two companies, heavily promoted, nationwide typewriting contests played a major role. Here, however, Remington was regularly beaten by Underwood. This was the context for Gilbreth being tasked with the commission of using his film-based method to train a group of typists the ten-finger system on the new machine. Underwood's supremacy in the typewriting contests had to be broken. The goal of the commission was less to develop structural forms of motion rationalization, and more to increase the typing speed of a few individuals whose high-level performances were effective for publicity purposes. These performances were subsequently to be used in advertisements as an argument for the superiority of Remington's typewriters.[82]

Due to the prescribed QWERTY keyboard, the typewriter did not permit any ergonomic changes. Hence, the Gilbreths concentrated on the development of a training system that would allow for beginners to make progress in their learning as quickly as possible. Additionally, Underwood participants in the contest's

---

[80] L. Gilbreth, *The Psychology of Management*, 38–39.

[81] The Remington Typewriter plant in Illion, New York, was rationalized by Henry L. Gantt a few years earlier in 1910. See Chandler, *The Visible Hand*, 277.

[82] See advertisement for the *Remington Typewriter Company* in *The Rotarian* 8, no. 1 (1916): 59.

category of professional typists had a very high typing speed, which Gilbreth's charges could not meet in the time they had available to them. So they concentrated on the amateur (novice) category. Between 1890 and 1910, the number of typists and stenographers in American companies rose from 33,418 to 316,693.[83] There was a palpable need to train new typists. It was thus precisely the argument that beginners would make quick and easy progress by learning to type with a Remington that represented the machine's practical superiority and distinguished it from the more fabled record of the Underwood typists, who, from this perspective, were more remote from practical reality.

> The question of typewriter merit is not determined by what the exceptional operator of exceptional training can do, *but what the average operator can do* [emphasis in original]. And the best answer to this question, afforded by any speed contest, is, *what can the novice do?* [emphasis in original]—for the novice stage is the stage through which all operators must pass.[84]

Since the Gilbreths proceeded with the principle of learning from abstract models, the test subjects were initially not supposed to practice their movements on a typewriter. Instead, the Gilbreths prepared paper models of the keyboard, which were color-coded for the finger that needed to be used with each key. It was only when the positions of the individual keys were learned and the first attempts at typing on the paper model had been undertaken that the subjects could switch to specially prepared training typewriters. The keys were covered with dark caps, so that the finger coordination learned with a model could be translated to the typewriter "blindly."[85]

Once they had successfully mastered this step, then they had to pinpoint any remaining efficiency potential and further increase typing speed. For this purpose, the typists were filmed in a motion study laboratory (Figs. 81 and 82), in order to recognize and subsequently alter inefficient movements. In the laboratory, the Gilbreths had recourse to various shot sizes, with which they filmically captured the basic hand movements of typing. Alongside shots of the typists, which captured the movements of paper and line changes (Fig. 83), they also took close-ups that focused on the fingers and the movements they traced (Fig. 84). As such, they prepared cyclegraphic recordings, in order to make the deviations of individual fingers visible.[86] At the same time, film

[83] See Wootton and Kemmerer, "The Emergence of Mechanical Accounting in the U.S. 1880–1930," 109.

[84] Advertisement for the Remington Typewriter Company, *The Rotarian* 8, no. 1 (1916): 59.

[85] Gilbreth Jr. and Gilbreth-Carey, *Cheaper by the Dozen*, 54–58.

[86] Ibid., 59.

Figure 81 A motion study laboratory for the commission with Remington Typewriter Company. Visible in the photograph are the chronocyclegraphic device, a Gilbreth clock, the lighting elements for film recording, as well as the obligatory graphic backdrop, in this case a simple chalkboard.

Figure 82 A proud typist in front of the film set in the motion study laboratory.

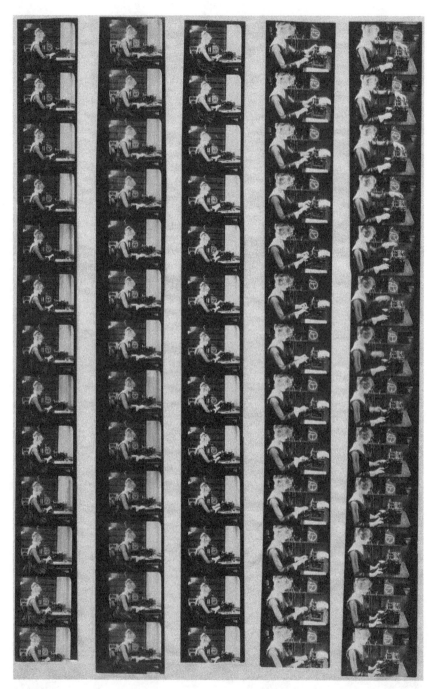

Figure 83 Images of a typist in a motion study laboratory.

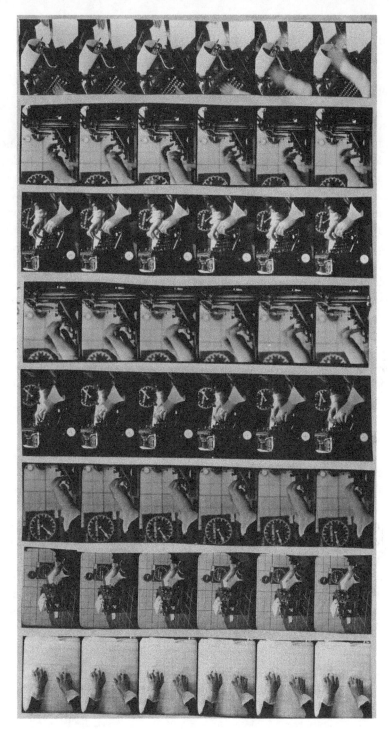

Figure 84 Image details for controlling motion sequences, as reaction tests and for on-selling to American weekly newsreels. The upper film strip shows the increases in efficiency through the principle of continuous form paper.

footage represented instruments of control, which determined the progression or regression of the typists.

The hand movements deviating from the prescribed "one best way," to be avoided if the desired typing speed of up to 140 words per minute was to be attained, were analyzed and thenceforth corrected through the use of slow-motion viewing in the motion study laboratory. Some of the trained typists made great progress in only a very short amount of time. There were two main reasons for this. First, the Gilbreths not only accelerated the actual process of writing, but also optimized the movements made during the page and line changes.[87] Through a meaningful coordination of both arms, the time consumed by inserting a new piece of paper in the typewriter was reduced to less than two seconds. They communicated these optimized movements to the typists with the aid of film footage. The movements recorded were translated into "Simo-Charts" (simultaneous-motion charts),[88] where the movements of both hands could be graphically represented in detailed fashion.

On the other hand, they were successful in enduringly motivating the typists to adopt their form of training. As I mentioned earlier, they managed this through integrating the typist into the research process itself. The typists no longer functioned as mere objects of observation and investigation, but actively intervened in the research process. They were, after all, the most important component of the motion studies carried out. They were supposed to internalize the improvements that needed to be attained and thereby win contests.

The Gilbreths adroitly used film footage for this purpose—not only as a device of scientific analysis, but also as a motivational tool. While the direct address of the individual was already given through close and intensive collaboration within the motion study laboratory (Figs. 85 and 86), the Gilbreths also filmed the typists outside of the framework of the motion studies themselves. A paradigmatic example of this is a close-up of the face of typists wearing a hat (Fig. 86). In doing so, the Gilbreths gave the participants the feeling of being something special. The motivation resources were unleased by cannily using the film culture that was popular among employees for their motivation strategy. This address also took place in the context of an increase in appeals to women as consumers.[89]

---

[87] Apart from this, Gilbreth experimented with the color of the typewriters. Instead of black machines, he made white machines, in order to reduce the contrast with the white writing paper. This was intended to delay ocular fatigue. See Gilbreth, "Address Before the Eye Sight Conservation Council," Lecture, 1922.

[88] See "Simo Chart Hortense S. Stollnitz," Gilbreth LOM, SPCOLL, Purdue University Libraries, NF 51/297-2.

[89] See, for instance, Jean V. Matthews, The Rise of the New Woman: The Women's Movement in America, 1875–1930 (Chicago: I.R. Dee, 2003); Michele Ramsey, "Selling Social Status: Woman and Automobile Advertisements from 1910–1920," Women and Language 28, no. 1 (2005): 26–38; Margaret Finnegan, Selling Suffrage: Consumer Culture & Votes for Women (New York: Columbia University Press, 1999); Ricia Anne Chansky, "Time to Shop: Advertising Trade Card Rhetoric and

Figure 85 Intensive collaboration in the motion analysis is ensured by the cooperation and motivation of the participants.

The footage enabled the typists to later watch themselves on the screen, much like the great silent film stars of the time.[90] Moreover, the film footage was usually produced before a collection of external visitors.[91] The association with the bustling energy surrounding a star on a feature film set was also possible in the laboratory film set. The use of the film medium ensured the atmosphere of cooperation and participation judged to be essential by the Gilbreths. In the close-ups, we can see the relaxed atmosphere that prevailed on the set, which was in fact a training camp for typists. Even a certain shyness and helplessness in front of the camera can be discerned. It was precisely the aspect of novelty that contributed to boosting motivation. The fascination for the still unfamiliar medium did not bring about mistrust, but motivation.

The disciplinary Taylor clock and the distrust among the workers it aroused was replaced by the Gilbreth clock, a control concept that was not based on

the Construction of a Public Space for Women in the United States, 1880–1890," *ATENEA* 29, no. 1 (2009): 151–66. I would like to thank Thomas Elsaesser for this reference.

[90] See also Richard Lindstrom, "'They all believe they are undiscovered Mary Pickfords': Workers, Photography, and Scientific Management," *Technology and Culture* 41 (2000): 725–51.

[91] See Figure 42.

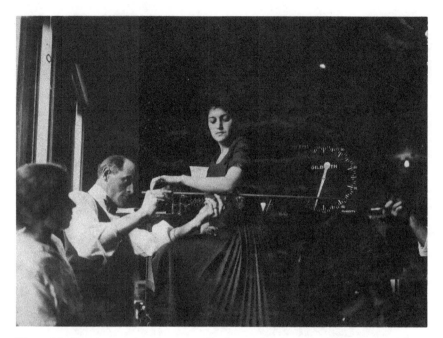

Figure 86 Creating motion awareness. Setting up the chronocyclegraphic recording instruments for Hortense S. Stollnitz, who was later the 1916 amateur world typing champion. To the right, Lillian Gilbreth accompanies the preparations.

dividing workers but on bringing them together. The film camera was ideally suited for speaking to individual people and motivating them. The resulting footage shows areas for potential improvement to the typists in concrete motion processes and replaced unspecific appeal to increasing performance. Here, the Gilbreths developed an initial concept that was consciously premised on the workers' competency for self-leadership, a strategy of employee leadership which would only become widespread many decades later. The close-ups also arose in the framework of a project in which the Gilbreths sought to understand the visual and reactive behaviors of typists. They were also part of the motivation complex that ensured the success of the training program. It was precisely the ambivalent position of this footage, between scientific recording and cinematic fascination, that made it so productive as a tool for excitation and motivation.

By combining a system of media excitation with a few fundamental improvements to workers' movements, the Gilbreths were successful, up to a certain limit. For instance, one of their trainees, Hortense S. Stollnitz, won the International Novice Champion Typewriter Contest in New York on October 25, 1915,

Figure 87 The "film star" in the laboratory. Increasing motivation among typists through film recordings allowing for flirting with the film camera and enabling their own subjectivity.

with 114 words per minute.[92] In 1916, she became the International Amateur Champion Typist with 137 words per minute, and later set a new world speed record for amateurs with 147 words per minute.[93] The title of "National Amateur Typewriting Champion" was also won by a trainee of the Gilbreths, Anna Gold, with 132 words per minute. In this contest, organized by the Chicago Business Show, Stollnitz came in second, with 129 words per minute.[94] But when Stollnitz entered the category of professionals, although she achieved the highest number of keystrokes in the field of contestants, she had by far the highest error rate, and thus came in seventh place. Places one to six were won by typists from rival

[92] Advertisement for the Remington Typewriter Company, *The Rotarian* 8, no. 1 (1916): 59.
[93] Gilbreth and Gilbreth, *Applied Motion Studies*, 36–37.
[94] Advertisement for the Remington Typewriter Company, in *Journal of Education* 84 (1916).

company Underwood. Their typists may well have typed more slowly, but their error rate was up to ten times less.[95] This was a sign that, although the Gilbreths were capable of generating euphoria and motivation among their typists, their actual training method left a lot to be desired.[96]

The promotional coup of a victory in the amateur class demanded by the client was reached, but Gilbreth lacked any long-term viability. Nonetheless, the studies for the consultancy firm Gilbreth, Inc. represented a major publicity success. He relied on the chronocylegraph footage, photographs, and film produced there, which showed the immaculate superiority of lab-based consulting. This impression became more widespread through the notices posted by Remington, such as through American newsreels, which screened some of this film footage.[97]

Incentive Systems in Big Business

In order to be successful with their method of lab-based consulting, it was clear to the Gilbreths that the workers affected by the restructuring of labor processes should not completely reject their method. After all, the Gilbreths' rather open approach did not exclusively rest on the principle of discipline through the dyad of surveillance and punishment. In the case of the Remington typists, this was relatively simple to achieve. The training practices undertaken there had little in common with the classical form of workplace education and training. Instead, the typists were provided with an intensive, individualized training that was directed toward a concrete target: winning contests. In this sense, it was necessary to achieve optimal performances of only a few minutes duration. The combination of the laboratory setting and the film camera automatically placed the typists in the center of attention. The ensuing individual address by the film camera and the participation of motion experts ensured their willingness to

---

[95] "Official Records International Championship Typewriting Contest New York City," October 17, 1921, Gilbreth LOM, SPCOLL, Purdue University Libraries, NF 57/417-4.

[96] Gilbreth followed a special learning principle, which was distinct from conventional training techniques. He did not start out by training the movements in a slowed-down form, in order then to steadily increase the temp. Gilbreth believed that the "One Best Way" could never be reached through a slowed-down training of motion sequences, since different, and therefore false, motion lines lay at the basis of these slowed-down movements. He thus had them practice, from the very beginning, the motion sequences at the targeted maximum speed. Instead of slowly increasing speed and thus guaranteeing a motion sequence with the fewest possible errors, Gilbreth deliberately had workers trained at high speed, even if they made errors. It was his task to gradually minimize the errors. With the film recordings, he had an instrument that allowed precisely this retrospective control. A typing speed of up to 140 words a minute could no longer be carried out with the naked eye. The high error rate in the 1921 typing contests reveals that Gilbreth had little success with this method.

[97] See Lancaster, *Making Time*, 200ff.

cooperate. In fact, this situation more closely resembled a scientific investigation or a sports training camp[98] than the realities of industrial workplace training.

In the production sites of major industrial enterprises, there was no direct connection between the motion analysis in the laboratory and the awareness of movement. Due to the great number of workers who needed to be trained and the limited possibilities of the media technologies available at the time, it was essential to separate motion *analysis* from motion *training*.[99] The motion analysis of previous motion sequences needed to be communicated to the employees as quickly as possible. Filming and training every worker in a motion study laboratory would have been simply too expensive and time-consuming. For the training of entire departments, Frank Gilbreth had to resort to other means, like the labor study film and wire models of movements. With this, he wanted to bring knowledge out of the motion study laboratory and into the workplace.[100] This meant, however, that the direct motivation of the workers through individual contact within the laboratory was lacking. The necessary willingness to cooperate that was evident among the typists within the laboratory situation had to be achieved, here, through other means. Using media with front-of-class teaching, so much was clear to Gilbreth, would not lead to the kind of motion-aware worker upon whom the optimal implementation of his consulting method was predicated.

In his activities in the business world, Gilbreth therefore had to tackle this problem differently. He needed to develop techniques that, in spite of the absence of a personal training situation, as was the case with the Remington commission, allowed for an individual approach toward the employees.

Exemplary, in this sense, was the approach he took with the restructuring of the New England Butt Company in Providence, Rhode Island. This business produced machine parts for wire production and refining. From 1913 on, Gilbreth introduced a raft of measures in order to ensure the success of his rationalization program. "The Gilbreths used a mixture of personnel management, vocational education, industrial democracy, and psychology to persuade the workers to accept what the 'experts' thought was best for them."[101] They oriented themselves to the form, originally developed in Germany,[102] of company paternalism and

---

[98]   On this, see also the collaboration between Gilbreth and the training specialist Walter Camp in Chapter 5 of this volume, "Media Contract Acquisition: Film and Fencing in the Wilhemine Era".

[99]   In Chapter 4 of this volume, "Epistemological Effects of Early Cinema," I give a detailed overview of the technical reasons that led to the concept of the hermetically closed-off motion laboratory imposing itself, with no film recordings made directly on the factory floor.

[100]   Details of this can be found in Chapter 3 of this volume, "Knowledge Transfer through Motion Awareness."

[101]   Lancaster, *Making Time*, 136.

[102]   See also Jane Lancaster "Frank and Lillian Gilbreth Bring Order to Providence: The Introduction of Scientific Management at the New England Butt Company, 1912–13," *Rhode Island History* 55, no. 199 (1997): 76.

patriarchy.[103] These included methods of worker leadership, which sought to secure the stability and productivity of a business through auxiliary sociopolitical measures.[104] Designated in the United States as *industrial betterment*, this incorporated the introduction of company pensions or the provision of cheap living quarters and subsidized food.[105] The goal was a general improvement in working conditions, thereby gaining the loyalty of workers. As corporate consultants, however, the Gilbreths were not concerned with long-term measures. They had to demonstrate short-term success. As such, Gilbreth installed custom-made instruments in order to ensure the success of the restructuring process of the company and the raising of productivity on the assembly line. The Gilbreths' approach "included clean bathrooms, lunchrooms, and regular rest periods. It also involved education for the workers, including the provision of libraries and lectures."[106] Gilbreth particularly emphasized the educational aspect, but he wanted to realize the ideal of motion-aware workers, and thereby raise productivity. For this, he not only required a healthy and loyal staff, but also a certain basic understanding of his method among the workers. After all, the concept of motion-aware workers also demanded an act of abstraction from the workforce. An educational offensive, Gilbreth thought, would have two advantages. On the one hand, the comprehension and the acceptance among the workers of his scientific techniques would be higher, while on the other hand it would be easier for educated workers to engage in a training process and successfully see it through to the end. Exemplary for this approach is the *home reading box scheme* that Gilbreth designed (Fig. 88). This system gave the workers access to magazines and books.

Gilbreth established a retrieval system for used magazines across the entire metropolitan area of Providence, which would then be made available to workers in the Butt Company free of charge.[107] "The Home Reading Box movement was part of the optimistic progressive spirit of the time: give the worker access to knowledge and they will use it."[108] Alongside the *home reading box scheme*, he also introduced an employee suggestion scheme, for which the *suggestion box*

---

[103] See Gerhard Albert Ritter and Klaus Tenfelde, *Arbeiter im Deutschen Kaiserreich, 1871 bis 1914* (Bonn: Dietz, 1992); Klaus Tenfelde, *Arbeiter im 20. Jahrhundert* (Stuttgart: Klett-Cotta, 1991).

[104] This model was characteristic of the corporate culture in Krupp, Stumm, Bosch, Zeiss, and other firms. Gilbreth's esteem for this form of corporate management is clear from the praise he gave to the organizational form of the Zeiss plant in Jena, for which he was briefly active as a corporate consultant.

[105] Hartmut Berghoff, "Unternehmenskultur und Herrschaftstechnik: Industrieller Paternalismus.: Hohner von 1857 bis 1918," *Geschichte und Gesellschaft: Zeitschrift für historische Sozialwissenschaft* 23, no. 2 (1997): 167–204.

[106] Lancaster, *Making Time*, 138.

[107] See "Route Plan Home Reading Movement Providence," Gilbreth LOM, SPCOLL, Purdue University Libraries, NF 162/0299-11.

[108] Lancaster, *Making Time*, 139.

Figure 88 The *home reading box* and *suggestion box* in the New England Butt Company. Here, the workers could borrow magazines for educational purposes. Moreover, a delivery and retrieval service was also offered which transported books and magazines across the entire metropolitan area of Providence, Rhode Island.

was conceived. A higher level of education, he thought, could not only positively change the attitudes of workers toward the impending rationalization efforts. With the suggestion scheme, the Gilbreths wanted to actively involve the workers in the restructuring process. After all, the workers were in the best position to know where there were inefficient work processes to overcome.[109] In order to help make this system a success, the workers needed to participate in the new system and not block it through a lack of interest. The motivation to strengthen the workers was correspondingly the actual goal of his participatory approach, which he sought to attain through instruments like the home reading box scheme, or the conscious instrumentalization of media technologies and practices.

The Star System of the Industrial Film

Alongside general measures to encourage worker motivation, Gilbreth also introduced the targeted favoring of cooperative workers as an instrument of business management. He had already gained experience with this approach in

[109] Ibid.

his activities in the construction industry, where he had abolished the practice of *blacklisting*, the active exclusion of unwanted workers, in favor of *whitelisting*. Instead of active repression, Gilbreth introduced the favoring of particularly good workers as a tool of worker management.[110]

A filmic pendant to this principle was introduced in 1918, for a commission for the Ball Brothers Glass Manufacturing Company, a business that had specialized in the packaging of long-lasting food. Here he used the system trialed with the Remington Typewriter Company of involving the workers in the transformation of workplace conditions. Since he did not carry out a detailed individual training suited to each worker, he used film in a different way as an instrument of worker motivation. If the film footage shot for Remington still stood in direct relation to the motion analysis carried out in the motion study laboratories, Gilbreth produced films for Ball Brothers in which he "rewarded" selected workers with filmic presence, thereby elevating them from the crowd of their coworkers: "The worker receives not only a money reward, but also publicity."[111] Based on Lillian Gilbreth's work in industrial psychology, they created the "star system" of the industrial film, a media incentive system which was intended to elicit an increase in the filmic attention economy among participating workers. An intertitle always preceded the footage of the individual worker in the framework of a film which thematized the improvement of specific production processes. It contained the name of the worker subsequently shown, which further contributed to personalizing the footage. Sometimes common nicknames the workers had were also used.

This gimmick further bolstered the personalized approach, while also constructing an implicit proximity with the workers depicted. The selection of close-up shot sizes (Figs. 89 and 90) also contributed to the individualization of the film images. Instead of an impersonal system, individual workers were shown who were intended to paradigmatically represent and also popularize the system.

With the introduction of the film as a bearer of symbolic capital,[112] the Gilbreths also created a symbolic hierarchy within the company, in which the workers had to position themselves. During his time in the construction industry years earlier, Frank had already had recourse to this instrument of worker leadership. There, he organized bricklayer contests, whose winners were symbolically rewarded, in full public view, with an American flag. At Ball Brothers, film

---

[110] For more details on "whitelisting" in the construction industry, see Chapter 3 of this volume, " 'Lay some brick . . .': From Businessman to Consultant.

[111] L. Gilbreth, *The Psychology of Management*, 186.

[112] On the concept of symbolic capital, see Pierre Bourdieu, *Distinction: A Social Critique of the Judgement of Taste*, 8th ed., trans. Richard Nice (Cambridge, MA: Harvard University Press, 1996 [1984]).

Figure 89 The star system of the industry film. Film material taken by Gilbreth in 1918 in a factory in Muncie, Indiana, for the Ball Brother Glass Manufacturing Company.

Figure 90 Filmic representation of work groups. The use of "nicknames" suggests a good atmosphere within the group.

took over the function of manifesting visibility and social prestige in the public domain.

Alongside individuals who were elevated by being filmed, small work groups also became part of the star system. Of course, Gilbreth primarily focused on the specific worker, the individual, but the implementation and adaptation of the changes demanded by him took place on the factory floor. The work structures there consisted above all of work groups, who generally bore responsibility for a given assembly process. Cooperation within the group was essential for a frictionless production process, and so the internal group relations also had to be filmically represented. In order to avoid the impression of a random group image and retain the individual character of the footage, which would have been lost with camera positions that were too far away from the subjects, a maximum of only two workers could be seen on the screen at any one time. With camera pans, the other members of the group were integrated into the filmic representation and designated as a part of the group.

These personalized images were part of a filmic training material which was intended to communicate changes in working methods to the staff. The personalized worker images in the film thus had a dual purpose. On the one hand, they focused on the person depicted and created a new hierarchy of media visibility among the company's employees. On the other hand, they also need to convince the workers to actually implement this method. Sociopolitical measures such as the establishment of libraries, together with the introduction of media incentive systems, formed part of an attempt to secure the practical adaptation of the new knowledge from the motion study laboratories to the factory floors.

Finally, these films also represented evidence for the superiority of Gilbreth's model of corporate consulting. They were suited to being ideal promotional vehicles for his consulting knowledge. After all, the film image showed that Gilbreth was successful in convincing the workers of his approach. The reality of the film images was remote from the protestations and resistance of the workforce that the rationalization projects of Scientific Management regularly incited. In this context, the personal proximity they suggested aroused the impression that the Gilbreth method could be integrated in existing business structure without too many problems.

The idea of conceptualizing the factory space as a laboratory space invariably met with success when Gilbreth worked in companies which were not union organized, like the New England Butt Company. Here he was able to get the workers to cooperate with his transparent method. He deliberately exhibited the media technology utilized and thus integrated staff directly into the process of analysis. In union-organized workplaces, however, his method generally failed.[113] As soon as Gilbreth sought to implement his media incentive system in a workplace in which a stable symbolic and social hierarchy already existed, and

[113] See Chapter 5 in this volume for a failed consulting project in Berlin.

a high level of union organization signified nothing else, he could not manage it. The perspective I suggest—not to reduce Gilbreth's usage of media to the actual motion studies, but to understand his media method more as an incentive system—provides a possible explanation for these failures.

In union-organized workplaces, he was unable to implement his media-based form of a symbolic hierarchy predicated on social prestige against the pre-existing order. As a rule, the intended restructuring process also failed. Without symbolically obtaining interpretative sovereignty within the firm, he was not in a position to implement the new knowledge gained in the motion laboratory.

That Gilbreth could not prevail against the existing order was also due to the fact that he overestimated the efficacy of media incentive systems. The enthusiasm of the audience for the film medium, which Gilbreth experienced in his visits to the movie theaters of Berlin,[114] could not be so easily transferred from the cinema *dispositif* to the reality of the business world. His concept of the participatory integration of workers was strongly oriented to his notions of a bourgeois eagerness for education. Like Montessori in her conception of pedagogy, Gilbreth assumed that people would freely grow and develop if they were given the opportunity.[115] This idea of an early form of control through self-management was, at the time, still a profoundly bourgeois convention which had little to do with the lived reality of the working class.

Nonetheless, the Gilbreths forged a new path with their conception of media and the management tools derived from it. They transformed the idea of the paternalistic factory system from the nineteenth century into a variety of applicable media strategies and adapted them to the new situation of integrated big businesses.

What the Gilbreths anticipated in their conception of media and the media practice derived from it would later be described as the *Hawthorne effect*. This referred to the observation that scientific investigations of workers can result in increased performances per se, because the workers enjoy a higher estimation of their value. This effect was first scientifically defined more than a decade later by a research team from the Harvard Business School, which investigated the Hawthorne Works of the Western Electric Company in Chicago from 1924 to 1932 for the effects of factory lighting levels on labor productivity. The completely random changes in productivity, according to their conceptions and methods, could in the end be explained by this so-called Hawthorne effect, which simply meant that worker productivity could be influenced through the workers' social relations and the labor environment. To this can be added the attention that the researchers gave to the workers.

---

[114] See Chapter 4 of this volume, " 'I go to the movies most every night': Cinema and Management."
[115] See Chapter 4 of this volume, "Media and Montessori: Senses—Nerves—Motoricity."

The history of science and business sees the Hawthorne experiments as the origin of a fundamental paradigm shift in the scientific preoccupation with commercial and industrial processes. Workers are now no longer seen as human machines, but as social beings.[116] For academic research this may indeed be true. But those active as corporate consultants or managers did not have to be notified of this scientific "discovery" in order to take this circumstance into account in their daily decisions. As an analysis of their conception of media demonstrates, Frank and Lillian Gilbreth were aware of this effect, at least as the implicit basis of their work, more than a decade before it was studied. Unlike the scientists from an academic background, they were less concerned with the theoretical determination of this effect. Instead, they sought to productively introduce it into their activities as corporate consultants. In this sense, they turned the factory space into a laboratory space. This move was not only for the purposes of scientific discovery. Above all, it was grounded in their desire to increase the motivation of the workers and thereby garner new consulting commissions.

Epistemological Effects of Early Cinema

The Gilbreths' corporate consulting model relied on filmic and media processes and the principle of the laboratory space. This combination was not only dependent on strategic considerations of using the principle of "scientificity" as a motivational resource and as their unique selling point in the field of the consulting branch. A similarly decisive role was played by the media technology available at this time. The possibilities arising from this, as well as the limitations associated with it, considerably contributed to the Gilbreths establishing the form of lab-based consulting as a model of modern industrial and commercial management. Technical and economic aspects of early cinema, together with the laboratory-based motion analysis, developed in physiological settings, formed the epistemological background for the model.[117]

Here, we must refer to the basic paradox that their model came up against. As outlined earlier, they followed an "open," participatory approach. With this, they wanted to speak to workers individually and motivate them. At the same time, they represented a model of producing, analyzing, and synthesizing knowledge, which was based on the spatial structure of the laboratory. The participatory approach was diametrically opposed to the concept of a knowledge

[116] See Charles D. Wrege, *Facts and Fallacies of Hawthorne* (New York: Garland, 1986); Richard Gillespie, *Manufacturing Knowledge: A History of the Hawthorne Experiments* (Cambridge: Cambridge University Press, 1991).

[117] For details on the value Gilbreth placed on physiological laboratory settings, see Hoof, "'The One Best Way.'"

production located in a geographically closed-off laboratory. Whereas the former presupposed the visibility of knowledge production, the hermetic space of the laboratory prevented precisely this necessary visibility of recording and analysis processes. The laboratory as a participatory framework with an equitable treatment of experts and workers was accordingly only perceived by those workers who found themselves *inside* the laboratory.

On a purely hypothetical level, other models, not reliant on the principle of the closed-off laboratory, could have been offered. With the mobile devices of film, laboratory units were conceivably visible for everyone on the factory floors. Instead of taking place in a closed-off laboratory setting, the motion studies were carried out directly in the workplaces in question. The model of a mobile film laboratory unit could have cultivated an open, participatory atmosphere. Film footage was accessible and visible to all employees. Interestingly, however, this did not happen. Instead of that, the concept of lab-based consulting garnered a vehement dynamic of inclusion and exclusion, which only increased the longer the Gilbreths incorporated it into their consulting business as a unique selling point. But why did Frank Gilbreth close off these processes in a difficult-to-access laboratory? Why did he go against the Gilbreths' own approach, which relied on the participatory integration of workers? Doing so was not, as the thesis presented here argues, a decision consciously made by Gilbreth. It was also a result of the costs and technical limitations of early cinema.

The adaptation of filmic techniques for industry created a series of serious problems. Whereas in 1906 the film company Gaumont built the biggest film studio in the world, the Cité Elgé in the Buttes-Chaumont in Paris, erecting large glass studio roofs in order to have maximum light exposure for film recording, Gilbreth wanted to film with a similar recording technique in near windowless, dusty, and "perfectly dark factory spaces."[118] This was a daring undertaking and required suitable illumination systems, which also had to be compact, transportable, and robust (see Figs. 91 and 92).[119] For this reason, only arc lamps were taken into consideration, since they were equipped with carbon rods for illumination.

Nonetheless, their introduction was connected with a substantial generation of heat, and the lights also produced a high level of ultraviolet radiation. In order to guarantee enough brightness for the takes, it was essential to position the person filming close to the illuminating lamps. Whereas it was relatively simple to protect the film crew "through the use of dark glasses against the light of the lamps,"[120] the workers filmed were exposed to harmful rays and heat. Eye inflammations and skin damage similar to sunburn were the

---

[118] Fritze, "Kinematographie im Dienste der Industrie," 124.
[119] See R. Thun, *Der Film in der Technik* (Berlin: VDI-Verlag), 156–57.
[120] Ibid., 163.

Figure 91 The *Jupiter-Industrie-Lampe Typ 26* could be made mobile. It was quick to assemble and disassemble and required only a standard electricity connection. But the lamp offered only a low luminocity.

result.[121] Additionally, there was a blinding effect produced by the open lamps that was not to be underestimated, which restricted the coordination and vision of the filmic protagonists. With chronocyclegraphic recordings, the lights and wires attached to the limbs of workers led to burns.[122] Certainly, there now arose the possibility of directly recording labor processes in the authentic work

---

[121] Ibid., 162.
[122] F. B. Gilbreth, letter to L. M. Gilbreth, January 12, 1914, Gilbreth LOM, SPCOLL, Purdue University Libraries, NF 91/813-6.

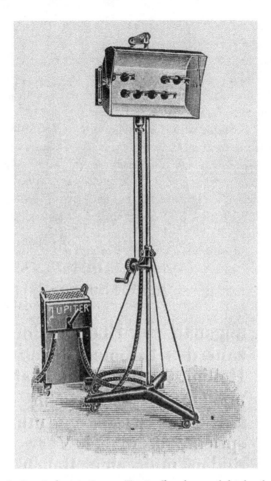

Figure 92 The *Jupiter-Industrie-Lampe Typ 3* offered a much higher luminosity, but it could only be used in stationary film studios. This model was too bulky and heavy to transport, and it also required a high-voltage electricity connection.

situation of the factory. But the equipment used created such distortions that any advantage was erased. There could no longer be any talk of a "realistic" work situation when the worker was distracted by the heat and brightness of the lights.

Apart from the technical problems, the sheer cost of filmic analysis processes also contributed to the motion studies being carried out in the stationary laboratory.[123] Due to the dust emissions in the factory, it was also necessary to use the

---

[123] That the attendant costs of the film generally prevented its introduction in industry can also be discerned from publications of the period, such as the article by M. Nelzow, "Billige Lichtbilder," *Werkstattstechnik* 18. no. 16 (1924): 427.

expensive "double coating" technique on the film stock,[124] in order to protect the celluloid from being scratched.[125]

Gilbreth reacted to the high costs of the film stock and development[126] with a convoluted technique of multiple exposure for reducing costs. Additionally, he introduced a matte in order to cover a part of the film during a take. With this method, the same film stock, as can be seen in Figure 93, could be used up to eight times.[127] Each one of the four image series consisted in turn of two alternating exposed series of takes. In this example, the filmed worker wore a hat during a take so that he could be more easily distinguished, and in take that immediately followed, the hat was gone.

Nonetheless, multiple exposure led to a reduction in the resolution of the film footage. In order to be able to valorize it, devices for optical image enlargement were necessary (Fig. 94). Concomitantly, the film footage only served as an auxiliary tool for carrying out motion studies within the laboratory.[128] For the standard projectors and screening instruments, this footage was no longer suitable (Fig. 95). The method did decrease the price, but also limited the visibility of the films. As instructive images for worker training, they were no longer appropriate.[129] The images were now tied with the context of the laboratory and found only restricted usage outside of it.

As long as Gilbreth continued to film in the 35mm format in the early 1910s, and with commonly available camera technology, the footage from the laboratories could still be directly used for training or motivational purposes. This direct connection was lost with the professionalization of his film techniques and processes. By persistently developing new special devices for the preparation of motion studies, he departed from the cinema *dispositif* and the path of technical development associated with it. He transformed film into a technique for underpinning the paradigm of scientific visibility.[130] Similar to the principle of other

[124] Motionscope Company, letter to F. B. Gilbreth, November 11, 1914, Gilbreth LOM, SPCOLL, Purdue University Libraries, NF 37/265-4.

[125] From 1915 on, Frank B. Gilbreth began to prepare his films in this manner. See F. B. Gilbreth, letter to L. M. Gilbreth, May 23, 1915, Gilbreth LOM, SPCOLL, Purdue University Libraries, NF 92/813-5.

[126] In particular, the costs for the external development of the film stock, which in the case of the Auergesellschaft contract was the Messter Filmgesellschaft, had to be reduced. See I. Witte, letter to F. B. Gilbreth, November 29, 1915, TECHNOSEUM, Witte Nachlass, Sig. 992, No. 6/2-14.

[127] In the end, Gilbreth was able to reuse a film strip up to twenty-four times. See Witte, *Kritik des Zeitstudienverfahrens*, 30–31.

[128] See Horace B. Drury, *Scientific Management: A History and Criticism* (New York: Columbia University Press, 1915), 112.

[129] Witte, *Kritik des Zeitstudienverfahrens*, 31.

[130] On this, see also the distinction made by Curtis between spectatorship and observation; Scott Curtis, "Between Observation and Spectatorship. Medicine, Movies and Mass Culture in Imperial Germany," in *Film 1900: Technology, Perception, Culture*, ed. Annemone Ligensa and Klaus Kreimeier (New Barnet: John Libbey, 2009), 87–98.

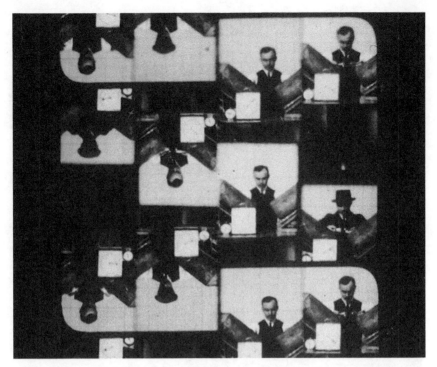

Figure 93 Rationalization of rationalization: efficient filming through multiple exposure.

Figure 94 A magnification apparatus necessary for the multiple exposure of film material used in motion analyses. The image derives from an analysis laboratory, which Gilbreth installed in Berlin during his time as a consultant for the Auergesellschaft.

Figure 95   Reduced visibility of the film image in the laboratory. Film became a discreet vehicle of data. "Projector Box for Film Reading in Daylight-Room" from the year 1921.

graphic recording systems, it charted a flow of data, which would be later used for analysis. At the beginning of his activities, a haphazard usage of filmic evidence and visibility prevailed, as could be observed in the commission for the Remington Typewriter Company,[131] but this had to be specially prepared for the changed conditions in each new case. If film now appeared as a tool for training, motivation, or advertising, then it was no longer a matter of a contingent excess of media signification coming out of the laboratory, but a planned filmic, media strategy. This was necessary for opening the hermetic, invisible laboratory space up to the outside world. Film was part of the scientific laboratory space and no longer the guarantor of a transparent and participatory corporate restructure. It was turned into material data for management and became the basis for planning

---

[131] Such as the close-up shot, for instance, which served to analyze eye movements, but also turned the person under analysis into a film protagonist and was capable of releasing further motivation resources. See Chapter 4 of this volume, "Typing Faster."

and decision-making processes, which were displaced to the motion laboratory, charting departments, and planning departments.

The model of lab-based consulting was due less to a conscious decision for the scientific process of the laboratory studies and more to the technical and economic conditions of early film technology. In the stationary location of the laboratory, the standards of film studios for firmly installing lighting equipment could be adopted. This in turn enabled the introduction of incandescent lamps for film lighting, which had less of an effect on the recording process.

No Participation Without Visibility

With the forced displacement of the work studies into the laboratory situation, hermetically sealed off from everyday production processes, Gilbreth drew on the guiding principles of scientificity. The laboratory was to be a guarantor for the scientific One Best Way. At the same time, he lost direct contact with the staff. Processes within the motion laboratory eluded the gaze of the workers. The atmosphere of cooperation and participatory coexistence attested by him was made impossible with the uncoupling of labor studies from actual production. The collaboration of the workers in the studies now meant cooperation in the isolated conditions of the laboratory. In concrete terms, for the workers this meant a significant paring back of their possibilities for informal participation in the organization of the firm.[132] If the employees previously had information about the department and the concrete work phase which was to be subject to change, they could no longer follow these practices within the motion laboratory. They were no longer able to enact changes to the workplace directly on the factory floor with the aid of informal discussions. Considered from this perspective, the introduction of laboratory knowledge was also a risky enterprise directed against the existing patterns of knowledge and action in the workplace.

---

[132] A series of studies into labor and organizational sociology has established, in this context, that industrial corporations not only represent models of an ideal command structure, but that they must be understood as a space of social interaction. The functional ability of an organization thus relied not only on their explicit rules and spheres of responsibility. Just as important are the informal acts of social activity. This micropolitics lies at cross-purposes to the predetermined formal structures of an organization. See, for example, Michel Crozier and Erhard Friedberg, *Actors & Systems: The Politics of Collective Action*, trans. Arthur Goldhammer (Chicago: The University of Chicago Press, 1980); Karl Lauschke and Thomas Welskopp, *Mikropolitik in Unternehmen: Arbeitsbeziehungen und Machtstrukturen in industriellen Großbetrieben des 20. Jahrhunderts* (Essen: Klartext, 1994); Willi Küpper and Günther Ortmann, *Mikropolitik: Rationalität, Macht und Spiele in Organisationen* (Opladen: Westdeutscher Verlag, 1988); Geßner, "Zur Bedeutung von Macht in Beratungsprozessen: Sind mikropolitische Ansätze praxistauglich?" in *Soziologische Beratungsforschung: Perspektiven für Theorie und Praxis der Organisationsberatung*, ed. Nina Degel et al. (Opladen: Leske und Budrich, 2001), 39–54.

Taken literally the "one best way" approach suggests that there is a unique so-lution for any given work methods problem which will maximize production rates. This could only happen if there were no conflicting requirements on work methods, but this is obviously impossible. [. . .] There simply is no "one best way" in terms of all the requirements that must be considered in any real-life problem. There only can be an optimal way in which the various viewpoints and, hence, requirements are given appropriate weight. The "one best way" con-cept is nothing more than a quasi-moral postulate that an ideal state of stand-ardization for work methods should be achieved in real life.[133]

By generating knowledge in the artificial space of the laboratory, without veri-fying it first-hand against his own business aptitude, Gilbreth heightened the risk that the adaptation process would backfire. There, the fixation on the laboratory turned against his approach. This concerned the so-called scientific methods of engineering science, and in particular approaches of:

work measurement, where experimental results depend directly on the envi-ronment in which they are made. A laboratory investigation, for example, can hardly be expected to reveal much about the performance characteristics of workers in a factory environment.[134]

The laboratory studies, as implemented by the Gilbreths, were an extremely pre-carious affair. The accumulation of investigations in the laboratory guaranteed scientific objectivity. At the same time, however, they prevented the adaptation of this knowledge. For a successful transfer of knowledge from the laboratory, the Gilbreths, after all, were dependent on the workers. Laboratory knowledge by itself was not sufficient to integrate it successfully into workplace procedures. Only the workforce possessed the production knowledge needed for actually implementing the improvements. If they were not incorporated into the planned measures for change, it was easy for them to block said changes.

Taken together, this provides a plausible explanation for why Frank and Lillian Gilbreth were extremely successful in garnering commissions but encountered numerous failures in the concrete execution of their consulting jobs. Inadequate lighting equipment, the high costs of film production, and the fear of industrial espionage[135] excluded film footage from being taken directly on the factory floor.

---

[133] Abruzzi, *Workers and Work Measurement*, 242.

[134] Ibid., 9.

[135] See the restrictive control over the Universum-Filmgesellschaft's film footage of the Daimler production plant. "Tagesmitteilung Nr. 457," June 12, 1923, Mercedes-Benz Archiv, DMG 38, and "Tagesmitteilung Nr. 458," June 14, 1923, Mercedes-Benz Archiv, DMG 38. Even Gilbreth himself had difficulties in receiving permission for film recording, as was the case with his contract for Carl

Even if the Gilbreths were exposed to the model of a mobile, "open" laboratory, they could not realize it in the given circumstances. The technical reality lagged behind the visionary power of their participatory model. Additionally, unlike their predecessors in physiology, they had to contend with the changing conditions of ongoing factory production. Their utopian ideas about media immediacy, and the participatory and educational effects associated with it, were far in advance of the technical possibility and the widespread discourse at the time around work and business management. As such, their model appears in retrospect as a pioneering act of business management which for this very reason was a failure in everyday reality.

Zeiss Jena. The company's management was concerned that he would take pictures of secret production techniques. See F. B. Gilbreth, letter to L. M. Gilbreth, May 24, 1914, Gilbreth LOM, SPCOLL, Purdue University Libraries, NF 91/813-6.

5

Failing in Style

Business Consulting in Wartime Berlin

It was in the year 1914 that the Gilbreths first began to implement their consulting method on a major scale, with the restructuring of the Berlin-based Auergesellschaft. This commission will form the focus of the ensuing chapter. My case study will show the gap produced between the aspirations of their method and the reality of their concrete consulting activity, but also the high value that media techniques were given in this process.

The first phase of their consulting activity involved impressing the client with the scientific potential of Gilbreth's filmic techniques. In Berlin, Gilbreth carried out filmed studies of fencing. If he had retained the commission, he would have installed a motion study laboratory as well as a planning department, which would have guided the restructuring of the business from a central position, allowing him to gather and visually handle data. Gilbreth developed and combined a series of data visualization techniques and scenario analyses, which were to support him in devising new production processes. He used the chronocyclographic method, but also had recourse to other visualization techniques from the *graphic method media network*. At the same time, he installed training spaces, which were equipped with the latest media projection technology. Here, he sought to educate management and convey to them the main traits of his new system.

Gilbreth's consulting approach was a failure in Berlin. The reasons for this lie in global political circumstances and the resistance put up by workers and middle management, which he was incapable of overcoming. In spite of the difficult circumstances, he was nonetheless able to delay the termination of the contract. This can be understood as a success for his strategy of media-based consulting. The kind of practices and models of visual knowledge transfer and adaptation Gilbreth used in Berlin corresponded to a modern form of consulting knowledge that has remained stable until the present day. In the production of this visual consulting knowledge, the purpose of its application was always taken into consideration. Whereas early corporate consultants like Emerson, Gantt, and Taylor still relied heavily on the written form to legitimize their method, Gilbreth concentrated on the visual evidence of his media devices. Together with his partner Lillian, he lay the cornerstone for a form of consulting that is still valid today. Gilbreth was not only a pragmatic consultant; he also developed the

Angels of Efficiency. Florian Hoof, Oxford University Press (2020) © Oxford University Press.
DOI: 10.1093/oso/9780190886363.003.0001

first abstract-theoretical conceptions of management practice, which rested on the visual and media-based decision-making practices.

Media Contract Acquisitions: Film and Fencing in the Wilhelmine Era

In January 1914, before the beginning of his consulting activity for the Auergesellschaft in Berlin, Gilbreth carried out motion studies with the newly developed technique of chronocyclegraphy, which was not directly connected to the actual commission. "I am planning to cyclegraph a famous fencer and send the pictures to the Kaiser and director Remane [*sic*] wants to get into it also."[1] The planned cyclegraphs were part of a public relations offensive, to secure the desired long-term consulting contract with the Auergesellschaft (Fig. 96). Hermann Remané was the corporation's boss. At the same time, Gilbreth attempted to gain a private audience with Kaiser Wilhelm II.

For this purpose, Gilbreth carried out a series of fencing studies on January 16 and January 28, 1914.[2] The morning of January 16 alone saw the production of a total of "300 feet of movie and 50 or more stereoscopic cyclegraphs and chronocyclegraphs"[3] of a German and Russian fencer with "pictures of standard procedures of fencing and also broad sword exercise."[4] The fencers participating in this study "are supposed to be the best in all Germany and are retained by the army."[5] The archival holdings lack details about the concrete payment methods or who assigned this commission. It is probable, however, that Gilbreth carried out the studies at his own expense. The fact that he had hired the cameraman Roger Freeman on his personal account, in order "to develop motion pictures and cyclegraph pictures about 2 hours per day per week" is evidence of this.[6] The film recordings on January 16 lasted two hours and took place on site in the Auergesellschaft's premises in the Berlin borough of Friedrichshain.

The first recordings were botched. Technical problems immediately arose because the lamps of the cyclegraphic recording device were constantly

[1] F. B. Gilbreth, letter to L. M. Gilbreth, January 14, 1914, Gilbreth Library of Management (LOM), Special Collections (SPCOLL), Purdue University Libraries, NF 91/813-6.

[2] F. B. Gilbreth, letter to L. M. Gilbreth, January 15, 1914, Gilbreth LOM, SPCOLL, Purdue University Libraries, NF 91/813-6.

[3] F. B. Gilbreth, letter to L. M. Gilbreth, January 16, 1914, Gilbreth LOM, SPCOLL, Purdue University Libraries, NF 91/813-6.

[4] F. B. Gilbreth, letter to L. M. Gilbreth, January 15, 1914, Gilbreth LOM, SPCOLL, Purdue University Libraries, NF 91/813-6.

[5] F. B. Gilbreth, letter to L. M. Gilbreth, January 16, 1914, Gilbreth LOM, SPCOLL, Purdue University Libraries, NF 91/813-6.

[6] F. B. Gilbreth, letter to L. M. Gilbreth, January 7, 1914, Gilbreth LOM, SPCOLL, Purdue University Libraries, NF 91/813-6.

Figure 96 Stereoscopic image of participants in the fencing studies Frank B. Gilbreth, second from the left, next to him on the right, the privy-councilor Bernhard Dernburg, former state secretary of the Imperial Colonial Bureau and later Imperial Vice-Chancellor and finance minister in Scheidemann's cabinet, flanked on either side by Russian and German fencers, after the first, unsuccessful, film recording of the morning. The date on the photograph, January 15, 1914, does not concord with the date of January 16, 1914, given by Gilbreth in a letter to his wife.

extinguished by the swords during the fencing bouts. This problem could be overcome, but extended the originally planned recording time of one to two hours. Since the fencers, much like the attending privy councilor Bernhard Dernburg, seemed fascinated by the possibilities of filmic recording, they rescheduled a planned visit to a member of the German aristocracy in order to complete the recordings.[7] More seriously, however, it turned out afterward that the lamps they used emitted insufficient illumination. The recordings were thus too dark and had no viable usefulness.[8] It is also possible, however, that Gilbreth and his cameraman had incorrectly lit the takes and simply placed the blame on the lamps provided by the Auergesellschaft. After all, in a later letter, Gilbreth spoke in general terms about the recordings "not tak[ing] enough light."[9] In the

---

[7] F. B. Gilbreth, letter to L. M. Gilbreth, January 16, 1914, Gilbreth LOM, SPCOLL, Purdue University Libraries, NF 91/813-6.

[8] F. B. Gilbreth, letter to L. M. Gilbreth, January 23, 1914, Gilbreth LOM, SPCOLL, Purdue University Libraries, NF 91/813-6.

[9] F. B. Gilbreth, letter to L. M. Gilbreth, January 16, 1914, Gilbreth LOM, SPCOLL, Purdue University Libraries, NF 91/813-6.

end, he worked with new film and photography equipment form the Ernemann company, which the Auergesellschaft had made available to him only a few days beforehand, and with which he had thus garnered very little practical experience.[10] Due to the first setback, he prepared a new recording session, which took place on January 28, and achieved the desired results. The roughly fifty stereocyclegraphs from this date preserved in the Gilbreth archives authorize the conclusion that the film recordings had a similar scope as the first attempt on January 16. The day after, Gilbreth wrote with satisfaction: "We got the pictures of the fencers and they are very fine, yet I don't know exactly what to do with them now that I've got them."[11] Why he should film fencing studies, of all things, was less due to coincidence, and more due to his marketing calculations already tested out in the United States. This consisted of making motion studies of popular sporting activities, for which there was a certain interest among potential clients.

Sporting Studies, the Public, and Winning Contracts

Gilbreth varied this principle for different sports. Thus, he carried out a series of similar sporting motion studies for the perfect golf swing. In May 1913 already, before his stay in Berlin, he investigated the pitching and hitting movements in baseball during a game between the New York Giants and the Philadelphia Phillies (Fig. 97). With these studies, he was able to measure the speed of the ball and the necessary time requirements for a few standard plays. A real improvement in pitching technique resulting from this study, however, is not documented.[12] Above all, the goal of these studies was to make his own name, and the method of motion studies associated with it, more prominent. This happened against the backdrop of his recent move to Providence due to a consulting contract. It was there that he sought to build up his newly founded consulting business. Along with the baseball studies, he filmed nearby athletes from Brown University at track meets, in particular the 100-yard dash. These films were "advertising gimmicks"[13] for his consulting business.

A few years later, Gilbreth found an application for the general knowledge about the elementary movement of pitching he had gained. In a 1916 commission for the American military, he trained soldiers in how to throw hand

[10] F. B. Gilbreth, letter to L. M. Gilbreth, January 12, 1914, Gilbreth LOM, SPCOLL, Purdue University Libraries, NF 91/813-6.
[11] Brief to F. B. Gilbreth and L. M. Gilbreth, January 31, 1914, Gilbreth LOM, SPCOLL, Purdue University Libraries, NF 91/813-6.
[12] Lancaster, *Making Time*, 144.
[13] Ibid.

Figure 97 Baseball pitching studies, recorded on May 31, 1913, during a home game of the New York Giants against the Philadelphia Phillies in the Polo Grounds stadium. The gridded background was to allow for pitch deviations from balls crossing the lines to be detected.

grenades as efficiently as possible, in preparation for their intervention into World War I.[14] The extent to which the pitching motion in baseball resembled that of a combat situation was of secondary concern. At the very least, however, Gilbreth could refer to these studies when realizing his commissions, and point to pre-existing experiences with the filmic investigation of throwing movements. This approach, as I will argue, exhibited a certain resemblance to the fencing studies that Gilbreth carried out in Berlin. How he proceeded with the results of his filmic studies already corresponded to a form of publicity, very widespread today, which for reasons of popular acceptance does not take the form of overt advertising, but of a supposedly scientific study.[15]

---

[14] For details, see Florian Hoof, "'Between the Frontlines': Military Training Films, Machine Guns and the Great War," in *Cinema's Military Industrial Complex*, ed. Lee Grieveson and Haidee Wasson (Berkeley: University of California Press, 2018), 177–91.

[15] Present-day corporate consultancies rely on pro bono projects in order to conquer new markets, such as the public sector. Potential clients can thus be convinced of their methods without running any financial risk.

Together with Walter Camp, one of the founding figures of American football, a former coach at Yale University and an early fitness guru, Gilbreth carried out other sport studies (Fig. 98).[16] At the beginning of this collaboration, for which they specifically hired a public relations manager,[17] Gilbreth considered setting up a corporate partnership with Camp if the project was successful. Under the motto "speed, skill, strength,"[18] they were to concentrate on the analysis of sport. It was far from a coincidence that Gilbreth should discover an interest in sports studies shortly after his return from Berlin, when he had to traverse a period with a low number of commissions. A campaign initiated by Frederick W. Taylor against his method (and his person) had its effects, and it made attracting new consulting contracts difficult. The main motivation for studying sports was less his abstract interest in motion studies and more his concern about a lack of clients. Applied sports studies were still not very widespread and represented an auspicious new field of business. Moreover, the lack of contracts threatened Gilbreth's presence in the media, and with it the reputation of his corporate consulting in the public sphere.

Gilbreth's cooperation with Camp is also an example of the fact that the targeted intermingling of business, private, and scientific motives was not without its problems and required precise guidance. Consulting knowledge was a delicate commodity. On the one hand, it required objective, scientifically grounded criteria to legitimize the corporate transformation processes desired. On the other hand, this knowledge, and its attendant method, simply had to be communicated. The one-sided focus on sports studies shook the fragile balance between abstract scientificity and its easy accessibility. This is documented in a letter Gilbreth wrote to Camp. The latter had used pictures taken from Gilbreth's golf studies in an article for the August 1916 edition of *Vanity Fair*, without gaining his permission.

> I saw this month's *Vanity Fair* and was greatly pained to see the way our name was mentioned in connection with the moving pictures of golf. This certainly looks as though we had gone into the motion picture business.[19]

---

[16] Walter Camp published a series of guidebooks aimed at improving fitness, such as *Keeping Fit All the Way: How to Obtain and Maintain Health, Strength and Efficiency* (New York: Harper & Brothers, 1919).

[17] Lindstrom, " 'They all believe they are undiscovered Mary Pickfords'," 732.

[18] Pencil sketch, Gilbreth LOM, SPCOLL, Purdue University Libraries, NF 45/293.

[19] F. B. Gilbreth, letter to Walter Camp, 28.12.1916, Gilbreth LOM, SPCOLL, Purdue University Libraries, NF 45/293.

Figure 98 Different camera angles from a motion study of golf swings. Problems in the exposure of the outdoors shots can be seen, while the film images taken under laboratory conditions (below right) appear to be usable.

If the project of studying sports was initially a nonbinding trial balloon, Gilbreth was now concerned with his reputation as a serious, scientific corporate consultant.

In the early years of his career as a business consultant, film was still an ill-defined, relatively new technology that incited a playful approach toward it. This changed with the advent of entertainment cinema and the concomitant emergence of genres and stable narrative forms. The controversy over the portrayal of sex and violence in film, such as the "white slave" films of the 1910s in Chicago and New York, and later the scandals surrounding drug abuse, adultery, and rape in the orbit of the Hollywood star system, changed the public's perception of film.[20] It was no longer just an innovative technology that offered new perceptual and aesthetic forms. Film became a projection screen for the morally reprehensible and the indecent. This resulted in a serious image problem for film, to which

---

[20] See Grieveson, *Policing Cinema*, 151–91; Shelley Stamp Lindsey, "'Oil upon the Flames of Vice': The Battle over White Slave Films in New York City," *Film History* 9, no. 4 (1997): 351–64; Gary Alen Fine, "Scandal, Social Conditions, and the Creation of Public Attention: Fatty Arbuckle and the 'Problem of Hollywood,'" *Social Problems* 44, no. 3 (1997): 297–323; Kenneth Anger, *Hollywood Babylon* (New York: Simon & Schuster, 1975).

Gilbreth had to respond. In any case, he wanted to avoid appearing to be part of the morally controversial film industry. In the light, too, of the military contracts he received from 1917 on, Gilbreth henceforth sharply distinguished his films from commercial cinema and its usual designation of "motion pictures." "These films do not fall under the classification of 'motion pictures.' They are devices for visual education."[21] As such, he moved away from his earlier orientation of marketing film as a scientifically accurate recording apparatus. Instead, film now became a pedagogical promise that would guarantee the "transfer of skills."[22]

A further reason for Gilbreth's growing reluctance was due to technical difficulties in the sports recordings. The equipment for the chronocyclegraphs easily came apart from the golf clubs, as had already happened in the Berlin fencing studies. In addition, the sheer weight of the recording equipment had a major impact on the actual movement and falsified the results. In addition, exposure problems made it difficult to obtain assessable data.[23]

Fencing and Film

Whereas baseball, athletics, and golfing were entrenched popular pastimes in the United States, fencing represented a sport with equal cultural identification potential for the elites of Wilhelmine Germany. The rise of fencing in the German Reich accelerated from 1880 onward with the advent of student dueling associations, or *Mensurs*, and at the beginning of the twentieth century the sport reached its highpoint. Although the *Mensurs* had earlier met with police bans and the threat of imprisonment, as occurred in Tübingen before 1888, this offense was no longer pursued consistently in the following years. Around 1910, the *Mensur* was an indispensable cultural component of the aggressive militarism of the Wilhelmine era.[24] At the same time, fencing began to assert itself in broader society. This was witnessed by the wave of founding fencing clubs, which began at the beginning of the twentieth century and culminated in 1911 in the establishment of the Deutscher Fechterbund (German Fencing Association). As Norbert Elias notes, the "merciless habitus"[25] which is ineluctably associated with the *Mensur*, was supplemented with the goal of perfecting athletic movements.

[21] F. B. Gilbreth, lecture notes for "Technical War Films and Vocational Training," ASME Meeting June 4–7, 1918, Gilbreth LOM, SPCOLL, Purdue University Libraries, NF 126/887.

[22] Lillian M. Gilbreth and Frank B. Gilbreth, *Modern Methods of Transferring Skill*, illustrated by Military Films, undated booklet, ca. 1921–22, Gilbreth LOM, SPCOLL, Purdue University Libraries, VT 2/0019.

[23] Lindstrom, " 'They all believe they are undiscovered Mary Pickfords,'" 732.

[24] Sonja Levsen and Helmut Berding, *Elite, Männlichkeit und Krieg: Tübinger und Cambridger Studenten 1900–1929* (Göttingen: Vandenhoeck & Ruprecht 2005), 102–104.

[25] Norbert Elias, *The Germans*, trans. Eric Dunning and Stephen Mennell (Cambridge: Polity Press, 1996), 107.

Figure 99 Stereocyclegraphs of Berlin fencing studies from January 15, 1914.

Gilbreth's fencing studies were, epistemologically considered, not physiological studies, but part of a publicity campaign to win people over to his model of filmic and media-based corporate consulting. They did not aim for the penetration of bodily movement sequences, but the penetration of the German elites. There, the motion studies of fencing generated the work of winning people over to the commercial application of his method in factories and for the military. It is unclear how Gilbreth arrived at the idea of studying fencing and using this reservoir of identification for his own purposes. He himself showed very little interest in fencing.[26]

In any case, the images produced were not suitable as physiological studies aimed at improving fencing, because the standard movements recorded were not easily recognizable (Fig. 99). Even the fencers involved in the recordings had difficulty assigning the developed stereocyclegraphs to the respective sequences of movements. "They were delighted with the pictures, but they could not tell what they were—only 5 out of dozens."[27] Whether for a physiological analysis of the actual movements or for possible pedagogical purposes, they were of little

[26] Sigfried Giedion defends the thesis that Gilbreth was in principle interested in all movements, because he wanted to develop a universal grammar of motion. This teleological narrative is not, however, confirmed by the archives. See Siegfried Giedion, *Mechanization Takes Command*, 100–12.
[27] F. B. Gilbreth, letter to L. M. Gilbreth, January 28, 1914, Gilbreth LOM, SPCOLL, Purdue University Libraries, NF 91/813-6.

use. Instead, they served only to convince potential clients of his method. The visual brilliance required for this purpose was undoubtedly inherent to the correctly exposed images in the second experiment. They represented a form of objectifiable knowledge and represented this with a corresponding aesthetic.[28] This aesthetic was highly responsive to the transformations that were taking place in the artistic regime—from a figurative to an abstract aesthetic and concept of art.[29] Gilbreth's approach of visualizing movements through abstraction in a new, previously unknown way resembled practices that simultaneously prevailed in the field of art. The visual evidence of his consulting knowledge did not just come from a convincing method. There arose an aesthetic homology between his cinematic and photographic visualizations and artistic forms of expression. In addition, his graphic lines of movement in industry met with the drive toward medialization that took place at the end of the nineteenth century. Taken together, the graphs, charts, and nomograms of this period formed a *visual culture* of industrial management,[30] which Gilbreth could seamlessly connect with his visual consultancy knowledge and which at the same time he had a decisive influence on.

The power of persuasion that Gilbreth was able to generate for and with his method was not just based on the aesthetic qualities of successful film and photo recordings. His filmic form of acquiring commissions was also successful because the guests invited to the fencing shots were themselves part of the motion studies. As viewers, they could either directly follow all the steps up to the finished study on the film set, or they were directly involved as recording objects in the analysis process. Gilbreth also encouraged his guests both to let themselves be filmed during a movement and to subsequently examine and analyze it. Later, he pursued a similar strategy in touring exhibitions and fairground booths, which he designed for his motion studies (Fig. 100). They contained various photographic and cinematic exhibits, as well as a small, fully functional motion laboratory. There, selected visitors could create motion studies of themselves.[31] Gilbreth deliberately used the fascination with new media for his own purposes: his contract acquisition was also successful because he did not reduce the potential client to the role of the viewer. Instead, he actively involved them in the media environment. This gave them the impression that they did not acquire an abstract systematics, as represented, for example, by the schematic method

[28] See W. Jack Duncan, Peter M. Ginter, and Terrie C. Reeves, "Motion Study in Management and the Arts: A Historic Example," in *Frank and Lillian Gilbreth: Critical Evaluations in Business and Management*, ed. Michael C. Wood and John C. Wood (London: Routledge, 2003), 420–44.

[29] On the parallel develops of visual abstraction in the artistic sphere, see Rosalind Krauss, *The Originality of the Avant-Garde and Other Modernist Myths*, 9–22.

[30] See Chapter 1 of the current volume.

[31] See the information brochure, "The One Best Way to Do Work," TECHNOSEUM, Witte Nachlass, Sig. 996, N. 2/1-116.

Figure 100 View of an exhibition stand on motion studies conceived by Gilbreth. At the back left, in the brightly lit corner, there is a functioning motion study laboratory.

advocated by the proponents of Scientific Management. Instead, it was a system that could be flexibly adjusted to individual operational specificities.[32] In addition, it is clear that the fascination exerted by the new media technologies of the day played a decisive role.

Motion studies of sports were particularly well suited to this form of contract acquisition because they were not tied to any corporate particularities. There could be no danger that the corporate secrets of earlier clients would be revealed. Because it was not a matter of concrete examples of rationalization, Gilbreth had no need to worry that the methods shown would, if he did not gain the commission, be plagiarized. This danger was a constant one, as Gilbreth's approach in his work for the Carl Zeiss company in Jena showed.

[32] Thus, privy-councilor Leopold Koppel and Bernhard Dernburg visited Gilbreth in his new offices at the Auergesellschaft and were shown chronocyclegraphs and stereoscopes. F. B. Gilbreth, letter to L. M. Gilbreth, January 12, 1914, Gilbreth LOM, SPCOLL, Purdue University Libraries, NF 91/813-6.

In May 1914, he presented his methods in Jena in a twelve-day trial phase, with the goal of securing a longer-term consulting contract. Here, he showed film recordings from earlier commissions and motion studies, which he had previously taken in a Berlin hospital, and the baseball studies carried out in the United States.[33] In order to be persuasive in such a short period of time, he also carried out motion studies of concrete work processes and gave instructions in written forms, as to how Scientific Management foresaw them. He gave a skeptical summary of this task:

> This job is a dancy [sic]. Each day they say that they are much pleased with my lectures and that of course is pleasing also they say each day is better than the day before. But of course they are most excited about the forms. I treat the forms like they were glasses of rare beer and they with my permission photograph and blueprint each one.[34]
>
> Each day I take them some pictures or photographs of my work so as to impress them and they ask each day if they may photo them and I say, "Sure" and they think they have the system.[35]

The problem of plagiarism was not present in the use of film recordings from the sphere of sports. At the same time, it was advantageous that the media surplus value linked with the method should be especially emphasized. In the artificial situation of a sports study, there was no chance of commercial details distracting the viewer from the method itself, the filmed motion study.

Attracting Potential Clients

With his fencing studies, Gilbreth pursued the goal of making his method of motion analysis better known in Germany, without giving away too much of his approach. In this context, he had three concrete target groups in view, whom he wanted to convince of his consulting method and who were easily reached through the cultural connotations of fencing.

In the first place, there was the upper-level management of the Auergesellschaft, which in the following weeks had to make a decision about securing a long-term, expensive consulting contract with Gilbreth. At this time, Gilbreth worked, as

[33] F. B. Gilbreth, letter to L. M. Gilbreth, May 22, 1914, Gilbreth LOM, SPCOLL, Purdue University Libraries, NF 91/813-6.
[34] F. B. Gilbreth, letter to L. M. Gilbreth, May 27, 1914, Gilbreth LOM, SPCOLL, Purdue University Libraries, NF 91/813-6.
[35] F. B. Gilbreth, letter to L. M. Gilbreth, May 28, 1914, Gilbreth LOM, SPCOLL, Purdue University Libraries, NF 91/813-6.

he later would with Carl Zeiss, in a trial phase lasting a few weeks. Within this period, he needed to convince management of his method, in order to secure the desired one- or two-year contract.[36]

In addition to this, he used the militaristic aspect of fencing to make his first contacts with the German army. From this side, he hoped to win potential commission in the framework of modernizing and rationalizing the armed forces.[37] Later, he used the same approach to gain permission for filming the frontline and hospitals near the front. He then wanted to sell this footage to the newsreel department of the Universal Film Company in New York.[38] Unfortunately, Universal's policy of only purchasing undeveloped film stock, in combination with German film censorship, which only allowed the export of developed film, stymied Gilbreth's potential career as a film producer.

Apart from this, he intended to send the footage directly to Kaiser Wilhelm II. In this way, he attempted to obtain a personal audience with the Kaiser. The extent to which Gilbreth was informed of Wilhelm's keen interest in film cannot be discerned from the archives.[39] In any case, he imagined that he would be able to convince the Kaiser in a short lecture of the relevance of his methodology and persuade the monarch to be a promoter of a newly founded institute for motion studies and labor rationalization.

Auergesellschaft

His strategy was successful, at least among the upper management of the Auergesellschaft, which was overwhelmingly composed of parts of the progressive new bourgeoisie and was oriented less to Wilhelmine militarism than to American-style ideas of modernity.[40] Here, it was not so much the "content" of the studies that was the source of enthusiasm, but the advanced media technology and the scientific techniques associated with it.

[36] See Price, "One Best Way," 229.

[37] A photograph dated April 17, 1915, from the Irene Witte archive indicates that Gilbreth was in close contact with the German military. The status of this image is unclear. Whether it was a filmed trial cannot be reconstructed. It is a stereographic recording of a soldier in German uniform, holding a saber. In Gilbreth's correspondence with his wife, there was no mention of such activities, possibly due to wartime mail censorship. See TECHNOSEUM, Bildarchiv, PVZ: 2005/0872.

[38] F. B. Gilbreth, letter to L. M. Gilbreth, March 12, 1915, March 21, 1915, August 11, 1915, Gilbreth LOM, SPCOLL, Purdue University Libraries, NF 92/813-5.

[39] On the dealings that Kaiser Wilhelm II had with the medium of film, see the filmed images from 1914 in the documentary film *Wilhelm II: Majestät brauchen Sonne* (Peter Schamoni, 1999).

[40] Thus, the June 12, 1910 *New York Times* reported on the resignation of Bernhard Dernburg as state secretary for the colonies, describing it under the headline "Herr Dernburg's Fall" as a triumph of reactionaries over the "American trained" Dernburg. "Herr Dernburg's Fall," *New York Times*, October 12, 1912.

Everyone present during the fencing studies, including the fencers themselves, were members of exclusive, influential Berlin social circles, with the best connections to the Prussian nobility. The fencers already had undertaken combat shows in front of the Kaiser and were among the best fencers in the German Empire.[41] The equally present privy councilor Bernhard Dernburg, who provided the contacts for the fencers, was directly involved in the decision whether to give Gilbreth a consulting contract. Dernburg, a former state secretary for the colonies, with the rank of a minister, and from 1919 minister of finance and vice-chancellor of the Reich under Philip Scheidemann, was the link to Leopold Koppel, the privy councilor for commerce, whose banking company Koppel & Co made a major contribution to financing and controlling the Auergesellschaft through venture capital investment.[42] As chairman of the supervisory board and the main stockholder of the Auergesellschaft, Koppel was "practically its owner,"[43] and he was the final authority to decide on whether to grant Gilbreth his consulting commission. Gilbreth therefore had a major interest in convincing Dernburg of his methods. Fencing studies were particularly suited to this purpose. They provided conversation material as well as legitimizing the methodological basis of the motion studies and giving Gilbreth the possibility of showing a few films and images from his earlier commissions after the end of the fencing studies, in order to underscore the breadth and viability of his approach. "I showed them some of our handkerchief cyclegraphs, the stereoscope and they were carried away by the results and possibilities. I am sure that it will be the greatest hit there ever was."[44] With his media campaign of persuasion, Gilbreth was extremely successful. By the end of January he had signed off on a two-year contract that would bring in $54,000 per year. Included in this contract were the costs for himself, his manager S. E. Whitaker, and five assistants. After accounting for all these costs, Gilbreth still had a stately profit of $25,000 per year.[45] Certainly, these developments, which in the end led to the signing of the contract, were not only a result

[41] F. B. Gilbreth, letter to L. M. Gilbreth, January 14, 1914 and January 16, 1914, Gilbreth LOM, SPCOLL, Purdue University Libraries, NF 91/813-6.

[42] In 1907, as a representative of the National-Liberal Party, Bernhard Dernburg was named Minister for the Colonies, in order to develop a new direction in colonial policy after the German genocide of the Herero people in what was then known as German South-West Africa. Dernburg was against a further violent expansion of overseas territories. Instead, he subjected the local resource industry to a rationalization process, in order to increase profits from the colonies. See also Bernhard Dernburg, *Von beiden Ufern* (Berlin: Kronen Verlag, 1916; Bernhard Dernburg, *Zielpunkte des Deutschen Kolonialwesens* (Berlin: Mittler, 1907).

[43] Friedrich Klauer, *Geschichte der Auergesellschaft. Von der Gründung im Jahre 1892 bis zum Jahre 1958* (Berlin: Auer 1960), 12.

[44] F. B. Gilbreth, letter to L. M. Gilbreth, January 16, 1914, Gilbreth LOM, SPCOLL, Purdue University Libraries, NF 91/813-6.

[45] See Price, "One Best Way," 251.

of the fencing studies. Their influence as an additional, trust-building measure is not to be underestimated.

The intermingling of general sports footage with a concrete business agenda was not an exception but corresponded to the regulated approach with which Gilbreth would acquire contracts in the future. His film studies were less concerned with physiological-scientific aspects. Rather, they secured the necessary acceptance of his consulting method among the economic elites of the day. He sensitized them to ergonomic methods, which, while they were not entirely opposed to the dominant ideal of orthodox factory discipline, nonetheless stressed quite different accents. He honed the profile of his consulting enterprise by foregrounding his usage of media technology as an exclusive selling point. His consulting knowledge not only consisted of an abstract concept that was to be implemented. The potential commissioners "can hardly refute the friendly offer"[46] made by Gilbreth's media ensemble, consisting of film, stereoscopy, photographs, and charts. With the media novelty of the motion study film and his recourse to the *graphic method media network*, Gilbreth succeeded in materializing his consulting performance in the concrete form of visual representations.

Military Contracts

Apart from the decision makers in the Auergesellschaft, he additionally sought contact with the officers of the German military. This was what the fencing studies were predestined for, since they had a direct relation to militarism. After all, it was in fact a way of practicing battle conduct. Fighting with swords and daggers was in no way an innovation in military warcraft, and this was not a disadvantage. In the context of the strong cultural significance of fencing in this period, Gilbreth's fencing studies appeared to his customers less as a form of advertising his consulting services, and more as a manifestation of his interest in this aspect of Wilhelmine military culture. They allowed for acquaintances to be made in a less formal setting than, for instance, when Gilbreth sought contact with his footage for an improved method of loading and unloading machine guns. This is not to mention the risks of plagiarism. This gave Gilbreth, a social climber from humble roots, access to the social elites. The cultivated atmosphere that prevailed among them, their cultural habitus,[47] was alien to him. By orienting his media devices to a core component of their cultural identity, he could deliberately cover

---

[46] K. H. Condit, "Management Methods and Principles of Frank B. Gilbreth, Inc.—II," *American Machinist* 1 (1923), 293.

[47] On the concept of habitus, see Pierre Bourdieu, "Structures, Habitus, Practices," in *The Logic of Practice*, 52–65; Pierre Bourdieu, *Distinction: A Social Critique of the Judgement of Taste*.

up this circumstance. In this manner, he involved potential clients in occupying themselves with his methodology and could in time steer conversation toward his consulting services. Since this step was not necessarily predetermined, there was no danger that in the case of a rejection one of the participants would feel snubbed. In the end, the playful, nonbinding nature of the meeting was retained, and it could be returned to if necessary. The film studies on baseball, golf, or fencing, divorced from business considerations, could also be interpreted as a particular interest in these specific sports. If this was not sufficient, then there remained the rationale of the origins of motion studies from Leonardo da Vinci up to the industrial age. Such conversations took place in the common dinners in the villa of privy councilor Koppel attended by Gilbreth, who was impressed by the Rubens and Titian paintings hanging on the walls.[48]

In a way, his approach resembled that of the French physiologist Étienne-Jules Marey, who astounded the Parisian bourgeoisie with sports footage of musclebound men or dynamic racehorses. Like baseball, golf, and fencing, they were part of the cultural identity of the relevant social elites. If Marey successfully elicited attention and goodwill in the future distribution of research funds, Gilbreth used a very similar approach to persuade decision makers in industry of the advantages of his motion studies. In place of generous research funds, Gilbreth was motivated by lucrative consulting contracts from the private sphere.

Details as to whether Gilbreth had successfully made contact with the German military are not to be found in the archival holdings. Nonetheless, there seems to have been at least a few partial successes. Thus, a correspondence arose with Senior Lieutenant Hermann Schlüpmann from the 6th Fresh Meat Transport Column of the 2nd Bavarian Army Corps. In 1915, he inquired as to whether Gilbreth could explain the fundamental rules of Scientific Management to him. Gilbreth, who had moved back to America after the termination of his contract with the Auergesellschaft, nonetheless answered this inquiry in great detail.[49] The intensification of the war and the fact that the sea voyage to Europe was no longer safe made a commission from the German military a purely hypothetical matter. Instead, from 1916 Gilbreth worked for the opposite side, the US armed forces. There, as he had offered to the German military two years earlier, he trained American soldiers to load machine guns more rapidly.

---

[48] F. B. Gilbreth, letter to L. M. Gilbreth, January 23, 1914, Gilbreth LOM, SPCOLL, Purdue University Libraries, NF 91/813-6.
[49] F. B. Gilbreth, letter to H. Schlüpmann, July 19, 1915, Gilbreth LOM, SPCOLL, Purdue University Libraries, NF 94/816-20.

Seeing the Kaiser

The fencing studies not only served to open doors to the German military; they also had an even more important purpose. Gilbreth wanted to see the Kaiser. He was convinced that he could gain a private audience with Wilhelm II merely by dint of sending him the cyclegraphs taken of fencers. "I'll send them to the Kaiser I think and that will pay for them other than in money."[50] This sheds light on the fact that Gilbreth himself, in spite of his calculating, strategic usage of media techniques, suffered from a certain media overestimation of himself. On the one hand, he wanted to use the meeting to offer his services to the cause of rationalizing the military. He saw concrete potential for improvement in the handling of machine guns, which he wanted to record and then convey to the soldiers with filmic and choroncyclegraphic images. "I will show him how to load his guns faster."[51] On the other hand, he intended to propose to the Kaiser a cooperation between representatives of German industrial engineering and his newly established summer school in the United States. Here, in an annual three-week course, he trained American students, professors, and managers in the use of motion studies. Additionally, the summer school enabled him to recruit new colleagues for his corporate consultancy.

> I have told prof. S. [Schlesinger] that I desire to meet the Kaiser to invite him to send two representatives (college professors) to America and attend the Summer School. Prof. S. at first laughed and sneered at my nerve. I told him that he must not forget I was the Emperor of S.M. [Scientific Management] and we Emperors had much in common that he could not understand.[52]

Even though Schlesinger considered this desire to be somewhat naïve and utopian, Gilbreth succeeded, in the end, in motivating him to become active in this matter. Since Gilbreth's motion studies in Germany were understood less as a new scientific methodology and more as an extension of his pedagogical arsenal, Georg Schlesinger initially tried to attain an audience for Gilbreth through the minister for education.[53] When this failed, he sent a letter to privy councilor Dernburg with the request to set up an audience in the brief time remaining: "Frank B. Gilbreth has expressed the burning desire to find an

---

[50] F. B. Gilbreth, letter to L. M. Gilbreth, January 31, 1914, Gilbreth LOM, SPCOLL, Purdue University Libraries, NF 91/813-6.

[51] F. B. Gilbreth, letter to L. M. Gilbreth, January 18, 1914, Gilbreth LOM, SPCOLL, Purdue University Libraries, NF 91/813-6.

[52] F. B. Gilbreth, letter to L. M. Gilbreth, January 15, 1914, Gilbreth LOM, SPCOLL, Purdue University Libraries, NF 91/813-6.

[53] G. Schlesinger, letter to B. Dernburg, January 21, 1914, Gilbreth LOM, SPCOLL, Purdue University Libraries, NF 91/813-6.

opportunity to personally inform His Majesty the Kaiser of his science during his stay."[54] Here, he placed special emphasis on Gilbreth's media innovations and the fact that he had, with his "motion studies and the inscription of the movement of the human hand on a photographic plate, laid the capstone for the so-called corporate science methods."[55]

When the private audience failed to materialize,[56] Gilbreth, together with Schlesinger, attempted to convince the financier of the Auergesellschaft, privy-councilor Leopold Koppel, to fund a joint research institute for motion studies. At this time, Koppel supported the Kaiser Wilhelm-Gesellschaft zur Förderung der Wissenschaften through his Leopold Koppel Stiftung. It was responsible, among other things, for Albert Einstein's salary, which he obtained as member of the Königlich-preußischen Akademie der Wissenschaft (Royal Prussian Academy of Science). In spite of several common dinners and accompanying film screenings, this plan for a joint institute also foundered. If even one of the projects had been realized, Gilbreth planned to emigrate with his family to Germany, particularly since a campaign initiated by Frederick W. Taylor was attacking him in the United States and had already caused him to lose one consulting contract. In Germany, he thought, he would be the unquestioned authority in the sphere of Scientific Management. Moreover, he perceived a greater understanding for his philosophy of workplace organization and leadership in this country.[57]

Failed Consulting in Berlin: Auergesellschaft

Even if Gilbreth was thwarted from gaining a private audience with Kaiser Wilhelm II and had no success with his desired commissions from the German military, he nonetheless attained his most important goal. He secured a long-term consulting contract with the Auergesellschaft/Deutsche Gasglühlicht AG, one of the then largest industrial corporations in Berlin. In 1913, this company

[54] "Frank B. Gilbreth hegt den heissen Wunsch, eine Gelegenheit zu finden, während seines Aufenthalts hier Sr. Majestät dem Kaiser über seine Wissenschaft persönlich vortragen zu dürfen." G. Schlesinger, letter to B. Dernburg, January 21, 1914, Gilbreth LOM, SPCOLL, Purdue University Libraries, NF 91/813-6.

[55] G. Schlesinger, letter to B. Dernburg, January 21, 1914, Gilbreth LOM, SPCOLL, Purdue University Libraries, NF 91/813-6.

[56] In her study, Elspeth H. Brown erroneously reports of an audience held with Kaiser Wilhelm III (sic). See Elspeth H. Brown, The Corporate Eye: Photography and the Rationalization of American Commercial Culture, 1884–1929 (Baltimore: Johns Hopkins University Press, 2005), 102.

[57] Along with the spread of the movement of industrial betterment in Germany, the local principle of the specialist industrial worker contributed to this. In the end, Gilbreth wanted to make workers motion-aware. Well-educated specialist workers were better suited to this than uneducated workers without any special training, who in the United States represented the lion's share of the workforce.

Figure 101　View of Building A of the *Lampenstadt* from the direction of Naglerstraße, with the Oberbaumbrücke in the background.

employed more than 7,000 workers in the production of gas lamps and lightbulbs alone, without counting staff in management and operations.[58] At the time, it was the world's largest industrial complex, and the goal was to reorganize it according to the system of Scientific Management.

The company was originally founded as a venture capital investment by the Koppel & Co bank, together with other Berlin financial institutions, in order to valorize its gaslight patent.[59] The main shareholder, privy councilor Leopold Koppel, had enabled the company to develop into a complex conglomerate through a series of acquisitions of various other firms.[60] The endpoint of this expansion drive was the beginning, in 1907, of the construction of the so-called *Lampenstadt* ("City of Light," see Figs. 101 and 102).

---

[58]　Klauer, *Geschichte der Auergesellschaft*, 27.

[59]　As a shareholder-owned company, the Auergesellschaft was particularly resistant to innovations. Unlike in traditionally organized family businesses, here the ownership structures were separated from the structure of the company's operational management. Similar structures could be seen in the railway companies investigated by Yates, which in the United States played a pioneering role in the introduction of systematic management methods. See Yates, *Control Through Communication*.

[60]　Klauer, *Geschichte der Auergesellschaft*, 12–13.

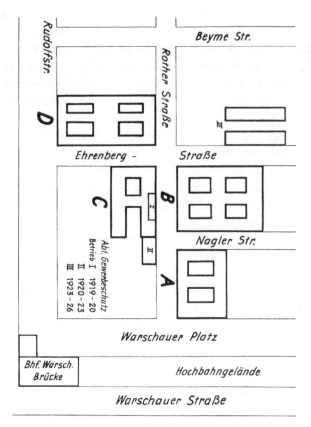

Fabrikkomplex an der Warschauer Straße Berlin O17

Figure 102 Blueprint of the factory layout, the so-called *Lampenstadt* in Friedrichshain, Berlin. The building housed production and research facilities as well as the warehousing and delivery departments.

Subsequently, the Auergesellschaft's production capacities, which were previously strewn across all of Friedrichshain, were concentrated in an expansive industrial complex, stretching over several blocks in the Berlin borough. Despite its industrial expansion, the financial health of the company in the mid-1910s was not optimal. On the one hand, it had lost a legal battle over the exclusive rights to the gaslight patent, and the company was now confronted with competition in this area. On the other hand, the market for gaslights met with a tendency toward saturation. Whereas dividends in the 1893–1894 business year were still a robust 130%, by 1899 they were reduced to 28%.[61] Alongside these financial difficulties, there was also the need to undertake an alteration of the product portfolio. The market for gaslights, in which the company was still producing over 50 million items in the year, was stagnant, while sales of electric lightbulbs represented the future of growth in the industry.[62] The company had to be restructured, so that the trend toward the new type of illumination would not be missed. It was in this extremely difficult business situation that Gilbreth was given the commission to restructure the *Lampenstadt* with the aid of Scientific Management, and thereby make it more profitable.

There were two ways in which this consulting commission was a paradigmatic example for the media-based approach to corporate consulting pursued by Gilbreth. First, attracting clients with the help of chronocyclegraphic sport studies, as described earlier, was a typical method for Gilbreth, and as a rule it was extremely successful. Gilbreth used his filmic techniques to pinpoint the mindset of potential clients and address their thoughts about matters of efficiency. He mastered the latest techniques for visualizing business data and knew how to use this advantage for his own purposes. His approach confronted the visual culture of the medialization drive which was taking place in the business world. The affinity with techniques of data visualization arising here played directly into his hands. Moreover, Gilbreth's method gained in credibility: his approach toward industrial rationalization combined the latest practices in film and visualization and thus appeared to be oriented toward the newest developments in media, technology, and science.

Second, his various graphic visualization techniques not only served promotional purposes. They also assumed a central role in the implementation of his commission. For the first time in the world, a corporate consultant utilized the entire spectrum of visualization techniques available at the time, including filming methods, in the framework of a single consulting contract.

The commission itself ended in complete disaster. Gilbreth's concept failed across the board. The production system he conceived was never implemented in the way he envisaged. It is precisely for this reason that this case is particularly well suited to illustrating the functioning of the media-based consulting model deployed by Gilbreth. The problems and difficulties in the implementation of his commission produced a constant verification pressure with respect to his clients. For this reason, Gilbreth frequently had recourse to visualization techniques in order to verify individual methods in order to legitimize the commission as a whole, or discredit specific rivals in his field. Incessant conflicts in the enterprise led to many details being documented, which in a consulting contract that had

---

[61] Ibid., 6.
[62] Ibid., 17.

proceeded without any problems would not have found their way into the archives. It was due to the lack of success in the attempted corporate restructuring,
then, that this case study can be reconstructed as a paradigm for the functioning
of the principle of corporate consulting in the 1910s. It was in this decade that
the branch established itself as an ongoing component in the field of business
management. At its center were the visualization techniques used by Gilbreth as
vehicles of the form of consulting knowledge used in a given workplace.

Even today, the fundamental traits of "corporate consulting" that emerged
here still mark the branch's practices. Changes undertaken or conceived in the
framework of a consulting commission had to be verified with the clients and
communicated within the company. It was only in this way that innovations
could, in the end, be successfully enacted. The consulting knowledge necessary
for this had very particular requirements. It had to be modular and flexible, as
well as follow a persuasive, stable internal logic.

In order to secure the acceptance of his restructures and the cooperation of
the workforce, Gilbreth also introduced the tools of *industrial betterment* that
had already been trialed in the New England Butt Company. He installed a library for employees,[63] and he sought to erect the *home reading box* scheme[64]
and the principle of the *suggestion box*.[65] Moreover, he implemented his system
of personnel planning in the area of sales staff and technicians,[66] the "Three
Position Plan of Promotion."[67] As a principle, this was a transparent, systematic
regulation of incentives within the company. It sought to ensure the motivation
of employees and their long-term loyalty toward the company, by declaring the
progressive rise within the corporate hierarchy through incentives to be standard
practice. Incentives were altered from an arbitrary measure to an instrument for
controlling the workforce. The idea of the Three Positions referred to individual
employees. They were supposed to always declare their role in the company as
a relation between three positions: the lower positions (1), which they had before their current position (2), and the future higher position (3), which they
could obtain through good performance in the workplace. This automation of

[63] F. B. Gilbreth, letter to D. M. Pratsch, June 15, 1913, Gilbreth LOM, SPCOLL, Purdue University Libraries, NF 94/816-20.
[64] F. B. Gilbreth, letter to L. M. Gilbreth, April 3, 1914, Gilbreth LOM, SPCOLL, Purdue University Libraries, NF 91/813-6.
[65] *Auergesellschaft Report*, 44–45, Gilbreth LOM, SPCOLL, Purdue University Libraries, NF 76/695-2.
[66] *Auergesellschaft Report*, Gilbreth LOM, SPCOLL, Purdue University Libraries, NF 76/695-2; F. B. Gilbreth, letter to L. M. Gilbreth, October 26, 1914, Gilbreth LOM, SPCOLL, Purdue University Libraries, NF 92/813-5.
[67] Frank B. Gilbreth and Lillian Gilbreth, "The Three Position Plan," in *Applied Motion Study: A Collection of Papers on the Efficient Method to Industrial Preparedness* (New York: Sturgis &Walton Company, 1917), 188ff.

incentives was supposed to unleash additional reserves of motivation and reduce the high turnover rate of workers.

Another area for raising acceptance was related less to the concept of industrial betterment and more to the attempt at willful deception. With all the means available to him, Gilbreth sought to conceal the fact that he was still working with the methods of *Taylorism*.[68] In order to hide the parallels and connections between his and Frederick W. Taylor's methods of Scientific Management, he even considered halting the translation and publication of one of his books[69] by Springer Verlag.[70] He was concerned that the translator Colin Ross sought to create a too obvious connection between him and Taylor. "I fear being put in Speedy's [the derogatory contemporary nickname for Taylor] class by the worker."[71] If, in Germany, he was primarily perceived as a supporter of Taylorism, the chances were poor of constructing a participatory, cooperative work atmosphere in the union-organized Auergesellschaft. In the end, he fundamentally failed at this attempt to distance himself from Taylor, even though his approach actually was distinct from orthodox Taylorism in several regards.

Reasons for Failure

So why, then, did he falter in Berlin with the approach he had successfully deployed a year earlier in the United States with the New England Butt Company? Two circumstances considerably contributed to his failure. Gilbreth encountered a local conflict situation that was extremely unfavorable to his approach. The borough of Friedrichshain, the red, proletarian east of Berlin, where the Auergesellschaft works were located, was also the core of the blossoming German workers movement. With his concept of participatory collaboration and the idea that the interests of workers and capitalists could be united with transparent scientific procedures, he was directly opposed to figures such as Friedrich Engels, who, twenty years earlier, only a few streets from the *Lampenstadt*, lay the foundations of the German workers movement. It was not least for this reason, and due to its location in a traditional working-class neighborhood, that the Auergesellschaft exhibited a high degree of union organization. In Berlin, unlike

---

[68] F. B. Gilbreth, letter to L. M. Gilbreth, February 1, 1914, Gilbreth LOM, SPCOLL, Purdue University Libraries, NF 91/813-6.

[69] This was Frank B. Gilbreth, *Das ABC der wissenschaftlichen Betriebsführung* (Berlin: Springer, 1917), the German translation of the handbook published in English in 1912 as *Primer of Scientific Management* (New York: D. van Nostrand Company 1912).

[70] F. B. Gilbreth, letter to L. M. Gilbreth, May 27, 1914, Gilbreth LOM, SPCOLL, Purdue University Libraries, NF 91/813-6.

[71] F. B. Gilbreth, letter to L. M. Gilbreth, May 27, 1914, Gilbreth LOM, SPCOLL, Purdue University Libraries, NF 91/813-6.

in the New England Butt Company, which was not union organized, he was not in a position to convince either the workers, or even middle management (which proved to be even more consequential), of his approach. Instead of the desired participatory collaboration, an unstinting atmosphere of mistrust and hostility prevailed.

Consequently, he was unable to fulfil the central promises of his consulting approach. Here the weaknesses of his method of lab-based consulting were made manifest. He did not succeed in anchoring his film-based laboratory motion studies as a model of participation.[72] Instead, Gilbreth's closed system of knowledge, which relied on motion experts and laboratory studies, provoked the mistrust of workers. His approach was not suited to practice and functioned only under ideal-typical prerequisites, such as were present in the commission for training the Remington Typewriter Company typists.[73] However, as soon as the media recording devices were not perceived as participatory possibilities of workforce cooperation, they automatically appeared as an even more perfidious form of Taylorism. If this was the prevailing mood of the workforce, then his approach was condemned to failure from the start. After all, the precise details of the concept of the "motion-aware" workers could only be realized if there was a minimum of willingness to cooperate on the part of the workforce.

In Berlin this was not the case. The Auergesellschaft workers never accepted the film recordings from Gilbreth's laboratory motion studies as a neutral, mediating entity between workers and management. Considered from the viewpoint of corporate organization, his filmic laboratory studies did not possess the necessary prerequisites for becoming a boundary object of knowledge transfer between the laboratory and the workers. The necessary low-threshold possibilities for participation were simply not available. The scientifically objective[74] character of filmic techniques on which Gilbreth speculated was not sufficient for justifying their introduction into an existing organizational structure. The project was opposed, with both overt and covert means, not only by the workers, but also by the department supervisors and other representatives of middle management. Although, in his theoretical writings, Gilbreth grounded his use of media in the strengthening of collaboration between workers and managers, he was not able to overcome the resistance of the workforce. On the contrary, his presence provoked the open rejection of his approach. In April 1914, a meeting of about 600 Auergesellschaft workers took place, in which their consent to the planned restructuring was demanded. In the same month, an article rejecting Taylorism

---

[72] See the detailed reasons for this given in Chapter 4 of this volume, "No Participation Without Visibility".

[73] See Chapter 4 of this volume, "Typing Faster."

[74] Lorraine Daston and Peter Galison, "The Image of Objectivity," *Representation* 132, no. 40 (1992): 81–128.

appeared in a popular German magazine,[75] which was illustrated with pictures of Gilbreth's rationalization commission from the New England Butt Company. As a result, he was not only equated with Taylor, but due to his usage of media was considered the more perfidious of the two. If Taylorism still relied on the schematic idea of separating manual and intellectual labor, Gilbreth's filmic studies managed to penetrate into areas of the labor process which had been closed off to Taylor and his work inspectors. Even the smallest movement of the worker could become the starting point for efficiency measures. This met with general rejection: "Gilbreth is the worst of all because he puts the movies after the poor peepul [sic]."[76] His film-based model of industrial rationalization, taking ergonomic aspects into consideration and thus, apparently, particularly friendly to the worker, was converted into its opposite, a filmic dystopia of control. The increasing rejection of Taylorism in trade union circles[77] led to another meeting of the workers. The decision taken there demanded a general prohibition on Gilbreth setting foot in the Auergesellschaft's factories.[78]

Successful Corporate Restructurings

This was the context in which Gilbreth decided to concentrate mainly on the training and further education of middle management. It was only by the end of 1914 that Gilbreth and his assistants had made hesitant progress in the alteration of the production process on the factory floor, even though this was the sole basis of his activity as a corporate consulting. His supposed success relied on winning the trust of *an* employee, who enjoyed a certain reputation among his colleagues.[79] He declared himself ready to take part in filmic recordings and advocated the idea of Scientific Management. In the given circumstances, this success was nonetheless relativized.

Due to the general mobilization in August 1914, the younger members of the workforce were drafted to the military.[80] Hence, those workers who were hostile

---

[75] The title of the magazine can unfortunately not be determined from the archival documents available.

[76] F. B. Gilbreth, letter to L. M. Gilbreth, 23.04.1914, Gilbreth LOM, SPCOLL, Purdue University Libraries, NF 91/813-6.

[77] At the same time, the US Senate convened the Hoxie Commission to investigate the effects of Taylorism. European trade union circles soon received the commission's critical comments. For the final report of the Hoxie Commission, see Robert F. Hoxie, *Scientific Management and Labor* (New York: D. Appleton and Company, 1915).

[78] F. B. Gilbreth, letter to L. M. Gilbreth, April 23, 1914, Gilbreth LOM, SPCOLL, Purdue University Libraries, NF 91/813-6.

[79] Price, "One Best Way," 287.

[80] Liste der zum Kriegsdienst Eingezogenen (Lists of military service conscripts), A Rep. 231, No. 1529, Firmenarchiv Osram GmbH, Landesarchiv Berlin.

Figure 103 "Nailing corner cushions." Chronocyclegraphic recordings of the movements of the worker Geyer, taken on May 6, 1915, a month before the termination of the consulting contract.

to Gilbreth simply disappeared into the trenches. This situation, favorable as it was to a restructuring process, was recognized by the Auergesellschaft's corporate management, and emboldened Gilbreth to act quickly. A major part of the workforce was, at this point, already probably dead, or had returned from the war as invalids. Indeed, enabling war invalids to re-enter the workplace with the aid of motion studies would prove to be the next lucrative area of work, which Gilbreth turned his attentions toward after the end of World War I.

The absence of cooperation from the workers did not allow for any rationalization measures in the actual production process. Out of necessity, Gilbreth initially began by restructuring the departments of sales, warehousing,[81] operations, and management, along the principles of Scientific Management.[82] In the process, his team relied on strategies which had already been successful in reorganizing the New England Butt Company. They reorganized parts of the bureaucracy in newly created open-plan offices and introduced techniques for

[81] F. B. Gilbreth, letter to L. M. Gilbreth, January 7, 1914, Gilbreth LOM, SPCOLL, Purdue University Libraries, NF 91/813-6

[82] The packing department overwhelmingly employed women. The resistance expected there was less than in the production department, which was characterized by a high level of trade union organization. Similar reasons favored progress in reshaping management.

Figure 104 "Establish the price." Chronocyclegraphic study of office activities in the Auergesellschaft.

accelerating typewriting among the secretaries that had already been tested out in the United States (Fig. 105).[83] The concentration of specific activities such as data processing with a typewriter in a central site in the company had first become possible through an improvement in corporate communication. For this purpose, Gilbreth created a messenger system, which served to regulate communication across the expansive premises of the *Lampenstadt*. It consisted of thirty messenger boys who were responsible for ensuring the transmission of written communication between the individual departments.[84] In the corporate departments, Gilbreth installed a total of 500 baskets—two per worksite: one each for incoming and outgoing mail (Figs. 103 and 104).[85] The company's internal messenger service allowed written notes to be transported from one corporate department to another in a maximum of fifteen minutes. The planned reconstruction of the company could only be tackled if these communication structures remained intact. In combination with the previously created central administration units, whole spheres of the company could be restructured

[83] Price, "One Best Way," 253.

[84] Group photograph of the messenger staff, Gilbreth LOM, SPCOLL, Purdue University Libraries, NF 162/10, Vol. VI, No. 14.

[85] F. B. Gilbreth, letter to L. M. Gilbreth, April 6, 1914, Gilbreth LOM, SPCOLL, Purdue University Libraries, NF 91/813-6.

Figure 105 Rationalized workplaces in the administration of the Auergesellschaft.

from the "planning department" (also known as the "Gilbreth Office"), and these processes could be supervised and directed with the aid of this communication system.

The only area close to production which Gilbreth was able to restructure according to the principles of Scientific Management was the company's warehouse sector. Here, he instated a reorganization plan of all commodity flows relevant to the warehouse. The goal was to formalize the ordering process, by documenting the respective jurisdictions of the participating departments, and thereby making the process of a central management entity accessible from the outside. For this purpose, the Gilbreth Office developed a flow chart[86] that outlined, in written and visual form, all the commodity flows within the company's existing organizational structure. In this way, warehouse expenses could be reduced.[87] Additionally, his consulting team could implement the models for the optimal structuring of packing processes in the delivery and packing departments,

[86] Schematic display of the work process for an order in the manufacturing of gas mantles, TECHNOSEUM, Witte Nachlass, Sig. 992, No. 3/10-9.

[87] F. B. Gilbreth, letter to L. M. Gilbreth, November 1, 1914, Gilbreth LOM, SPCOLL, Purdue University Libraries, NF 92/813-5.

Figure 106 Group photo of the employees directly involved in the rationalization measures. In the foreground sit the assistants from Gilbreth's office; behind them are the typists and management staff from the sales department.

which they had already developed in earlier commissions in the United States. As part of this work, they prepared filmic motion studies of various loading and unloading activities.[88]

Within the company's management, the sales department proved to be cooperative (Fig. 106).[89] It was entirely restructured according to the new system.[90] This was no coincidence, since, in the end, the planned changes to the factory system automatically led to a greater sphere of responsibility for the management of the sales department. Although the employees were overwhelmingly cooperative, here, too, there were serious problems that hindered the new system. If the workers on the factory floor felt threatened by a higher labor tempo and increased control over their activity, in the white-collar departments, it was the department managers and supervisors who felt cornered in by Scientific Management. Here, resistance was provoked due to a fear of the division of competencies and the concomitant devaluation of their own activity. Such suppositions did not seem unjustified if the principles of Scientific Management were followed. In the context of the financial difficulties in which the Auergesellschaft found itself, this gained extra urgency. In addition to the workers, now sections of middle and

[88] See "Method of Packing Soap," in *Original Films of Frank B. Gilbreth: The Quest of the One Best Way*, Gilbreth Library of Management Videos, SPCOLL, Purdue University Libraries.

[89] *Auergesellschaft Report*, 13, Gilbreth LOM, SPCOLL, Purdue University Libraries, NF 76/695-1.

[90] F. B. Gilbreth, letter to L. M. Gilbreth, September 21, 1914 and September 28, 1914, Gilbreth LOM, SPCOLL, Purdue University Libraries, NF 92/813-5.

upper managements began to torpedo Gilbreth's efforts. Recommendations were not carried out, were delayed, or were fundamentally questioned.

> No one of the bunch will give up their ancient rights and consequently all are scared to give up any information or assist in perfecting a function because they think that their power may be lessened or that the secret of their life may be discovered.[91]

There was also a concerted attempt to discredit the suitability and competence of Gilbreth and his assistants.[92] Modest advances in rationalization and the onset of World War I, which was, according to Gilbreth, "about the 50th unexpected thing to keep me from being rich,"[93] ensured that the Auergesellschaft terminated the consulting contract in 1915.[94] Subsequently, changes that had already been implemented were reverted to the way things were before.[95]

Successful Failure

Gilbreth failed in the concrete implementation of his proposals. In his actual core business of corporate consulting, the sale of ideas and concepts, he was, however, rather successful, considering the extremely unfavorable surrounding circumstances. As was the case with obtaining the contract, Gilbreth was able to maintain the interest of his clients in his method and procedures, in spite of the minimal progress he had made in the actual rationalization of the workplace. In this respect, his visualization techniques were of considerable help. With this visual consulting knowledge, he involved upper management already in the conception and strategic planning of restructuring measures. There he created precisely the atmosphere of cooperation which he had sought to foster among the workers. He generated a consulting situation in which management accepted his proposals, not least due to the visual evidence of his consulting practice.

An important step in this regard was the opening of the planning department (the Gilbreth Office) in the second story of Building D of the Auergesellschaft

---

[91] F. B. Gilbreth, letter to L. M. Gilbreth, June 3, 1914, Gilbreth LOM, SPCOLL, Purdue University Libraries, NF 91/813-6.

[92] Price, "One Best Way," 255.

[93] F. B. Gilbreth, letter to L. M. Gilbreth, October 10, 1914, Gilbreth LOM, SPCOLL, Purdue University Libraries, NF 92/813-5.

[94] The Auergesellschaft delivered protective equipment to the Reichswehr for use in gas warfare, and it was assessed to be a business essential for war needs. It was expressly forbidden from employing foreign staff, which included Gilbreth's rationalization team.

[95] Irene Witte, letter to F. B. Gilbreth, August 10, 1915, Gilbreth LOM, SPCOLL, Purdue University Libraries, NF 104/116-187.

Figure 107 Stereoscopic view of the central planning room at the Auergesellschaft.

on April 28, 1914 (Fig. 107).[96] The planning and direction competence of the business was combined into a central location. Moreover, Gilbreth collected personnel in these spaces, which was responsible for the fabrication of different visualization tools. They formed the basis for the conception and planning phase, from which he subsequently wanted to tackle the restructuring of production processes.

This was where the implicit and explicit organizational knowledge of management had been made visible, thus forming the basis for the impending restructuring of the plant. In order to have the appropriate framework for the representation of visual consulting knowledge at his disposal, Gilbreth installed a film projection space for management, which was equipped with the latest media technology for the presentation of films, slides, and stereoscopic images (Fig. 108).[97] Here he discussed the planned workplace rationalization measures with the managers affected. "[The planning department] is going to make a wonderful showing. Nothing ever seen like it before in the history of S.M. [Scientific Management]."[98] The planning room was the heart of the

---

[96] See the factory blueprint in Figure 102.
[97] F. B. Gilbreth, letter to L. M. Gilbreth, September 21, 1914, Gilbreth LOM, SPCOLL, Purdue University Libraries, NF 92/813-5.
[98] F. B. Gilbreth, letter to L. M. Gilbreth, April 28, 1914, Gilbreth LOM, SPCOLL, Purdue University Libraries, NF 91/813-6.

Figure 108 "An Office Group looking at motion pictures of their work."

department: information from the company flowed in and was then processed by his assistants. "The Planning Department is the central place from which all planning orders and directions are issued and to which all reports regarding performance are sent."[99] It thus formed the cornerstone of the new production system to be implemented according to the model developed by Scientific Management.

The system was based on the consequent written record of all business communication in the form of work instruction cards. For this purpose, Gilbreth installed a large board on which the respective instruction cards were appended (Fig. 109). The whole complex of the Gilbreth Office still consisted of the personal offices of Frank B. Gilbreth and his colleagues S. E. Whitaker and Russ Allen. The remaining personnel of the planning room were made up of employees who were sent there from the individual corporate departments.

They had the task of directing production in their respective departments from a central location, with the aid of these instruction cards. The managerial

[99] *Auergesellschaft Report*, 5, Gilbreth LOM, SPCOLL, Purdue University Libraries, NF 76/695-1.

Figure 109 Provisional table for the storage of work instruction cards.

competency of the individual departments was centralized within the newly
founded planning department and withdrawn from the departments that were
previously responsible for it. In the course of the restructuring process, this also
took care of its vehement rejection in some sectors of the company.[100] In addition, the instruction cards contained, in the case of a mechanical failure or a disruption to the production flow, details on the activities that needed to be carried
out in place of the planned work phases. Hence, valuable labor time during disruptions needed to be immediately channeled in a productive manner. Beyond
this, dialogue partners were also given in the case of an inquiry or a problem.
After the end of a work phase, the card had to be immediately forwarded to the
relevant authority, who was also listed on the card. The system not only functioned as a system of commands, but also as a feedback system. Rewinding the
cards showed the state of labor in the production process. The board used as a re-
pository system for the work cards was a provisional step. In fact, Gilbreth strove
for the installation of a so-called Taylor Flying Machine (Fig. 110), which had
been specially developed for management to rapidly access the work instruction
cards.[101] But in Germany it could not be easily procured.

The planning department was part of the Taylorist factory system, which
had the goal of translating into written form all production tasks in the form of

---

[100] Layton sees this uncompromising approach as one of the main reasons for the failure of the
Taylorist factory system. See Layton, *The Revolt of the Engineer*, 139.
[101] *Auergesellschaft Report*, 2, Gilbreth LOM, SPCOLL, Purdue University Libraries, NF 76/695-1.

Figure 110 Professional data organization and processing with the Taylor Flying Machine in the New England Butt Company. This guaranteed quick access to relevant data for organizational and planning tasks in factory management.

work instruction cards. At the same time, it was also the prototype for a central planning and strategy department (Fig. 111). Due to the problems on the factory floor, daily training for middle and upper management became an involuntary kernel of his rationalization project. Over the course of several weeks, training sessions in the planning department took place nearly every day, in which Gilbreth explained his system and discussed concrete steps with corporate management for its implementation. "I lecture to about ten of them from 9:00 to 11:30 daily and make a great hit every time."[102] He carried out his training sessions in the film projection room of the planning department. Here, he discussed the chronocyclegraphic recordings, advocated reworkings of the organizational structure, and repeatedly showed films from his previous consulting projects in the United States.[103] The planning department was the site in which *consulting*

[102] F. B. Gilbreth, letter to L. M. Gilbreth, January 27, 1914, Gilbreth LOM, SPCOLL, Purdue University Libraries, NF 91/813-6.

[103] *Auergesellschaft Report*, 41, Gilbreth LOM, SPCOLL, Purdue University Libraries, NF 76/695-2.

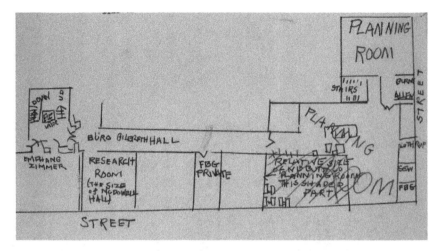

Figure 111 Sketch of the planning department realized in the Auergesellschaft.

knowledge manifested itself in the company. This consulting knowledge assumed two main functions for Gilbreth. On the one hand, he was occupied with the actual restructuring of the business, while on the other hand he wanted to show management everything that had yet to be achieved and what possibilities his system still offered. In other words, the training sessions were daily justifications to management. At the same time, Gilbreth used this context to subtly advocate for the subsequent extension of his consulting mandate. Depending on the circumstances, the visual techniques were transformed from practical tools of corporate consulting to visual promises. They were intended to reinforce the potential of his method every day: "We have [. . .] the photograph, the movies and stereo, and so with the combination of all these things we have a fairly good scheme for the visualization of our problem."[104] The statistical, kinetic and calculative techniques collected there enabled Gilbreth to communicate a conception of his method, without actually applying even a single one of these aspects.

The media techniques represented a prototypical form of visual consulting knowledge: knowledge of potentiality, which vacillated between the ideal-typical media entity and its profane realization. It had to address the utopian character of possible transformations in the future, while at the same time appearing practicable and applicable. For this purpose, Gilbreth introduced a series of rationalization tools. They were intended to make visible the gulf between profane

[104] *Visualizing the Problem of Management*, 10, typescript, ca. 1921, Gilbreth LOM, SPCOLL, Purdue University Libraries, NF 74/675-1.

improvement and utopian efficiency potential, which only needed to be tapped into. For example, he promised to reach an increase in efficiency of 200% on average by means of his filmed motion studies. In individual departments, even a productivity increase of 500% was deemed to be realistic.[105] In connection with such major, almost fantastic promises, the visual consulting knowledge that Gilbreth took into account in this context functioned as a system of stabilization. It was only by dint of this that such statements could even be possible in the first place.

Visual Consulting Knowledge

Here, Gilbreth developed and collected a series of data visualization and scenario analysis techniques, which were to support him in devising new production processes. On the one hand, he used chronocyclegraphic techniques that he had specifically developed for this purpose, while on the other hand he had recourse to visualization techniques such as Gantt charts and harmonographs, as described in Chapter 2 of this study. Gilbreth assembled his visual consulting knowledge from these different techniques. At the same time, in the framework of his consulting commission, the fundamentals of visual management also had to be made clear. Unlike with Gantt, Adamiecki, or in the use of nomographic techniques through the booming science of engineering, Gilbreth united the entire media network into a new configuration of knowledge. He had a major influence on management, and he was part of the gestation process of modern managerial practices. These new forms of business knowledge and visualization techniques utilized there can be classified according to the three ideal types of the graphic method media network (static, kinetic, and calculative). Which forms of visualization, then, did Gilbreth introduce in Berlin? How did he concretely proceed, and which forms did his consulting knowledge and the practice of visual management associated with it assume?

Data Visualization Through Charting and Diagrams

Gilbreth utilized the established forms of visualization that the graphic method media network had made available at this time. He used bar graphs and curve diagrams together with other techniques of graphic data visualization in the framework of his lectures and training sessions. With this, he documented the

---

[105] *Auergesellschaft Report*, 15, Gilbreth LOM, SPCOLL, Purdue University Libraries, NF 76/695-1.

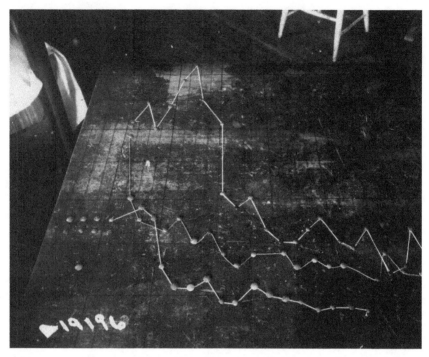

Figure 112   Flexible consulting knowledge. Early techniques of data visualization for the fast comparison of data.

progress of his activities or demanded concrete changes in the business. Even in the official interim reports to the Auergesellschaft on the progress of the commission, Gilbreth frequently used graphic forms of visualization.[106]

For this day-to-day work he also had recourse to very simple and quickly produced visualization techniques. For example, he implemented a system made out of thumbtacks and thread (Fig. 112). With this simple principle, gridded wooden boards could quickly and straightforwardly translate data into a diagram chart. The possibility for data visualization through charting appeared to him to be so important that he envisaged setting up a department dedicated purely to charts.[107] As "the greatest visualizing device of all,"[108] it had the exclusive task of collecting production data from all departments and translating

---

[106] *Auergesellschaft Report*, Gilbreth LOM, SPCOLL, Purdue University Libraries, NF 76/695-2.
[107] On the implementation of "Charting-Rooms," see also Yates, "Graphs as a Managerial Tool."
[108] *Visualizing the Problem of Management*, 28, typescript, ca. 1921, Gilbreth LOM, SPCOLL, Purdue University Libraries, NF 74/675-1.

it into charts.[109] These were made available the next day to management in the planning department, and they enabled an overview in graphic form of the company's individual departments.

> The planning department bulletin board enables you to visualize how many jobs are ahead, and how long ahead. You can also visualize who will be the next man at the machine. You can visualize if there is going to be a change. You can visualize that the planning department is at fault in not getting work in the second set of hooks. You can visualize the names of the best workers. The shop bulletin board will enable you to visualize the sequence of jobs at any one machine, whether or not the machine is apt to become idle, and it will enable you to visualize as much information on this job as you are willing to put any time on. Your chart department is the greatest visualizing device of all.[110]

The charting anticipated for this process was based on the ideal-typical form of static data representation. But Gilbreth developed it further for its introduction into the workplace. A mere transformation of factory data into a scaled graphic form of representation was inadequate for the actual purpose of this graphic display, which was to prepare *decision-making knowledge* for upper management. The processing and selection of data were associated with the process of visualization. The data had to be marked and hierarchized according to importance.

Much like Henry L. Gantt, who furnished his charts with "danger lines," in order to highlight essential information for factory operations,[111] Gilbreth inserted "exception principle zones" into the charts (Fig. 113). These markings had two functions. They served, in analogous fashion to the "danger lines" of the Gantt charts, to emphasize deviations in a single chart. Such deviations did not have to be recognized through intensive comparisons, but were directly highlighted through graphic means. The data presented itself, following the perceptual principle of visual management, "at a glance."[112] These charts "should have 'exception principle zones' to save the time of high priced men and managers. 'Exception principle zones' allow the main things on a chart to be seen at a glance."[113] Apart from that, the exception principle zones represented a point of

---

[109] *Auergesellschaft Report*, 21, Gilbreth LOM, SPCOLL, Purdue University Libraries, NF 76/695-2.

[110] *Visualizing the Problem of Management*, 28–29, typescript, ca. 1921, Gilbreth LOM, SPCOLL, Purdue University Libraries, NF 74/675-1.

[111] See Chapter 2 of this volume, "'Charting': Corporate Management through Visual Routines."

[112] For details on this mode of visual perception, see Chapter 1 of this volume, "The Popularization of the 'Graphic Method Media Network.'"

[113] *Auergesellschaft Report*, 21, Gilbreth LOM, SPCOLL, Purdue University Libraries, NF 76/695-2.

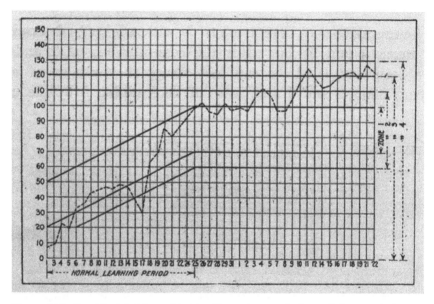

Figure 113 Graphic data hierarchization through an early form of chart analysis. When defined tolerance corridors were exceeded, the charts were automatically forwarded to company management.

selection. They exhibited a sphere of tolerance, which defined those deviations from the production plan that remained within this zone as unproblematic.

It was only when this area was exceeded that the data were transformed into knowledge relevant for administrative purposes. The charts that corresponded to this data were subsequently forwarded by the charting department to the responsible manager. The exclusion of irrelevant data "can be obtained by having the executives determine *zones* on the chart, it being understood that as long as the points fall within the zone he is not to see the charts [. . .]. He is, however, to have sent to him, for initialing, any chart having a point that falls outside his excluded zone."[114] Insignificant information, the "background noise" of the factory floor, was separated from information relevant for administrative purposes.

Between visual management and the previously standard oral or written management practices, there was a fundamental distinction. In practice, visual management not only collected workplace data; it also provided this information in a form that made it compatible for management's administrative and planning processes. The visualizations of business data in its charts already represented a

---

[114] Gilbreth, "Graphical Control on the Exception Principle for Executives," 312.

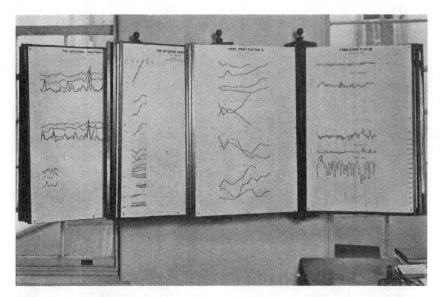

Figure 114 Graphic tableaux as decision-making knowledge in an office situation.

further processing of corporate data. This process obeyed the principle of *static* data representation. The combination of this principle with that of the exception principle zones transformed the charts into vehicles of visual decision-making knowledge.

Ordered in the form of a visual tableau, they appeared—in spite of their heterogeneity—as a coherent data surface (Fig. 114). The logic of *static* representation gave way to *kinetic* logic. The surface corresponded to the modeling and registration of a process. It formed itself into visual decision-making knowledge, which was based on corporate data but which, on the level of its visual representation, took the form of a decision-making tableau (Fig. 115). Similar to the graphic barometers that were commonly used in social and economic meteorology,[115] they enabled extremely diverse data from the production process to be observed and compared in the form of graphic representation. They were transformed into a graphic machine of differentiation, which due to its visual form was interpreted as an integrated knowledge. Decisions were no longer based on static data, but also on the types of media action of the visual ensemble. The graphic data could be *statically* compared, while also serving the modeling and representation of complex *kinetic* processes, such as a production chain or the workforce's patterns of behavior recognizable in Gantt charts.

---

[115] See Chapter 1 of this volume, "The 'Static' Mode of Graphic Representation."

Figure 115 Representing visual management. A stereographic representation of early forms of graphic decision-making knowledge in the Auergesellschaft.

Route Models

Whereas graphic representations like charting were an adaptation of commonly used graphic methods of static visualization, Gilbreth developed, with his *route models*, a genuine innovation in strategic business planning. For the conception of new production facilities and the restructuring of existing work processes, Gilbreth adapted for factory management techniques that were already standard practice in the military.[116] In the tradition of planning games and strategic simulation play, he introduced *route models*, in order to simulate possible changes and play them out. These route models consisted of tables which depicted the building foundations of the Auergesellschaft's plant, on which scale models of the required machines could be arranged. Brackets allowed the individual tables,

---

[116] See Philipp von Hilgers, *War Games: A History of War on Paper*, trans. Ross Benjamin (Cambridge, MA: The MIT Press, 2012), 43–51.

representing the first and second floors, to be placed on top of one another. This enabled a playful planning process of production facilities not only for individual floors, but also for multistory buildings. Different scenarios could be trialed and weighed up against each other. Gilbreth had already developed this principle in his activity for the New England Butt Company:

> At the Butt Company he had built a small route model of the factory, with moveable machines that could be placed in any series of locations to determine the best sequence of material from one machine to another in continuous movement, until the product left the plant.[117]

Unlike in the Butt Company, in Berlin Gilbreth had access to the Auergesellschaft's well-equipped photography department, which, as he himself recognized, enabled him to manufacture route models with a precision and graphic splendor that "were never seen before (see Figs. 116 and 117)."[118]

The use of route models was accompanied by the special situation in the Auergesellschaft. Unlike in many other commissions involving the introduction of scientific management, it was not only the transformation of existing structures that was under focus. It was also necessary to develop entirely new production processes and structures. "It is a new thing in management to start a job from the beginning in management."[119]

This situation, that of a completely new construction which paid no heed to the limitations of pre-existing structures, required tools for translating the necessary planning process in a regulated form. Since there were no existing structures that formed the point of departure of the planning process, Gilbreth had recourse to his *route models*, which represented the building floor plans and depicted the beginning of the planning process (Fig. 118). Within this artificial planning space, all combinations of the required machines were possible. In addition, he had so-called process flow charts drawn up (Fig. 119). "The process flow chart [. . .] was created [. . .] as another means of portraying graphically the sequence of steps in a plant's operation."[120] In this combination, the predetermined production pathway and the ultimate spatial setup in the factory building combined into a visual simulation game, which opened new perspectives for factory planning. In the planning situation, all three action types of the graphic method media network—the static, kinetic, and calculative—came together. Process charts

---

[117] Yost, *Frank and Lillian Gilbreth*, 217.

[118] F. B. Gilbreth, letter to L. M. Gilbreth, April 16, 1914, Gilbreth LOM, SPCOLL, Purdue University Libraries, NF 91/813-6.

[119] F. B. Gilbreth, letter to L. M. Gilbreth, April 24, 1914, Gilbreth LOM, SPCOLL, Purdue University Libraries, NF 91/813-6.

[120] Yost, *Frank and Lillian Gilbreth*, 217.

and route models represented static production data, as well as serving the kinetic simulation of manufacturing processes. The visual surfaces of these displays could in turn be transformed into raw data for calculation purposes. With their to-scale depiction of the real-life factory, these route models and processes charts could be measured and described as mathematical calculations. The different scenarios which were conceived with the visual techniques could not only be compared with each other "at a glance." They could also be accounted for in the search for the "one best way" to structure the factory. The measured lines and intervals were transformed into calculative parameters, with which various production and process scenarios could be calculated.

Corporate Consulting as a Participatory Process

The models and charts were not only a component of a planning process carried out by Gilbreth's consulting team. They also enabled the active integration of company management and the directly affected department supervisors in the planning phase. Alongside the major route models in the planning department, Gilbreth developed to-scale models of the machines and assembly lines required in the factory. He gave each of the department supervisors a set of these models that could fit inside a small suitcase to be taken home with them, so that new ideas for the optimal integration of production processes could be developed.

> It is a small portable box 11"x18" full of shelves for small route models (simply the floors). We let the head of depts. concerned take these home to study. [. . .] Think of letting the head men take these home, and how they will boast about.[121]

This set of planning toys allowed the department supervisors to construct different production scenarios and then apply the ideas and machine configurations simulated with the route models to concrete suggestions for change.

In the planning department of the factory management's newly created central exchange, recourse was also had to *flow charts* in the evaluation of these planning games. They were used to depict the production situations of individual departments on long strips of paper.

> Good management methods [. . .] meant being able to visualize and to help others visualize each part of a plant's operation in relationship to the whole and

---

[121] F. B. Gilbreth, letter to L. M. Gilbreth, April 24, 1914, Gilbreth LOM, SPCOLL, Purdue University Libraries, NF 91/813-6.

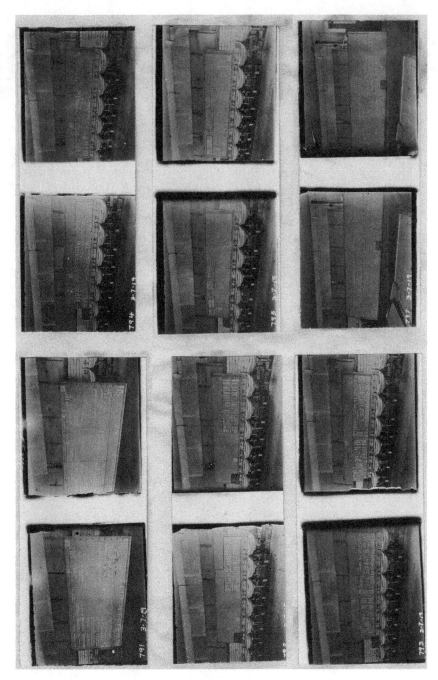

Figure 116 Readymade visualization of factory floors. A table contained the blueprint of a firm's factory floor. A washroom is used as an improvised warehouse for the components of the route models.

Figure 117 Visualization workers fabricating route models.

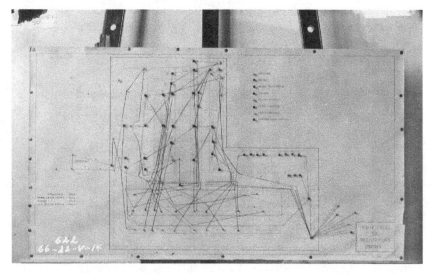

Figure 118 Route model of the messenger system in the Auergesellschaft.

Figure 119 Visualizing and calculating. Processes charts as a surface and a point of departure for mathematical calculations.

to see, merely through looking at the chart, where efficiency was lost through back-tracking.[122]

The route models offered these possibilities of visualization or the preparation of visual surfaces for the managerial personnel employed in the Auergesellschaft (Fig. 120). Gilbreth presided over the design process, making the forms and possibilities of visualization available to management. In this sense, they were *boundary objects*, which brought together different groups and presented them with low-threshold offers of participation.

For cooperative managers, these visualizations offered the possibility of positioning themselves as particularly progressive figures within the company. For instance, the leader of the accounting division, Mr. Radzig, proved to be particularly engaged. He transformed his department according to Gilbreth's guidelines.

An example of what can be done with Processes Charts can be seen in Mr. Radzig's room, where he has a small box containing Processes Charts that he can take home with him at night and study. As a result of his study, he has made the lines of the paths of papers shorter and much more direct.[123]

[122] Yost, *Frank and Lillian Gilbreth*, 217.
[123] *Auergesellschaft Report*, 13, Gilbreth LOM, SPCOLL, Purdue University Libraries, NF 76/ 695-2.

Figure 120 A route model of a three-piece factory plant allowed for the simulation of various factory layouts.

Radzig has turned his dept. of 100 clerks into a model place.[124]

Not the least of his reasons for doing so was the fact that the concept that stood behind the planned restructures necessarily led to an expansion of corporate bureaucracy. Central departments, such as the accounting divisions, would be granted extended responsibilities. Radzig could be rather certain to increase his position of power in the company if the restructure was a success.

With his visual consulting knowledge, Gilbreth was also able to interest impartial sectors of management in his methods, such as Dr. Feuer, the head of the gaslight department. Due to the looming rebuilding in the company, he was not a proponent of any corporate restructuring. The Auergesellschaft strove for a total conversion of production from gas to electric lights. He feared a loss of influence should this conversion take place.

Director Feuer of the Gas Mantle Factory has held off—delayed—dallied—and billingsgated and today fell in a heap over a route model showing proposed

---

[124] F. B. Gilbreth, letter to L. M. Gilbreth, September 21, 1914, Gilbreth LOM, SPCOLL, Purdue University Libraries, NF 91/813-6.

changes in his factory store's functions. One never knows what will make the hit.[125]

But even he could be impressed by Gilbreth's route models, as the latter observed with satisfaction. Gilbreth used visual methods in order to test new factory layouts, develop scenarios, and weigh them up against one another. This was a case of managerial practices of future anticipation, which concerned both middle and upper management. At the same time, Gilbreth used his visual consulting knowledge to demonstrate transparency and the ability to take action to his clients at the uppermost executive level of the company—such as during a visit from privy-councillor Bernard Dernburg, the general manager of the Auergesellschaft.

> His Excellency asked to visit me today and I permitted him to come. [. . .] He was excited about the route model, which had the path string of the path of an order of lamps from the first man to the express wagon. [. . .] Then we showed him cyclegraphs of Stronck [Gilbreth's assistant] inspecting incandescent lamps. Then I showed him the pictures of you [Lillian Gilbreth] sorting photos and of you sorting when we took the first chronocyclegraph.[126]

Gilbreth used the route models to gain a *kinetic* comprehension of the factory. With this, he could register and represent the various contributing processes. The model was used to reduce an extremely heterogeneous combination of different components to a process description. At the same time, they also assumed a *static* representational function. Visualizations and film screenings allowed him to speak about his actual core business. The visualization represented an enunciatory system, a grammar, which helped to objectify the activity of the corporate consultant. The depiction of abstract principles in route models, process charts, flow charts, stereoscopic images, chronocyclegraphic photographs, and film recordings created the necessary methodological evidence for his activity as a corporate consultant. The concrete steps became so tangible that he was able to insert the client, in this case Dernburg, directly into the mindset of efficiency maximization:

> I then showed him the best film of folding handkerchiefs, and he said, "I can see a better way myself. Fold three times and crease once." I said, "How did

[125] F. B. Gilbreth, letter to L. M. Gilbreth, October 21, 1914, Gilbreth LOM, SPCOLL, Purdue University Libraries, NF 91/813-6.
[126] F. B. Gilbreth, letter to L. M. Gilbreth, January 12, 1914, Gilbreth LOM, SPCOLL, Purdue University Libraries, NF 91/813-6.

Figure 121 Gilbreth as management guru. Stylization and demarcation from competitors in the consulting field through the targeted exhibition of new media technologies, in this case the phonograph.

you know when you have seen only the film?" [. . .] He blushed for his own modesty, and walked away. [. . .] I could see that he was greatly pleased and surprised.[127]

This visual consulting knowledge documented the work of a corporate consultant and made it visible for the first time. Without such visualization techniques, Gilbreth would surely not have succeeded in making his consulting knowledge appear as consistent and legitimate within the space of less than two years (against the backdrop of the stagnation of the company's actual turnover).

That this was in no way a coincidental side effect, but planned practice, can be seen in another area. Lillian Gilbreth sent her husband Frank a *phonograph*, a predecessor of the dictaphone (Fig. 121). The purpose of this device, however, was less its practical facilitation of working life, but the technological device in and of itself: "The phonograph makes a great hit everywhere—it was very smart of you to think of it. It shows them that we are ingenious and can do everything better than can other people."[128] The static, kinetic, and calculative visualization techniques used by Gilbreth served the same purpose: the stabilization of fragile consulting knowledge. They were supposed to show that the corporate consultancy Gilbreth, Inc. "can do everything better than can other people."[129]

[127] Ibid.
[128] F. B. Gilbreth, letter to L. M. Gilbreth, April 28, 1914, Gilbreth LOM, SPCOLL, Purdue University Libraries, NF 91/813-6.
[129] Ibid.

Visual Control

The use of charts was not only restricted to the level of the company's executives; it was also deployed on the factory floor. Here, too, Gilbreth's and Gantt's approaches resemble each other. Like Gilbreth, Gantt also employed the rapid transparency of graphic displays as a tool of *visual control* over the employees. The daily depiction of the productivity of individual departments over the previous day and the previous week was intended, as Gilbreth explained, to motivate the workers to achieve an equally high level of performance.

> The by-products of a properly operated chart system are even more valuable than its direct product. We find that the psychological effect of the variable "promptness" itself makes the curves representing outputs and costs fall more nearly in the proximity of the established norms and locations prophesied on the charts.[130]

If productivity went backward in one department, then this was seen not only by the workers employed there, but also all the other workers of the factory. Poor work operations immediately became known beyond the relevant department and were supposed to impel the employees to work better. If a repressive moment was connected with the overt visualization of work performance, then these performance charts were supplemented with organization charts which showed the "path of possible promotion."[131] They were to spur the workforce by using graphic tools to show them the future prospects for promotion. The system of incentives was also part of this system of visual control. Whoever consistently delivered good work results could expect to attract rewards. Gilbreth expanded the technique of visual control developed by Gantt at the turn of the century and supplemented it with a positive, motivational side. Gilbreth used all the possibilities of visualization available to him in order to exploit the "psychological side"[132] of the employees as a new resource for management. He extended methods of visual control with mobile pieces of visual display.

[130] Gilbreth, "Graphical Control on the Exception Principle for Executives," 311.
[131] *Auergesellschaft Report*, 22, Gilbreth LOM, SPCOLL, Purdue University Libraries, NF 76/ 695-2.
[132] L. Gilbreth, *The Psychology of Management*.

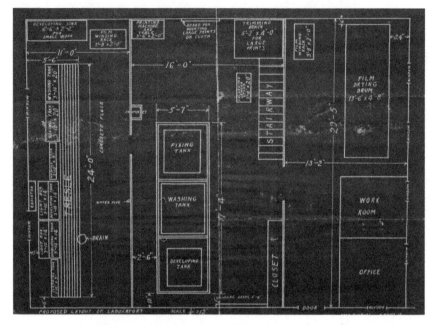

Figure 122   Floor plan of a film laboratory, which was also being planned for the Auergesellschaft. The blueprint probably derives from a consulting contract for the Erie Forge Steel Company.

The Infrastructure of Visual Management

Visual management incorporated different spheres of planning and administration as well as practices of employee supervision. The visualization of workplace knowledge was highly valued during Gilbreth's consulting commission in the Auergesellschaft.

This was reflected in the considerable efforts that Gilbreth invested in the erection of facilities and infrastructure, which were all intended to serve the purpose of data visualization. Apart from a charting department, he also wanted to attach a film laboratory to the Auergesellschaft's planning department.[133] The layout of a film laboratory that Gilbreth planned five years later gives us an idea of the scope of such an installation (Fig. 122). It contained all the necessary appliances for the development, enlargement, and processing of films and photographs. Gilbreth had the goal of creating a self-sufficient visualization headquarters. It would justify his approach toward corporate restructures. The visualizations it produced

---

[133] For the planned film laboratory, the Auergesellschaft acquired used equipment for film development.

would place him in a position to appropriately communicate the changes needed in the business. Significant areas of the planning department were not, as could be expected, preoccupied with the concrete planning of the company's restructure. Instead, they were tasked with producing the visualization of corporate data in a variety of forms. As a consequence, considerable financial sums were directed toward the production of visual consulting knowledge.

A Theory of Management

Gilbreth had not gone through any kind of education in engineering science. He was not one of those classical engineering consultants who primarily concentrated on technical changes to the production process. His goal was not exhausted in the rationalization of the production process on the factory floor. Additionally, he wanted to use his graphic method to improve decision-making procedures on the level of management and the bureaucracy associated with it. In other words: Gilbreth had an overarching theoretical conception of the "managerial." His approach was not restricted to a succession of individual (technical) improvements. Following the principles of the division of labor and motion efficiency, he defined the manager as a *pure* decision-making authority. "The personal work of the executive should consist as much as possible of making decisions and as little as possible of making motions."[134] Their task did not consist of generating or selecting information, but more in making decisions in the visual data arena of the central planning room.

> The motions that an executive would expend in getting information by such old methods as, for example, walking through the works to see with his unreliable eyes conditions which are not typical, partly owing to his presence, bring results of little value compared with the results that can be obtained by the same amount of time and motions concentrated on those facts and conditions which cause the great fluctuations from the desired output.[135]

Instead of directly garnering the required information from the factory floor, the manager was better off concentrating on the data drawn together in the planning departments. A meticulous analysis of these data sets would lead to better, more objective decisions. The previous practice rested on ostensibly direct information from the individual departments. In contrast to the graphic-visual

---

[134] Gilbreth, "Graphical Control on the Exception Principle for Executives," 311.
[135] Ibid.

information, however, these were, as Gilbreth argued, always distorted by the presence of an observer.

The principle of visualization[136] represented a departure from the idea that the direct, physical presence of the manager was necessary for the observation, comprehension, and evaluation of the situation in the workplace. The practices of direct, oral management still adhered to this mentality. The persistent presence of the supervisor in the factory was to guarantee the orderly nature of production operations. Gilbreth departed from this viewpoint by implicitly defining a sphere of decision making. A good decision did not require a direct confrontation with the local state of play. In contrast, it was beneficial to be somewhat withdrawn from it. It was only at a distance, with the scenario at hand reflected in the available data, that there was a basis for a "good" decision to be made. The abstraction and selection performance on the level of the visual was central to this approach. It forced management, as Auerbach and von Pirani had already argued, to adopt new forms of thinking and reflection. The system of visual management used by Gilbreth "presents facts in a new way that enables the manager to see 'tendencies' of development."[137] Von Pirani made similar observations about the possibilities of "visual interpolation."[138] The conception that attached surplus value to the visual, and which also took aspects of intuition and creativity into account, was incorporated into Gilbreth's system.

The consulting contract at the Auergesellschaft was the last testing station of Gilbreth's management system. In December 1917 he presented it publicly for the first time at the annual conference of the ASME. Apart from that, a detailed description of his visual management system is available in a manuscript with the title *Visualizing the Problem of Management*.[139] Possibly due to the early and abrupt death of Gilbreth, this text was never published. This is another reason why the value of the early corporate consultants for management theory has long been underestimated.[140]

"Lab-Based Consulting": Doesn't Work? Doesn't Matter!

If the circumstances that accompanied the consulting commission in Berlin are taken into consideration, then Gilbreth's failure was an overall success. He

---

[136] *Visualizing the Problem of Management*, typescript, ca. 1921, Gilbreth LOM, SPCOLL, Purdue University Libraries, NF 74/675-1.

[137] *Auergesellschaft Report*, 7, Gilbreth LOM, SPCOLL, Purdue University Libraries, NF 76/695-1.

[138] See Chapter 1 of this volume, "Applied Industrial Research."

[139] *Visualizing the Problem of Management*, typescript, ca. 1921, Gilbreth LOM, SPCOLL, Purdue University Libraries, NF 74/675-1.

[140] Such as in the account given by McKenna, who precisely denies the epistemological relevancy of corporate consultants. See McKenna, *The World's Newest Profession*, 26–50.

nonetheless had to contend with a series of setbacks. The Auergesellschaft found itself in a generally precarious situation. Certainly, it was a leader in the manufacturing of gas lightbulbs, but this status was acutely threatened through the advent of electricity. Added to this was the rising hostility the German trade unions had toward Taylorism, which advanced from a marginal tendency in management theory to a thoroughly politicized term of combat. The simultaneous onset of World War I did not help matters. The restructuring of the company ended in disaster, with all the transformations undertaken by Gilbreth and his team reversed.

More than the unfavorable circumstances of his commission, however, the internal contradictions of his method were chiefly responsible for this situation. Gilbreth's conception of media relied on the notion of a participatory involvement of the workforce. Without their cooperation, his goal of the motion-aware worker could not be attained. But, as shown in the previous chapters on his conception of media and the technical prerequisites of his method, this approach could not be redeemed, due in large part to the limitations in the technical implementation of his ideas and his inclination for the scientific form of the laboratory study. The visibility necessary for participatory access could not be attained with the black box of the motion study laboratory. Instead, it unleashed deep mistrust within the union-organized workforce, which Gilbreth, even with the help of film, was incapable of dispelling.

As a corporate consultant in the narrower sense—that is, a seller of knowledge—he was nonetheless thoroughly successful. Over the course of almost two years, he was able to convince his clients that the restructuring would, in the end, be a success—even after the entire male workforce was drafted into the military, with the remaining factory workers consisting of old men and uneducated, newly employed women, and the factory only operating a couple of days a week. With his form of visual consulting knowledge, Gilbreth did not propose a clear, well-trodden path. Flow charts, route models, cyclegraphs, and processes charts generated an almost surreal form of managerial consulting and administrative knowledge capable of meeting all contingencies through the use of media, in the middle of a country at war. That this would end in success remained the conviction of his clients in the *Lampenstadt*, even when Gilbreth, on his daily walk to the Auergesellschaft, increasingly came to walk past bloodied, crippled soldiers returned from the front, and even when he was arrested on the suspicion of being an English spy, or when market stall holders tried to sell him the latest fad in Berlin children's toys: Russian hangmen in doll form.

All this did not seem to diminish the evidence and effectiveness of Gilbreth's visual consulting knowledge, which was composed of filmic techniques as well as visualization techniques from the graphic method. His method was not only successful, and accepted as such, due to its visual aesthetic of media regulation techniques. Just as much credit could be attributed to the potential media action associated with it. Gilbreth's ensemble of media visualization techniques optimally covered the *graphic method media network*'s three dimensions of action. With the route models, corresponding to the kinetic action type, complex processes could be modeled and molded to be accessible to management. Flow charts allowed for the assembly of static representations of relevant data. When needed, the same visualizations could subsequently be measured, enumerated, and calculatively compared in different scenarios.

In the graphic method's three dimensions of action, media techniques of visualization joined with the company's concrete practices. Visual consulting knowledge not only included abstract representations, kinetic modelings, or visual comparative calculations. It also consisted of fully valued managerial instruments, which combined practical action options with a visual surface, an aesthetic of administration, regulation, and the "managerial" in general. This connection of visual aesthetics with concrete action options made the *graphic method media network* into an ideal vehicle of knowledge and a tool for the branch of corporate consulting.

This was representative of a visual culture in management which between 1880 and 1930 considerably established itself in the business world through the practice of corporate consulting. These processes shaped and stabilized the drive toward medialization in business described earlier. They contributed to the form of visual management succeeding the previously standard managerial modes: those of *oral* and *written* management.

In the 1910s and 1920s already, advanced theoretical reflection on visual management systems was developed on this basis. This is evidence that the corporate consultants of the day were not exclusively restricted to the rationalization of production, as Christopher McKenna assumes.[141] Rather, in the visual models and practices of the engineering consultants investigated in my study, we can discern a logic that is also quite relevant for the present-day branch of corporate consulting.

[141] Ibid.

Conclusion

Consulting and the "Managerial"

In my preceding historical analysis, I investigated corporate consulting media and the early visual practices of management that were closely associated with them. I described these as part of a structurally transformative drive toward medialization in the commercial-industrial sphere, which took place between 1880 and 1930. This gave rise to the form of *visual management*.

I ascribed this change to three developments, which fundamentally changed business's knowledge structure after 1880. First, an independent form of managerial activity was developed in the business world, with which specific management tools were associated. Second, in the same period the branch of corporate consulting began to establish itself. Third, with the *graphic method media network*, a set of visualization practices was developed which was made available to management and corporate consultants around 1880. These three developments favored and shaped the medialization drive in business I described earlier.

Contemporary microeconomic theory describes the visualization possibilities of the graphic method as an exit point for breaking free from established, standardized patterns of thought. The graphic-visual form was intended to counteract tendencies toward bureaucratization and standardization, and enable an intuitive momentum when reaching decisions. It was even ascribed with prognostic potential. These attributions were part of the popularization process of the graphic method in the early twentieth century. Visualization techniques were positioned as a universally applicable mode of representation. They were used to visualize, take stock of, and graphically compare data, but also to photochemically depict, model, or graphically register previously imperceptible processes.

Parallel to their rise in popular culture, these techniques also established themselves in industry. With *Gantt charting* and Karol Adamiecki's system of the *harmonograph*, both of which were graphic management systems for factory administration, workplace routines could be comprehended and translated into knowledge relevant to the tasks of administration. The visual techniques here not only served the purposes of control and surveillance. Rather, they were supposed to facilitate intuitive decision making by managerial staff in opaque or unclear workplace situations.

Angels of Efficiency. Florian Hoof, Oxford University Press (2020) © Oxford University Press.
DOI: 10.1093/oso/9780190886363.003.0001

Alongside the introduction of graphic techniques through corporate consultants and engineering experts, they also found favor on the level of everyday labor practices. With *nomography*, an easily accessible graphic calculation system, mathematic and scientific principles were established in the business sphere. They found an entryway into the sphere of production and the sales departments of corporations. The medialization drive was not only based on individual projects of corporate restructuring, which were generally the responsibility of external consultants. It also held sway within the corporation, in its various departments. This development thus gained additional stability and dynamism.

There arose a *visual culture* of industrial-commercial corporate management based on the *graphic method media network*. This provided concrete options for action that guaranteed a practical surplus value of graphic-visual techniques. These in turn enabled the *static* representation of complex sets of data, the modeling and simulation of *kinetic* processes, and their *calculative* accounting, which gave rise, *avant la lettre*, to visual *decision environments*, allowing management to make rapid decisions "at a glance."

In this context, the introduction of media was understood as a progressive, consequential development of management practices. Graphic-visual methods were thus able to increasingly gain acceptance. This tendency permitted corporate consultants to specifically introduce visualization techniques as a tool for winning clients and legitimizing their method. They used the interest in media techniques among management and business in order to combine the graphic method with their consulting services. Exemplary for this practice was the corporate consultancy Gilbreth, Inc., which deliberately utilized media, and especially film, as a unique selling proposition when trying to attract commissions. Filmic motion studies guaranteed an aesthetic of efficiency and thus also legitimized the consultants' approach.

As shown at the beginning of this study, where I discussed the consulting model of the Wheel of Motion popularized by Frank B. Gilbreth, consulting knowledge was marked by very particular challenges. It had to be modular and flexible, and at the same time follow a stable, persuasive internal logic. Changes carried out or proposed in the framework of a consulting commission had to be verified by the clients and communicated within the company. Consulting knowledge vacillated between an ideal-typical entity, like the filmic cyclegraph or the model of the Wheel of Motion, and its profane realization as "transferable data."[1] It had to address the visionary character of potential future changes in the workplace, while also appearing practicable and implementable. *Visual consulting knowledge* stood in for this split between profane improvement and

[1] Frank B. Gilbreth and Lillian M. Gilbreth, "Applications of Motion Studies: Its Use in Developing the Best Methods of Work," *Management* and *Administration* 8, no. 3 (1924): 296.

visionary efficiency potential, which only needed to be exploited. And it was not least the latest media technology used here that represented the "state of the art" modern consulting business.

In this context, media techniques appear not only as tools oriented toward functionality. They are also constitutive for the development of modern commercial and industrial management. Media techniques and apparatuses function as discursive channels and *borrowed systems of enunciation* for those aspects that were until then incapable of being articulated or represented. Engineers, corporate consultants, and company owners used media to speak about an as yet nonexistent theory of management. As such, media like film left their mark on the representational world of consultants, as well as on the concrete practices of management. With the graphic method, there subsequently arose the first concretion of managerial practice, which took the form of methods of future anticipation, scenario analysis, and simulation.

Visual Management

The *graphic method media network* formed the basis for *visual consulting knowledge* and *visual management*. These two spheres had a reciprocal relationship with one another. On the one hand, the prototypical form of visual consulting knowledge was instated and became an accepted component of business administration options. On the other hand, the form of visual management established itself, a managerial practice which even more strongly than the previous oral and written regimes of managements foregrounded "pure" managerial administrative and decision-making knowledge. In contrast to consulting knowledge, this is not a knowledge of potentiality, but concrete practice in the workplace. It manifested itself in technological apparatuses of direction and planning and in contemporary descriptions of management practices. Visual consulting knowledge and visual management shaped and marked the visual culture of the "managerial," as it established itself in the business world after 1880.

The drive toward medialization was part of corporate management's new basis for taking action. An interventionist, top-down model gave way to the principle of lateral communication and constant readjustment. This model of readjustment was dependent less on tried and tested national procedures of exercising state power, which primarily rested on macro-instruments like statistics. Rather, the "politics of large numbers"[2] has been replaced by the micropolitics of flexible, action-oriented consulting services. It can be seen that, independently of the

2 Alain Desrosières, *The Politics of Large Numbers: A History of Statistical Reasoning*, trans. Camille Naish (Cambridge, MA: Harvard University Press, 2002).

technology available, action practices in business that amounted to forms of *simulation* or *feedback systems* were already widespread by the end of the nineteenth century. Computers, or fantasies of cybernetic control and regulation, were not necessary for giving rise to this form of managerial thinking. In this context, my analysis can contribute to a better understanding of why concepts of flexible regulation could be so smoothly implemented after the end of World War II. In the end, the corporate world had already introduced and tested out (proto-)cybernetic techniques, which I describe here under the rubric of *visual management*. On account of their orientation and the proven nature of their application, these techniques crossed the threshold between proto-cybernetics and cybernetics, in spite of being entirely absent of data processing.

Consulting Knowledge

Closely related to this, and a decisive driving force behind its development, is the parallel formation of the consulting industry. Here, a certain virtuosity in the deployment of visualization practices arose, which led to the actual service of providing consulting knowledge entering into a tight symbiosis with the visualization techniques that were available at the time. They appeared to be particularly well suited as vehicles for consulting knowledge, even if the knowledge produced had to be flexibly adapted to a company's specific local conditions. At the same time, the predetermined form of visual representation prevented the impression of total randomness, even if the local situation pre-existing the consulting commission is subordinated to an ensemble of methods and apparatuses in the form of graphics, charts, and visual inscription, and to a certain extent visually standardized. The form of visual knowledge thus partly coincides with the form of consulting knowledge. It not only represents the concrete data of the respective local business situation, but also exhibits, and at the same time characterizes, the external character of consulting knowledge. The visual form in and of itself creates the difference to daily production routines necessary for the process of transforming an organization.

At the same time, visual consulting knowledge is suitable for the growing number of corporate consultants as a practical instrument for attracting clients. The visual evidence of these techniques and their associated appearance of "mechanical objectivity" was used by Frank B. Gilbreth, for example, as a unique selling proposition for his form of corporate consulting. Whether the media techniques actually played a substantial role in increasing efficiency is a secondary consideration. Of primary concern is the fact that media techniques were a suitable tool for addressing the expectations of his potential clients. With them, Gilbreth was able to make "inefficiency" visible. Subsequently, he provided techniques for correcting any, equally visual, "erroneous developments." For the business owners and shareholder boards, this visual consulting knowledge amounted to a wager on the economic efficiency and adequate administrative and decision-making routines in management.

This is also conditioned by the fact that the visual forms of consulting knowledge not only addressed an understanding of economic efficiency and rationality. A similarly abstract language of forms established itself in the sphere of art,[3] theater, and dance.[4] The potential clients were thus confronted with visual forms that were not entirely new. Visual consulting knowledge was linked with an aesthetic discourse,[5] an aesthetic regime,[6] that also succeeded in other areas of society. It is an aesthetic that not only stood for regressive conservation, but also for progressive, reform-oriented modernity. It promised the exploitation of not yet exhausted reserves of efficiency with the aid of scientific-methodical precision. This combination of a progressive aesthetic with the goal of movement rationalization was the basis for the success and the acceptance of *visual consulting knowledge*.

Mediated through the sphere of corporate consulting, the graphic method was also able to establish itself in industrial production. The consulting branch's visual consulting knowledge is not only part of an overarching visual aesthetic. Consultants were also successful because they encountered pre-existing visualization practices that had already been introduced into the workplace. These are two developments that intersect with one another, reciprocally stabilizing each other and thereby becoming the motor force for visual management.

The "Visual Culture" of Management

The medialization drive influenced the corporate consulting industry and the forms of *visual management* realized in the workplace. Beyond this, it also played a central role in the establishment and professionalization of management. In trade journals, shortly after his death, Frank. B Gilbreth had already risen to

---

[3] Rosalind E. Krauss, *The Originality of the Avant-Garde and Other Modernist Myths*, 6th ed. (Cambridge, MA: MIT Press, 1989), 9–22.

[4] Similar aesthetics also existed in the dance theater of Rudolf von Laban or in the theater of François Delsarte and Émile Jacques-Dalcroze. See W. Jack Duncan, Peter M. Ginter, and Terrie C. Reeves, "Motion Study in Management and the Arts: A Historic Example," in *Frank and Lillian Gilbreth: Critical Evaluations in Business and Management*, ed. Michael C. Wood and John C. Wood (London: Routledge, 2003), 420–44.

[5] Michel Foucault, "The Order of Discourse," in *Untying the Text: A Post-Structuralist Reader*, ed. Robert Young (London: Routledge & Kegan Paul, 1981).

[6] Jacques Rancière, *Aesthetics and Its Discontents*, trans. Steve Corcoran (Cambridge: Polity Press, 2009).

become *the* central protagonist and pioneer of developing management. Unlike the disputed figure Frederick W. Taylor, he became an emblem of modern, scientific management, a figure of identification for the new *imagined community* of salaried factory managers. Neither trade journals like the German *REFA-Bücher*[7] nor generalist historical treatises[8] failed to discuss his cyclegraphs, charts, motion study laboratories, and the media technologies used within. Films were made about him, and in the 1950s, a biographical novel about his life became a bestseller in the United States and Germany.[9] His graphic techniques and his definition and application of these visual objects acquired the status of boundary objects, toward which later generations of management oriented themselves, and which provided an initial framework for understanding what "management" actually is. The visual culture of the "managerial" that arose out of this stabilized and shaped the formation of the discourse of management theory.

But it was not only on the level of a metahistory of management that the visual techniques and representations were part of the gestation process of the "managerial." Graphic forms of corporate knowledge also facilitated communication between managers. Abstract aspects of administration could be visualized in the form of graphic displays (Fig. 123). Subsequently, the charts could be discussed and debated. Chart analysis helped in articulating and clarifying executive decision making. In this context, the graphic techniques also served the self-ascertainment of the rising profession of the *salaried manager*. At the end of the nineteenth and beginning of the twentieth century, this profession enjoyed neither a good reputation nor a particularly high social standing.[10] With graphic techniques, they possessed, for the first time, a common representational potential for their activity, divided as it was between various spheres and activities.

---

[7] The books published by the Reichsausschuss für Arbeitsstudien (Imperial Commission for Labor Studies) were the accepted standard for calculating wage costs in Germany. See REFA, *Zweites REFA—Buch: Erweiterte Einführung in die Arbeitszeitermittlung* (Berlin: Beuth, 1939); REFA, *REFA—Buch vol. I: Arbeitsgestaltung: Mit einer Einführung in das Arbeitsstudium*, 2nd ed. (Munich: Carl Hanser, 1952); REFA, *REFA—Buch vol. I. Arbeitsgestaltung*, 5th ed. (Munich: Carl Hanser, 1955); REFA, *REFA—Buch vol. I. Arbeitsgestaltung*, 9th ed. (Munich: Carl Hanser, 1960).

[8] Such as Shaw, *The Purpose and Practice of Motion Study*.

[9] Frank B. Gilbreth Jr. and Ernestine Gilbreth Carey, *Cheaper by the Dozen* (New York: Crowell, 1948). The 1950 film adaptation of this book by the Twentieth Century Fox Film Corporation also had the title *Cheaper by the Dozen*.

[10] See Jürgen Kocka, "Legitimationsprobleme und -strategien der Unternehmer und Manager im 19. und frühen 20. Jahrhundert," *Zeitschrift für Unternehmensgeschichte* 44 (1999), 18; Jürgen Kocka, "Class Formation, Interest Articulation and Public Policy: The Origins of the German White Collar Class in the Late Nineteenth and Early Twentieth Centuries," in *Organizing Interests in Western Europe: Pluralism, Corporatism, and the Transformation of Politics*, ed. Suzanne Berger (Cambridge: Cambridge University Press, 1988), 63–81; Heike Franz, "Kulturelles Milieu und Disziplinbildung: Die Entstehung der Betriebswirtschaftslehre in Deutschland 1900 bis 1933," *Wissenschaftsgeschichte heute: Festschrift für Peter Lundgreen* (Verlag für Regionalgeschichte, 2001), 251–77.

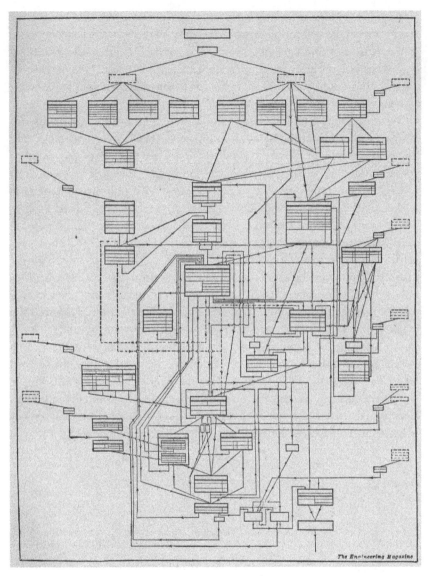

The Engineering Magazine

Figure 123 The "pure" knowledge of visual management. This system could only be published on the condition that all the details that referred to the specific type of factory had to be deleted. "Graphical Representation of Processes and Routing in a Representative Plant. Names of the departments and operations are omitted by request of the proprietors of the establishment in which this chart was made."

Graphic techniques *represented* the "managerial," administrative knowledge and promoted the self-conception of an established profession. They functioned in this sense as *media boundary objects*. The graphic representation of a Gantt chart translated the heterogeneous fields of management into a loose visual coupling: the basic prerequisite for the definition of generally valid concepts, and the formation of an accepted canon of managerial methods.

It was precisely the abstract visual form of the graphic method that manifested itself as a major advantage. Hence, administrative knowledge was no longer tied to concrete things, processes, or products, and, freed from all of this, could be communicated as "pure" administrative knowledge. Managers from different spheres or competing firms could now exchange views on various aspects of business administration, without having to betray company secrets such as special production processes. Concrete details were dissolved in abstract administrative knowledge. The visual culture of the "managerial" that thus arose consisted of many different media boundary objects.[11] It was not only *within* the firms that they contributed to the creation of administrative knowledge. They also enabled and facilitated its circulation within the new elite functionary of the salaried manager. Thus, they became aware of their actual task and formed their own self-conception. At the end of the time frame analyzed here, 1880 to 1930, *the* ultimate theory of business management was constituted. In 1929, Erich Gutenberg published his first description of the theory of factors, the seminal text of German managerial doctrine.[12] For the abstract factors described there, Gutenberg also had recourse to the graphic method. It was initially in the different visualized curves (such as "quantity cost curves"[13]) that individual components of the "managerial" could be concretized and communicated.[14]

[11] Florian Hoof, "The Media Boundary Objects Concept: Theorizing Film and Media," in *Media Matter: The Materiality of Media, Matter as Medium*, ed. Bernd Herzogenrath (New York: Bloomsbury, 2015), 180–200.

[12] Erich Gutenberg, *Die Unternehmung als Gegenstand betriebswirtschaftlicher Theorie* (Berlin: Gabler, 1929).

[13] Ibid., 49–50.

[14] See also Fritz Nordsieck, "Die schaubildliche Erfassung und Untersuchung der Betriebsorganisation" (PhD diss., Stuttgart, 1930); Fritz Nordsieck, "Harmonogramme: Ein Beitrag zur schaubildlichen Untersuchung der Betriebs-Organisation," *Zeitschrift für Organisation (ZfürO)* 5, no. 5 (1931): 106–12; Fritz Nordsieck, "Erfassung der Betriebsorganisation durch Organisations-Schaubilder," *Zeitschrift für Organisation (ZfürO)* 4, no. 18 (1930): 487–91; Fritz Nordsieck, "Graphische Darstellung der formalen Fehlerkontrollen in der Bankbuchhaltung unter besonderer Berücksichtigung der Kontokorrentkontrolle," *Zeitschrift für handelswissenschaftliche Forschung* 23 (1929): 145–69; Fritz Nordsieck, "Die organisations-technische Darstellung von Arbeitsabläufen in der Buchhaltung: Eine Erweiterung der Richtlinien des AWF," *Zeitschrift für Organisation (ZfürO)* 1, no. 16 (1928): 440–42.

The Graphic Method Media Network

For the period between 1880 and 1930, the *graphic method media network* was decisive. Specific techniques enabled a selection of data, like the charts introduced by Gilbreth with their *exception principle zones*. They had the capacity to be able to accomplish the preparation and visualization of a particular quantity of business data. The actual innovation of the visual method was the ability to transform *statistical* into *kinetic* techniques. This enabled concrete individual case analyses and not only the representation of statistically mediated data. Visual displays were not only a form of "representation," but also calculation, modeling, and planning spaces. Nevertheless, these kinetic techniques immediately came up against their limitations. To use the terms of the computer age, the graphic method simply had too little processing capacity and a resolution that was difficult to scale. Graphic techniques were appropriate for simple selection processes. With multilevel calculations or voluminous data sets, the graphic method quickly met its limits. Instead of extracting the relevant data from the background noise of the company's daily operational data, these techniques themselves began to produce background noise (Fig. 124). Through this, they devolved from a kinetic technique of modeling, scenario analysis, and simulation to a statistical process. This statistical process, in turn, offered a general impression of a given situation. "No specific or detailed impression is possible because of the conglomeration of lines."[15]

Even if the graphic method soon came up against its limits, it was still historically significant. As the epistemological environment for management, it was constitutive. It allowed management to grapple with the new dynamics of industrial, technical, and commercial developments. Media administrative knowledge contributed to propelling the factory system of the nineteenth century into a new, altered form in the twentieth century.

Media History of Consulting

I began this study with the media-epistemological inquiry of the two histories formulated by George Canguilhem: "that of lapsed knowledge and that of sanctioned knowledge, i.e. science which is still current because still being used."[16] Having disappeared, as a fleeting "entr'acte in history,"[17] the *graphic*

---

[15] Willard C. Brinton, *Graphic Presentation* (New York: Brinton Associates, 1939), 72.

[16] Georges Canguilhem, "The Object of the History of Science," in *Continental Philosophy of Science*, ed. Garry Gutting (Oxford: Blackwell, 2005), 201.

[17] Siegfried Zielinski, *Audiovisions: Cinema and Television as Entr'actes in History* (Amsterdam: Amsterdam University Press, 1999).

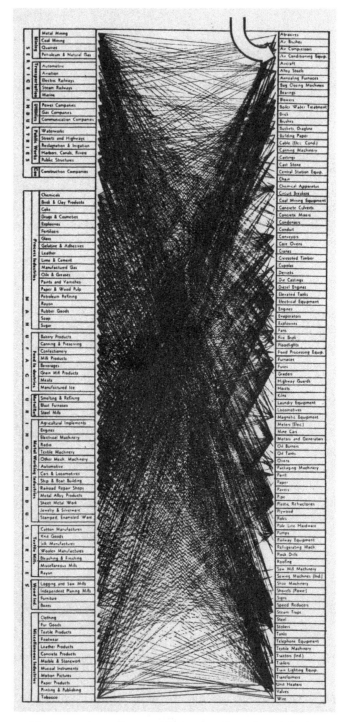

Figure 124 The limits of visualization. The overtaxed graphic method turns into noisy data.

method media network in the concrete sense of the term turned out to be the factor unleashing the historical potential conditions for the advent of *visual management* and *visual consulting knowledge.*The position of media technology in the present day no longer has much in common with the situation prevailing at that time.

This status also corresponds to the existing, extremely piecemeal state of research into corporate consulting.[18] Here, it is argued that the development of this branch divides roughly into six phases. The time frame I have investigated between 1880 and 1930 partly overlaps with the first initialization phase between 1900 and 1930. Following this is the *professionalization* phase, lasting until 1960, which then gave way to a phase of *internationalization* and, from 1970 on, of *differentiation*. From 2000, we can see a process of *consolidation* and *revitalization*. The markers for this delineation of phases are either external factors, such as a change in the legal framework, macroeconomic caesuras, a changed market environment, or innovations, such as an altered strategic concept, which stemmed directly from the consulting industry and fundamentally transformed its business activities.[19] My analysis focuses less on external factors, in order to describe the changes to the consulting industry. Instead, I have been interested in the questions as to why this branch has proven itself to be so stable in the first place? And how did consultants react to these diverse challenges, such that they emerged out of it as an independent profession?

Which conclusions can be drawn from this historical analysis for determining the contemporary situation of the consulting industry, without falling into the trap of a historicism referring to the present,[20] or, alternatively, of updating a linear historical teleology through the search for predecessors as "transitory teleology"?[21] Which epistemologically formed expressions are possible about consulting practices arising in the context of Taylorist and Fordist machinery? Can a modus operandi of currently similar relations or patterns be found, in order to better understand the consulting industry?

[18] Charles D. Wrege, Regina A. Greenwood, and Sakae Hata, "What We Do Not Know about Management History: Some Categories of Research and Methods to Uncover Management History Mysteries," *Journal of Management History* 5, no. 7 (1999): 414–24.

[19] Dietmar Fink, *Strategische Unternehmensberatung* (Munich: Frank Vahlen, 2014); Christopher McKenna, *The World's Newest Profession: Management Consulting in the Twentieth Century* (Cambridge, MA: Cambridge University Press, 2006); Christopher McKenna, "The Origins of Modern Management Consulting," *Business and Economic History* 24, no. 1 (1995): 51–58.

[20] Walter Benjamin, "On the Philosophy of History," in *Illuminations: Essays and Reflections*, ed. Hannah Ahrendt and trans. Harry Zohn (New York: Schocken Books, 1969), 253–64.

[21] Thomas Elsaesser, "The New Film History as Media Archaeology," *Cinémas: Revue d'études Cinématographiques* 14, no. 2–3 (2004): 89.

Media and Consulting as Loose or Solid Coupling

As a supplement to the existing approaches on the history of corporate consulting, I have, in my historical case studies, reconstructed consulting knowledge as a *coupling* of *media* and *consulting*. I take it as a given that it was not only external factors that determined the field of corporate consulting. Its epistemological constitution, its models, and knowledge structures also played a role, and, as I have shown, it was tightly allied with the graphic method media network. It is precisely this coupling that is visible in consulting media and characterizes the flexible and adaptive system of corporate consulting. This was how the industry succeeded for more than a hundred years in adapting itself to different conditions and ruptures. And yet the requisite changes were not, as is somewhat implied in the historical phase models of corporate consulting, innovations of the branch. They are components that had already arisen and been tested out in the context of Taylorist machine configurations and the *graphic method media network*. Up to the present day, fundamental visualization techniques have been preserved. Certainly, contemporary management no longer uses charts that are fabricated with the aid of thumbtacks and twine on wooden tables. They have been replaced by Powerpoint presentations and automated statistical models of calculation-based accounting systems. The principle, however, of the practices developed between 1880 and 1930 and the visual culture associated with it, has proven to be astonishingly stable.

What insights does this allow into the present-day situation of corporate consulting? In the key moments of the consulting industry of the last hundred years, it is frequently the coupling of media technology and consulting which predetermines its course, and which has retrospectively proven itself to be particularly successful.

In the 1910s, Frank B. Gilbreth connected the new medium of film with his film-based consulting service. Similarly, the corporate consultancy Arthur Anderson proceeded to establish an "IT Practice" department in the 1950s. Its consultants used it for the first time in 1954, in a commission for the introduction of a mainframe computer system for payroll accounts in a General Electric plant in Louisville, Kentucky. Whereas with Gilbreth it was the promise of increasing efficiency in physical work that resulted from the coupling of the latest filmic media technology and corporate consulting, Arthur Anderson joined the architecture of the mainframe computing system with the promise of lowering fixed administrative costs through data automation. Up until the 1970s and 1980s, Arthur Anderson was so successful in this sphere that the business analysis company finally decided to separate off its consulting activities from its actual analysis business.

Similar tendencies permeate the current situation. Classical corporate consultancies like McKinsey, the Boston Consulting Group, and Roland Berger have increasingly succumbed to the pressure of competition from rivals who were previously foreign to the market. Not only corporate analysis concerns like KPMG or PWC, but also information technology (IT) service firms like Accenture or Cap Gemini have given them serious competition. On the basis of their core competency in the IT sector, they extended their activities in the prestigious and highly profitable market of strategic consulting. As a reaction to these new market conditions, corporate consultants merged with IT service companies to become *total service providers*. One of the most recent examples of this is the Omnetric Group, a joint venture that incorporates Siemens IT products and Accenture's consulting skills. Alongside these direct connections between the consulting media technology associated with it, classical strategic consultants like McKinsey have reacted to the changed situation with an expansion of their palette of services offered. It is no longer only the ideal-typical consulting knowledge in the form of the McKinsey 7-S Framework that is at the center of its activity. Visual consulting knowledge is supplemented through downstream maintenance and service offers. "Model factories," in which workers were trained, were supposed to reinforce customer loyalty and bring in new contracts. Historically considered, these are not innovations, but the recurrence of Frank B. Gilbreth's applied strategy of erecting motion laboratories and *better-man rooms* on site. These served to integrate both workers and management in the consulting process. They were supposed to conclude with the emergence of the motion-aware worker, but the apparatuses used also served the purpose of acquiring contracts. They were supposed to illustrate to potential clients that Gilbreth was in a position to convert abstract concepts, like his grammar of movement the Wheel of Motion, into practice. McKinsey pursued a similar strategy with its "model factories." By coaching the workforce into becoming "error-aware" employees, they could exhibit their own competency in the method and at the same time hope for follow-up commissions. The construction of training centers represented an attempt to reinforce the loose coupling of consulting and its *unique selling proposition*, the promise of efficiency, such that it could be foreseeably converted into a *return on investment*. This represented a turn away from the model of the omniscient consultant communicating knowledge through charts and Powerpoint slides—a model that was only plausible under the conditions of an asymmetrical knowledge situation. Here, consulting knowledge is a step away from the situation of early consultants I have explored earlier. It is no longer only the consultant, or the recruiting strategy and consulting philosophy of the firm standing behind them, that embodies the surplus value of consulting knowledge. Whereas with Frank B. Gilbreth, it was the route models with which the consultants and management commonly sought the optimal workflow in the shaping of factory floors in the Auergesellschaft, now consultants worked on the optimization of logistics chains in "model factories." Incorporating local knowledge into the consulting process from the very beginning was, as was already the case with Gilbreth, intended to help forestall misfires in its subsequent implementation in the workplace. This tension between the ideal-typical model and its concrete realization determines, up to the present, the predetermined breaking point of consulting knowledge. At the same time, it is this relational connection which today is one of the distinguishing features of consulting knowledge. It is the difference between a low-threshold, flexible access and its inherent "hard core," as described using the principle of the *boundary object*, that gives consulting knowledge its form.

Here, consulting has had recourse to media technology as a *borrowed system of enunciation*. Surfeits of signification produced by media prompt us to speculate on reserves of efficiency that have not yet been exhausted. This connection of concrete realization and imaginary excess is not a side effect, but constitutive for consulting. Media is central for consulting, because it transforms efficiency potential into a form that is at once binding yet imprecise: binding, because the graphic form presupposes a stable method, imprecise because the system of enunciation is *borrowed* and still little understood.

If this coupling between consulting and media imagination is disrupted, the principle of consulting knowledge and the business model of the consulting industry is weakened. One possible response to this situation is to once again strengthen this coupling. Consulting firms like McKinsey, for instance, speak of seeking to return back to "real life."[22] An overly flexible and unspecific consulting service was to be replaced by a reinforced coupling of concrete media-technology practices, which restores the equilibrium between flexible adaptation and the hard core, as described by the concept of the *boundary object*.

Another strategy lies in exploiting the "newness" of media, as Frank B. Gilbreth had already practiced with the aesthetics of the then new medium of film. In this case, the industry had to *borrow* a new medium, after film and mainframe computing systems, for its purposes. Clayton M. Christensen, an expert who teaches at the Harvard Business School, together with two consultants previously employed in the industry, has speculated about this:

> Only a limited number of consulting jobs can currently be productized, but that will change as consultants develop new intellectual property. New IP leads to further automation and technology products. We expect that as artificial intelligence and big data capabilities improve, the pace of productization will increase.[23]

[22] Dietmar Student, "Hai-Alarm," *Manager Magazin* 1 (2014): 30.

[23] Clayton M. Christensen, Dina Wang, and Derek van Bever, "Consulting on the Cusp of Disruption: The Industry That Has Long Helped Others Sidestep Strategic Threats Is Itself Being Upended," *Harvard Business Review* 10 (2013): 112.

This diagnosis of the contemporary situation of the consulting industry contains the quintessence of the cyclical coupling and uncoupling of consulting and media. Whereas Gilbreth's film studies promised managers previously untapped efficiency reserves in the terra incognita of the human body, now algorithmic data analysis and Artificial Intelligence suggest a similarly limitless and imprecise access to a previously unattainable level of economic reality.

If the principle of corporate consulting relies on the coupling of borrowed (media) systems of enunciation with actual consulting, then the success of this industry over the last hundred years or more should not only be attributed to its operative business model, which mainly consists of the localization and realization of efficiency reserves. Consulting can henceforth be understood as a signifying system, which legitimizes techniques and actions and only then becomes a practicable alternative.

Considered from the subjective perspective of management, the access to consulting services represents an attempt to profit from capitalism's "creative destruction."[24] Considered on a macroeconomic level, this perspective is eminently paradoxical, since, following the fundamental laws of free market economics, there must always be losers. In this light, consulting promises the reconciliation of two obviously irreconcilable goals: profit without risk, or at least profit without a risk to oneself. Considered systematically, since competitors, the intended losers, can also have recourse to consultants, corporate consulting is a signifying system that lives off of the symbolic-transcendental, but which for the most part does not function on the symbolic level, instead producing, as I have shown, very concrete effects. These *angels of efficiency*, who have in the last hundred years transformed themselves from film pioneers to IT infrastructure experts and then data analysts, remain the same: savants, who on account of their "Brahmanic" consulting knowledge are in a position to do things that only they can do—precisely because they are savants.

Consulting, therefore, is ostensibly more than the sum of its parts, and it should above all be understood as a culture. It is a practice that is not only determined by the corporate logic of rationalization and calculation. As I outlined at the beginning of this study, it is paradoxically rational consultants who make a considerable contribution to the "disenchantment of the world" observed by Max Weber,[25] and who repeatedly re-enter the meaning that has distanced itself from them. They become a second-order signifying system, which is responsible

---

[24] Joseph Alois Schumpeter, *Capitalism, Socialism and Democracy* (New York: Routledge Chapman Hall, 2005 [1946]).
[25] Max Weber, "Science as a Vocation," in *From Max Weber: Essays in Sociology*, ed. and trans. H. H. Gerth and C. Wright Mills (New York: Oxford University Press, 1946), 129–56.

for the re-entry of meaning into business contexts. However, as I have shown, this system does not follow an anthropological constant of differentiation, but forges its own tangled pathways as a cultural practice.

Latent Society

If the world is disenchanted, then consulting culture protrudes in the vacancies left behind. It is a culture in which the direct menace of bodily discipline—with which Frederick W. Taylor, for one, was thoroughly familiar—was just as little available as an instance of unquestioned authority. From this point on, conflicts and ruptures tended to be put off. This also concerned social and societal relations. If the staging of conflicts was forestalled, they did not disappear, but remained virulent and therefore had to be managed. In the case of consulting, they were enduringly positioned, as I have shown, as *media boundary objects*, and thus robbed of their acute intensity. The option of ignorance provided by these media boundary objects, the disguising of social complexity, enabled the coexistence of different social worlds, and thus ensured social peace, at least for a time. What it meant for a society to retain conflicts in latent form rather than solve them, as described earlier, is an open question. My study illustrates that such a society committed itself to a consulting culture that functioned as a signifying system. This consulting complex appeared, in any case, to be in a position to dissipate tensions. The price for this was accepting the structures of consulting knowledge. It is a form of knowledge which distinguishes itself from "knowledge" understood in the sense of a noble Enlightenment term. Consulting knowledge is not a democratic and transparent knowledge. Nor does it produce the conditions for "domination-free communication."[26] Quite the contrary: it is to a large degree a tactical and strategic knowledge, and becomes significant precisely when it generates asymmetries of knowledge. Here, a society that has displaced its conflicts and ruptures to a latent level once more comes up against these tensions and in the end delegates them to the work of *angels of efficiency*.

In 2002, I held an interview with a partner of one of the world's five largest consulting firms, which specialized in financial services. This promising new field, he was convinced, would be boosted by the deregulation of the state banking system in Europe. In particular, the German mutual societies and credit unions were faced with a major transformation in the following five years due to Europe-wide deregulation measures, with a correspondingly large number of consulting

---

[26] Jürgen Habermas, *Theory of Communicative Action vol. I: Reason and the Rationalization of Society*, trans. Thomas A. McCarthy (Boston: Beacon Press, 1983).

commissions expected to be given out. As we know, things turned out differently. Instead of the deregulation of the European banking system within five years, the world saw the collapse of Lehman Brothers. The ensuing financial crisis led to more rather than less regulation.

For the consulting branch in the finance sector, this outcome, in comparison with the scenario envisaging a deregulation of state banks, is possibly the more lucrative development. They are the ones implementing the new banking regime of the *Basel I* and *Basel III* accords. The fallout of latent economic processes in the finance sector—in this case "toxic" assets and an opaque concatenation of legal agreements within the banks—led to new, lucrative business opportunities for consultants. Only highly specialized financial consultants are in a position to maneuver around state regulation authorities attempting to regulate the banking sector.

If we understand consulting in this context as a culture, then the rise of the "corporate consulting" signifying system should be understood as the symptom of a society which has not resolved its conflicts, but retained them in latent form. Here, consulting processes convert decisions not yet made into a process of reworking that is deemed legitimate. This development should be understood as a structural hallmark of a differentiated society that merits being investigated. Consulting is a cultural practice that is characterized by media, and which had and has significant epistemological effects. It suggests the expansion of options for action through the incorporation of new practices and knowledge sets, while also setting limits on one's own sovereignty and ability to take action. How our society will handle this in the future represents the open-ended experiment of Western democracies. In any case, consulting, a cultural technology mediating between the abstract and the concrete, has a long future ahead of it.

Sources and References

Archives

Landesarchiv Berlin, Firmenarchiv Osram GmbH

Library of Congress, Washington, Motion Pictures, Broadcasting and Recorded Sound Division, Prelinger Collection

Mercedes-Benz Archiv, Daimler AG, Stuttgart

Mikrofilmarchiv der deutschsprachigen Presse e.V. Institut für Zeitungsforschung, Dortmund

Purdue University Archives and Special Collections (SPCOLL), West Lafayette, IN, Gilbreth Library of Management (LOM), abbreviated in the chapters as (Gilbreth LOM, SPCOLL, Purdue University Libraries)

Stiftung Preußischer Kulturbesitz, Staatsbibliothek zu Berlin, Kartenabteilung

TECHNOSEUM. Stiftung Landesmuseum für Technik und Arbeit in Mannheim, Nachlass Witte; Bildarchiv PVZ, abbreviated in the chapters as (TECHNOSEUM, Witte Nachlass)

Journals

American Machinist. Vol. 1880–1930.

Archiv für Sozialwissenschaft und Sozialpolitik. Vol. 1904–1930.

AWF-Nachrichten (Ausschuss für wirtschaftliche Fertigung), published as a supplement in *Maschinenbau. Gestaltung, Betrieb, Wirtschaft; Zeitschrift für angewandte Mathematik und Mechanik.* Vol. 1921–1930.

Der Betrieb. Vol. 1918–1921.

Betriebswirtschaftliche Rundschau und Archiv für das Revisions—und Treuhandwesen. Vol. 1924–1928.

The Journal of the American Society of Mechanical Engineers. Vol. 1908–1918.

Maschinenbau. Gestaltung, Betrieb, Wirtschaft. Vol. 1921–1923, before 1924 published in individual installments as *Maschinenbau/Betrieb, Maschinenbau/Gestaltung,* and *Maschinenbau/Wirtschaft.*

Organisation. Zeitschrift für Betriebswissenschaft, Verwaltungspraxis u. Wirtschaftspolitik. Vol. 1898–1925.

Transactions of the American Society of Mechanical Engineers. Vol. 1880–1930.

Werkstattstechnik. Vol. 1907–1913; 1920–1930.

Zeitschrift für Betriebswissenschaft, Verwaltungspraxis und Wirtschaftspolitik. Vol. 1898–1925.

Zeitschrift für Handelswissenschaft und Handelspraxis. Vol. 1908–1930.

Zeitschrift für handelswissenschaftliche Forschung. Vol. 1906–1930.

Zeitschrift für Physik. Vol. 1920–1930.

ZfürO (Zeitschrift für Organisation). Vol. 1927–1934.
References to individual journal articles can be found in "References and Other Sources."

References and Other Sources

Abelshauser, Werner. "Umbruch und Persistenz: Das deutsche Produktionsregime in historischer Perspektive." *Geschichte und Gesellschaft. Zeitschrift für historische Sozialwissenschaft* 27, no. 4 (2001): 503–23.

Abruzzi, Adam. *Work, Workers and Work Measurement*. New York: Columbia University Press, 1956.

Acland, Charles, ed. *Residual Media*. Minnesota: University of Minnesota Press, 2007.

Adamiecki, Karol. "Harmonizacja jako jedna z głównych podstaw organizacji naukowej." *Przegl d Techniczny*, no. 49/52/53 (1924).

Adamiecki, Karol. "Harmonograf." *Przegl d Organizacji*, no. 1 (1931).

Adamiecki, Karol. "Metoda wykreślna organizowania pracy zbiorowej w walcowniach." *Przegl d Techniczny*, no. 17/18/19/20 (1909).

Aley, Robert Judson. *Graphs*. New York: C. Heath & Co., 1902.

Amar, Jules. *The Physiology of Industrial Organisation and the Re-employment of the Disabled*. London: The Library Press Limited, 1918.

Anderson, Benedict. *Imagined Communities: Reflections of the Origin and Spread of Nationalism*. Rev. ed. London: Verso, 2006.

Anger, Kenneth. *Hollywood Babylon*. New York: Simon & Schuster, 1975.

Anthony, Robert N. "Management Accounting: A Personal History." *Journal of Management Accounting Research* 15, no. 1 (2003): 249–53.

Armbrüster, Thomas. *The Economics and Sociology of Management Consulting*. Cambridge, MA: Cambridge University Press, 2006.

Armbrüster, Thomas. *Management and Organization in Germany*. Hampshire, UK: Ashgate, 2005.

Armytage, Walter H. G. *A Social History of Engineering*. 4th ed. London: Faber & Faber, 1976.

Arnst, Paul. "Die Normalisierungsbestrebungen im deutschen Baugewerbe." *Zeitschrift für handelswissenschaftliche Forschung* 17 (1923): 303–20.

Ascher, Kurt. "Der Industriefilm, seine Anwendung und Verbreitung." In *Das Kulturfilmbuch*, edited by Edgar Beyfuss and Alex Kossowsky, 160–65. Berlin: Carl P. Chryselius'scher Verlag, 1924.

Assmann, Bruno. *Technische Mechanik: Kinematik und Kinetik*. 2nd ed. Munich: Oldenbourg, 1975.

Auerbach, Felix. *Die Furcht vor der Mathematik und ihre Überwindung*. Jena: Fischer, 1924.

Auerbach, Felix. *Die graphische Darstellung: Eine allgemeinverständliche, durch zahlreiche Beispiele aus allen Gebieten der Wissenschaft und Praxis erläuterte Einführung in den Sinn und den Gebrauch der Methode*. Leipzig: Teubner, 1914.

Auerbach, Felix. "Die graphische Darstellung." *Die Naturwissenschaften* 1, no. 6 (1913): 139–45.

Auerbach, Felix. "Die graphische Darstellung." *Die Naturwissenschaften* 1, no. 7 (1913): 159–64.

Auerbach, Felix. *"Das Zeisswerk und die Carl-Zeiss-Stiftung in Jena: Ihre wissenschaftliche, technische und soziale Entwicklung und Bedeutung."* 5th ed. Jena: Fischer, 1903.

AWF Ausschuss für wirtschaftliche Fertigung. "Richtlinien für die organisations-technische Darstellung von Arbeitsabläufen: Vorentwurf vom 5.12.1927." *Zeitschrift für Organisation (ZfürO)* 4, no. 1 (1927): 631–41.

AWF-Mitteilungen. "AWF-Getriebefilme: Vollständiges Verzeichnis der Trickfilme." *AWF-Mitteilungen* 6, no. 5 (1927): 250–51.

AWF-Mitteilungen. "Getriebefilme und stereoskopische Aufnahmen von Getriebemodellen." *AWF-Mitteilungen* 6, no. 18 (1927a): 923.

AWF-Mitteilungen. "Stereoskopische Aufnahmen von Getriebemodellen." *AWF-Mitteilungen* 6, no. 5 (1927): 251–52.

Ayres, Leonard Porter. *The War with Germany: A Statistic Summary.* Washington, DC: US Government Printing Office, 1919.

Babbage, Charles. *On the Economy of Machinery and Manufactures.* London: Charles Knight, 1832.

Bachelard, Gaston. *Épistémologie: Textes Choisis.* Paris: PUF, 1971.

Baecker, Dirk. *Die Form des Unternehmens.* Frankfurt a. M.: Suhrkamp, 1993.

Baecker, Dirk. *Postheroisches Management: Ein Vademecum.* Berlin: Merve, 1994.

Banta, Martha. *Taylored Lives: Narrative Productions in the Age of Taylor, Veblen, and Ford.* Chicago: University of Chicago Press, 1993.

Barley, Stephen R., and Gideon Kunda. "Design and Devotion: Surges of Rational and Normative Ideologies of Control in Managerial Discourse." *Administrative Science Quarterly* 37 (1992): 363–99.

Barth, Carl G. "Slide Rules as Part of the Taylor System." *Transactions of the American Society of Mechanical Engineers* 25 (1904): 49–62.

Barthes, Roland. *Camera Lucida: Reflections on Photographie.* Translated by Richard Howard. New York: Hill and Wang, 1981.

Beck, Robert H. "Kilpatrick's Critique of Montessori's Method and Theory." *Studies in Philosophy and Education* 1, no. 4/5 (1961): 153–62.

Beckenbach, Niels. *Industriesoziologie.* Berlin: Walter de Gruyter, 1991.

Bellinger, Andréa, and David Krieger. *ANThology: Ein einführendes Handbuch zur Akteur-Netzwerk-Theorie.* Bielefeld: transcript, 2006.

Beniger, James R. "Communication and the Control Revolution." *OAH Magazine of History* 6 (1992): 10–13.

Beniger, James R. *The Control Revolution.* Cambridge, MA: Harvard University Press, 1986.

Beniger, James R., and Dorothy L. Robyn. "Quantitativ Graphics in Statistics." *The American Statistician* 32, no. 1 (1978): 1–11.

Benjamin, Walter. "Theses on the Philosophy of History." In *Illuminations: Essays and Reflections*, edited by Hannah Arendt. Translated by Harry Zohn. 253–64. New York: Schocken Books, 1969.

Benjamin, Walter. "The Work of Art in the Age of Mechanical Reproduction." In *Illuminations: Essays and Reflections*, edited by Hannah Arendt. Translated by Harry Zohn. 217–52. New York: Schocken Books, 1969.

Benner, Dietrich, and Jürgen Oelkers, eds. *Historisches Wörterbuch der Pädagogik.* Weinheim: Beltz, 2004.

Berghoff, Hartmut. "Unternehmenskultur und Herrschaftstechnik: Industrieller Paternalismus: Hohner von 1857 bis 1918." *Geschichte und Gesellschaft. Zeitschrift für historische Sozialwissenschaft* 23, no. 2 (1997): 167–204.

Berghoff, Hartmut, and Jakob Vogel. "Wirtschaftsgeschichte als Kulturgeschichte: Ansätze zur Bergung transdisziplinärer Synergiepotentiale." In *Wirtschaftsgeschichte als*

Kulturgeschichte: Dimensionen eines Perspektivenwechsels, edited by Hartmut Berghoff and Jakob Vogel, 9–41. Frankfurt a.M.: Campus Verlag, 2004.

Bericht der Schriftleitung. "Berichte der Schriftleitung: Die Verwendung des 'Arbeitsaufzeichners' zur Feststellung des Wirkungsgrades." *Werkstattstechnik* 10, no. 16 (1916): 341–42.

Bericht der Schriftleitung. "Berichte der Schriftleitung: Mechanische Aufzeichnungen der geleisteten Arbeit." *Werkstattstechnik* 10, no. 16 (1916): 337–40.

Bericht der Schriftleitung. "Berichte der Schriftleitung: Photographisches Festhalten von Maschineneinrichtungen." *Werkstattstechnik* 17, no. 1 (1923): 24.

Bernet, Brigitta, and David Gugerli. "'Sputniks Resonanzen': Der Aufstieg der Humankapitaltheorie im Kalten Krieg." *Historische Anthropologie* 19, no. 3 (2011): 433–46.

Beudels, Wolfgang. "'Ich fühle was du nicht hörst und das schmeckt rot': Wahrnehmung, Wahrnehmungsstörungen und Wahrnehmungsförderung in der Montessori-Pädagogik und der Psychomotorik." In *Montessori-Pädagogik und frühe Kindheit—Eine Revolution in der Erziehung?*, edited by Reinhard Fischer, Christian Fischer, and Harald Ludwig, 70–86. Münster: Lit Verlag, 2004.

Beyfuss, Edgar, and Alexander Kossowsky. *Das Kulturfilmbuch*. Berlin: Carl P. Chryselius'scher Verlag, 1924.

Bieberbach, Ludwig. "Über Nomographie." *Die Naturwissenschaften* 10, no. 36 (1922): 775–82.

Biswas, Sugata, and Daryl Twitchell. *Management Consulting: A Complete Guide to the Industry*. 2nd ed. New York: John Wiley & Sons, 2002.

Bivins, Percy A. *The Ratio Chart in Business*. New York: Codex, 1926.

Bock, Fr. "Versuche mit einem neuen Torsionsmesser." *Werkstattstechnik* 5, no. 1 (1911): 12–17.

Boehm, Gottfried, and Maurice Merleau-Ponty. *Was ist ein Bild?*. Munich: Fink, 1994.

Bönig, Jürgen. *Die Einführung von Fließbandarbeit in Deutschland bis 1933*. Münster: Lit Verlag, 1993.

Bolter, Jay David, and Richard Arthur Grusin. *Remediation: Understanding New Media*. Cambridge, MA: MIT Press, 2000.

Böttger, Walter. "Stereoskop-Bilder." *Film und Lichtbild* 1, no. 5 (1912): 56–61.

Booker, Peter Jeffrey. *A History of Engineering Drawing*. London: Northgate, 1979.

Booth, Charles, and Michael Rowlinson. "Management and Organizational History: Prospects." *Management & Organizational History* 1, no. 1 (2006): 5–30.

Borchert, Ernst. *Die Lehre von der Bewegung bei Nicolaus Oresme*. Münster: Aschendorffsche Verlagsbuchhandlung, 1934.

Borck, Cornelius, Volker Hess, and Henning Schmidgen. *Maß und Eigensinn: Studien im Anschluß an George Canguilhem*. Munich: Wilhelm Fink, 2005.

Bottomore, Stephen. "Rediscovering Early Non-Fiction Film." *Film History* 13, no. 2 (2001): 160–73.

Bourdieu, Pierre. *Distinction: A Social Critique of the Judgement of Taste*. Translated by Richard Nice. 8th ed. Cambridge, MA: Harvard University Press, 1996.

Bourdieu, Pierre. *The Logic of Practice*. Translated by Richard Nice. Stanford, CA: Stanford University Press, 2008. First published 1980 by Les Éditions de Minuit (Paris).

Bourdieu, Pierre. "Postface à Architecture gothique et pensée scolastique de E. Panofsky." In *Achitecture gothique et pensée scolastique: Précédé de l'abbé suger de Saint-Denis*, edited by Erwin Panofsky. Translated and postface by Pierre Bourdieu. 135–67. Paris: Les Éditions de Minuit, 1967.

Bourdieu, Pierre. "Structuralism and Theory of Sociological Knowledge." *Social Research* 35, no. 4 (1968): 681–706.

Bowker, Geoffrey C., and Susan Leigh Star. *Sorting Things Out: Classification and Its Consequences*. Cambridge, MA: MIT Press, 2000.

Bowser, Eileen. *History of the American Cinema vol. II: The Transformation of Cinema, 1907–1915*. New York: Macmillan, 1990.

Braun, F. "Die nomographische Berechnung der Laufzeit bei Arbeiten auf der Bilgram-Kegelhobelmaschine." *Werkstatttechnik* 21, no. 10 (1927): 281–84.

Braun, Marta. *Picturing Time: The Work of Étienne-Jules Marey (1830–1904)*. Chicago: University of Chicago Press, 1992.

Braverman, Harry. *Labor and Monopoly Capital: The Degradation of Work in the Twentieth Century*. 25th anniversary ed. New York: Monthly Review Press, 1974.

Bredekamp, Horst. "Towards the Iconic Turn." *Hardware: Kritische Berichte*, no. 1 (1998): 85ff.

Brinton, Willard C. *Graphic Methods for Presenting Facts*. New York: The Engineering Magazine Co., 1919.

Brinton, Willard C. *Graphic Presentation*. New York: Brinton Associates, 1939.

Bröckling, Ulrich, and Eva Horn. *Anthropologie der Arbeit*. Tübingen: Narr, 2002.

Brodetsky, Selig. *A First Course in Nomography*. London: G. Bell and Sons, 1920.

Brown, Elspeth H. *The Corporate Eye: Photography and the Rationalization of American Commercial Culture: 1884–1929*. Baltimore: John Hopkins University Press, 2005.

Brundage, Percival F. "Milestones on the Path of Accounting." *Harvard Business Review* 29, no. 4 (1951): 71–81.

Burnham, James. *The Managerial Revolution*. Harmondsworth, UK: Penguin Books, 1962.

Busch, Bernd. *Belichtete Welt: Eine Wahrnehmungsgeschichte der Fotografie*. Frankfurt a. M.: Fischer, 1997.

Callon, Michel. "Some Elements of a Sociology of Translation: Domestication of the Scallops and the Fisherman of St. Brieuc Bay." In *Power, Action, and Belief: A New Sociology of Knowledge*, edited by John Law, 196–233. London: Routledge & Kegan Paul, 1986.

Calmes, Albert. "Die statistische Abteilung im Fabrikbetrieb." *Zeitschrift für Handelswissenschaft und Handelspraxis* 3, no. 9 (1910): 313–19.

Calvert, Monte A. *The Mechanical Engineer in America 1830–1910: Professional Cultures in Conflict*. Baltimore: Johns Hopkins, 1967.

Camp, Walter. *Keeping Fit All the Way: How to Obtain and Maintain Health, Strength and Efficiency*. New York: Harper & Brothers, 1919.

Canback, Staffan. "The Logic of Management Consulting. Part 1." *Journal of Management Consulting* 10, no. 2 (1998): 3–11.

Canback, Staffan. "The Logic of Management Consulting. Part 2." *Journal of Management Consulting* 10, no. 3 (1999): 3–12.

Canguilhem, Georges. *Études d'Histoire et de Philiosophie des Sciences Concernant les Vivants et la Vie*. Paris: Vrin, 1968.

Canguilhem, Georges. *Ideology and Rationality in the History of the Life Sciences*. Translated by Arthur Goldhammer. Cambridge, MA: MIT Press, 1988.

Canguilhem, Georges. "The Object of the History of Science." In *Continental Philosophy of Science*, edited by Garry Gutting, 198–207. Oxford: Blackwell, 2005.

Canguilhem, Georges. "Die Rolle der Epistemologie in der heutigen Historiographie der Wissenschaft." In *Wissenschaftsgeschichte und Epistemologie: Gesammelte Aufsätze*, edited by Georges Canguilhem, 38–58. Frankfurt a. M.: Suhrkamp, 1979.

Chandler Jr., Alfred D. *Strategy and Structure: Chapters in the History of the Industrial Enterprise*. Cambridge, MA: MIT Press, 1969.

Chandler Jr., Alfred D. *The Visible Hand: The Managerial Revolution in American Business*. 16th ed. Cambridge, MA: Harvard University Press, 2002.

Chandler Jr., Alfred D., and James W. Cortada. *A Nation Transformed by Information: How Information Has Shaped the United States from Colonial Times to the Present*. New York: Oxford University Press, 2003.

Chansky, Ricia Anne. "Time to Shop: Advertising Trade Card Rhetoric and the Construction of a Public Space for Women in the United States, 1880–1890." *ATENEA* 29, no. 1 (June 2009): 151–66.

Christensen, Clayton M., Dina Wang, and Derek van Bever. "Consulting on the Cusp of Disruption: The Industry That Has Long Helped Others Sidestep Strategic Threats Is Itself Being Upended." *Harvard Business Review* 91, no. 10 (2013): 106–14.

Chun, Wendy Hui Kyong. "Did Somebody Say New Media?." In *New Media Old Media: A History and Theory Reader*, edited by Wendy Hui Kyong Chun, and Thomas Keenan, 1–10. London: Routledge, 2006.

Clark, Peter. "The Treatment of History in Organisation Studies: Towards an 'Historic Turn'?." *Business History* 46, no. 3 (2004): 331–52.

Clark, Wallace. *The Gantt Chart: A Working Tool of Management*. New York: Ronald Press Company, 1922.

Clausewitz, Carl von. *On War*. Translated and edited by Michael Howard and Peter Paret. Princeton, NJ: Princeton University Press, 1989.

Condit, K. H. "Management Methods and Principles of Frank B. Gilbreth, Inc." *American Machinist* 58, no. 1 (1923): 33–35.

Condit, K. H. "Management Methods and Principles of Frank B. Gilbreth, Inc.—II." *American Machinist* 58, no. 8 (1923): 293–95.

Corwin, Sharon. "Picturing Efficiency: Precisionism, Scientific Management, and the Effacement of Labor." *Representations* 84 (2003): 139–64.

Crozier, Michel, and Erhard Friedberg. *Actors and Systems: The Politics of Collective Action*. Translated by Arthur Goldhammer. Chicago: The University of Chicago Press, 1980.

Curtis, Scott. "Between Observation and Spectatorship: Medicine, Movies and Mass Culture in Imperial Germany." In *Film 1900: Technology, Perception, Culture*, edited by Annemone Ligensa and Klaus Kreimeier, 87–98. New Barnet, UK: John Libbey, 2009.

Curtis, Scott. "Images of Efficiency: The Films of Frank B. Gilbreth." In *Films That Work: Industrial Film and the Productivity of Media*, edited by Vinzenz Hediger and Patrick Vonderau, 85–99. Amsterdam: Amsterdam University Press, 2009.

Curtis, Scott. *The Shape of the Spectatorship: Art, Science, and Early Cinema in Germany*. New York: Columbia University Press, 2015.

D'Ocagne, Maurice. *Le Calcul Simplifié: Graphical and Mechanical Methods for Simplifying Calculation*. Translated by J. Howlett and M. R. Williams. 3rd ed. Cambridge, MA: MIT Press, 1986.

D'Ocagne, Maurice. *Cours de géométrie pure et appliquée de l'Ecole polytechnique*. Paris: Gauthier-Villars, 1917/1918.

D'Ocagne, Maurice. *Nomographie: Les Calculs usuels effectués au moyen des abaques: Essai d'une théorie Générale*. Paris: Gauthier-Villars, 1891.

D'Ocagne, Maurice. *Principes usuels de nomographie: Avec application à divers problèmes concernant l'artillerie et l'aviation*. Paris: Gauthier-Villars, 1920.

D'Ocagne, Maurice. *Traité de nomographie*. 2nd ed. Paris: Gauthier-Villars, 1921.

Daston, Lorraine, and Peter Galison. "The Image of Objectivity." *Representations* 132, no. 40 (1992): 81–128.

Daum, Andreas W. *Wissenschaftspopularisierung im 19. Jahrhundert: Bürgerliche Kultur, naturwissenschaftliche Bildung und die deutsche Öffentlichkeit, 1848–1914.* Munich: Oldenbourg, 1998.

Degele, Nina, Tanja Münch, Hans J. Pongratz, and Nicole J. Saam. *Soziologische Ber atungsforschung: Perspektiven für Theorie und Praxis der Organisationsberatung.* Opladen: Leske und Budrich, 2001.

Deleuze, Gilles, and Félix Guattari. *A Thousand Plateaus: Capitalism and Schizophrenia.* vol. 2. London: Bloomsbury, 2013.

Dernburg, Bernhard. *Von beiden Ufern.* Berlin: Kronen Verlag, 1916.

Dernburg, Bernhard. *Zielpunkte des Deutschen Kolonialwesens.* Berlin: Mittler, 1907.

Desrosières, Alain. *The Politics of Large Numbers: A History of Statistical Reasoning.* Translated by Camille Naish. Cambridge, MA: Harvard University Press, 2002.

Dobbeler, C. v. "Grundlagen der Nomographie." *Maschinenbau/Gestaltung* 3, no. 4 (1923): 99–107.

Down, Simon: "Knowledge Sharing Review the Use of History in Business and Management, and Some Implications for Management Learning." *Management Learning* 32, no. 3 (2001): 393–414.

Drury, Horace B. *Scientific Management: A History and Criticism.* New York: Columbia University, 1915.

Duncan, W. Jack, Peter M. Ginter, and Terrie C. Reeves. "Motion Study in Management and the Arts: A Historic Example." In *Frank and Lillian Gilbreth: Critical Evaluations in Business and Management,* edited by Micheal C. Wood and John C. Wood, 420–44. London: Routledge, 2003.

Earle, Edward W., Howard Saul Becker, Thomas W. Southall, and Harvey Green. *Points of view: The Stereograph in America: A Cultural History.* Rochester, NY: Visual Studies Workshop Press, 1979.

Edwards, Richard. *Contested Terrain: The Transformation of the Workplace in the Twentieth Century.* New York: Basic Books, 1979.

Eisner, F. "Die Nomographie, ein Hilfsmittel wirtschaftlicher Gestaltung und schärfster Selbstkostenermittlung." *Maschinenbau/Gestaltung* 1, no. 1 (1922): 11–20.

Elias, Norbert. *The Germans: Power Struggles and the Development of Habitus in the Nineteenth and Twentieth Centuries.* Edited by Michael Schröter. Translated by Eric Dunning and Stephen Mennell. Cambridge: Polity Press, 1996.

Elsaesser, Thomas. "The New Film History as Media Archaeology." *Cinémas: Revue d'études Cinématographiques* 14, no. 2/3 (2004): 75–117.

Emerson, Harrington. *Efficiency as a Basis for Operation and Wages.* New York: The Engineering Magazine Co., 1911.

Emerson, Harrington. *The Twelve Principles of Efficiency.* New York: The Engineering Magazine Co., 1913.

Falkner, Roland P. "Uses and Perils of Business Graphics." *Administration: The Journal of Business Analysis* 3, no. 1 (1922): 52–56.

Faltus, Franz. *Fünfzehn Nomogramme für den Eisenbau: Einfache Lösung häufiger Aufgaben des Eisenbaues durch Nomogramme mit Feinablesung.* Geislingen an der Steige: NBW Verlag Dipl. Ing. P. Leybold, 1927.

Felix, Friedrich. "Der plastische Film." *Film und Lichtbild* 3, no. 7 (1914): 106–109.

Felix, Friedrich. "Statistische Lichtbilder." *Film und Lichtbild* 1, no. 6 (1912): 83–84.

Ferguson, Michael. *The Rise of Management Consulting in Britain*. Aldershot, UK: Ashgate, 2002.

Fienberg, Stephen E. "Graphical Methods in Statistics." *The American Statistician* 33, no. 4 (1979): 165–78.

Fine, Gary Alen. "Scandal, Social Conditions, and the Creation of Public Attention: Fatty Arbuckle and the 'Problem of Hollywood.'" *Social Problems* 44, no. 3 (1997): 297–323.

Fink, Dietmar. *Strategische Unternehmensberatung*. Munich: Frank Vahlen, 2014.

Finnegan, Margaret. *Selling Suffrage: Consumer Culture & Votes for Women*. New York: Columbia University Press, 1999.

Fleischman, Richard K., and Thomas N. Tyson. "Cost Accounting During the Industrial Revolution: The Present State of Historical Knowledge." *Economic History Review* 46, no. 3 (1993): 503–17.

Fligstein, Neil. *The Transformation of Corporate Control*. Cambridge, MA: Harvard University Press, 1990.

Foucault, Michel. *The Archaeology of Knowledge and the Discourse on Language*. Translated by Sheridan Smith. New York: Pantheon Books, 1972.

Foucault, Michel. *Discipline and Punishment: The Birth of the Prison*. London: Penguin Press, 1991.

Foucault, Michel. "The Order of Discourse." In *Untying the Text: A Post-Structuralist Reader*, edited by Robert Young, 48–78. Boston: Routledge & Kegan Paul, 1981.

Foucault, Michel. *Security, Territory, Population: Lectures at the Collège de France 1977–1978*. Basingstoke, UK: Palgrave Macmillan, 2009.

Foucault, Michel. *Selected Interviews and Other Writings 1972–1977*. Edited by Colin Gordon. Translated by Colin Gordon, Leo Marshall, John Mephan, and Kate Soper. New York: Pantheon Books, 1980.

Foville, A. de. "Essai de Meteorologie Economique et Social." *Journal de la Société de Statistique de Paris* (1888): 243–49.

Francastel, Pierre. *Art & Technology in the Nineteenth and Twentieth Centuries*. New York: Zone Books, 2000.

Francastel, Pierre. *Etudes de Sociologie de l'art*. Enlarged ed. Paris: Gallimard, 1989.

Franz, Heike. "Kulturelles Milieu und Disziplinbildung: Die Entstehung der Betriebswirtschaftslehre in Deutschland 1900 bis 1933." In *Wissenschaftsgeschichte heute: Festschrift für Peter Lundgreen*, edited by Jürgen Büschenfeld, Heike Frank, and Frank M. Kuhlemann, 251–77. Gütersloh: Verlag für Regionalgeschichte, 2001.

French, Joseph L. "Itard, Jean-Marie-Gaspard." In *Encyclopedia of Psychology (8 vols.)*, edited by Alan E. Kazdin. Washington, DC: American Psychological Association, 2000.

Frenz, Gustav. *Kritik des Taylor-Systems: Zentralisierung—Taylors Erfolge: Praktische Durchführung des Taylor-Systems: Ausbildung des Nachwuchse*. Berlin: Julius Springer Verlag, 1920.

Freund, Oskar. "Über die Anwendbarkeit graphischer Darstellungsweisen in industriellen Betrieben." *Werkstattstechnik* 13, no. 1 (1919): 5–9.

Friendly, Michael. "The Golden Age of Statistical Graphics." *Statistical Science* 23, no. 4 (2008): 502–35.

Fritze, G. A. "Kinematographie im Dienste der Industrie." *Bild und Film. Zeitschrift für Lichtbilderei und Kinematographie* 3, no. 6 (1913): 124–28.

Funkhouser, H. Gray. "Historical Development of the Graphical Representation of Statistical Data." *Osiris* 3 (1937): 269–404.

Galison, Peter. *Image and Logic: A Material Culture of Microphysics*. Chicago: The University of Chicago Press, 1997.

Gantt, Henry L. "A Graphical Daily Balance in Manufacture." *Transactions of the American Society of Mechanical Engineers* 24 (1903):1322–36.

Gantt, Henry L. *Industrial Leadership*. New Haven, CT: Yale University Press, 1916.

Gantt, Henry L. *Organizing for Work*. New York: Harcourt, Brace and Howe, 1919.

Gantt, Henry L. *Work, Wages, and Profits*. 2nd ed. New York: The Engineering Magazine Co., 1919.

Garncarz, Joseph. "Über die Entstehung der Kinos in Deutschland 1896–1914." *KINtop. Jahrbuch zur Erforschung des frühen Films* 11 (2002): 144–58.

Gasteff, A. K. "Bewegungsstudien und Arbeiterschulung in Russland." *Maschinenbau. Gestaltung, Betrieb, Wirtschaft* 5, no. 1 (1926): 16–18.

Gaycken, Oliver. *Devices of Curiosity: Early Cinema and Popular Culture*. New York: Oxford University Press, 2015.

Geimer, Peter. *Ordnungen der Sichtbarkeit: Fotografie in Wissenschaft, Kunst und Technologie*. Frankfurt a. M.: Suhrkamp, 2002.

Geimer, Peter. "Was ist kein Bild? Zur 'Störung der Verweisung.'" In *Ordnungen der Sichtbarkeit: Fotografie in Wissenschaft, Kunst und Technologie*, edited by Peter Geimer, 313–41. Frankfurt a. M.: Suhrkamp, 2002.

George, Claude S. *The History of Management Thought*. 2nd ed. Englewood Cliffs, NJ: Prentice-Hall, 1972.

Geßner, Andreas. "Zur Bedeutung von Macht in Beratungsprozessen: Sind mikropolitische Ansätze praxistauglich?," In *Soziologische Beratungsforschung: Pe rspektiven für Theorie und Praxis der Organisationsberatung*, edited by Nina Degele, Tanja Münch, Hans J. Pongratz, and Nicole J. Saam, 39–54. Opladen: Leske und Budrich, 2001.

Giedion, Sigfried. *Mechanization takes Command: A Contribution to Anonymous History*. Minneapolis: University of Minnesota Press, 2013. First published 1948 by Oxford University Press.

Giese, Fritz. *Psychologisches Wörterbuch vol. VII*. Leipzig: Teubner, 1928.

Gilbreth, Frank B. *Das ABC der wissenschaftlichen Betriebsführung*. Translated and edited by Collin Ross. Berlin: Springer, 1917.

Gilbreth, Frank B. *Bricklaying System*. New York: The Myron C. Clark Publishing Co., 1909.

Gilbreth, Frank B. "Concrete System." In *The Writings of the Gilbreths*, edited by William R. Spriegel, William R., and Clark E. Myers, 19–65. Homewood, IL: Richard D. Irwin, Inc., 1953.

Gilbreth, Frank B. Discussion on "The Present State of Art of Industrial Management." *Transactions of the American Society of Mechanical Engineering* 34 (1912): 1224–26.

Gilbreth, Frank B. "The Effect of Motion Study upon the Workers." *The ANNALS of the American Academy of Political and Social Science* 65, no. 1 (1916).

Gilbreth, Frank B. *Field System*. New York: The Myron C. Clark Publishing Co., 1908.

Gilbreth, Frank B. "Graphical Control on the Exception Principle for Executives." *The Journal of the American Society of Mechanical Engineers* 39, no. 4 (1917): 311–12.

Gilbreth, Frank B. *Motion Study: A Method for Increasing the Efficiency of the Workman*. New York: D. Van Nostrand Company, 1921.

Gilbreth, Frank B. *Primer of Scientific Management*. New York: D. van Nostrand Company, 1912.

Gilbreth, Frank B., and Lillian M. Gilbreth. "The Achievements of Motion Psychology." Speech for the Taylor Society, Cambridge, MA, April 25, 1924.

Gilbreth, Frank B., and Lillian M. Gilbreth. "Address Before the Eye Sight Conservation Council." Lecture at the The Eye Sight Conservation Council, New York, 1922.

Gilbreth, Frank B., and Lillian M. Gilbreth. "Applications of Motion Studies: Its Use in Developing the Best Methods of Work." *Management* and *Administration* 8, no. 3 (1924): 295–97.

Gilbreth, Frank B., and Lillian M. Gilbreth. *Applied Motion Studies.* New York: Sturgis & Walton Company, 1917.

Gilbreth, Frank B., and Lillian M. Gilbreth. "Classifying the Elements of Work: Methods of Analyzing Work into Seventeen Subdivisions." *Management and Administration* 7, no. 8 (1924): 151–54.

Gilbreth, Frank B., and Lillian M. Gilbreth. *Ermüdungsstudien: Eine Einführung in das Gebiet der Ermüdungsstudien.* Berlin: VDI Verlag, 1921.

Gilbreth, Frank B., and Lillian M. Gilbreth. *Fatigue Study: The Elimination of Humanity's Greatest Unnecessary Waste: A First Step in Motion Study.* 2nd ed. New York: The Macmillan Company, 1919.

Gilbreth, Frank B., and Lillian M. Gilbreth. "Measurement of the Human Factor in Industry." Lecture at the National Conference of the Western Efficiency, May 22–25, 1917.

Gilbreth, Frank B., and Lillian M. Gilbreth. "Motion Models: Their Use in the Transference of Experience and the Presentation of Comparative Results in Educational Methods." Lecture at the American Association for the Advancement of Science, Columbus, Ohio, December 27, 1915–January 01, 1916.

Gilbreth, Frank B., and Lillian M. Gilbreth. "Scientific Management in Other Countries Than the United States." Lecture at the Taylor Society, January 26, 1924.

Gilbreth, Frank B., and Lillian M. Gilbreth. "Time and Motion Study: As Fundamental Factors in Planning and Control." Lecture at the Taylor Society, New York, December 16, 1920.

Gilbreth, Lillian M. *F. B. Gilbreth. Das Leben eines amerikanischen Organisators.* Stuttgart: Poeschel Verlag, 1925.

Gilbreth, Lillian M. *The Psychology of Management: The Function of the Mind in Determining, Teaching and Installing Methods of Least Waste.* New York: Sturgis & Walton Company, 1914.

Gilbreth Jr., Frank B., and Ernestine Gilbreth Carey. *Cheaper by the Dozen.* New York: Crowell, 1948.

Gillespie, Richard. *Manufacturing Knowledge: A History of the Hawthorne Experiments.* Cambridge: Cambridge University Press, 1991.

Gilman, S. *Graphic Charts for the Business Man.* Chicago: La Salle Extension University, 1917.

Gitelman, Lisa. *Always Already New: Media, History, and the Data of Culture.* Cambridge, MA: MIT Press, 2006.

Gitelman, Lisa, and Geoffrey B. Pingree. "What's New about New Media?" In *New Media, 1740–1915,* edited by Lisa Gitelman, xi–xxii. Cambridge, MA: MIT Press, 2003.

Göllner, Peter. *Ernemann Cameras: Die Geschichte des Dresdner Photo-Kino-Werks.* Hückelhoven: Wittig, 1995.

Goergen, Jeanpaul. "Cinema in the Spotlight: The Lichtspiel-Theaters and the Newspapers in Berlin, September 1913: A Case Study." In *Kinoöffentlichkeit*

(1895–1920): Entstehung—Etablierung—Differenzierung, edited by Corinna Müller and Harro Segeberg, 66–86. Marburg: Schüren Verlag, 2008.

Gotcher, J. Micheal. "Assisting the Handicapped: The Pioneering Efforts of Frank and Lillian Gilbreth." In *Frank and Lillian Gilbreth: Critical Evaluations in Business and Management*, edited by Michael C. Wood and John Wood, 393–402. London: Routledge, 2003.

Graham, Laurel. "Lillian Gilbreth and the Mental Revolution at Macy's, 1925–1928." *Journal of Management History* 6, no. 7 (2000): 285–305.

Grieveson, Lee. "Feature Films and Cinema Program." In *The Silent Cinema Reader*, edited by Lee Grieveson and Peter Krämer, 187–95. London: Routledge, 2004.

Grieveson, Lee. "Fighting Films: Race, Morality, and the Governing of Cinema, 1912–1915." In *The Silent Cinema Reader*, edited by Lee Grieveson and Peter Krämer, 169–86. London: Routledge, 2004.

Grieveson, Lee. *Policing Cinema: Movies and Censorship in Early-Twentieth-Century America*. Berkeley: University of California Press, 2004.

Grieveson, Lee, and Peter Krämer. *The Silent Cinema Reader*. London: Routledge, 2003.

Griffiths, Alison. *Wondrous Difference: Cinema, Anthropology, & Turn-of-the-Century Visual Culture*. New York: Columbia University Press, 2002.

Grimshaw, Robert. "Aus dem Merkbuch eines Organisators." *Werkstattstechnik* 8, no. 7 (1914): 200–2.

Groezinger, W. *Fluchtlinientafeln zur Berechnung des cos ϕ*. Berlin: Springer, 1925.

Gugerli, David, and Barbara Orland. *Ganz normale Bilder: Historische Beiträge zur visuellen Herstellung von Selbstverständlichkeit*. Zurich: Chronos, 2002.

Guillén, Mauro F. *Models of Management: Work, Authority, and Organization in a Comparative Perspective*. Chicago: University of Chicago Press, 1994.

Guillén, Mauro F. "Scientific Management's Lost Aesthetics: Architecture, Organization, and the Taylorized Beauty of the Mechanical." *Administrative Science Quarterly* 42, no. 4 (1997): 682–715.

Gunning, Tom. "Before Documentary: Early Nonfiction Films and the 'View' Aesthetic." In *Uncharted Territory: Essays on Early Nonfiction Film*, edited by Daan Hertogs and Nico de Klerk, 9–24. Amsterdam: Nederlands Filmmuseum, 1997.

Gunning, Tom. "The Cinema of Attractions: Early Film, Its Spectators and the Avant-Garde." In *Early Film*, edited by Thomas Elsaesser and Adam Barker, 56–62. London: BFI, 1989.

Gunning, Tom. *D. W. Griffith and the Origins of American Narrative Film: The Early Years at Biograph*. Urbana: University of Illinois Press, 1991.

Gutenberg, Erich. *Die Unternehmung als Gegenstand betriebswirtschaftlicher Theorie*. Berlin: Gabler, 1929.

Gysin, J. *Tafeln zum Abstecken von Eisenbahn- und Strassen-Kurven: In neuer Teilung (Centesimal-Teilung)*. Liestal: Lüdin, 1885.

Habermas, Jürgen. *The Theory of Communicative Action, vol. I: Reason and the Rationalization of Society*. Translated by Thomas McCarthy. Boston: Beacon Press, 1984.

Hänsel, Sylvaine, and Angelika Schmitt. *Kinoarchitektur in Berlin. 1895–1995*. Berlin: Reimer, 1995.

Hak, J. "Über eine neue Art von Rechentafeln." *Zeitschrift für angewandte Mathematik und Mechanik* 1, no. 2 (1921): 154–57.

Haller, Lea. "Angewandte Forschung? Cortison zwischen Hochschule, Industrie und Klinik." In *Jenseits des Labors: Labor, Wissen, Transformation*, edited by Florian Hoof, Eva-Maria Jung, and Ulrich Salaschek, 171–98. Bielefeld: transcript, 2011.

Hankins, Thomas L. "Blood, Dirt and Nomograms: A Particulare History of Graphs." *Isis* 90, no. 1 (1999): 50–80.

Hankins, Thomas L., and Robert J. Silverman. *Instruments and the Imagination*. Princeton, NJ: Princeton University Press, 1995.

Haskell, Allan C. *How to Make and Use Graphic Charts*. New York: Codex, 1919.

Havelock, Eric. A. *The Literate Revolution in Greece and Its Cultural Consequences*. Princeton, NJ: Princeton University Press, 1982.

Hebeisen, Walter. *F. W. Taylor und der Taylorismus: Über das Wirken und die Lehre Taylors und die Kritik am Taylorismus*. Zurich: vdf Verlag, 1999.

Hediger, Vinzenz, and Patrick Vonderau. *Films that Work: Industrial Film and the Productivity of Media*. Amsterdam: Amsterdam University Press, 2009.

Hediger, Vinzenz, Florian Hoof, and Yvonne Zimmermann. *Films That Work Harder: The Global Circulation of Industrial Cinema*. Amsterdam: Amsterdam University Press, forthcoming.

Hegner, K. "Maschinenkarten." *Maschinenbau. Gestaltung, Betrieb, Wirtschaft* 5, no. 13/14 (1923): 575–78.

Heider, Fritz. "Thing and Medium." In *On Perception, Event, Structure, and Psychological Environment: Selected Papers, Psychological Issues* 1, no. 3, edited by Fritz Heider, 1–34. New York: International Universities Press, 1959.

Hellborn, A. V. "Wie entsteht eine nomographische Netztafel für Gleichungen mit mehreren Veränderlichen?" *Maschinenbau. Gestaltung, Betrieb, Wirtschaft* 5, no. 1 (1926): 1–6.

Henning, Friedrich-Wilhelm. *Das industrialisierte Deutschland: 1914 bis 1992*. 9th ed. Stuttgart: UTB Verlag, 1997.

Henning, Friedrich-Wilhelm. *Die Industrialisierung in Deutschland: 1800–1914*. 9th ed. Paderborn: Schöning, 1995.

Henning, Karl W. "Zur graphischen Darstellung organisatorischer Arbeitsabläufe." *Zeitschrift für Organisation (ZfürO)* 4, no. 1 (1930): 12–17.

Herrmann, Christian. v. "Pensum—Spur—Code: Register der Arbeitswissenschaft bei Taylor, Gilbreth und Bernstein." In *Anthropologie der Arbeit*, edited by Ulrich Bröckling and Eva Horn, 193–208. Tübingen: Narr, 2002.

Hesse, Jan-Otmar. *Im Netz der Kommunikation: Die Reichs-Post- und Telegraphenverwaltung 1876–1914*. Munich: Beck, 2002.

Heßler, Martina, and Dieter Mersch. *Logik des Bildlichen: Zur Kritik der ikonischen Vernunft*. Bielefeld: transcript, 2009.

Hildebrandt, Reinhardt. *Mathematisch-graphische Untersuchungen über die Rentabilitätsverhältnisse des Fabrikbetriebes*. Berlin: Springer, 1925.

Hilger, Philipp von. *War Games: A History of War on Paper*. Translated by Ross Benjamin. Cambridge, MA: MIT Press, 2012.

Hillecke, Matthias. "Arbeitsplatzgestaltung in den Gießereien der DaimlerChrysler AG. Ein historischer Rückblick." *Zeitschrift für Arbeitswissenschaft* 59 (2005): 353–59.

Hirschfeld, F., and K. Kustin. "Anwendung der Nomographie auf die Vorkalkulation bei spananhebender Bearbeitung." *Maschinenbau: Gestaltung, Betrieb, Wirtschaft* 7, no. 18 (1928): 857–62.

Hirschman, Albert O. *Exit, Voice, and Loyalty: Responses to Decline in Firms, Organizations, and States*. Cambridge, MA: Harvard University Press, 1970.

Hoff, E. H., and L. A. Geddes. "Graphic Recording Before Carl Ludwig: An Historical Summary." *Archives internationales d'Histoire des Science* 50 (1959): 3–25.

Hoff, E. H., and L. A. Geddes. "Graphic Registration before Ludwig: The Antecedents of the Kymograph." *Isis* 50 (1959): 5–21.

Hoffmann, Karl. "Anwendung der Nomographie zur Ermittlung der Schnittzeit für geradlinig spanabhebende Werkzeugmaschinen." *Maschinenbau/Gestaltung* 3, no. 4/5 (1923): 109–10.

Homburg, Heidrun. "Anfänge des Taylorsystems in Deutschland vor dem ersten Weltkrieg: Eine Problemskizze unter besonderer Berücksichtigung der Arbeitskämpfe bei Bosch 1913." *Geschichte und Gesellschaft: Zeitschrift für historische Sozialwissenschaft* 4, no. 1 (1978): 170–94.

Hoof, Florian. "'Between the Frontlines': Military Training Films, Machine Guns and the Great War." In *Cinema's Military Industrial Complex*, edited by Lee Grieveson and Haidee Wasson, 177–91. Berkley: University of California Press, 2018.

Hoof, Florian. "Between Recognition and Abstraction: Early Vocational Training Films." In *The Image in Early Cinema: Form and Material*, edited by Scott Curtis, Philippe Gauthier, Tom Gunning, and Joshua Yumibe, 111–19. Bloomington: Indiana University Press, 2018.

Hoof, Florian, and Sebastian K. Boell. "Culture, Technology, and Process in 'Media Theories': Towards a Shift in the Understanding of Media in Organizational Research." *Organization* 26, no. 4 (2019): 636–654.

Hoof, Florian. "Decision|Culture: Das Ornament der Finanzkrise." In *Spekulantenwahn: Zwischen ökonomischer Rationalität und medialer Imagination*, edited by Christina Braun and Dorothea Dorn, 111–34. Berlin: Neofelis, 2015.

Hoof, Florian. "Film—Labor—Flow-Charting: Mediale Kristallisationspunkte moderner Managementtheorie." In *Medien in Raum und Zeit: Maßverhältnisse des Medialen*, edited by Ingo Köster and Kai Schubert, 239–66. Bielefeld: transcript, 2009.

Hoof, Florian. "'Have We Seen It All Before?' A Sociomaterial Approach to Film History." In *At the Borders of (Film)History, Temporality, Archaeology*, edited by Alberto Beltrame and Andrea Mariani, 347–57. Proceedings XXI International Film Studies Conference, Udine: Forum, 2015.

Hoof, Florian. "Ist jetzt alles Netzwerk? Mediale 'Schwellen- und Grenzobjekte'." In *Jenseits des Labors: Labor, Wissen, Transformation*, edited by Florian Hoof, Eva-Maria Jung, and Ulrich Salaschek, 45–62. Bielefeld: transcript, 2011.

Hoof, Florian. "The Media Boundary Objects Concept: Theorizing Film and Media." In *Media Matter: The Materiality of Media, Matter as Medium*, edited by Bernd Herzogenrath, 180–200. New York: Bloomsbury, 2015.

Hoof, Florian. "Medien managerialer Entscheidungen: Decision-Making 'At a Glance'." *Soziale Systeme: Zeitschrift für soziologische Theorie* 20, no. 1 (2015): 23–51.

Hoof, Florian. "'The One Best Way': Bildgebende Verfahren der Ökonomie als strukturverändernder Innovationsschub der Managementtheorie ab 1860." *montage a/v* 15, no. 1 (2006): 123–38.

Hoof, Florian, Eva-Maria Jung, and Ulrich Salaschek. *Jenseits des Labors: Labor, Wissen, Transformation*. Bielefeld: transcript, 2011.

Hoxie, Robert F. *Scientific Management and Labor*. New York: D. Appleton and Company, 1915.

Huhtamo, Erkki, and Jussi Parikka. *Media Archaeology: Approaches, Applications, and Implications*. Berkley: California University Press, 2011.

Innis, Harold A. *The Bias of Communication.* Toronto: University of Toronto Press, 1951.

Innis, Harold A. *Empire and Communications.* 2nd ed. Toronto: University of Toronto Press, 1972.

Innis, Harold A. "Minerva's Owl." In *The Bias of Communication.* 2nd ed., 3–32. Toronto: University of Toronto Press, 2008.

Ivins, William Mills. *On the Rationalization of Sight: With an Examination of Three Renaissance Texts on Perspective.* 1938. Reprint, New York: Da Capo Press, 1975.

Ivins, William Mills. *Prints and Visual Communication.* Cambridge, MA: MIT Press, 1978.

Jacques, Roy Stager. *Manufacturing the Employee: Management Knowledge from the 19th to 21st Centuries.* London: Sage, 1996.

Jacques, Roy Stager. "History, Historiography and Organization Studies: The Challenge and the Potential." *Management & Organizational History* 1, no. 1 (2006): 31–49.

Jason, Alexander. *Der Film in Ziffern und Zahlen: 1895–1925.* Berlin: Deutsches Druck- und Verlagshaus, 1925.

Jenkins, Henry. *Convergence Culture: Where Old and New Media Collide.* New York: New York University Press, 2006.

Johnson, Thomas H. "Management Accounting in an Early Multidivisional Organization: General Motors in the 1920s." *The Business History Review* 52, no. 4 (1978): 490–517.

Joint Committee on Standards for Graphical Presentation. "Preliminary Report of Inviting Suggestions for the Benefit of the Committee." *The Journal of Industrial Engineering Chemistry* 7, no. 10 (1915): 894–95.

Kaes, Anton, Wolfgang Jacobsen, and Hans Helmut Prinzler. *Geschichte des deutschen Films.* Stuttgart: J.B. Metzler, 2004.

Kaminsky, G., and H. Schmidtke. *Arbeitsablauf- und Bewegungsstudien.* Munich: Carl Hanser, 1960.

Kanigel, Robert. *The One Best Way: Frederick Winslow Taylor and the Enigma of Efficiency.* London: Abacus, 2000.

Kaplan, Robert S. "The Evolution of Management Accounting." *Accounting Review* 59, no. 3 (1984): 390–418.

Karsten, K. G. *Charts and Graphs: An Introduction to Graphic Methods in the Control and Analysis of Statistics.* New York: Prentice-Hall, 1925.

Kazdin, Allan E. *Encyclopedia of Psychology.* 8 vols. Washington, DC: American Psychological Association, 2000.

Keil, Charlie, and Ben Singer. *American Cinema of the 1910s: Themes and Variations.* New Brunswick, NJ: Rutgers University Press, 2009.

Kelley, James E., and Morgan A. Walker. "Critical-Path Planning and Scheduling." *Proceedings of the Eastern Joint Computer Conference,* 1959.

Khurana, Rakesh. *From Higher Aims to Hired Hands: The Social Transformation of American Business Schools and the Unfulfilled Promise of Management as a Profession.* Princeton, NJ: Princeton University Press, 2007.

Kieser, Alfred. "Rhetoric and Myth in Management Fashion." *Organization* 4, no. 1 (1997): 49–74.

Kilpatrick, Willian Heard. *The Montessori System Examined.* Cambridge, MA: The Riverside Press, 1914.

Kipping, Matthias. "Consultancies, Institutions and the Diffusion of Taylorism in Britain, Germany and France, 1920s to 1950s." *Business History* 39, no. 4 (1997): 67–83.

Kipping, Matthias. *Management Consultancies in Germany, Britain and France, 1900–60*. An Evolutionary and Institutional Perspective, *University of Reading: Discussion Papers in Economica and Management, Series A*. No. 350 (1996), 1–27.

Kipping, Matthias, and Lars Engwall. *Management Consulting: Emergence and Dynamics of a Knowledge Industry*. Oxford: Oxford University Press, 2001.

Kirsch, Hans. "Die Anwendung maschineller Hilfsmittel im Rechnungswesen der Industriebetriebe." *Zeitschrift für handelswissenschaftliche Forschung* 19 (1925): 404–52.

Kittler, Friedrich. *Discourse Networks 1800/1900*. Translated by Michael Metteer and Chris Cullens. Stanford, CA: Stanford University Press, 1990. First published 1985 by Fink (Paderborn).

Kittler, Friedrich. "Dracula´s Legacy." In *Literature, Media, Information Systems: Essays*, edited by John Johnston. Abingdon, UK: Routledge, 2012.

Kittler, Friedrich. *Gramophone Film Typewriter*. Translated by Geoffrey Winthrop-Young and Michael Wutz. Stanford, CA: Stanford University Press, 1999. First published 1986 by Brinkmann & Bose (Berlin).

Klauer, Friedrich. *Geschichte der Auergesellschaft: Von der Gründung im Jahre 1892 bis zum Jahre 1958*. Berlin: Auer, 1960.

Knorr-Cetina, Karin. *Epistemic Cultures: How the Sciences Make Knowledge*. Cambridge, MA: Harvard University Press, 1999.

Kocka, Jürgen. "Class Formation, Interest Articulation and Public Policy: The Origins of the German White Collar Class in the Late Nineteenth and Early Twentieth Centuries." In *Organizing Interests in Western Europe: Pluralism, Corporatism, and the Transformation of Politics*, edited by Suzanne Berger, 63–81. Cambridge: Cambridge University Press, 1988.

Kocka, Jürgen. "Industrielles Management, Konzeptionen und Modelle in Deutschland vor 1914." *Vierteljahresschrift für Wirtschafts- und Sozialgeschichte* 56, no. 3 (1969): 332–72.

Kocka, Jürgen. "Legitimationsprobleme und -strategien der Unternehmer und Manager im 19. und frühen 20. Jahrhundert." *Zeitschrift für Unternehmensgeschichte* Beiheft 44, (1983): 7–22.

Kocka, Jürgen. "Management in der Industrialisierung: Die Entstehung und Entwicklung des klassischen Musters." *Zeitschrift für Unternehmensgeschichte* 44, no. 1 (1999): 135–49.

König, Wolfgang. "Spezialisierung und Bildungsanspruch: Zur Geschichte der Technischen Hochschulen im 19. und 20. Jahrhundert." *Berichte zur Wissenschaftsgeschichte* 11, no. 4 (1988): 219–25.

König, Wolfgang. "Stand und Aufgaben der Forschung zur Geschichte der deutschen Polytechnischen Schulen und Technischen Hochschulen im 19. Jahrhundert." *Technikgeschichte* 48, no. 1 (1981): 47–67.

Konorski, B. M. *Die Grundlagen der Nomographie*. Berlin: Springer, 1923.

Koselleck, Reinhart. *Futures Past: On the Semantics of Historical Time*. Translated by Keith Tribe. New York: Columbia University Press, 2004.

Kracauer, Siegfried. *The Salaried Masses: Duty and Distraction in Weimar Germany*. Translated by Quintin Hoare. London: Verso, 1998.

Krämer, Sybille. "Operative Bildlichkeit: Von der 'Grammatologie' zu einer 'Diagrammatologie'? Reflexionen über erkennendes 'Sehen.'" In *Logik des Bildlichen: Zur Kritik der ikonischen Vernunft*, edited by Martina Heßler und Dieter Mersch, 94–122. Bielefeld: transcript 2009.

Krauss, Fritz. *Die Nomographie oder Fluchtlinienkunst.* Berlin: Springer, 1922.

Krauss, Rosalind E. *The Originality of the Avant-Garde and Other Modernist Myths.* 6th ed. Cambridge, MA: MIT Press, 1989.

Krauss, Rosalind E. *Le Photographique–Pour une Théorie des Escarts.* Translated by Marc Bloch and Jean Kempf. Paris: Macula Editions, 1990.

Krauß, Hans. "Die Werkbücherei: Ein Beitrag zur Bildungsarbeit der Industrie." *Zeitschrift für Handelswissenschaft und Handelspraxis* 17, no. 1 (1924): 17–23.

Kretzschmar, H. E. "Schaubilder über die Wirtschaftlichkeit von Werkzeugmaschinen." *Maschinenbau: Gestaltung, Betrieb, Wirtschaft* 5, no. 1 (1926): 13–16.

Küpper, Willi, and Günther Ortmann. *Mikropolitik: Rationalität, Macht und Spiele in Organisationen.* Opladen: Westdeutscher Verlag, 1988.

Kugler, Anita. *Arbeitsorganisation und Produktionstechnologie der Adam-Opel-Werke (von 1900 bis 1929).* Berlin: Wissenschaftszentrum Berlin, 1985.

Kugler, Anita. "Von der Werkstatt zum Fließband: Etappen der frühen Automobilproduktion in Deutschland." *Geschichte und Gesellschaft: Zeitschrift für historische Sozialwissenschaft* 13 (1987): 304–39.

Kyrtsis, Alexandros-Andreas. "Diagrammatic Rhetoric in Business and Architecture." Lecture at the Imagining Business Oxford University Said Business School, June 26–27, 2008.

Lacmann, Otto. *Die Herstellung gezeichneter Rechentafeln: Ein Lehrbuch der Nomographie.* Berlin: Springer, 1923.

Ladenthin, Volker. "Zur Pädagogik Jean Itards und zu Aspekten ihrer Rezeption bei Maria Montessori." *Pädagogische Rundschau* 51 (1997): 499–515.

Lancaster, Jane. "Frank and Lillian Gilbreth Bring Order to Providence: The Introduction of Scientific Management at the New England Butt Company, 1912–13." *Rhode Island History* 55, no. 2 (1997): 69–84.

Lancaster, Jane. *Making Time: Lillian Moller Gilbreth, A Life Beyond 'Cheaper by the Dozen'.* Lebanon, Beirut: Northeastern University Press, 2004.

Larson, Magali Sarfatti. *The Rise of Professionalism: A Sociological Analysis.* Berkeley: University of California Press, 1977.

Lassally, Arthur. *Bild und Film im Dienst der Technik: 2. Teil: Betriebskinematographie.* Halle: Verlag Wilhelm Knapp, 1919.

Lassally, Arthur. *Film und Bild im Dienst der Technik. 1. Teil: Betriebsphotographie.* Halle: Verlag Wilhelm Knapp, 1919.

Lassally, Arthur. "Kinematographische Bewegungsstudien." *Werkstattstechnik* 14, no. 2 (1920): 47–48.

Latour, Bruno. "Drawing Things Together." In *Representation in Scientific Practice*, edited by Michael Lynch and Steve Woolgar, 19–68. Cambridge, MA: MIT Press, 1990.

Latour, Bruno. *Science in Action: How to Follow Scientists and Engineers Through Society.* 6th ed. Cambridge, MA: Harvard University Press, 1994.

Latour, Bruno, and Steve Woolgar. *Laboratory Life: The Construction of Scientific Facts.* Princeton, NJ: Princeton University Press, 1986.

Lauke, Herbert L. "Graphische Fertigungs-Berichte." *Zeitschrift für Organisation (ZfürO)* 5, no. 6 (1931): 246–48.

Lauschke, Karl, and Thomas Welskopp. *Mikropolitik in Unternehmen: Arbeitsbeziehungen und Machtstrukturen in industriellen Großbetrieben des 20. Jahrhunderts.* Essen: Klartext, 1994.

Layton, Edwin. "Mirror-Image Twins: The Communities of Science and Technology in 19th-Century America." *Technology and Culture* 12, no. 4 (1971): 562–80.

Layton, Edwin. *The Revolt of the Engineers: Social Responsibility and the American Engineering Profession.* Baltimore: The Johns Hopkins University Press, 1986.

Le Bon, Gustave. *The Crowd: A Study of the Popular Mind.* First published in 1895. Translated into English 1986. New York: MacMillan, 1896.

Lee, G. A. "The Concept of Profit in British Accounting, 1760–1900." *The Business History Review* 49, no. 1 (1975): 6–36.

Leonhard, Karin. "Bild und Zahl: Das Diagramm in Kunst und Naturwissenschaft am Beispiel Wassily Kandinsky und Felix Auerbachs." In *Sichtbarkeit und Medium: Austausch, Verknüpfung und Differenz naturwissenschaftlicher und ästhetischer Bildstrategien,* edited by Anja Zimmermann, 231–45. Hamburg: Hamburg University Press, 2005.

Levsen, Sonja, and Helmut Berding. *Elite, Männlichkeit und Krieg: Tübinger und Cambridger Studenten 1900–1929.* Göttingen: Vandenhoeck & Ruprecht, 2005.

Lewin, C. M. "Technische oder Fabrik-Statistik." *Zeitschrift für Handelswissenschaft und Handelspraxis* 3, no. 8 (1910): 279–83.

Leyensetter, A. "Die Graphische Darstellung als Hilfsmittel zur Regelung und Überwachung der Produktion." *Maschinenbau/Betrieb* 5, no. 19 (1923): 765–67.

Lindsey, Shelley Stamp. "'Oil upon the Flames of Vice': The Battle over White Slave Films in New York City." *Film History* 9, no. 4 (1997): 351–64.

Lindstrom, Richard. "'They all believe they are undiscovered Mary Pickfords': Workers, Photography, and Scientific Management." *Technology and Culture* 41 (2000): 725–51.

Lindstrom, Richard. *Science and Management: Popular Knowledge, Work, and Authority in the Twentieth-Century United States.* PhD diss., Purdue University, 2000.

Link, Jürgen. *Versuch über den Normalismus: Wie Normalität produziert wird.* Opladen: Westdeutscher Verlag, 1997.

Linnenbrügge, Hans. *Über eine neue graphische Methode zur Untersuchung der Schiffsschaufelräder.* Sondershausen: Eupel, 1925.

Lipka, Joseph. *Graphical and Mechanical Computation: Part 2: Experimental Data.* New York: Wiley & Sons, 1918.

Litterer, Joseph A. *The Emergence of Systematic Management as shown by the Literature of Management from 1870–1900.* New York: Garland, 1986.

Litterer, Joseph A. "Systematic Management: The Search for Order and Integration." *The Business History Review* 35, no. 4 (1961): 461–76.

Lord, Chester B. "Management by Exception." *Transactions of the American Society of Mechanical Engineers* 53 (1931): 49–58.

Lowry, Stewart M., Harold B. Maynard, and G. J. Stegemerten. *Time and Motion Study and Formulas for Wage Incentives.* New York: McGraw-Hill, 1940.

Luckey, Paul. *Einführung in die Nomographie, Teil 1: Die Funktionsleiter.* Leipzig: Teubner, 1918.

Luckey, Paul. *Einführung in die Nomographie, Teil 2: Die Zeichnung als Rechenmaschine.* Leipzig: Teubner, 1920.

Luhmann, Niklas. *Legitimation durch Verfahren.* Neuwied: Luchterhand, 1969.

Lynch, Michael, and Steve Woolgar. *Representation in Scientific Practice.* Cambridge, MA: MIT Press, 1990.

Majetschak, Stefan. "Sichtvermerke: Über Unterschiede zwischen Kunst- und Gebrauchsbildern." In *Bild-Zeichen: Perspektiven einer Wissenschaft vom Bild*, edited by Stefan Majetschak, 97–121. Munich: Fink, 2005.

Malcolm, D. G., J. H. Roseboom, C. E. Clark, and W. Fazar. "Application of a Technique for Research and Development Program Evaluation." *Operations Research* 7, no. 5 (1959): 646–69.

Manegold, Karl-Heinz. "Geschichte der technischen Hochschulen." In *Technik und Bildung*, edited by Laetitia Boehm and Charlotte Schönbeck, 204–34. Düsseldorf: VDI Verlag, 1989.

Marey, Étienne-Jules. "La Chronophotographie: Nouvelle Méthode pour analyser le Mouvement dans les Sciences Physiques et Naturelles." *Extrait de la Revue Génerale des Sciences Pures et Appliquées* 2, no. 21 (1891): 689–719.

Marey, Étienne-Jules. *La Méthod Graphique dans les Science Expérimentales et Principlement en Physiologie et en Médecine*. Paris: G. Masson, 1878.

Marsh, Edward R. "The Harmonogram of Karol Adamiecki." *The Academy of Management Journal* 18, no. 2 (1975): 358–64.

Martyniak, Zbigniew. "Karol Adamiecki—Precursor wspólczesnych Nauk o Zarzadzaniu." *Przegląd Organizacji*, no. 6. (1996).

Marvin, Carolyn. *When Old Technologies Were New*. New York: Oxford University Press, 1988.

Matthews, Jean V. *The Rise of the New Woman: The Women's Movement in America, 1875–1930*. Chicago: I. R. Dee, 2003.

Mayer, Joh. Eugen. *Das Rechnen in der Technik und seine Hilfsmittel: Rechenschieber, Rechentafeln, Rechenmaschinen usw*. Leipzig: Göschen, 1908.

McCraw, Thomas K. *Creating Modern Capitalism: How Entrepreneurs, Companies, and Countries Triumphed in Three Industrial Revolutions*. 2nd ed. Cambridge, MA: Harvard University Press, 1999.

McKenna, Christopher. "The Origins of Modern Management Consulting." *Business and Economic History* 24, no. 1 (1995): 51–58.

McKenna, Christopher. *The World's Newest Profession: Management Consulting in the Twentieth Century*. Cambridge, MA: Cambridge University Press, 2006.

McLuhan, Marshall. *Understanding Media: The Extensions of Men*. 1964. Reprint, London: Routledge Classics, 2001.

Mehrtens, Herbert, and Werner Sohn. *Normalität und Abweichung: Studien zur Theorie und Geschichte der Normalisierungsgesellschaft*. Opladen: Westdeutscher Verlag, 1999.

Meiksins, Peter. "The 'Revolt of Engineers' Reconsidered." *Technology and Culture* 29, no. 2 (1988): 219–46.

Merkle, Judith A. *Management and Ideology: The Legacy of the International Scientific Management Movement*. Berkeley: University of California Press, 1980.

Michel, Eduard. *Wie macht man Zeitstudien?* Berlin: Verlag des Vereins deutscher Ingenieure, 1920.

Michel, V. "Die graphische Darstellung in der Geschäftsstatistik." *Zeitschrift für Handelswissenschaft und Handelspraxis* 4, no. 3 (1911): 102–4.

Mildebrath, Georg. "Der Fließ-Band—oder Wandertischbetrieb: Wesen und betriebswirtschaftliche Bedeutung." *Zeitschrift für Handelswissenschaft und Handelspraxis* 19, no. 10 (1926): 234–36.

Mills, F. C. *Statistical Methods Applied to Economics and Business*. New York: Henry Holt, 1924.

Mincer, Jacob. "Investment in Human Capital and Personal Income Distribution." *The Journal of Political Economy* 66, no. 4 (1958): 281–302.

Minck, Friedrich M. "Zeitstudien in Mittelbetrieben." *Zeitschrift für Organisation (ZfürO)* 10, no. 3 (1930): 119–21.

Mitchell, W. J. T. "Diagrammatology." *Critical Inquiry* 7, no. 3 (1981): 622–33.

Mitchell, W. J. T. *Picture Theory*. Chicago: University of Chicago Press, 1995.

Montessori, Maria. *The Montessori Method: Scientific Pedagogy as Applied to Child Education in 'The Children's Houses'*. New York: Frederick A. Stokes Company, 1912.

Montessori, Maria. *The Secret of Childhood*. Edited and translated by Barbara Barclay Carter. London: Sangam Books, 1983.

Moon, Francis C. *The Machines of Leonardo Da Vinci and Franz Reuleaux: Kinematics of Machines from the Renaissance to the 20th Century*. Dordrecht, the Netherlands: Springer, 2007.

Morgan, Gareth. *Images of Organization*. 2nd ed. Thousand Oaks, CA: Sage, 1997.

Mühl-Benninghaus, Wolfgang. "German Film Censorship during World War I." *Film History* 9, no. 1 (1997): 71–94.

Müller, Corinna. "Variationen des Kinoprogramms: Filmform und Filmgeschichte." In *Die Modellierung des Kinofilms: Zur Geschichte des Kinoprogramms zwischen Kurzfilm und Langfilm 1905/06–1918*, edited by Corinna Müller and Harro Segeberg, 43–76. Munich: Fink, 1998.

Müller, Corinna, and Harro Segeberg. *Kinoöffentlichkeit (1895–1920): Entstehung. Etablierung: Differenzierung*. Marburg: Schüren, 2008.

Müller, F. G. "Ein Vermittlungsvorschlag zur organisations-technischen Darstellung von Arbeitsläufen." *Zeitschrift für Organisation (ZfürO)* 4, no. 13 (1930): 350–51.

Müller-Kalkberge, Gustav. "Über die Umsatzstatistik." *Zeitschrift für handelswissenschaftliche Forschung* 5 (1910/11): 322–26.

Münsterberg, Hugo. "The Photoplay: A Psychological Study." In *Hugo Münsterberg on Film. The Photoplay: A Psychological Study and Other Writings*, edited by Allan Langdale, 45–162. 1916. Reprint, New York: Routledge 2002.

Münsterberg, Hugo. "Why We Go to the Movies." In *Hugo Münsterberg on Film. The Photoplay: A Psychological Study and Other Writings*, edited by Allan Langdale, 171–82. 1916. Reprint, New York: Routledge 2002.

Mulhall, Michael G. *The Balance Sheet of the World: For Ten Years, 1870–1880*. London: Edward Stanford, 1881.

Mulhall, Michael G. *The Progress of the World in Arts, Agriculture, Commerce, Manufactures, Instruction, Railways, and Public Wealth Since the Beginning of the Nineteenth Century*. London: Edward Stanford, 1880.

Nadworny, Milton J. "Frederick Taylor and Frank Gilbreth: Competition in Scientific Management." *The Business History Review* 31, no. 1 (1957): 23–34.

Nash, Gerald D. "The Conflict Between Pure and Applied Science in Nineteenth-Century Public Policy: The California State Geological Survey, 1860–1874." *Isis* 54, no. 176 (1963): 217–28.

Nelson, Daniel. *Frederick W. Taylor and the Rise of Scientific Management*. Madison: University of Wisconsin Press, 1980.

Nelson, Daniel. *A Mental Revolution: Scientific Management since Taylor*. Columbus: Ohio State University Press, 1992.

Nelson, Daniel. "Scientific Management in Retrospect." In *A Mental Revolution. Scientific Management since Taylor*, edited by Daniel Nelson, 5–39. Columbus: Ohio State University Press, 1992.

Nelson, Daniel. "Scientific Management, Systematic Management, and Labor, 1880–1915." *The Business History Review* 48, no. 4 (1974): 479–500.

Nelson, Daniel, and Stuart Campbell. "Taylorism Versus Welfare Work in American Industry: H. L. Gantt and the Bancrofts." *The Business History Review* 46, no. 1 (1972): 1–16.

Nelzow, M. "Billige Lichtbilder." *Werkstattstechnik* 18, no. 16 (1924): 427.

Neuendorff, R. *Praktische Mathematik.* 1911. Reprint, Leipzig: B. G. Teubner, 1918.

Noble, David F. *America by Design: Science, Technology, and the Rise of Corporate Capitalism.* Oxford: Oxford University Press, 1979.

Nolan, Mary. *Visions of Modernity: American Business and the Modernization of Germany.* Oxford: Oxford University Press, 1994.

Nordsieck, Fritz. "Erfassung der Betriebsorganisation durch Organisations-Schaubilder." *Zeitschrift für Organisation (ZfürO)* 4, no. 18 (1930): 487–91.

Nordsieck, Fritz. "Graphische Darstellung der formalen Fehlerkontrollen in der Bankbuchhaltung unter besonderer Berücksichtigung der Kontokorrentkontrolle." *Zeitschrift für handelswissenschaftliche Forschung* 23 (1929): 145–69.

Nordsieck, Fritz. "Harmonogramme: Ein Beitrag zur schaubildlichen Untersuchung der Betriebs-Organisation." *Zeitschrift für Organisation (ZfürO)* 5, no. 5 (1931): 106–12.

Nordsieck, Fritz. "Die organisations-technische Darstellung von Arbeitsabläufen in der Buchhaltung: Eine Erweiterung der Richtlinien des AWF." *Zeitschrift für Organisation (ZfürO)* 1, no. 16 (1928): 440–42.

Nordsieck, Fritz. *Die schaubildliche Erfassung und Untersuchung der Betriebsorganisation.* PhD diss., Stuttgart, 1930.

Normblattentwürfe: "Sinnbilder für Rohrleitungen." *Maschinenbau: Gestaltung, Betrieb, Wirtschaft* 7, no. 21/22 (1924): 836–38.

Notiz: "Aus der amerikanischen Werkstatt: Bestimmung von Formänderungen an Maschinenteilen mittels Photographie." *Werkstattstechnik* 6, no. 9 (1912): 484.

Oberhoff, Eugen. "Arbeitsgestaltungsstudien mit der Poppelreuter'schen Arbeitsschauuhr: Was kommt bei der Rationalisierung wirklich heraus?." *Rationalisierung* 1, no. 9 (1950).

Ong, Walter J. *Orality and Literacy: The Technologizing of the Word.* Rev. ed. London: Methuen, 1987.

Oresme, Nicole, Tractatus de latitudinibus formarum. 1486 [1320–1382]. Padua: Mathaeus Cerdonis.

Orlikowski, Wanda J., and Scott, Susan V. "Sociomateriality: Challenging the Separation of Technology, Work and Organization." *Academy of Management Annals* 2, no. 1 (2008): 433–74.

Palmer, A. R. *The Use of Graphs in Commerce and Industry.* London: G. Bell and Sons, 1921.

Parsons, Talcott, and Neil J. Smelser. *Economy and Society: A Study in the Integration of Economic and Social Theory.* London: Routledge and Kegan Paul, 1956.

Pascale, Richard T., and Anthony G. Athos. *The Art of Japanese Management: Applications for American Executives.* New York: Simon & Schuster, 1981.

Peddle, John B. *The Construction of Graphical Charts.* New York: McGraw-Hill, 1910.

Peters, Raymond W. *Communication Within Industries.* New York: Harper, 1949.

Peters, Tom Frank. *Building the Nineteenth Century.* Cambridge, MA: MIT Press, 1996.

Peters, Thomas J., and Robert H. Waterman. *In Search of Excellence: Lessons from America's Best-Run Companies.* New York: Harper & Row, 1982.

Peterson, Peter B. "The Evolution of the Gantt Chart and Its Relevance Today." *Journal of Managerial Issues* 3, no. 2 (1991): 131–55.

Pfennig. "Die symbolischen Zeichen in der Maschinenindustrie." *Maschinenbau. Gestaltung, Betrieb, Wirtschaft* 5, no. 18 (1926): 854–57.

Phillips, Tom. *The Postcard Century: 2000 Cards and Their Messages.* London: Thames & Hudson, 2000.

Pias, Claus. *Cybernetics—Kybernetik: The Macy-Conferences 1946–1953.* Zurich: Diaphanes, 2003.

Pirani, Marcello v. *Graphische Darstellung in Wissenschaft und Technik.* Berlin: Göschen, 1914.

Playfair, William. *The Commercial and Political Atlas and Statistical Breviary.* 1786. Reprint, London: Cambridge University Press, 2005.

Pörksen, Uwe. *Weltmarkt der Bilder: Eine Philosophie der Visiotype.* Stuttgart: Klett-Cotta, 1997.

Pohl, Manfred. "Die Geschichte der Rationalisierung: Das RKW 1921 bis 1996." *RKW*, 2001. http://www.rkw.de/rkwportrait/d_rkw_geschichte/aufsatz.pdf. Accessed June 6, 2009.

Pokorny, Rita. *Die Rationalisierungsexpertin Irene M. Witte (1894–1976): Biographie einer Grenzgängerin.* PhD diss., Technische Universität Berlin, 2003.

Polanyi, Michael. *The Tacit Dimension.* Chicago: The University of Chicago Press, 2009. First published 1966.

Pollard, Sidney. *The Genesis of Modern Management: A Study of the Industrial Revolution in Great Britain.* Aldershot, UK: Gregg Revivals, 1993.

Polnisches Rationalisierungs-Institut Warschau. "Diagramograph und Harmonograph: Neue Hilfsmittel für Planung, Statistik und Kontrolle." *Zeitschrift für Organisation (ZfürO)* 20, no. 5 (1931): 221–23.

Pouchet, Louis-Ezéchiel. *Arithmétique linéaire.* Rouen: n.p., 1795.

Pouchet, Louis-Ezéchiel. *Tableau des Nouveaux: Poids, mesures et monnoies de la République française.* Rouen: n.p., 1796.

Price, Brian. "Frank and Lillian Gilbreth and the Manufacture and Marketing of Motion Study: 1908–1924." *Business and Economic History* 18, no. 2 (1989): 88–97.

Price, Brian. "Frank and Lillian Gilbreth and the Motion Study Controversy: 1907–1930." In *A Mental Revolution: Scientific Management Since Taylor*, edited by Daniel Nelson, 58–76. Columbus: Ohio State University Press, 1992.

Price, Brian. "One Best Way: Frank and Lillian Gilbreth's Transformation of Scientific Management, 1885–1940." Phd diss., Purdue University, 1987.

Priestley, Joseph. *A Chart of Biography.* London: J. Johnson, St. Paul's Church Yard, 1765.

Rabinbach, Anson. *The Human Motor: Energy, Fatigue and the Origins of Modernity.* Berkeley: University of California Press, 1992.

Ramsey, Michele. "Selling Social Status: Woman and Automobile Advertisements from 1910–1920." *Women and Language* 28, no. 1 (2005): 26–38.

Rancière, Jacques. *Aesthetics and Its Discontents.* Translated by Steve Corcoran. Cambridge: Polity Press, 2009.

Rancière, Jacques. *The Politics of Aesthetics: The Distribution of the Sensible.* Translated by Gabriel Rockhill. New York: Continuum International, 2009.

Reeves, Terrie C., W. Jack Duncan, and Peter M. Ginter. "Motion Study in Management and the Arts: A Historical Example." *Journal of Management Inquiry* 10, no. 2 (2001): 137–49.

REFA. *REFA—Buch vol. I: Arbeitsgestaltung: Mit einer Einführung in das Arbeitsstudium.* 2nd ed. Munich: Carl Hanser, 1952.

REFA. *REFA—Buch vol. I: Arbeitsgestaltung.* 5th ed. Munich: Carl Hanser, 1955.

REFA. *REFA—Buch vol. I: Arbeitsgestaltung.* 9th ed. Munich: Carl Hanser, 1960.

REFA. *Zweites REFA—Buch: Erweiterte Einführung in die Arbeitszeitermittlung.* Berlin: Beuth, 1939.

Reichelt, A. "Einführung von Zeitstudien." *Werkstattstechnik* 21, no. 13 (1927): 385–88.

Reishaus, M. "Die Lichtpause im modernen Fabrikbetrieb." *Werkstattstechnik* 4, no. 4 (1910): 220–26.

Reuleaux, Franz. *The Kinematics of Machinery: Outlines of a Theory of Machines.* Translated and edited by Alex Kennedy. London: Macmillan and Co., 1876.

Rheinberger, Hans-Jörg. *Experiment, Differenz, Schrift: Zur Geschichte epistemischer Dinge.* Marburg: Basilisken-Presse, 1992.

Rheinberger, Hans-Jörg. "Strukturen des Experimentierens: Zum Umgang mit dem Nicht-Wissen." In *Wissenschaft als kulturelle Praxis, 1750–1900*, edited by Hans Erich Bödeker, Peter Hans Reill, and Jürgen Schlumbohm, 415–24. Göttingen: Vandenhoeck und Ruprecht, 1999.

Rheinberger, Hans-Jörg. *Toward a History of Epistemic Things: Synthesizing Proteins in the Test Tube.* Stanford, CA: Stanford University Press, 1997.

Rheinberger, Hans-Jörg, and Michael Hagner. *Die Experimentalisierung des Lebens: Experimentalsysteme in der biologischen Wissenschaft 1850–1950.* Berlin: Akademie Verlag, 1993.

Rhyn, Heinz. "Sinnlichkeit/Sensualismus." In *Historisches Wörterbuch der Pädagogik*, edited by Dietrich Benner and Jürgen Oelkers, 866–85. Weinheim: Beltz, 2004.

Rieger, Stefan. *Schall und Rauch: Eine Mediengeschichte der Kurve.* Frankfurt am Main: Suhrkamp, 2009.

Riggleman, J. R. *Graphic Methods for Presenting Business Statistics.* New York: MacGraw-Hill, 1926.

Ritter, Gerhard Albert, and Klaus Tenfelde. *Arbeiter im Deutschen Kaiserreich, 1871 bis 1914.* Bonn: Dietz, 1992.

Rose, T. G. *Business Charts: A Clear Explanation of the Various Types of Charts Used in Business and of the Principles Governing the Correct Presentation of Facts by Graphical Methods.* London: Sir Isaac Pitman and Sons, 1930.

Rosenstock-Huessy, Eugen. *Werkstattaussiedlung: Untersuchungen über den Lebensraum des Industriearbeiters.* Berlin: Springer, 1922.

Ross, Colin. "Das Wesen der wissenschaftlichen Betriebsführung." In *Das ABC der wissenschaftlichen Betriebsführung*, edited and translated by Colin Ross and Frank Gilbreth, 1–15. Berlin: Springer, 1917.

Rothe, Rudolf. "Die Nomographie als Gegenstand der Ingenieurausbildung an den Technischen Hochschulen." *Maschinenbau/Wirtschaft* 3, no. 5 (1923): 113–14.

Rousseau, Jean-Jacques. *Emile, or On Education.* Translated by Allan Bloom. New York: Basic Books, 1979.

Russo, Marcell. "Versuch einer Einführung des Taylorsystems." *Werkstattstechnik* 8, no. 5 (1914): 129–32.

Sammond, Nicholas. "Picture This: Lillian Gilbreth's Industrial Cinema for the Home." *Camera Obscura* 21, no. 3 (2006): 103–33.

Sarasin, Philipp. *Geschichtswissenschaft und Diskuranalyse.* Frankfurt a. M.: Suhrkamp, 2003.

Sarasin, Philipp. "Die Rationalisierung des Körpers: Über 'Scientific Management' und 'biologische Rationalisierung.'" In *Geschichtswissenschaft und Diskuranalyse*, edited by Philipp Sarasin, 61–99. Frankfurt a. M.: Suhrkamp, 2003.

Sarasin, Philipp. *Reizbare Maschinen: Eine Geschichte des Körpers: 1765–1914*. Frankfurt a. M.: Suhrkamp, 2001.

Sarasin, Phillipp, and Jakob Tanner. *Physiologie und industrielle Gesellschaft*. Frankfurt a. M.: Suhrkamp, 1998.

Schaaps, Franz. "Statistik und graphische Darstellung im Dienste des Kaufmanns." *Zeitschrift für Handelswissenschaft und Handelspraxis* 3, no. 4 (1910): 125–28.

Schilling, Albert Carl. *Graphische Darstellungen zur Psychologie*. Leipzig: Ernst Wunderlich, 1901.

Schilling, Friedrich. *Über die Nomographie von M. D'Ocagne*. Leipzig: Teubner, 1900.

Schleif, Fr. "Kontrolle der Arbeitszeit." *Maschinenbau: Gestaltung, Betrieb, Wirtschaft* 6, no. 13 (1924): 440–41.

Schleif, Fr. "Die Nomographie in Anwendung bei der Zeitberechnung für Reck- und Freiformschmiedearbeiten." *Maschinenbau: Gestaltung, Betrieb, Wirtschaft* 3, no. 11 (1924): 366–69.

Schlesinger, Georg. "Brennende Probleme der Betriebsorganisation und ihre natürliche Lösung." *Werkstattstechnik* 18, no. 10 (1924): 269–72.

Schlesinger, Georg. "Die Entwicklung der deutschen Organisationswissenschaft für industrielle Betriebe." *Werkstattstechnik* 17, no. 5 (1923): 152–54.

Schmaltz, Gustav. "Über Methoden zur photographischen Registrierung geradliniger Schwingungsbewegungen." *Maschinenbau/Gestaltung* 2, no. 5/6 (1922): 150–60.

Schmidt, Gunnar. *Anamorphotische Körper: Medizinische Bilder vom Menschen im 19. Jahrhundert*. Cologne: Böhlau, 2001.

Schmidt, K. H. "Betriebswissenschaftliche Grundlagen für die Einführung der Fließarbeit." *Maschinenbau. Gestaltung, Betrieb, Wirtschaft* 4, no. 9 (1925): 409–15.

Schmidt, K. H. "Über einige Anwendungsmöglichkeiten der Nomographie in der Betriebswirtschaft." *Zeitschrift für Handelswissenschaft und Handelspraxis* 19, no. 11 (1926): 257–61.

Schneider, Alexandra. *'Die Stars sind wir': Heimkino als filmische Praxis*. Marburg: Schüren, 2004.

Schneider, L. "Zeitmessungen in Bürobetrieben." *Zeitschrift für Handelswissenschaft und Handelspraxis* 19, no. 11/12. (1926): 254–57; 279–81.

Schroyer, Helen Q. "Contributions of the Gilbreths to the Development of Management Thought." *Academy of Management Proceedings*, no. 1 (1975): 7–9.

Schulz-Mehrin, Otto. *Die industrielle Spezialisierung, Wesen, Wirkung, Durchführungsmöglichkeiten und Grenzen: Auf Grund der Untersuchungen des Ausschusses für Wirtschaftliche Fertigung*. Berlin: VDI Verlag, 1920.

Schultze, Arthur. *Graphic Algebra*. Norwood, MA: Norwood, 1908.

Schumpeter, Joseph Alois. *Capitalism, Socialism and Democracy*. 1942. Reprint, London: Routledge, 2005.

Schwerdt, Hans. *Einführung in die praktische Nomographie*. Berlin: Salle, 1927.

Schwerdt, Hans. *Lehrbuch der Nomographie auf abbildungsgeometrischer Grundlage*. Berlin: Springer, 1924.

Secord, James A. "Knowledge in Transit." *Isis* 95 (2004): 654–72.

Séguin, Édouard. *Traitement Moral, Hygiène et Éducation des Idiots*. Paris: Bailliere, 1846.

Seyffert, Rudolf. "Die Statistik des Plakats." *Zeitschrift für Handelswissenschaft und Handelspraxis* 10, no. 11 (1918/19): 228–35.

Shannon, C. E. "A Mathematical Theory of Communication." *The Bell System Technical Journal* 27, no. 7/10 (1948): 379–423; 623–56.

Shaw, Anne G. *The Purpose and Practice of Motion Study.* Manchester, UK: Columbine Press, 1960.

Shenhav, Yehouda. "From Chaos to Systems: The Engineering Foundations of Organization Theory, 1879–1932." *Administrative Science Quarterly* 40 (1995): 557–85.

Sinclair, Bruce. *A Centennial History of the American Society of Mechanical Engineers 1880–1980.* Toronto: University of Toronto Press, 1980.

Singer, Ben. "Manhattan Nickelodeons: New Data on Audiences and Exhibitors." *Cinema Journal* 34, no. 3 (1995): 5–35.

Singer, Ben. *Melodrama and Modernity: Early Sensational Cinema and Its Context.* New York: Columbia University Press, 2001.

Sombart, Werner. *War and Capitalism (European Sociology).* North Stratford, NH: Ayer, 1975. First published 1913 by Duncker & Humblot (Munich).

Spence, Ian. "No Humble Pie: The Origins and Usage of a Statistical Chart." *Journal of Educational and Behavioral Statistics* 30, no. 4 (2005): 353–68.

Spence, Ian. "William Playfair and His Graphical Inventions: An Excerpt From the Introduction to the Republication of His Atlas and Statisitcal Breviary." *The American Statistician* 59, no. 3 (2005): 224–29.

Spence, Ian, and Howard Wainer. "Introduction." In *The Commercial and Political Atlas and Statistical Breviary*, edited by William Playfair, 1–35. London: Cambridge University Press, 2005.

Spence, Ian, and Howard Wainer. "Who Was Playfair?." *Chance* 10, no. 1 (1997): 35–37.

Stahl, Bernhard. "Preisberechnung bei veränderlichen Grundpreisen unter Zuhilfenahme der Rechentafel." *Maschinenbau/Wirtschaft* 3, no. 5 (1923): 115–17.

Stahlmann, Michael. *Die erste Revolution in der Autoindustrie: Management und Arbeitspolitk von 1900–1940.* Frankfurt a. M.: Campus Verlag, 1993.

Stahlmann, Michael. "Vom Handwerk zur Fließbandarbeit: Die erste Revolution der Arbeitsorganisation bei Opel und Daimler-Benz." *WSI Mitteilungen* Oktober (1995): 646–53.

Staiger, Janet. "Combination and Litigation: Structures of US Film Distribution, 1896–1917." In *Early Cinema: Space, Frame, Narrative*, edited by Thomas Elsaesser, 189–210. London: BFI, 1990.

Star, Susan Leigh, and James R. Griesemer. "Institutional Ecology, 'Translations' and Boundary Objects: Amateurs and Professionals in Berkeley's Museum of Vertebrate Zoology, 1907–39." *Social Studies of Science* 19 (1989): 387–420.

Star, Susan Leigh, and James R. Griesemer. "The Structure of Ill-Structured Solutions: Boundary Objects and Heterogeneous Distributed Problem Solving." In *Distributed Artificial Intelligence (Vol. 2)*, edited by Les Gasser and Michael N Huhns, 37–54. London: Pitman, 1989.

Stefanic-Allmayer, Karl. "Graphische Statistik der Außenstände." *Zeitschrift für Organisation (ZfürO)* 3, no. 23 (1929): 623–27.

Stefanic-Allmayer, Karl. "Schaubildliche Darstellung von Kontenplänen und von Buchungszusammenhängen." *Zeitschrift für Organisation (ZfürO)* 3, no. 13 (1929): 341–46.

Stein, O. "Die Kinematographie im Ausstellungswesen." *Film und Lichtbild* 3, no. 6 (1914): 88–92.

Streible, Dan. *Fight Pictures: A History of Boxing and Early Cinema*. Berkeley: University of California Press, 2008.

Student, Dietmar. "Hai-Alarm." *Manager Magazin*, no. 1 (2014): 28–38.

Talbot, William Henry Fox. *The Pencil of Nature*. 1844.

Tama, M. "Graphische Rechentafeln." *Werkstattstechnik* 11, no. 1 (1917): 1–4.

Taylor, Frederick W. "On the Art of Cutting Metals." *Transactions of the American Society of Mechanical Engineers* 28 (1906): 31–279.

Taylor, Frederick W. *On the Art of Cutting Metals*. New York: The American Society of Mechanical Engineers, 1906.

Taylor, Frederick W. *The Principles of Scientific Management*. Norwood, MA: Plimpton Press, 1911.

Taylor, Frederick W. "Shop Management." *Transactions of the American Society of Mechanical Engineers* 24 (1903): 1337–480.

Taylor, Frederick W. *Shop Management*. New York: Harper & Brothers, 1911.

Tenfelde, Klaus. *Arbeiter im 20: Jahrhundert*. Stuttgart: Klett-Cotta, 1991.

Thun, R. "Die Auswertung arbeitswissenschaftlicher Filme." *Maschinenbau: Gestaltung, Betrieb, Wirtschaft* 6, no. 13 (1924): 454–58.

Thun, R. "Die Bedeutung kinematographischer Zeit- und Bewegungsuntersuchungen." *Maschinenbau/Betrieb* 5, no. 4 (1922): 18–122.

Thun, R. "Bemerkungen zum technischen Film." *Maschinenbau. Gestaltung, Betrieb, Wirtschaft* 5, no. 21 (1926): 1002–105.

Thun, R. *Der Film in der Technik*. Berlin: VDI-Verlag, 1925.

Tischner, Bruno. "Registrierapparat für Zeitstudien." *Maschinenbau/Betrieb* 5, no. 4 (1922): 123–24.

Tobies, Renate. "Zur Position von Mathematik und Mathematiker/innen in der Industrieforschung vor 1945." *NTM. Zeitschrift für Geschichte der Wissenschaft, Technik und Medizin* 15, no. 4 (2007): 241–70.

Tooze, J. Adam. "Die Vermessung der Welt: Ansätze zu einer Kulturgeschichte der Wirtschaftsstatistik." In *Wirtschaftsgeschichte als Kulturgeschichte: Dimensionen eines Perspektivenwechsels*, edited by Hartmut Berghoff and Jakob Vogel, 325–51. Frankfurt a. M.: Campus Verlag, 2004.

Tramm, Karl A. *Psychotechnik und Taylor-System*. Berlin: Springer, 1921.

Urwick, Lyndall. *The Golden Book of Management: A Historical Record of the Life and Work of Seventy Pioneers*. London: Newman Neame, 1956.

Wachsmann, J. "Nomogramm für die Dimensionierung von städtischen Kanalnetzen." *Gesundheits-Ingenieur* 48, no. 48 (1925): 605–607.

Waddell, Laurence Austine. *The Buddhism of Tibet or Lamaism, with Its Mystic Cult, Symbolism and Mythology, and in Its Relation to Indian Buddhism*. London: Allen, 1895.

Waffenschmidt, Walter G. "Graphische Methode in der theoretischen Oekonomie, dargestellt in Anlehnung an das Tauschproblem." *Archiv für Sozialwissenschaft und Sozialpolitik* 39 (1915): 438–81; 795–818.

Wagner, H. "Über die Kontrolle eines gemischten Werkes der Großeisenindustrie." *Zeitschrift für Handelswissenschaft und Handelspraxis*, no. 1 (1913): 4–12.

Warne, Frank J. *Warne's Book of Charts: A Special Feature of Warne's Elementary Course in Chartography*. Washington, DC: n.p., 1916.

Weber, Arnold E. "Das Konten-Schaubild als Spiegel der Buchhaltung." *Zeitschrift für Organisation (ZfürO)* 2, no. 14 (1928): 382–87.

Weber, Max. *Gesammelte Aufsätze zur Wissenschaftslehre*. 3rd rev. ed. Tübingen: J. C. B. Mohr, 1968.

Weber, Max. "Die Objektivität sozialwissenschaftlicher und sozialpolitischer Erkenntnis." In *Gesammelte Aufsätze zur Wissenschaftslehre*, edited by Max Weber, 146–214. Tübingen: Mohr, 1922.

Weber, Max. "Religious Groups (The Sociology of Religion)." In *Economy and Society: An Outline of Interpretive Sociology*, edited by Guenther Roth and Claus Wittich. Translated by Ephraim Fischoff, Hans Gerth, A. M. Henderson, Ferdinand Kolegar, C. Wright Mills, Talcott Parsons, Max Rheinstein, Guenther Roth, Edward Shils, and Claus Wittich, 399–634. Berkeley: University of California Press, 1978.

Weber, Max. "Science as a Vocation." In *From Max Weber: Essays in Sociology*, edited and translated by H. H. Gerth and C. Wright Mills, 129–56. New York: Oxford University Press, 1946.

Weber, Max. "The Social Categories of Economic Action." In *Economy and Society: An Outline of Interpretive Sociology*, edited by Guenther Roth and Claus Wittich. Translated by Ephraim Fischoff, Hans Gerth, A. M. Henderson, Ferdinand Kolegar, C. Wright Mills, Talcott Parsons, Max Rheinstein, Guenther Roth, Edward Shils, and Claus Wittich. 63–211. Berkeley: University of California Press, 1978.

Werkmeister, Paul. *Das Entwerfen von graphischen Rechentafeln (Nomographie)*. Berlin: Springer, 1923.

Werner, L. "Das Diagramm und seine Verwendung als Anschauungsmittel im Unterricht der Fortbildungsschule." *Werkstattstechnik* 18, no. 7/8 (1924): 210–14; 237–44.

Wesolowski, Zdzislaw P. "The Polish Contribution to the Development of Scientific Management." *Proceedings of the Academy of Managment* (1978): 12–16.

Wieske, Georg. "Die Anwendung von Registriermaschinen in der Depotdruckerei der Großbanken." *Zeitschrift für handelswissenschaftliche Forschung* 5 (1910/11): 97–107.

Willers, Friedrich A. "Bücherbesprechung: Graphisches Rechnen von K. Giebel." *Werkstattstechnik* 19, no. 22 (1925): 817.

Wilms, Fritz. *Lichtspieltheaterbauten*. Berlin: Friedrich Ernst Hübsch Verlag, 1928.

Wilson, James M. "Gantt Charts: A Centenary Appreciation." *European Journal of Operational Research* 149 (2003): 430–37.

Winkel, A. "Das Nomogramm in der Selbstkostenberechnung." *Werkstattstechnik* 17, no. 1 (1923): 12–14.

Winkel, H. *Selbstanfertigung von Rechentafeln: 4: Der Ausbau der Leitertafeln*. Berlin: Beuth, 1925.

Wirz, Wilhelm. "Taylors Betriebssystem." *Zeitschrift für Handelswissenschaft und Handelspraxis* 6, no. 5 (1918): 133–44.

Wissenschaftliche Arbeitsstelle der GfürO. "Organisationsschaubilder: Stellungnahme zum ÖNIG-Entwurf." *Zeitschrift für Organisation (ZfürO)* 4, no. 11 (1930): 293–95.

Wissenschaftliche Arbeitsstelle der GfürO. "Organisationstechnische Darstellung von Arbeitsabläufen: Auswertung des GfürO Preisausschreibens." *Zeitschrift für Organisation (ZfürO)* 5, no. 9 (1931): 200–203.

Witte, Irene. "Frank Bunker Gilbreth, Ein Lebens- und Charakterbild." *Betriebswirtschaftliche Rundschau* 1, no. 9 (1924): 203–206.

Witte, Irene. "Frank Gilbreth—A Philosopher." In *The Frank Gilbreth Centennial*, edited by The American Society of Mechanical Engineers, 102–109. New York: 1968.

Witte, Irene. *F. W. Taylor: Der Vater wirtschaftlicher Betriebsführung*. Stuttgart: Poeschel Verlag, 1928.

Witte, Irene. *Kritik des Zeitstudienverfahrens: Eine Untersuchung der Ursachen, die zu einem Mißerfolg des Zeitstudiums führen*. Berlin: Springer, 1921.

Witte, Irene. *Taylor, Gilbreth, Ford: Gegenwartsfragen der amerikanischen und europäischen Arbeitswissenschaft*. 2nd ed. Munich: R. Oldenburg, 1925.

Witting, A. *Soldaten—Mathematik*. Berlin: Teubner, 1916.

Wlach, Fritz. "Darstellung von Betriebs-Beziehungen kompositorisch oder im Netz." *Zeitschrift für Organisation (ZfürO)* 6, no. 3 (1932): 174–75.

Wlach, Fritz. "Organisations-technische Darstellung: Ihre Aufgabe und ihre bisherige Entwicklung." *Zeitschrift für Organisation (ZfürO)* 1, no. 16 (1927): 429–41.

Woldt, Richard. "Das Prämiensystem und die Arbeiter." *Werkstattstechnik* 3, no. 5 (1909): 270–72.

Wood, Michael C., and John C. Wood. *Frank and Lillian Gilbreth: Critical Evaluations in Business and Management*. London: Routledge, 2003.

Wootton, Charles W., and Barbara E. Kemmerer. "The Emergence of Mechanical Accounting in the U.S., 1880–1930." *Accounting Historians Journal* 34, no. 1 (2007): 91–124.

Wrege, Charles D. *Facts and Fallacies of Hawthorne*. New York: Garland, 1986.

Wrege, Charles D., Regina A. Greenwood, and Sakae Hata. "What We Do Not Know about Management History: Some Categories of Research and Methods to Uncover Management History Mysteries." *Journal of Management History* 5, no. 7 (1999): 414–24.

Wrege, Charles D., and Ronald G. Greenwood. *Frederick W. Taylor: The Father of Scientific Management: Myth and Reality*. Homewood, IL: Business One Irwin, 1991.

Wupper-Tewes, Hans. *Rationalisierung als Normalisierung*. Münster: Westfälisches Dampfboot, 1993.

Yates, JoAnne. *Control through Communication: The Rise of System in American Management*. London: John Hopkins University Press, 1989.

Yates, JoAnne. "Graphs as a Managerial Tool: A Case Study of Du Pont's Use of Graphs in the Early Twentieth Century." *The Journal of Business Communication* 22, no. 1 (1985): 5–33.

Yost, Edna. *Frank and Lillian Gilbreth: Partners for Life*. New York: Van Rees Press, 1949.

Zielinski, Siegfried. *Audiovisions: Cinema and Televsion as Entr'actes in History*. Amsterdam: Amsterdam University Press, 1999.

Zucker, Paul. *Lichtspielhäuser: Tonfilmtheater*. Berlin: Ernst Wasmuth, 1931.

Zucker, Paul. *Theater und Lichtspielhäuser*. Berlin: Ernst Wasmuth, 1926.

Zwer, Reiner. "Die statistische Konjunkturforschung in Vergangenheit und Gegenwart." *Statistische Hefte* 4, no. 1 (1963): 38–79.

List of Illustrations

Figures

Introduction

1. Gilbreth LOM, SPCOLL, Purdue University Libraries, NF 48/298.
2. Gilbreth, Lillian M., and Frank B. Gilbreth. "Applications of Motion Studies." *Management and Administration* 8, no. 3 (1924): 295.
3. Gilbreth LOM, SPCOLL, Purdue University Libraries, NF 151/0031-19, No. LG 1429.
4. Peters, Thomas J., and Robert H. Waterman. *In Search of Excellence: Lessons from America's Best-Run Companies.* New York: Harper & Row, 1982, 10.

Chapter 1

5. Oresme, Nicole. *Tractatus de latitudinibus formarum.* 1486 [1320–1382]. Padua: Mathaeus Cerdonis, n.p.
6. Playfair, William. *The Commercial and Political Atlas and Statistical Breviary.* 1786. Reprint, London: Cambridge University Press, 2005, 48.
7. Haskell, Allan C. *How to Make and Use Graphic Charts.* New York: Codex, 1919, 125.
8. de Foville, A. "Essai de Meteorologie Economique et Sociale." *Journal de la Société de Statistique de Paris* (1888): n.p.
9. Marey, Étienne-Jules. *La Méthode Graphique dans les Sciences Expérimentales et Particulièrement en Physiologie et en Médecine.* Paris: G. Masson, 1878, 560.
10. Marey, Étienne-Jules. *Die Chronophotographie*, 1893. Reprint, Frankfurt am Main: Deutsches Filmmuseum, 1985, 12.
11. TECHNOSEUM, Bildarchiv, PVZ: 2005/993.
12. D'Ocagne, Maurice. *Le Calcul Simplifié: Graphical and Mechanical Methods for Simplifying Calculation.* 3rd ed. Cambridge, MA: MIT Press, 1986, 89. First published 1894.
13. Bieberbach, Ludwig. "Über Nomographie." *Die Naturwissenschaften* 10, no. 36 (1922): 775.

14 & 15. Bieberbach, Ludwig. "Über Nomographie." *Die Naturwissenschaften* 10, no. 36 (1922): 776.

16. Hirschfeld, F., and K. Kustin. "Anwendung der Nomographie auf die Vorkalkulation bei spananhebender Bearbeitung." *Maschinenbau: Gestaltung, Betrieb, Wirtschaft* 7, no. 18 (1928): 858.

17. Faltus, Franz. *Fünfzehn Nomogramme für den Eisenbau.* Geislingen an der Steige: NBW Verlag Dipl. Ing. P. Leybold, 1927, n.p.

18. Brinton, Willard C. *Graphic Methods for Presenting Facts.* New York: The Engineering Magazine Co., 1919, 343.

19. Riggleman, John, R. *Graphic Methods for Presenting Business Statistics.* New York: MacGraw-Hill, 1926, 59.

20. Auerbach, Felix. *Die graphische Darstellung. Eine allgemeinverständliche, durch zahlreiche Beispiele aus allen Gebieten der Wissenschaft und Praxis erläuterte Einführung in den Sinn und den Gebrauch der Methode.* Leipzig: Teubner, 1914, 91.

21. Image Archive, INGV, Istituto Nazionale di Geofisica e Vulcanologia, Terremoto Messina, 1908.

22. Auerbach, Felix. *Die graphische Darstellung. Eine allgemeinverständliche, durch zahlreiche Beispiele aus allen Gebieten der Wissenschaft und Praxis erläuterte Einführung in den Sinn und den Gebrauch der Methode.* Leipzig: Teubner, 1914, 6.

23. Tama, M. "Graphische Rechentafeln." *Werkstattstechnik* 11, no. 1 (1917): 1.

24 & 25. Pirani, Marcello. *Graphische Darstellung in Wissenschaft und Technik.* Berlin: Göschen, 1914, 17–18.

Chapter 2

26. Gantt, Henry L. *Work, Wages, and Profits.* New York: The Engineering Magazine Co., 1919, 208. First published 1910.

27. Marsh, Edward R. "The Harmonogram of Karol Adamiecki." *The Academy of Management Journal* 18, no. 2 (1975): 362.

28. Polnisches Rationalisierungs-Institut Warschau. "Diagramograph und Harmonograph: Neue Hilfsmittel für Planung, Statistik und Kontrolle." *Zeitschrift für Organisation (ZfürO)* 20, no. 5 (1931): 223.

29. Polnisches Rationalisierungs-Institut Warschau. "Diagramograph und Harmonograph: Neue Hilfsmittel für Planung, Statistik und Kontrolle." *Zeitschrift für Organisation (ZfürO)* 20, no. 5 (1931): 222.

30. Taylor, Frederick W. *On the Art of Cutting Metals.* New York: The American Society of Mechanical Engineers, 1906, 173.

31. Taylor, Frederick W. *On the Art of Cutting Metals*. New York: The American Society of Mechanical Engineers, 1906, 31.

32. Barth, Carl. "Slide Rules as Part of the Taylor System." *Transactions of the American Society of Mechanical Engineers* 25 (1904): 54–55.

33. Barth, Carl. "Slide Rules as Part of the Taylor System." *Transactions of the American Society of Mechanical Engineers* 25 (1904): 59.

34. Hirschfeld, F., and K. Kustin. "Anwendung der Nomographie auf die Vorkalkulation bei spananhebender Bearbeitung." *Maschinenbau: Gestaltung, Betrieb, Wirtschaft* 7, no. 18 (1928): n.p.

35 & 36. Schmidt, K. H. "Über einige Anwendungsmöglichkeiten der Nomographie in der Betriebswirtschaft." *Zeitschrift für Handelswissenschaft und Handelspraxis* 19, no. 11 (1926): 259.

Chapter 3

37. TECHNOSEUM, Bildarchiv, PVZ: 2005/0880.

38. TECHNOSEUM, Bildarchiv, PVZ: 2005/0888.

39. TECHNOSEUM, Bildarchiv, PVZ: 1994/1203.

40. Image Archive, Gilbreth LOM, SPCOLL, Purdue University Libraries, NF 151/ 0031-19, No. GL 3.

41. Image Archive, Gilbreth LOM, SPCOLL, Purdue University Libraries, NF 152/ 0031-24, No. EF 197.

42. Image Archive, Gilbreth LOM, SPCOLL, Purdue University Libraries, NF 152/ 0031-24, No. EF 364.

43. TECHNOSEUM, Bildarchiv, PVZ: 1994/1228.

44. Film stills, *Original Films of Frank B. Gilbreth. The Quest of the One Best Way*, Library of Congress, Motion Pictures, Broadcasting and Recorded Sound Division, Prelinger Collection.

45. TECHNOSEUM, Bildarchiv, PVZ: 2005/0873.

46. TECHNOSEUM, Bildarchiv, PVZ: 2005/0772.

47. TECHNOSEUM, Bildarchiv, PVZ: 2005/0773.

48. TECHNOSEUM, Bildarchiv, PVZ: 1994/1241.

49. TECHNOSEUM, Bildarchiv, PVZ: 1994/1252.

50. Film stills, *Original Films of Frank B. Gilbreth: The Quest of the One Best Way*, Library of Congress, Motion Pictures, Broadcasting and Recorded Sound Division, Prelinger Collection.

51. Film stills, *Original Films of Frank B. Gilbreth: The Quest of the One Best Way*, Library of Congress, Motion Pictures, Broadcasting and Recorded Sound Division, Prelinger Collection.

52. TECHNOSEUM, Bildarchiv, PVZ: 2005/0759; original image description: Gilbreth LOM, SPCOLL, Purdue University Libraries, NF 56/299-12.

53. TECHNOSEUM, Bildarchiv, PVZ: 1994/1281.

54. Film stills, *Training of a Champion Typist, Original Films of Frank B. Gilbreth: The Quest of the One Best Way*, Library of Congress, Motion Pictures, Broadcasting and Recorded Sound Division, Prelinger Collection.

55. TECHNOSEUM, Bildarchiv, PVZ: 2005/0769.

56. TECHNOSEUM, Bildarchiv, PVZ: 1994/1205.

57. TECHNOSEUM, Bildarchiv, PVZ: 1994/1242.

58. TECHNOSEUM, Bildarchiv, PVZ: 2005/0843.

59. TECHNOSEUM, Bildarchiv, PVZ: 2005/0858.

60. TECHNOSEUM, Bildarchiv, PVZ: 2005/0839; Original Image Description: Gilbreth LOM, SPCOLL, Purdue University Libraries, NF 56/ 0299-12.

61. Film stills, *Gilbreth's Films, Odds and Ends #3*, Gilbreth Library of Management Videos, SPCOLL, Purdue University Libraries.

62. Film stills, *Gilbreth's Films, Odds and Ends #3*, Gilbreth Library of Management Videos, SPCOLL, Purdue University Libraries.

63. Film stills, *Gilbreth's Films, Odds and Ends #3*, Gilbreth Library of Management Videos, SPCOLL, Purdue University Libraries.

64. US-Pat. No. 1.199.980, submitted on May 23, 1913, patented on October 3, 1916; patent label: "Method and Apparatus for the Study and Correction of Motions." TECHNOSEUM, Witte Archive, Sig. 992, No. 3/6-10.

65. Gilbreth LOM, SPCOLL, Purdue University Libraries, NF 150/0031-17.

66. TECHNOSEUM, Bildarchiv, PVZ: 2005/0766.

67. Information brochure. "Gilbreth's The One Best Way to Do Work." TECHNOSEUM, Witte Archive, Sig. 992, No. 2/1-116.

68. Gilbreth LOM, SPCOLL, Purdue University Libraries, NF 62/868.

Chapter 4

69. Gilbreth LOM, SPCOLL, Purdue University Libraries, NF 146/0028, Vol. II, No. 200.566.

70. Pharusplan Berlin 1913, Staatsbibliothek zu Berlin, Stiftung Preußischer Kulturbesitz, Kartenabteilung, Karte No. 806.

71. Griffith, D. W. Film stills, *Judith von Bethulia*, 1914; American Mutoscope and Biograph Co.

Chapter 5

Conclusion

Plates

Index

Figures are indicated by *f* following the page number

For the benefit of digital users, indexed terms that span two pages (e.g., 52–53) may, on occasion, appear on only one of those pages.